MW01244259

The
Iroquois Handbook

originally published as

HISTORY,
MANNERS, AND CUSTOMS
OF
THE INDIAN NATIONS
WHO ONCE INHABITED PENNSYLVANIA AND THE NEIGHBOURING STATES

BY THE
REV. JOHN HECKEWELDER,
OF BETHLEHEM, PA.

1818

$\longleftrightarrow$

New and Revised Edition.
WITH AN
INTRODUCTION AND NOTES
BY THE
REV. WILLIAM C. REICHEL,
OF BETHLEHEM, PA.

PHILADELPHIA:

PUBLICATION FUND OF THE HISTORICAL SOCIETY OF PENNSYLVANIA, No. 820 SPRUCE STREET.

1881.

Publications
OF THE
Historical Society of Pennsylvania.

Knowledge Keepers edition, 2021

ISBN: 9798588708135

Cover design by Nicki Truesdell

Cover Photograph:

Mohican chief E Tow Oh Koam

National Portrait Gallery, Smithsonian Institution

John Hechewelder

Table of Contents

FOREWARD

Firsthand accounts, such as this one, are among the most valuable history books a nation can have. When it comes to the Indian tribes of North America, these printed firsthand accounts are very few, thus, all the more valuable.

In the case of Reverend Heckewelder's work, we are given a priceless gift: a book detailing every aspect of the lives and customs of the Iroquois nation, divided into short sections for ease of reading and research. This volume is packed with history, anecdotes, and wonderful descriptions of everyday life. It is, in my opinion, the perfect history book!

If lions had painters! This proverbial saying applies with equal force to the American Indians. They have no historians among them, no books, no newspapers, no convenient means of making their grievances known to a sympathising world. Why, then, should not a white man, a Christian, who has spent among them the greatest part of his life, and was treated by them at all times with hospitality and kindness, plead their honest cause, and defend them as they would defend themselves, if they had but the means of bringing their facts and their arguments before an impartial public? – Rev. Heckewelder

Many people ask, "How can we trust just the American's version of history, when they were the only people to write it down?" That's a very good question. And works such as this one answer it beautifully. Rev. Heckewelder loved the Indian people he went to live with. He resided among them for many years (as you will read). It was his earnest desire to portray them as honestly as possible.

The American story is filled with the clashing of the Indians and Europeans for many centuries, and each instance is unique, with varying outcomes. This book gives us a snapshot of the lives of the Iroquois nation during the 1700s. If you've ever read *The Leatherstocking Tales* (such as *Last of the Mohicans*) by James

Fennimore Cooper, or studied the French and Indian War, you'll enjoy this firsthand account of life with those very Indians.

In this newly printed edition, I have not changed the original text. I left the spelling and grammar as Rev. Heckewelder wrote them for historical accuracy. On occasion, I changed paragraph formatting, only to make the pages flow a little easier.

Part 1 of this book is Rev. Heckewelder's description of just about every part of Iroquois life. Part 2 is a very interesting correspondence between Heckewelder and the secretary of the Historical and Literary Committee of the American Philosophical Society. Part 3 is a valuable list of words and phrases in the Iroquois tongue with English translations. This is followed by Heckewleder's footnotes. Each part is littered with casual references to all sorts of American (and even European) history, languages, and geography. It is truly a wealth of information!

I hope you will add this and other Knowledge Keepers titles to your home library for the preservation of our true history.

Nicki Truesdell,

Founder of Knowledge Keepers

January 2021

INTRODUCTION
BY THE EDITOR

JOHN GOTTLIEB ERNESTUS HECKEWELDER, the author of "An Account of the History, Manners, and Customs of the Indian Nations who once inhabited Pennsylvania and the neighboring States," was born March 12th, 1743, at Bedford, England. His father, who was a native of Moravia, a few years after his arrival at Herrnhut, Saxony, was summoned to England to assist in the religious movement which his church had inaugurated in that country in 1734.

In his eleventh year, the subject of this sketch accompanied his parents to the New World, and became a resident of Bethlehem, Pennsylvania. Here he was placed at school, and next apprenticed to a cedar-cooper. While thus employed, he was permitted to gratify a desire he had frequently expressed of becoming an evangelist to the Indians, when in the spring of 1762 he was called to accompany the well-known Christian Frederic Post, who had planned a mission among the tribes of the then far west, to the Tuscarawas branch of the Muskingum. Here Post, in the summer of 1761, had built himself a cabin (it stood near the site of the present town of Bolivar), and here on the 11th day of April, 1762, the intrepid missionary and his youthful assistant began their labors in the Gospel.

But the times were unpropitious, and the hostile attitude of the Indians indicating a speedy resumption of hostilities with the whites, the adventurous enterprise was abandoned before the expiration of the year. Young Heckewelder returned to Bethlehem, and the war of Pontiac's conspiracy opened in the spring of 1763.

In the interval between 1765 and 1771, Mr. Heckewelder was, on several occasions, summoned from his cooper's shop to do service for the mission. Thus, in the summer of the first mentioned year, he spent several months at Friedenshütten, on the Susquehanna (Wyalusing, Bradford county, Pennsylvania), where the Moravian Indians had been recently settled in a body, after a series of most trying experiences, to which their residence on the frontiers and in the settlements of the Province subjected them, at a time when the inroads of the savages embittered the public mind indiscriminately against the entire race. This post he visited subsequently on several occasions, and also the town of Schechschiquanink (Sheshequin), some thirty miles north of Wyalusing, the seat of a second mission on the Susquehanna.

A new period in the life of Mr. Heckewelder opened with the autumn of 1771, when he entered upon his actual career as an evangelist to the Indians, sharing the various fortunes of the Moravian mission among that people for fifteen years, than which none perhaps in its history were more eventful. The well-known missionary David Zeisberger, having in 1768 established a mission among a clan of Monseys on the Allegheny, within the limits of what is now Venango county, was induced in the spring of 1770 to migrate with his charge to the Big Beaver, and to settle at a point within the jurisdiction of the Delawares of Kaskaskunk. Here he built Friedensstadt, and hither the Moravian Indians of Friedenshütten and Schechschiquanink removed in the summer of 1772.

Mr. Heckewelder was appointed Zeisberger's assistant in the autumn of 1771, and when in the spring of 1773 Friedensstadt was evacuated (it stood on the Beaver, between the Shenango and the Slippery Rock, within the limits of the present Lawrence county), and the seat of the mission was transferred to the valley of the Muskingum, Mr. Heckewelder became a resident of the Ohio country. Here in succession were built Schönbrunn, Gnadenhütten, Lichtenau and Salem, flourishing towns of Moravian

Indians, and here our missionary labored with his associates hopefully, and with the promise of a great ingathering, when the rupture between the mother country and her transatlantic colonies, gradually involved them and their cause in the most perplexing complications.

On the opening of the western border-war of the Revolution in the spring of 1777, the Moravian missionaries on the Muskingum realized the danger of their position. Strictly neutral as they and their converts were in reference to the great question at issue, their presence on debatable ground rendered them objects of suspicion alternately to each of the contending parties; and when, in 1780, the major part of the Delaware nation declared openly for the British crown, it was evident that the mission could not much longer hold its ground. It was for the British to solve the problem; and at their instigation, in the autumn of 1781, the missionaries and their converts in part were removed to Upper Sandusky, as prisoners of war, under suspicion of favoring the American cause. Thence the former were twice summoned to Detroit, the seat of British dominion in the then Northwest, and arraigned before the commandant of that post. Having established their innocence, and at liberty once more to resume their Christian work, the Moravians resolved upon establishing themselves in the neighborhood of Detroit, with the view of collecting their scattered converts, and gradually resuscitating the mission.

The point selected was on the Huron (now the Clinton), forty miles by water northwest of Detroit. Here they built New Gnadenhütten, in 1782. Four years later, New Gnadenhütten was abandoned, and a settlement effected on the Cuyahoga, in the present county of that name in northern Ohio. It was here that Mr. Heckewelder closed his missionary labors, and years memorable in his life, in the course of which he was "in journeyings often, in perils of waters, in perils of robbers, in perils of his countrymen, in perils by the heathen, in perils in the wilderness, in weariness, in watchings often, in hunger and thirst, in fastings often, in cold and nakedness," and yet spared, as to his life, to a good old age, in the quiet days of which, when resting from his labors, he drew up a narrative of this remarkable period in his own experience, and in the history of his church.

On severing his connection with the mission on the Cuyahoga, in the autumn of 1786, Mr. Heckewelder settled with his wife (Sarah m. n. Ohneberg, whom he married in 1780), and two daughters at Bethlehem. This change, however, brought him no rest, as much of his time for the next fifteen years was devoted to the interests of his church's work among the Indians, in behalf of which he made frequent and trying journeys to the west.

In the summer of 1792, Mr. Heckewelder was associated by Government with General Rufus Putnam (at that gentleman's request), to treat for peace with the Indians of the Wabash, and journeyed on this mission as far as Post Vincennes, where, on the 27th of September, articles of peace were formally signed by thirty-one chiefs of the Seven Nations represented at the meeting. This was a high testimonial of confidence in his knowledge of Indian life and Indian affairs. In the spring of the following year, he was a second time commissioned to assist at a treaty which the United States purposed to ratify with the Indians of the Miami of the Lake, through its accredited agents, General Benjamin Lincoln, Colonel Timothy Pickering, and Beverly Randolph. On this mission he travelled as far as Detroit. The remuneration Mr. Heckewelder received for these services, was judiciously economized for his old age, his immediate wants being supplied by his handicraft, and the income accruing from a nursery which he planted on his return from the western country. In the interval between 1797 and 1800, the subject of this sketch visited the Ohio country four times, and in 1801 he removed with his family to Gnadenhütten, on the Tuscarawas branch of the Muskingum. Here he remained nine years, having been entrusted by the Society of the United Brethren for Propagating the Gospel among the Heathen, founded at Bethlehem, in 1788, with the superintendence of a reservation of 12,000 acres of land on the Tuscarawas, granted by Congress to the said Society for the benefit of the Moravian Indians, as a consideration for the losses they incurred in the border-war of the Revolution. During his residence in Ohio, Mr. Heckewelder was also for a time in the civil service, being a postmaster, a justice of the peace, and an associate judge of the Court of Common Pleas.

In 1810 he returned to Bethlehem, built a house of his own, which is still standing, planted the premises with trees and shrubs from their native forest, surrounded himself with birds and wild flowers, and through these beautiful things of nature, sought by association to prolong fellowship with his beloved Indians in their distant woodland homes. He was called in 1815 to mourn the departure of his wife to the eternal world.

At a time when there was a growing spirit of inquiry among men of science in our country in the department of Indian archaeology, it need not surprise us that Mr. Heckewelder was sought out in his retirement, and called upon to contribute from the treasure-house of his experience. In this way originated his intimacy with Du Ponceau and Wistar of the American Philosophical Society, and that career of literary labor to which he dedicated the latter years of his life. In addition to occasional essays, which are incorporated in the Transactions of the Historical and Literary Committee of that society, Mr. Heckewelder, in 1818, published under its auspices, the "Account of the History, Manners, and Customs of the Indian Nations who once inhabited Pennsylvania and the neighboring States." His "Narrative of the Mission of the United Brethren among the Delaware and Mohican Indians," appeared in 1820, and in 1822 he prepared his well-known collection of "Names, which the Lenni Lenape, or Delaware Indians, gave to Rivers, Streams, and Localities within the States of Pennsylvania, New Jersey, Maryland, and Virginia, with their Significations." This was his last literary effort; another year of suffering, and on the 31st of January, 1823, the friend of the Delawares having lived to become a hoary old man of seventy-nine winters, passed away.

He left three daughters, Johanna Maria, born April 6, 1781, at Salem, Tuscarawas county, Ohio—the first white female child born within the borders of that State (she died at Bethlehem, September 19, 1868); Anna Salome, born August 13, 1784, at New Gnadenhütten, on the River Huron (Clinton), Michigan; she married Mr. Joseph Rice, of Bethlehem, and died January 15, 1857; and Susanna, born at Bethlehem, December 31, 1786; she married Mr. J. Christian Luckenbach, of Bethlehem, and died February 8, 1867.

Mr. Heckewelder was a fair representative of the Moravian missionaries of the last century, a class of men whose time was necessarily divided between the discharge of spiritual and secular duties; who preached the Gospel and administered the Sacraments in houses built by their own hands; who wielded the axe, as well as the sword of the Spirit, and who by lives of self-denial and patient endurance, sustained a mission among the aborigines of this country in the face of disappointments and obstacles, which would have discouraged any but men of their implicit faith in the Divine power of the Christian religion.

The subject of this notice made no pretensions to scholarship on taking the author's pen in hand. He was eminently an artless man, and artlessness is his characteristic as a writer. The fascinating volume to which this brief sketch is deemed a sufficient introduction, was received with almost unqualified approbation on its appearance in 1818. It was translated into German by Fr. Hesse, a clergyman of Nienburg, and published at Göttingen in 1821. A French translation by Du Ponceau appeared in Paris in 1822. True, there were those who subsequently took exception to Mr. Heckewelder's manifest predilection for the Lenape stock of the North American Indians, and others who charged him with credulity, because of the reception of their national traditions and myths upon the pages of his book. Knowing, as we do, that even the most prudent of men are liable to err in their search after truth, it would be presumptuous to claim infallibility for our author. It would, however, be as presumptuous to refuse his statements all claim to respect. Hence it may not be denied that John Heckewelder's contributions to Indian archaeology, touching their traditions, language, manners, customs, life, and character, while supplying a long-felt want, are worthy of the regard which is usually accorded to the literary productions of men whose intelligence, honesty, and acquaintance with their subject have qualified them to be its expounders.

In the preparation of his account, Mr. Heckewelder acknowledges his indebtedness to Moravian authorities, contemporaries, or colleagues of his in the work of missions among the aborigines of this country. He refers frequently to the Rev. J. Christopher Pyrlæus, and introduces extracts from the collection of notes and memoranda made by that clergyman during his sojourn in America. His references to Loskiel, the historian of the Moravian mission among the North American Indians, are more frequent. In fact, it is evident that he availed himself largely of the introductory chapters of that history, the material of which was furnished to Loskiel by the veteran missionary, David Zeisberger. In this way then, Mr. Heckewelder supplemented his personal experience, and the knowledge he had gained by intercourse with the Indians, touching those subjects of which he treats in his charming narrative.

Both the text and the author's footnotes, as found in the edition of 1818, are faithfully reproduced in the present issue; neither have been tampered with in a single instance. Such a course was deemed the only proper one, although it was conceded that the omission of occasionally recurrent passages, and a reconstruction of portions of the volume might render the matter more perspicuous, and the book more readable, without detracting from its value as a repository of well authenticated facts.[1]

x

Author's INTRODUCTION

The reader of the following pages, having already seen what has induced me to come forward with an historical account of the Indians, after so many have written on the same subject, will perhaps look for something more extraordinary in this than in other works of the kind which he has seen. Not wishing any one to raise his expectations too high, I shall briefly state that I have not written to excite astonishment, but for the information of those who are desirous of knowing the true history of those people, who, for centuries, have been in full possession of the country we now inhabit; but who have since emigrated to a great distance. I can only assure them, that I have not taken the information here communicated from the writings of others, but from the mouths of the very people I am going to speak of, and from my own observation of what I have witnessed while living among them. I have, however, occasionally quoted other authors, and in some instances copied short passages from their works, especially where I have thought it necessary to illustrate or corroborate my own statements of facts.

In what I have written concerning the character, customs, manners, and usages of these people, I cannot have been deceived, since it is the result of personal knowledge, of what I myself have seen, heard, and witnessed, while residing among and near them, for more than thirty years. I have however to remark, that this history, like other histories of former times, will not in every respect comport with the character of the Indians at the present time, since all these nations and tribes, by their intercourse with the white people, have lost much of the honourable and virtuous qualities which they once possessed, and added to their vices and immorality. Of this, no one can be a better judge than a missionary residing among them. And if,[2] what these people told us more than half a century ago; that lying, stealing, and other vicious acts, before the white men came among them, were considered as crimes, we may safely conclude—and we know it to be fact—that from that time to this, and especially within the last forty years, they have so much degenerated, that a delineation of their present character would bear no resemblance to what it was before.—It is therefore the history of early times, not of the present, that I have written; and to those times my delineations of their character must be considered to apply; yet, to shew the contrast, I have also delineated some of their present features.

It may be proper to mention in this place, that I have made use of the proper national name of the people whom we call *Delawares*, which is: "*Lenni Lenape*." Yet, as they, in the common way of speaking, merely pronounce the word "*Lenape*," I have, in most instances, when speaking of them, used this word singly. I have also made use of the word "*Mengwe*," or *Mingoes*, the name by which the *Lenape* commonly designate the people known to us by the name of the *Iroquois*, and *Five* or *Six Nations*. I shall give at the end a general list of all the names I have made use of in this communication, to which I refer the reader for instruction.

As the Indians, in all their public speeches and addresses, speak in the singular number, I have sometimes been led to follow their example, when reporting what they have said; I have also frequently, by attending particularly to the identical words spoken by them, copied their peculiar phrases, when I might have given their meaning in other words.

On the origin of the Indians, I have been silent, leaving this speculation to abler historians than myself. To their history, and notions with regard to their creation, I have given a place; and have also briefly related the traditions of the Lenape on the subject of their arrival at, and crossing the river Mississippi, their coming to the Atlantic coast, what occurred to them while in this country, and their retreat back again.

As the relation of the Delawares and Mohicans, concerning the policy adopted and pursued by the Six Nations towards them, may perhaps appear strange to many, and it may excite some astonishment, that a matter of such importance was not earlier set forth in the same light, I shall here, by way of introduction, and for the better understanding of the account which they give of this matter, examine into some facts, partly known to us already, and partly now told us in their relation; so that we may see how far these agree together, and know what we may rely upon.

It is conceded on all sides that the Lenape and Iroquois carried on long and bloody wars with each other; but while the one party assert, that they completely conquered the other, and reduced them by force to the condition of women, this assertion is as strongly and pointedly denied by the other side; I have therefore thought that the real truth of this fact was well deserving of investigation.

The story told by the Mingoes to the white people, of their having conquered the Lenape and made women of them, was much too implicitly believed; for the whites always acted towards the Delawares under the impression that it was true, refused even to hear their own account of the matter, and "shut their ears" against them, when they attempted to inform them of the real fact. This denial of common justice, is one of the principal complaints of the Lenape against the English, and makes a part of the tradition or history which they preserve for posterity.

This complaint indeed, bears hard upon us, and should, at least, operate as a solemn call to rectify the error, if such it is found to be; that we, in our history, may not record and transmit erroneous statements of those Aborigines, from whom we have received the country we now so happily inhabit. We are bound in honour to acquit ourselves of all charges of the kind which those people may have against us, who, in the beginning welcomed us to their shores, in hopes that "they and we would sit beside each other as brothers;" and it should not be said, that now, when they have surrendered their whole country to us, and retired to the wilds of a distant country, we turn our backs upon them with contempt.

We know that all Indians have the custom of transmitting to posterity, by a regular chain of tradition, the remarkable events which have taken place with them at any time, even often events of a trivial nature, of which I could mention a number. Ought we then, when such a source of information is at hand, to believe the story told by the Six Nations, of their having conquered the Lenape, (a powerful nation with a very large train of connexions and allies) and forcibly made them women? Ought we not, before we believe this, to look for a tradition of the circumstances of so important an event; for some account, at least, of the time, place, or places, where those battles were fought, which decided the fate of the Lenape, the Mohicans, and of a number of tribes connected with them? Are we to be left altogether ignorant of the numbers that were slain at the time, and the country in which this memorable event took place; whether on the St. Lawrence, on the Lakes, in the country of the conquerors, or of the conquered?

All these I am inclined to call *first* considerations, while a *second* would be: How does this story accord with the situation the first Europeans found these people in on their arrival in this country? Were not those who are said to be a conquered people, thickly settled on the whole length of the sea coast, and far inland, in and from Virginia to and beyond the Province of Maine, and had they not yet, at that very time, a great National Council Fire burning on the banks of the Delaware? Does not the joint tradition of the Delawares, Mohicans and Nanticokes, inform us, that their great National Council House[3] then extended from the head of the tide on the (now) Hudson river, to the head of the tide on the Potomack? All this we shall find faithfully copied or written down from their verbal tradition, and that this Council House "was pulled down by the white people!"[4] and of course was yet standing when they came into the country; which alone is sufficient to prove that the Lenape, at that time, were not a conquered people; and if they had been conquered since, we might expect to find the fact, with its particulars, somewhere on record.

It is admitted, however, by the Lenape themselves, that they and their allies were *made women* by the Iroquois. But how did this happen? Not surely by conquest, or the fate of battle. Strange as it may appear, it was not produced by the effects of superior force, but by successful intrigue. Here, if my informants were correct, and I trust they were, rests the great mystery, for the particulars of which, I refer the reader to the history of the Lenape and Mohicans themselves, as related in part by Loskiel in his "History of the Mission of the United Brethren among the North American Indians,"[5] and in this work.

In the first, he will find three material points ascertained, viz. 1st, "that the Delawares were too strong for the Iroquois, and could not be conquered by them by force of arms, but were subdued by insidious means. 2d, that the making women of the Delawares was not an act of compulsion, but the result of their own free will and consent; and 3d, that the whites were already in the country at the time this ceremony took place, since they were to hold one end of the great Peace Belt in their hands."[6] In the following History, which I have taken from the relation of the most intelligent and creditable old Indians, both Delawares and Mohicans, not only the same facts will be found, but also a more minute account of this transaction; in which it will be shewn, that the Dutch not only were present at, but were parties to it, that it was in this manner that the Six Nations were relieved from the critical situation they were in, at that very time, with regard to their enemies, the Delawares, Mohicans, and their connexions, and that the white people present coaxed and persuaded them to cause the hatchet to be buried, declaring at the same time[7] that they "would fall on those who should dig it up again;" which was, on the part of the Hollanders, a declaration of war against the Delawares and their allies, if they, or any of them, should attempt again to act hostilely against the Six Nations. All this, according to the tradition of the Lenape, was transacted at a place, since called "Nordman's Kill," a few miles from the spot where afterwards Albany was built, and but a short time after the Dutch had arrived at New York Island, probably between the years 1609 and 1620.

The Rev. Mr. Pyrlæus,[8] who had learned the Mohawk language of Conrad Weiser, and was stationed on the river of that name, for some time between the years 1742 and 1748, has noted down in a large manuscript book, that his friend there, the Mohawk chief, had told him, that at a place about four miles from Albany, now called Nordman's Kill,[10] the first covenant had been made between the Six Nations and the white people; which is in confirmation of the correctness of the above tradition of the Mohicans.[11]

This was then, according to the best accounts we have, the time when this pretended "conquest" took place; and the Delawares, (as the Six Nations have since said) were by them *made women*. It was, however, a conquest of a singular nature, effected through duplicity and intrigue, at *a council fire*, not *in battle*. "And, (say the Delawares and Mohicans, in their tradition,) when the English took the country from the *Dutchemaan*, (Hollanders) they stepped into the same alliance with the Six Nations, which their predecessors had established with them."

Colden, in his "History of the Five Nations,"[12] informs us, page 34, that this took place in the year 1664; and in page 36, gives us full proof of this alliance, by the following account—He says: "The Five Nations being now amply supplied by the English with fire-arms and ammunition, gave full swing to their warlike genius, and soon resolved to revenge the affronts they had at any time received from the Indian nations that lived at a greater distance from them. The nearest nations, as they were attacked, commonly fled to those that were further off, and the Five Nations pursued them. This, together with the desire they had of conquering, or ambition of making all the nations around them their tributaries, or to make them acknowledge the Five Nations to be so far their masters, as to be absolutely directed by them in all affairs of peace and war with their neighbours, made them overrun great part of North America. They carried their arms as far south as Carolina; to the northward of New England; and as far west as the river Mississippi; over a vast country, which extends twelve hundred miles in length, from north to south, and about six hundred miles in breadth; where they entirely destroyed many nations, of whom there are now no accounts remaining among the English," &c.

To what a number of important questions would not the above statement give rise? But I will confine myself to a few, and enquire first, for what purpose the Five Nations were armed, and so "amply supplied with ammunition?" and secondly, what use did they make of those arms? The Delawares and Mohicans believed that the white people, first the Dutch and then the English, did all that was in their power to make the Mengwe a great people, so that they might rule over them and all other nations, and "that they had done what they wanted them to do," &c. For an answer to the second question, we have only to believe what Colden himself tells us, of what the same Mengwe or Iroquois did, after having received arms and ammunition from the English, which it clearly appears they could not have done before. Now, if we even were willing to admit that they had only gone off, "to revenge the affronts they had at any time received from the Indian Nations," yet, we would be willing to know, of what nature those affronts had been; otherwise we might conclude, that they were no other than that those nations had refused "to become tributary to them; would not submit to their mandates, nor have them for their masters;" and therefore had beaten them off, when they came into their country for the purpose of bringing them under subjection, and perhaps also paid them a visit in return, after they had murdered some of their people.

If we were permitted to omit the words, "revenge the affronts they had received from other nations," &c., we need not one moment be at a loss to know precisely what they went out for, as the historian himself tells us, that they, soon after receiving fire-arms and ammunition, "gave full swing to their warlike genius, and went off with a desire of conquering nations—of making all those around them their tributaries, and compelling them all to acknowledge the Five Nations to be their masters, and to be absolutely directed by them, in all affairs of peace and war." We then know with certainty, what the object was for which they took the field.

We are here also told, of the vast tract of country over which the Six Nations had carried their arms, subduing, and even "so destroying many nations, that no account of them was now remaining with the English!"

In reply to this I might bring forward some sayings and assertions of the Delawares and Mohicans, which would not comport with the above story, nor apply to the great name the Six Nations have given themselves, which, as Colden tells us, is *Ongwe-honwe*, and signifies "men surpassing all others, superior to the rest of mankind:" but my object here is merely to discuss the fact, whether, previous to the white people's coming into the country, and while unsupplied with fire-arms, hatchets, &c., those Iroquois had done such wonders among nations as they report; or, whether all this was done since that time, and in consequence of their being put into possession of those destructive weapons which they had not before; for how are we to judge, and decide on the comparative bravery of two different nations, without knowing whether or not the combatants were placed on an equal footing with regard to the weapons they used against each other?

I might ask the simple question, whether the Dutch, and afterwards the English, have favoured their "brethren," the Delawares, Mohicans, and other tribes connected with them, who lived between them and the Six Nations, and on the land which they wanted to have, in the same manner that they have favoured their enemies?

Colden, in his Introduction to the History of the Five Nations, page 3, says: "I have been told by old men in New England, who remembered the time when the Mohawks made war on *their* Indians," (meaning here the Mohicans, or River Indians, as they often were called,) "that as soon as a single Mohawk was discovered in the country, *their* Indians raised a cry, from hill to hill, *a Mohawk! a Mohawk!* upon which they all fled, like sheep before wolves, without attempting to make the least resistance, whatever odds were on their side," and that, "the poor New England Indians immediately ran to the Christian houses, and the Mohawks often pursued them so closely, that they entered along with them, and knocked their brains out in the presence of the people of the house," &c.

This is indeed a lamentable story! It might be asked, How could the white people, whom those very Mohicans had hospitably welcomed, and permitted to live with them on their land, suffer an enemy to come into the country to destroy their benefactors, without making any opposition? Why did these Indians suffer this? Why did they not with spirit meet this enemy?

The answer to this last question will be found in their traditional history of the great meeting at Nordman's Kill, where they were expressly told, after they had consented to bury the hatchet, wherewith they warred against the Six Nations, "That whatsoever nation, (meaning the Mohicans and Delawares) should dig up the hatchet again, on them would the white people fall and take revenge!"

Thus, then, arms were put into the hands of the Six Nations, and with them the Dutch, and afterwards the English, sided; but the Delawares and Mohicans were compelled to remain unarmed, for fear of being cut up by the white people, who had taken part with their enemies. May we not conclude, that these poor New England Indians were placed between two fires?

We do not, I believe, find that in the then middle colonies, the Mohawks, or any of the Five Nations, had ventured so far in their hostile conduct against the Delawares, as they had done to the Mohicans of New England, though the alliance between the Dutch and the Five Nations, and afterwards between the English and the latter, was much against both, and indeed more against the Delawares than the Mohicans: yet, by turning to treaties and councils, held with these nations between the years 1740 and 1760, in Pennsylvania,[13] we find much insolent language, which the Iroquois were, I will say, permitted, but which, the people concerned say, they were "bid or hired to make against the Delawares, for the purpose of stopping their mouths, preventing them from stating their complaints and grievances, and asking redress from the colonial government."

The result of such high toned language, as that which was made use of to the Delawares, by the Six Nations, at a council held at the proprietors, in July, 1742, and at other times afterwards,[14] might easily have been foretold. For although now, these defenseless people had to submit to such gross insults, instead of seeing their grievances redressed, yet they were not ignorant of the manner in which they one day might take revenge, the door to the French, who were enemies to the English, being always open to them; they had but to go "on one side" (as they expressed themselves) to be out of the way of the Iroquois, and they could obtain from the possessors of Canada, and Louisiana, all that they wanted, fire-arms, hatchets, scalping-knives, ammunition, &c. They did so, and withdrew to the Ohio country, whither they were followed by others from time to time, and by the time the French war broke out, they were in perfect readiness, and joining the enemies of Britain, they murdered great numbers of the defenseless inhabitants of Pennsylvania, laid the whole frontier waste, and spread terror and misery far and wide by the outrages they committed; I have been myself a witness to those scenes, and to the distresses of hundreds of poor people, only in this one quarter.

A work, entitled: "An Enquiry into the Causes of the Alienation of the Delaware and Shawanese Indians from the British Interest," written by Charles Thompson,[15] Esq., and printed in London, in 1759, which some time since fell into my hands, well merits to be read with attention, on account of the correctness of the information that it contains.

By this time, the Delawares were sensible of the imposition which had been practiced upon them. They saw that a plan had been organized for their destruction, and that not only their independence, but their very existence, was at stake; they therefore took measures to defend themselves, by abandoning the system of neutrality into which they had been insidiously drawn.

It was not without difficulty that I obtained from them these interesting details, for they felt ashamed of their own conduct; they were afraid of being charged with cowardice, or at least with want of forethought, in having acted as they did, and not having discovered their error until it was too late.

And yet, in my opinion, those fears were entirely groundless, and there appears nothing in their whole conduct disparaging to the courage and high sense of honour of that brave nation. Let us for a moment place ourselves in the situation of the Delawares, Mohicans, and the other tribes connected with them, at the time when the Europeans first landed on New York Island. They were then in the height of their glory, pursuing their successes against the Iroquois, with whom they had long been at war. They were in possession of the whole country, from the sea coast to the Mississippi, from the River St. Lawrence to the frontier of Carolina, while the habitations of their enemies did not extend far beyond the great Lakes. In this situation, they are on a sudden checked in their career, by a phenomenon they had till then never beheld; immense canoes arriving at their shores, filled with people of a different colour, language, dress, and manners, from themselves! In their astonishment they call out to one another: "Behold! the Gods are come to visit us!"[16] They at first considered these astonishing beings, as messengers of peace, sent from the abode of the Great Spirit, and therefore, employed their time in preparing and making sacrifices to that Great Being who had so highly honoured them. Lost in amazement, fond of the enjoyment of this new spectacle, and anxious to know the result, they were unmindful of those matters which hitherto had taken up their minds, and had been the object of their pursuits; they thought of nothing else but the wonders which now struck their eyes, and their sharpest wits were constantly employed in endeavouring to divine this great mystery! Such is the manner in which they relate that event, the strong impression of which is not yet obliterated from their minds.

It was the *Delawares* who first received and welcomed these new guests on New York Island; the Mohicans who inhabited the whole of the North River above, on its eastern side, were sent for to participate in the joy which was felt on being honoured by such visitants. Their tradition of this event is clear and explicit. None of the enemy, say they, (meaning the Five Nations[17]) were present.

It may possibly be asked, how the Dutch could favour the Five Nations so much, when none of them were present at the meetings which took place on their arrival in America? how they came to abandon their first friends, and take part against them with strangers? and how the Dutch became acquainted with those strangers? I shall simply, in answer, give the traditional accounts of the Mohicans in their own words: "The Dutch Traders (say they) penetrating into our country, high up the Mohicanichtuck (the Hudson River), fell in with some of the Mingo warriors, who told them that they were warring against the very people, (the Delawares and Mohicans) who had so kindly received them; they easily foresaw, that they could not carry on their trade with their old friends, while this was the case; neither would the Mingoes suffer them to trade with their enemies, unless they (the Dutch) assisted them in bringing about a peace between them. They also made these traders sensible, that they at that time, were at war with a people of the same colour with theirs (meaning the French), who had, by means of a very large river which lay to the North, come into the country; that they (the Mengwe) were the greatest and most powerful of all the Indian nations; that if the people they belonged to, were friends to their enemies, and sided with them in their wars, they would turn their whole force against them; but if, on the other hand, the Dutch would join them in effecting a peace with them, so that their hatchet should be buried forever, they would support and protect them in all their undertakings;[18] that these traders being frightened, had returned home, and having stated the matter to their chief (the Dutch Governor), a vessel soon after went high up the river to an appointed place, where meeting with the Maqua (Five Nations), a conference was held, at which the Dutch promised them, that they would use their best endeavours to persuade their enemies to give up the hatchet to be buried, which, some time afterwards, actually took place."

These are (as they say) the circumstances which led to the league which was afterwards established between the white people and the Five Nations, which was the cause of much dissatisfaction, injustice, and bloodshed, and which would not have taken place, if the rights and privileges of the different nations and tribes had been respected, and each left to act for itself, especially in selling their lands to the Europeans.

Having seen how the Five, afterwards Six Nations, rose to power, we have next to state by what means they lost the ascendancy which they had thus acquired.

The withdrawing of the principal part of the Delawares, and the Shawanos, from the Atlantic coast, between the years 1740 and 1760, afforded them an opportunity of consulting with the western tribes, on the manner of taking revenge on the Iroquois for the many provocations, wrongs and insults they had received from them; when *ten* nations immediately entered into an alliance for that purpose, the French having promised to assist them.[19] In the year 1756, they agreed to move on in detached bodies, as though they meant to attack the English, with whom they and the French were then at war, and then turn suddenly on the Six Nations and make a bold stroke. Though, for various reasons, their designs could not at that time be carried into effect, yet they did not lose sight of the object, waiting only for a proper opportunity.

It would, however, have been next to impossible, under existing circumstances, and while the Six Nations were supported by such a powerful ally as the English, for the Delawares and their allies, to subdue, or even effectually to chastise them. These Nations, however, at the commencement of a war between the English nation and the Colonies, were become so far independent, that such of them as lived remote from the British stations or garrisons, or were not immediately under their eye, were at full liberty to side with whom they pleased; and though the Six Nations attempted to dictate to the Western Delawares, what side they should take, their spirited chief, Captain White Eyes, did not hesitate to reply, in the name of his nation: "that he should do as he pleased; that he wore no petticoats, as they falsely pretended; he was no woman, but a man, and they should find him to act as such." That this brave chief was in earnest, was soon after verified, by a party of Delawares joining the American army.

In 1781, when almost all the Indian nations were in the British interest, except a part of the Delawares, among whom were the Christian Indians between 2 and 300 souls in number,[20] the British Indian agent at Detroit applied to the great council of the Six Nations at Niagara, to remove those Christian Indians out of the country: the Iroquois upon this sent a war message to the Chippeways and Ottawas,[21] to this effect: "We herewith make you a present of the Christian Indians, to make soup of;[22]" which in the war language of the Indians, is saying: "We deliver these people to you to be murdered!" These brave Indians sent the message immediately back again with the reply: "We have no cause for doing this!"

The same message being next sent to the Wyandots, they likewise disobeyed their orders, and did not make the least attempt to murder those innocent people. The Iroquois, therefore, were completely at a loss how to think and act, seeing that their orders were every where disregarded.

At the conclusion of the revolutionary war, they had the mortification to see, that the trade which they had hitherto carried on, and to them was so agreeable and profitable, that of selling to the English the land of other nations, to which they had no possible claim, was at once and forever put an end to by the liberal line of conduct which the American Government adopted with the Indian Nations, leaving each at liberty to sell its own lands, reserving, only to themselves the right of purchase, to the exclusion of foreigners of every description.

In addition to this, the bond of connexion which subsisted between these Six Nations, if it was not entirely broken, yet was much obstructed, by a separation which took place at the close of that war, when a part, and the most active body of them, retired into Canada. No nation then any more regarded their commands, nor even their advice, when it did not accord with their will and inclination; all which became evident during the whole time the Western Nations were at war with the United States, and until the peace made with them in 1795.[23]

At last, being sensible of their humbled situation, and probably dreading the consequence of their former insolent conduct to the other Indian Nations, and principally the Delawares, whom they had so long and so much insulted, were they not to make some amends for all this contumely? They came forward, at the critical moment, just previous to the Treaty concluded by General Wayne, and formally declared the Delaware nation to be no longer *Women*, but MEN.

I hope to be believed in the solemn assertion which I now make: That in all that I have written on the subject of the history and politics of the Indian Nations, I have neither been influenced by partiality for the one, or undue prejudice against the other, but having had the best opportunities of obtaining from authentic sources, such information in matters of fact, as has enabled me to make up my mind on the subject, I have taken the liberty of expressing my opinion as I have honestly formed it, leaving the reader, however, at liberty to judge and decide for himself as he may deem most proper.

I wish once more to observe, that in this history it is principally meant to shew, rather what the Indians of this country were previous to the white people's arrival, than what they now are; for now, the two great nations, the Iroquois and the Delawares, are no longer the same people that they formerly were. The former, who, as their rivals would assert, were more like beasts than human beings, and made intrigue their only study, have, by their intercourse with the whites, become an industrious and somewhat civilised people; at least many of them are so, which is probably owing to their having been permitted to live so long, (indeed, for more than a century) in the same district of country, and while the British possessed it, under the protection of the superintendent of Indian affairs; while the latter have always been oppressed and persecuted, disturbed and driven from place to place, scarcely enjoying themselves at any place for a dozen years at a time; having constantly the lowest class of whites for their neighbours, and having no opportunity of displaying their true character and the talents that nature had bestowed upon them.

My long residence among those nations in the constant habit of unrestrained familiarity, has enabled me to know them well, and made me intimately acquainted with the manners, customs, character and disposition of those men of nature, when uncorrupted by European vices. Of these, I think I could draw a highly interesting picture, if I only possessed adequate powers of description: but the talent of writing is not to be acquired in the wilderness, among savages. I have felt it, however, to be a duty incumbent upon me to make the attempt, and I have done it in the following pages, with a rude but faithful pencil. I have spent a great part of my life among those people, and have been treated by them with uniform kindness and hospitality. I have witnessed their virtues and experienced their goodness. I owe them a debt of gratitude, which I cannot acquit better than by presenting to the world this plain unadorned picture, which I have drawn in the spirit of candour and truth. Alas! in a few years, perhaps, they will have entirely disappeared from the face of the earth, and all that will be remembered of them will be that they existed and were numbered among the barbarous tribes that once inhabited this vast continent. At least, let it not be said, that among the whole race of white Christian men, not one single individual could be found, who, rising above the cloud of prejudice with which the pride of civilisation has surrounded the original inhabitants of this land, would undertake the task of doing justice to their many excellent qualities, and raise a small frail monument to their memory.

I shall conclude with a few necessary remarks for the information of the reader.

Lenni Lenape being the national and proper name of the people we call "Delawares," I have retained this name, or for brevity's sake, called them simply *Lenape*, as they do themselves in most instances. Their name signifies "*original people*," a race of human beings who are the same that they were in the beginning, *unchanged* and *unmixed*.[24]

These people (the Lenni Lenape) are known and called by all the western, northern, and some of the southern nations, by the name of *Wapanachki*, which the Europeans have corrupted into *Apenaki, Openagi, Abenaquis,*[25] and *Abenakis.*[26] All these names, however differently written, and improperly understood by authors, point to one and the same people, the Lenape, who are by this compound word, called "people at the rising of the Sun," or as we would say, *Eastlanders*; and are acknowledged by near forty Indian tribes, whom we call nations, as being their grandfathers. All these nations, derived from the same stock, recognise each other as Wapanachki, which among them is a generic name.

The name "*Delawares,*" which we give to these people, is unknown in their language, and I well remember the time when they thought the whites had given it to them in derision; but they were reconciled to it, on being told that it was the name of a great white chief, Lord de la War, which had been given to them and their river. As they are fond of being named after distinguished men, they were rather pleased, considering it as a compliment.

The *Mahicanni* have been called by so many different names,[27] that I was at a loss which to adopt, so that the reader might know what people were meant. Loskiel calls them "Mohicans," which is nearest to their real name Mahicanni, which, of course, I have adopted.

The name "*Nanticokes*" I have left as generally used, though properly it should be *Néntico*, or after the English pronunciation *Nantico*.

The "*Canai,*" I call by their *proper* name. I allude here to those people we call *Canais, Conois, Conoys, Canaways, Kanhawas, Canawese*.

With regard to the Five, or Six Nations, I have called them by different names, such as are most common, and well understood. The Lenape (Delawares) are never heard to say "*Six Nations,*" and it is a rare thing to hear these people named by them otherwise than *Mengwe*; the Mahicanni call them *Maqua*, and even most white people call them *Mingoes*. When therefore I have said the *Five* or *Six Nations*, I have only used our own mode of speaking, not that of the Indians, who never look upon them as having been so many *nations*; but *divisions*, and *tribes*, who, as united, have become a nation. Thus, when the Lenape (Delawares) happen to name them as one body, the word they make use of implies "the five divisions together, or united," as will be seen in another place of this work. I call them also *Iroquois*, after the French and some English writers.

The *Wyandots*, or *Wyondots*, are the same whom the French call *Hurons*, and sometimes *Guyandots*. Father Sagard, a French Missionary, who lived among them in the 17th century, and has written an account of his mission, and a kind of dictionary of their language, says their proper name is *Ahouandâte*, from whence it is evident that the English appellation Wyandots has been derived.

There being so many words in the language of the Lenape and their kindred tribes, the sound of which cannot well be represented according to the English pronunciation, I have in general adopted for them the German mode of spelling. The *ch*, particularly before a consonant, is a strong guttural, and unless an Englishman has the use of the Greek χ, he will not be able to pronounce it, as in the words *Chasquem* (Indian corn), *Cheltol* (many), *Ches* (a skin), *Chauchschisis* (an old woman), and a great many more. Sometimes, indeed, in the middle of a word substitutes may be found which may do, as in the word *Nimachtak* (brethren), which might be written *Nemaughtok*, but this will seldom answer. This is probably the reason that most of the English authors have written Indian words so incorrectly, far more so than French authors.

The Delawares have neither of the letters R, F, nor V, in their language, though they easily learn to pronounce them. They have a consonant peculiar to them and other Indians, which is a sibilant, and which we represent by W. It is produced by a soft whistling, and is not unpleasant to the ear, although it comes before a consonant. It is not much unlike the English sound *wh* in *what*, but not so round or full, and rather more whistled. *W* before a vowel is pronounced as in English.

Part 1

History, Manners, and Customs
of
the Indian nations
who once inhabited Pennsylvania and
the neighbouring states

Chapter 1 ~
Historical traditions of the Indians

The Lenni Lenape (according to the traditions handed down to them by their ancestors) resided many hundred years ago, in a very distant country in the western part of the American continent. For some reason, which I do not find accounted for, they determined on migrating to the eastward, and accordingly set out together in a body. After a very long journey, and many nights' encampments[28] by the way, they at length arrived on the *Namœsi Sipu*,[29] where they fell in with the Mengwe,[30] who had likewise emigrated from a distant country, and had struck upon this river somewhat higher up. Their object was the same with that of the Delawares; they were proceeding on to the eastward, until they should find a country that pleased them. The spies which the Lenape had sent forward for the purpose of reconnoitring, had long before their arrival discovered that the country east of the Mississippi was inhabited by a very powerful nation, who had many large towns built on the great rivers flowing through their land. Those people (as I was told) called themselves *Talligeu* or *Talligewi*. Colonel John Gibson,[31] however, a gentleman who has a thorough knowledge of the Indians, and speaks several of their languages, is of opinion that they were not called *Talligewi*, but *Alligewi*, and it would seem that he is right, from the traces of their name which still remain in the country, the Allegheny river and mountains having indubitably been named after them. The Delawares still call the former *Alligéwi Sipu*, the River of the Alligewi. We have adopted, I know not for what reason, its Iroquois name, Ohio, which the French had literally translated into *La Belle Riviere*, The Beautiful River.[32] A branch of it, however, still retains the ancient name Allegheny.

Many wonderful things are told of this famous people. They are said to have been remarkably tall and stout, and there is a tradition that there were giants among them, people of a much

1

larger size than the tallest of the Lenape. It is related that they had built to themselves regular fortifications or entrenchments, from whence they would sally out, but were generally repulsed. I have seen many of the fortifications said to have been built by them, two of which, in particular, were remarkable. One of them was near the mouth of the river Huron, which empties itself into the Lake St. Clair, on the north side of that lake, at the distance of about 20 miles N. E. of Detroit. This spot of ground was, in the year 1786, owned and occupied by a Mr. Tucker. The other works, properly entrenchments, being walls or banks of earth regularly thrown up, with a deep ditch on the outside, were on the Huron river, east of the Sandusky, about six or eight miles from Lake Erie. Outside of the gateways of each of these two entrenchments, which lay within a mile of each other, were a number of large flat mounds, in which, the Indian pilot said, were buried hundreds of the slain Talligewi, whom I shall hereafter with Colonel Gibson call *Alligewi*. Of these entrenchments, Mr. Abraham Steiner, who was with me at the time when I saw them, gave a very accurate description, which was published at Philadelphia, in 1789 or 1790, in some periodical work the name of which I cannot at present remember.[33]

When the Lenape arrived on the banks of the Mississippi, they sent a message to the Alligewi to request permission to settle themselves in their neighbourhood. This was refused them, but they obtained leave to pass through the country and seek a settlement farther to the eastward. They accordingly began to cross the Namæsi Sipu, when the Alligewi, seeing that their numbers were so very great, and in fact they consisted of many thousands, made a furious attack on those who had crossed, threatening them all with destruction, if they dared to persist in coming over to their side of the river. Fired at the treachery of these people, and the great loss of men they had sustained, and besides, not being prepared for a conflict, the Lenape consulted on what was to be done; whether to retreat in the best manner they could, or try their strength, and let the enemy see that they were not cowards, but men, and too high-minded to suffer themselves to be driven off before they had made a trial of their strength, and were convinced that the enemy was too powerful for them. The Mengwe, who had hitherto been satisfied with being spectators from a distance, offered to join them, on condition that, after conquering the country, they should be entitled to share it with them; their proposal was accepted, and the resolution was taken by the two nations, to conquer or die.

Having thus united their forces, the Lenape and Mengwe declared war against the Alligewi, and great battles were fought, in which many warriors fell on both sides. The enemy fortified their large towns and erected fortifications, especially on large rivers, and near lakes, where they were successively attacked and sometimes stormed by the allies. An engagement took place in which hundreds fell, who were afterwards buried in holes or laid together in heaps and covered over with earth. No quarter was given, so that the Alligewi, at last, finding that their destruction was inevitable if they persisted in their obstinacy, abandoned the country to the conquerors, and fled down the Mississippi river, from whence they never returned. The war which was carried on with this nation, lasted many years, during which the Lenape lost a great number of their warriors, while the Mengwe would always hang back in the rear, leaving them to face the enemy. In the end, the conquerors divided the country between themselves; the Mengwe made choice of the lands in the vicinity of the great lakes, and on their tributary streams, and the Lenape took possession of the country to the south. For a long period of time, some say many hundred years, the two nations resided peaceably in this country, and increased very fast; some of their most enterprising huntsmen and warriors crossed the great swamps,[34] and falling on streams running to the eastward, followed them down to the great Bay River,[35] thence into the Bay itself, which we call Chesapeak. As they pursued their travels, partly by land and partly by water, sometimes near and at other times on the great Saltwater Lake, as they call the Sea, they discovered the great River, which we call the Delaware; and thence exploring still eastward, the *Scheyichbi* country, now named New Jersey, they arrived at another great stream, that which we call the Hudson or North River. Satisfied with what they had seen, they, (or some of them) after a long absence, returned to their nation and reported the discoveries they had made; they described the country they had discovered, as abounding in game and various kinds of fruits; and the rivers and bays, with fish, tortoises, &c., together with abundance of water-fowl, and no enemy to be dreaded. They considered the event as a fortunate one for them, and concluding this to be the country destined for them by the Great Spirit, they began to emigrate thither, as yet but in small bodies, so as not to be straitened for want of provisions by the way, some even laying by for a whole year; at last they settled on the four great rivers (which we call Delaware, Hudson, Susquehannah, and Potomack) making the Delaware, to which they gave the name of "*Lenapewihittuck*,"[36] (the river or stream of the Lenape) the centre of their possessions.

They say, however, that the whole of their nation did not reach this country; that many remained behind in order to aid and assist that great body of their people, which had not crossed the Namæsi Sipu, but had retreated into the interior of the country on the other side, on being informed of the reception which those who had crossed had met with, and probably thinking that they had all been killed by the enemy.

Their nation finally became divided into three separate bodies; the larger body, which they suppose to have been one half of the whole, was settled on the Atlantic, and the other half was again divided into two parts, one of which, the strongest as they suppose, remained beyond the Mississippi, and the remainder where they left them, on this side of that river.

Those of the Delawares who fixed their abode on the shores of the Atlantic divided themselves into three tribes. Two of them, distinguished by the names of the *Turtle* and the *Turkey*, the former calling themselves *Unâmis* and the other *Unalâchtgo*, chose those grounds to settle on, which lay nearest to the sea, between the coast and the high mountains. As they multiplied, their settlements extended from the *Mohicannittuck* (river of the Mohicans, which we call the North or Hudson river) to beyond the Potomack.

Many families with their connexions choosing to live by themselves, were scattered not only on the larger, but also on the small streams throughout the country, having towns and villages, where they lived together in separate bodies, in each of which a chief resided; those chiefs, however, were subordinate (by their own free will, the only kind of subordination which the Indians know) to the head chiefs or great council of the nation, whom they officially informed of all events or occurrences affecting the general interest which came to their knowledge. The third tribe, the *Wolf*, commonly called the *Minsi*, which we have corrupted into *Monseys*, had chosen to live back of the two other tribes, and formed a kind of bulwark for their protection, watching the motions of the Mengwe, and being at hand to afford their aid in case of a rupture with them. The Minsi were considered the most warlike and active branch of the Lenape. They extended their settlements, from the *Minisink*, a place named after them, where they had their council seat and fire, quite up to the Hudson on the east; and to the west or south west far beyond the Susquehannah: their northern boundaries were supposed originally to be the heads of the great rivers Susquehannah and Delaware, and their southern boundaries that ridge of hills known in New Jersey by the name of *Muskanecun*, and in Pennsylvania, by those of *Lehigh*, *Coghnewago*, &c. Within this boundary were their principal settlements; and even as late as the year 1742, they had a town, with a large peach orchard, on the tract of land where *Nazareth*, in Pennsylvania, has since been built;[37] another on *Lehigh* (the west branch of the Delaware), and others beyond the blue ridge, besides small family settlements here and there scattered.

From the above *three* tribes, the *Unâmis*, *Unalâchtgo*, and the *Minsi*, comprising together the body of those people we call *Delawares*, had in the course of time, sprung many others, who, having for their own conveniency, chosen distant spots to settle on, and increasing in numbers, gave themselves names or received them from others. Those names, generally given after some simple natural objects, or after something striking or extraordinary, they continued to bear even after they ceased to be applicable, when they removed to other places, where the object after which they were named was not to be found; thus they formed separate and distinct tribes, yet did not deny their origin, but retained their affection for the parent tribe, of which they were even proud to be called the grandchildren.

This was the case with the *Mahicanni* or Mohicans, in the east, a people who by intermarriages had become a detached body, mixing two languages together, and forming out of the two a dialect of their own: choosing to live by themselves, they had crossed the Hudson River, naming it Mahicannituck River after their assumed name, and spread themselves over all that country which now composes the eastern states. New tribes again sprung from them who assumed distinct names; still however not breaking off from the parent stock, but acknowledging the Lenni Lenape to be their grandfather: the Delawares, at last, thought proper to enlarge their council house for their Mahicanni grandchildren, that they might come to their fire, that is to say, be benefited by their advice, and also in order to keep alive their family connexions and remain in league with each other.

Much the same thing happened with a body of the Lenape, called *Nanticokes*, who had, together with their offspring, proceeded far to the south, in Maryland and Virginia; the council house was by their grandfather (the Delawares), extended to the Potomack, in the same manner and for the same motives as had been done with the *Mahicanni*.

Meanwhile the Mengwe, who had first settled on the great Lakes between them, had always kept a number of canoes in readiness to save themselves, in case the Alligewi should return, and their number also increasing, they had in time proceeded farther, and settled below the Lakes along the River St. Lawrence, so that they were now become, on the north side, neighbours of the Lenape tribes.

These Mengwe now began to look upon their southern neighbours with a jealous eye, became afraid of their growing power, and of being dispossessed by them of the lands they occupied. To meet this evil in time, they first sought to raise quarrels and disturbances, which in the end might lead to wars between distant tribes and the Lenape, for which purpose, they clandestinely murdered people on one or the other side, seeking to induce the injured party to believe, that some particular nation or tribe had been the aggressor; and having actually succeeded to their wishes, they now stole into the country of the Lenape and

6

their associates, frequently surprising them at their hunting camps, occasionally committing murders, and making off with the plunder. Foreseeing, however, that they could not go on in this way without being detected, they had recourse to other artful means, by which they actually succeeded in setting tribe against tribe, and nation against nation. As each nation or tribe has a particular mark on their war clubs, different from that of the others; and as on seeing one of these near the dead body of a murdered person, it is immediately known what nation or tribe has been the aggressor; so the Mengwe having left a war club, such as the Lenape made use of, in the Cherokee country, where they had purposely committed a murder, of course the Cherokees naturally concluding that it had been committed by the Lenape, fell suddenly upon them, which produced a most bloody war between the two nations. The treachery of the Mengwe, however, having been at length discovered, the Lenape determined on taking an exemplary revenge, and, indeed, nothing short of a total extirpation[38] of that deceitful race was resolved on; they were, besides, known to eat human flesh,[39] to kill men for the purpose of devouring them; and therefore were not considered by the Lenape as a pure race, or as rational beings; but as a mixture of the human and brutal kinds.

War being now openly declared against the Mengwe, it was carried on with vigour; until, at last, finding that they were no match for so powerful an enemy as the Lenape, who had such a train of connexions, ready to join them if necessity required, they fell upon the plan of entering into a confederacy with each other, by which they would be bound to make a common cause, and meet the common enemy with their united force, and not, as the present prospect was, be destroyed by tribes, which threatened in the end the destruction of the whole. Until this time, each tribe of the Mengwe had acted independent of the others, and they were not inclined to come under any supreme authority, which might counteract their base designs; for now, a single tribe, or even individuals of a tribe, by the commission of wanton hostilities, would draw the more peaceable among them into wars and bloodshed, as particularly had been the case with the Senecas, who were the most restless of the whole; and though the Lenape had directed their force principally against the aggressors, yet the body of the nation became thereby weaker; so that they saw the necessity of coming under some better regulations and government.[40]

This confederation took place some time between the 15th and 16th century;[41] the most bloody wars were afterwards carried on for a great length of time, between the confederated Iroquois, and the Delawares and their connexions, in which the Lenape say that they generally came off victorious. While these wars were carrying on with vigour, the French landed in Canada, and it was not long before they and the now combined Five Nations, or tribes, were at war with each other, the latter not being willing to permit that the French should establish themselves in that country. At last the Iroquois, finding themselves between two fires, and without any prospect of conquering the Lenape by arms, and seeing the necessity of withdrawing with their families, from the shores of the St. Lawrence, to the interior of the country, where the French could not easily reach them, fell upon a stratagem, which they flattered themselves would, if successful, secure to them not only a peace with the Lenape, but also with all the other tribes connected with them; so that they would then have but one enemy (the French) to contend with.

This plan was very deeply laid, and was calculated to deprive the Lenape and their allies, not only of their power but of their military fame, which had exalted them above all the other Indian nations. They were to be persuaded to abstain from the use of arms, and assume the station of mediators and umpires among their warlike neighbours. In the language of the Indians, they were to be made *women*.[42] It must be understood that among these nations wars are never brought to an end but by the interference of the weaker sex. The men, however tired of fighting, are afraid of being considered as cowards if they should intimate a desire for peace. It is not becoming, say they, for a warrior, with the bloody weapon in his hand, to hold pacific language to his enemy. He must shew to the end a determined courage, and appear as ready and willing to fight as at the beginning of the contest. Neither, say they, is it proper, to threaten and to sue in the same breath, to hold the peace belt in one hand, and the tomahawk in the other; men's words, as well as their actions, should be of a piece, all good or all bad; for it is a fixed maxim of theirs, which they apply on all occasions, that good can never dwell with evil. They also think that a treaty produced by threats or by force, cannot be binding. With these dispositions, war would never have ceased among Indians, until the extermination of one or the other party, if the tender and compassionate sex had not come forward, and by their moving speeches persuaded the enraged combatants to bury their hatchets, and make peace with each other. On these occasions they were very eloquent, they would lament with great feeling the losses suffered on both sides, when there was not a warrior, perhaps, who had not lost a son, a brother, or a friend. They would describe the sorrows of widowed wives, and, above all, of bereaved mothers. The pains of child-birth, the anxieties attending the progress of their sons from infancy to manhood, they had willingly and even cheerfully suffered; but after all these trials, how cruel was it for them to see those promising youths whom they had reared with so much care, fall victims to the rage of war, and a prey to a relentless enemy; to see them slaughtered on the field of battle, or put to death, as prisoners, by a protracted torture, in the midst of the most exquisite torments. The thought of such scenes made them curse their own existence, and shudder at the idea of bearing children. Then they would conjure the warriors by every thing that was dear to them, to take pity on the sufferings of their wives and helpless infants, to turn their faces once more towards their homes, families, and friends, to forgive the wrongs suffered from each other, to lay aside their deadly weapons, and smoke together the pipe of amity and peace. They had given on both sides sufficient proofs of their courage; the contending nations were alike high-minded and brave, and they must now embrace as friends those whom they had learned to respect as enemies. Speeches like these seldom failed of their intended effect, and the women by this honorable function of peace-makers, were placed in a situation by no means undignified. It would not be a disgrace, therefore; on the contrary, it would be an honour to a powerful nation, who could not be suspected of wanting either strength or courage, to assume that station by which they would be the means, and the only means, of preserving the general peace and saving the Indian race from utter extirpation.

Such were the arguments which the artful Mengwe urged to the Lenape to make them fall into the snare which they had prepared for them. They had reflected, they said, deeply reflected on their critical situation; there remained no resource for them, but that some magnanimous nation should assume the part and situation of the *woman*. It could not be given to a weak or contemptible tribe, such would not be listened to; but the Lenape and their allies would at once possess influence and command respect. As men they had been dreaded; as women they would be respected and honored, none would be so daring or so base as to attack or insult them; as women they would have a right to interfere in all the quarrels of other nations, and to stop or prevent the effusion of Indian blood. They entreated them, therefore, to become *the woman* in name and, in fact, to lay down their arms and all the insignia of warriors, to devote themselves to agriculture and other pacific employments, and thus become the means of preserving peace and harmony among the nations.

The Lenape, unfortunately for themselves, listened to the voice of their enemies. They knew it was too true, that the Indian nations, excited by their own unbridled passions, and not a little by their European neighbours, were in the way of total extirpation by each other's hands. They believed that the Mengwe were sincere, and that their proposal had no object in view but the preservation of the Indian race. In a luckless hour they gave their consent, and agreed to become *women*. This consent was received with great joy. A feast was prepared for the purpose of confirming and proclaiming the new order of things. With appropriate ceremonies, of which Loskiel has given a particular description,[43] the Delawares were installed in their new functions, eloquent speeches were delivered, accompanied, as usual, with belts of wampum. The great peace belt and the chain of friendship (in the figurative language of the Indians) was laid across the shoulders of the new mediator, one end of which, it was said, was to be taken hold of by all the Indian nations, and the other by the Europeans.[44] The Lenape say that the Dutch were present at that ceremony, and had no inconsiderable share in the intrigue.[45]

The old and intelligent Mahicanni, whose forefathers inhabited the country on the east side of the North river, gave many years since the following account of the above transaction:

- They said that their grandfather (the Lenni Lenape), and the nations or tribes connected with them, were so united, that whatsoever nation attacked the one, it was the same as attacking the whole; all in such cases would unite and make a common cause.
- That the long house (council house) of all those who were of the same blood, and united under this kind of tacit alliance, reached from the head of the tide, at some distance above where Gaaschtinick (Albany) now stands, to the head of the tide water on the Potomack.
- That at each end of this house there was a door for the tribes to enter at.
- That the Mengwe were in no way connected with those who had access to this house; but were looked upon as strangers.
- That the Lenape, with the Mohicans and all the other tribes in their connexion, were on the point of extirpating the Five Nations, when they applied to the *Dutchemaan*, who were now making a settlement at or near Gaaschtinick, to assist them in bringing about a peace with the Lenape.
- That accordingly these new comers invited the Lenape and Mohicans to a grand council, at a place situated at some distance from where Albany now stands, which the white people have since called by the name of *Nordman's Kill*.
- That when at length, by their united supplications and fair speeches, they had got the hatchet out of the hands of the Lenape, they buried that weapon at Gaaschtinick, and said that they would build a church over the spot, so that the weapon could never any more be got at, otherwise than by lifting up the whole church, and whatever nation should dare to do this, on them the Dutchemaan would take revenge.
- That now, having succeeded in getting the weapon out of the hands of the Lenape, the ceremony of placing them in the situation of "the woman," for the purpose of being

11

mediators, took place, when the Mengwe declared them henceforth to be their cousins, and the Mahicanni, they said, they would call their nephews.

The Mahicanni further say:

- That it was fear which induced the Dutchemaan to aid the Five Nations in bringing about this peace, because at the place where they were at that time making their settlement, great bodies of warriors would pass and repass, so that they could not avoid being interrupted in their undertakings, and probably molested, if not destroyed, by one or the other of the war parties, as their wars, at that time, were carried on with great rage, and no quarter was given.
- That in producing this peace, the white people had effected for the Mengwe, what no other nation could have done, and had laid the foundation of the future greatness of their Iroquois friends, as the same policy was pursued by the English, after they came into possession of this country.— So far the tradition of the Mahicanni.

The Rev. Mr. Pyrlæus, in his notes, after fixing as near as he could the time when the Five Nations confederated with each other, proceeds in these words:

> *"According to my informant, Sganarady, a creditable aged Indian, his grandfather had been one of the deputies sent for the purpose of entering into a covenant with the white Europeans; they met at a place since called Nordman's Kill, about four miles below where afterwards Albany was built, where this covenant of friendship was first established, and the Mohawks were the active body in effecting this work."*

From these three separate accounts of the Lenape, of the Mahicanni, and of the Mohawks, as related by Mr. Pyrlæus, it appears to be conclusively proved, that the Europeans were already in this country, when the Lenape were persuaded to assume the station of *the woman*, and that the Dutch were assisting in the plot, and were at least the instigators, if not the

12

authors of it. It was the *Dutch* who summoned the great council near Albany; the tomahawk was buried deep in the ground, and the vengeance of the *Dutch* was threatened if it should ever be taken up again; the peace belt was laid across the shoulders of the unfortunate Delawares, supported at one end by the Five Nations, and at the other by the *Europeans*; all these circumstances point so clearly to European intrigue, that it is impossible to resist the conclusion that the whites adopted this means to neutralize the power of the Delawares and their friends, whom they dreaded, and strengthen the hands of the Iroquois, who were in their alliance.

The Iroquois have denied that these machinations ever took place, and say that they conquered the Delawares in fair battle, and compelled them by force to become women, or in other words that they obliged them to submit to the greatest humiliation to which a warlike spirited people can ever be reduced; not a momentary humiliation, as when the Romans were compelled by the Samnites to pass under the Caudine forks, but a permanent disgrace, which was to last as long as their national existence. If this were true, the Lenape and their allies, who, like all other Indian nations, never considered a treaty binding when entered into under any kind of compulsion, would not have submitted to this any longer than until they could again have rallied their forces and fallen upon their enemy; they would have done long before the year 1755, what they did at last at that time, joined the French in their wars against the Iroquois and English, and would not have patiently waited more than a century before they took their revenge for so flagrant an outrage. Their numbers, acknowledged to have been far superior to that of their Indian enemies, and the vast extent of territory which they possessed, furnished them with ample means to have acted hostilely, if they had thought proper. On the contrary, they lived at peace with the Iroquois, and their European allies, until that decisive war, by which the French lost at once all their extensive possessions on the continent of America.

In addition to these positive proofs, negative evidence of the strongest kind may be adduced. The Iroquois say, indeed, that they conquered the Delawares and their allies, and compelled them to become women. But there is no tradition among them of the particulars of this important event. Neither Mr. Pyrlæus, nor Mr. Zeisberger,[46] who both lived long among the Five Nations, and spoke and understood their language well, could obtain from them any details relative to this supposed conquest; they ought, certainly, to have been able to say how it was effected; whether by one decisive fight or by successive engagements, or at least, when the last battle took place; who were the nations or tribes engaged in it; who the chiefs or commanders; what numbers fell on each side; and a variety of other facts, by which the truth of their assertion might have been proved: the total absence of such details appears to me to militate against them in the strongest manner, and to corroborate the statement of their adversaries.

The Delawares are of opinion, that this scheme of the Five Nations, however deeply laid, and meant essentially to injure them, would not, however, have operated against them, but on the contrary, have greatly subserved their national interest, if the Europeans had not afterwards come into the country in such great numbers, and multiplied so rapidly as they did. For their neutral position would greatly have favoured their increase, while the numbers of the other Indian nations would have been reduced by the wars in which they were continually engaged. But unfortunately for them, it happened that the Europeans successively invaded the country which they occupied, and now forms what are called the middle states, and as they advanced from the Atlantic into the interior, drove before them the Lenape and their allies, and obtained possession of their lands; while the Iroquois, who happened to be placed in the neighbourhood of Canada, between the French and English, who were frequently at war with each other, had an enemy, it is true, in the French nation, but had strong protectors in the English, who considered them as a check upon their enemies, and, being the most numerous people, were best able to afford them protection; thus they were suffered to increase and become powerful, while the Lenape, having no friend near them, the French being then at too great a distance, were entirely at the mercy of their English neighbours, who, advancing fast on their lands, gradually dispersed them, and other causes concurring, produced at last their almost entire destruction. Among those causes the

14

treacherous conduct of the Five Nations may be considered as the principal one.

Before that strange metamorphosis took place, of a great and powerful nation being transformed into a band of defenceless women, the Iroquois had never been permitted to visit the Lenape, even when they were at peace with each other. Whenever a Mengwe appeared in their country, he was hunted down as a beast of prey, and it was lawful for every one to destroy him. But now, *the woman* could not, consistently with her new station and her engagements, make use of destructive weapons, and she was bound to abstain from all violence against the human species. Her late enemies, therefore, found no difficulty in travelling, under various pretences, through her country, and those of her allies, and leaving here and there a few of their people to remain among them as long as they pleased, for the purpose, as they said, of keeping up a good understanding, and assisting them in the preservation of the general peace.

But while they were amusing the Lenape with flattering language, they were concerting measures to disturb their quiet by involving them in difficulties with the neighbouring nations. I shall relate one among many instances of a similar conduct:

> They once sent their men into the Cherokee country, who were instructed secretly to kill one of that nation, and to leave a war club near the person murdered, which had been purposely made after the manner and in the shape of those of the Delawares. Now leaving a war club in an Indian country, is considered by those nations as a formal challenge or declaration of war. The Cherokees, deceived by appearances, and believing that their grandfather the Lenape had committed the murder, collected a large party to go into their country and take their revenge.
>
> Meanwhile, the Iroquois sent a messenger to the Lenape, to inform them of the approach of an enemy, who, they had learned from their hunters, was coming towards their settlement, and to advise them to send a number of their men immediately to a certain place, where they would be

met by a large body of the Five Nations, who would take the lead, march in front, and fight their battles, so that they would have little else to do than to look on and see how well their friends fought for them.

The Lenape, being in no wise prepared to meet a powerful foe, assembled in haste a few of their men, and repaired to the place of rendezvous, where they were disappointed by not meeting any of their pretended protectors. The enemy, however, was close upon them; the Lenape fought with great courage, but were overpowered by an immense superiority of numbers, and defeated with considerable loss.

Now the Iroquois made their appearance, and instead of attacking or pursuing the Cherokees, loaded the Delawares with reproaches, for their temerity, as they called it, in having dared, being *women*, to take the lead in attacking *men*. They told them that the Five Nations being their superiors, they ought to have waited for them before they attacked the Cherokees, that then their protectors would have fought and defeated them, but that as they had thought proper to act by themselves, they had received the punishment justly due to their presumption.

It was thus that the Five Nations rewarded the confidence that the Delawares had placed in them. Their treachery was not, however, suspected for a long time; but it was at last discovered; it was even found out that in this last engagement, a number of the Iroquois had joined in fight against them with their enemies. The Lenape then determined to unite their forces, and by one great effort to destroy entirely that perfidious nation. This, they say, they might easily have done, as they were then yet as numerous as the grasshoppers at particular seasons, and as destructive to their enemies as these insects are to the fruits of the earth; while they described the Mengwe as a number of croaking frogs in a pond, which make a great noise when all is quiet, but at the first approach of danger, nay, at the very rustling of a leaf, immediately plunge into the water and are silent.

But their attention was now diverted by other scenes. The whites were again landing in great numbers on their coast, in the east and south, and this spectacle once more engaged all the capacity of their minds. They were lost in admiration at what they saw, and were consulting and deliberating together on what they should do. The Five Nations, who lived out of the reach of all danger, nevertheless also came; but bent on their own interest, while they were instigating the other nations to fall upon the new comers, or drive them off from their shores, by which they caused useless hostilities, in which they did not appear to participate, they were insinuating themselves into the favour of the powerful strangers, professing great friendship for them, persuading them that they were superior to the other Indian nations, that they had controul over them all, and would chastise those who should disturb their peace.

William Penn came, with his train of pacific followers. Never will the Delawares forget their elder brother *Miquon*, as they affectionately and respectfully call him. From his first arrival in their country, a friendship was formed between them which was to last as long as the sun should shine, and the rivers flow with water. That friendship would undoubtedly have continued to the end of time, had their good brother always remained among them, but in his absence, mischievous people, say they, got into power, who, not content with the land which had been given to them, contrived to get all that they wanted; and when the Lenape looked round for the friends of their brother Miquon, to hear their just complaints, and redress their wrongs, they could not discover them, and had the misfortune to see their greatest enemies, the Mengwe, brought on for the purpose of shutting their mouths, and compelling them to submit to the injustice done them.

They cannot conceive how the English could turn from the people by whom they had been so kindly received and welcomed with open arms; from those who had permitted them to sit down upon their lands in peace, and without fear of being molested by them; who had taken delight in supplying all their wants,[47] and who were happy in smoking the pipe of friendship with them at one and the same fire; how they could not only see them degraded and injured by a base and perfidious nation, but join with that nation in sinking them still lower.

For to the countenance of the English, they say, is entirely owing the great preponderance which the Iroquois at last attained: they complain that the English did support that enemy against them, that they even sanctioned their insolence, by telling them to make use of their authority as men, and bring these women (the Lenape) to their senses. That they were even insulted and treated in a degrading manner, in treaties to which the English were parties, and particularly in that which took place at Easton,[48] in Pennsylvania, in July, 1742,[49] when the Six Nations were publicly called on to compel the Delawares to give up the land taken from them by the long day's walk. But for these repeated outrages, they would not have taken part with the French in the memorable war of 1755.[50] Nor, perhaps, would they have done so, had not they been seduced into the measure by the perfidious Iroquois.

At the commencement of that war, they brought the war belt, with a piece of tobacco, to the Delawares, and told them: "Remember that the English have unjustly deprived you of much of your land, which they took from you by force. Your cause is just; therefore smoke of this tobacco, and arise; join with us our fathers, the French, and take your revenge. You are women, it is true, but we will shorten your petticoats, and though you may appear by your dress to be women, yet by your conduct and language you will convince your enemies that you are determined not tamely to suffer the wrongs and injuries inflicted upon you."

Yielding to these solicitations, the Delawares and their connexions took up arms against the English in favor of the French, and committed many hostilities, in which the Iroquois appeared to take no part. Sir William Johnson requested them to use their ascendancy and to persuade the hostile Indians to lay down the hatchet, instead of which, instead of conforming to the ancient custom of Indian nations, which was simply to take the war-hatchet back from those to whom they had given it, they fell on a sudden on the unsuspecting Lenape, killed their cattle, and destroyed their town on the Susquehannah, and having taken a number of them prisoners, carried them to Sir William Johnson, who confined and put them in irons. This cruel act of treachery, the Delawares say, they will never forget nor forgive.

Thus the Lenape, whose principal settlements were then on the frontier of Pennsylvania, took part with the French, and acted hostilely against the English during the whole of the war of 1755. The animosity which mutual hostilities produced between them and the settlers concurred, no doubt, with other causes, in producing the murder of the Conestogo Indians, which took place at the close of that war, in December, 1763, and is feelingly related by Loskiel, part I., ch. 14 and 15.[51]

The revolutionary war put an end to the exorbitant power of the Iroquois. They were, indeed, still supported by the British government, but the Americans were now the strongest party, and of course against them. They endeavored to persuade the other Indian nations to join them, but their expectations were deceived. At a meeting which took place at Pittsburg in 1775, for the express purpose of deliberating on the part which it became Indians to take in the disturbances which had arisen between the King of Great Britain and his subjects, Capt. White Eyes, a sensible and very spirited warrior of the Lenape,[52] boldly declared to a select body of the Senecas, that his Indians would never join any nation or power, for the purpose of destroying a people who were born on the same soil with them. That the Americans were his friends and brothers, and that no nation should dictate to him what part he should take in the existing war.

Anticipating the measure which the American Congress took in the succeeding year, he declared *himself*,[53] in behalf of his nation, free and independent of the Iroquois; they had pretended that they had conquered him, they had made a woman of him and dressed him in woman's apparel, but now he was again a man, he stood before them as a man, and with the weapons of a man he would assert his claim to all yonder country, pointing to the land on the west side of the Allegheny river; for to him it belonged, and not to the Six Nations, who falsely asserted that they had acquired it by conquest. In the year 1778 or 1779, the Lenape bravely asserted their national independence by joining Col.

Brodhead's troops in an expedition against the Senecas.[54] If they did not do as much in that war as might have been expected of them, and took only a partial revenge, it was owing to the death of their brave chief, White Eyes, who died of the small pox at Pittsburg, I think, in the year 1780. He was a Christian in his heart, but did not live to make a public profession of our religion, though it is well known that he persuaded many Indians to embrace it.[55]

Although the Lenape acted independently in the war of 1755, and made a formal declaration of their independence at the beginning of the revolutionary war, yet the Six Nations persevered in their pretensions, and still affected to consider them as women. Finding, however, that this obsolete claim was no longer acknowledged, and that it was useless to insist upon it any longer, they came forward of their own accord, about the time of Wayne's treaty, and formally declared that the Lenape and their allies were no longer women, but MEN.

The Delawares and Mohicans agree in saying:

- That from the time of the fatal treaty in which they were persuaded to assimilate themselves to women, and, indeed, ever since the Europeans first came into the country, the conduct of the Iroquois was treacherous and perfidious in the extreme
- That it was their constant practice to sally out secretly and commit depredations on the neighbouring nations, with intent to involve them in wars with each other.
- That they would also commit murders on the frontier settlers, from Virginia to New England, and charge the tribes who were settled in the neighbourhood with the commission of those crimes.
- That they would then turn negotiators, and effect a peace, always at the expense of the nation whom they had injured.
- They would sell the lands of other nations to the English and receive the money, pretending to a paramount right to the whole territory, and this, say the Lenape, was their manner of CONQUERING NATIONS!

CHAPTER 2

Indian account of the first arrival of the Dutch at New York Island

The Lenni Lenape claim the honour of having received and welcomed the Europeans on their first arrival in the country, situated between New England and Virginia. It is probable, however, that the Mahicanni or Mohicans, who then inhabited the banks of the Hudson, concurred in the hospitable act. The relation I am going to make was taken down many years since from the mouth of an intelligent Delaware Indian, and may be considered as a correct account of the tradition existing among them of this momentous event. I give it as much as possible in their own language.

"A great many years ago, when men with a white skin had never yet been seen in this land, some Indians who were out a fishing, at a place where the sea widens, espied at a great distance something remarkably large floating on the water, and such as they had never seen before. These Indians immediately returning to the shore, apprised their countrymen of what they had observed, and pressed them to go out with them and discover what it might be. They hurried out together, and saw with astonishment the phenomenon which now appeared to their sight, but could not agree upon what it was; some believed it to be an uncommonly large fish or animal, while others were of opinion it must be a very big house floating on the sea.

At length the spectators concluded that this wonderful object was moving towards the land, and that it must be an animal or something else that had life in it; it would therefore be proper to inform all the Indians on the inhabited islands of what they had seen, and put them on their guard. Accordingly they sent off a number of runners and watermen to carry the news to their scattered chiefs, that they might send off in every direction for the warriors, with a message that they should come on immediately. These arriving in numbers, and having themselves viewed the strange appearance, and observing that it was actually moving towards the entrance of the river or bay; concluded it to be a remarkably large house in which the Mannitto (the Great or Supreme Being) himself was present, and that he probably was coming to visit them.[56]

By this time the chiefs were assembled at York island, and deliberating in what manner in which[57] they should receive their Mannitto on his arrival. Every measure was taken to be well provided with plenty of meat for a sacrifice. The women were desired to prepare the best victuals. All the idols or images were examined and put in order, and a grand dance was supposed not only to be an agreeable entertainment for the Great Being, but it was believed that it might, with the addition of a sacrifice, contribute to appease him if he was angry with them.

The conjurers were also set to work, to determine what this phenomenon portended, and what the possible result of it might be. To these and to the chiefs and wise men of the nations, men, women, and children were looking up for advice and protection. Distracted between hope and fear, they were at a loss what to do; a dance, however, commenced in great confusion. While in this situation, fresh runners arrive declaring it to be a large house of various colours, and crowded with living creatures. It appears now to be certain, that it is the great Mannitto, bringing them some kind of game, such as he had not given them before, but other runners soon after arriving declare that it is positively a house full of human beings, of quite a different colour from that of the Indians, and dressed differently from them; that in particular one of them was dressed entirely in red, who must be the Mannitto himself.

They are hailed from the vessel in a language they do not understand, yet they shout or yell in return by way of answer, according to the custom of their country; many are for running off to the woods, but are pressed by others to stay, in order not to give offence to their visitor, who might find them out and destroy them. The house, some say, large canoe, at last stops, and a canoe of a smaller size comes on shore with the red man, and some others in it; some stay with his canoe to guard it. The chiefs and wise men, assembled in council, form themselves into a large circle, towards which the man in red clothes approaches with two others. He salutes them with a friendly countenance, and they return the salute after their manner.

They are lost in admiration; the dress, the manners, the whole appearance of the unknown strangers is to them a subject of wonder; but they are particularly struck with him who wore the red coat all glittering with gold lace, which they could in no manner account for. He, surely, must be the great Mannitto, but why should he have a white skin? Meanwhile, a large *Hackhack*[58] is brought by one of his servants, from which an unknown substance is poured out into a small cup or glass, and handed to the supposed Mannitto. He drinks—has the glass filled again, and hands it to the chief standing next to him. The chief receives it, but only smells the contents and passes it on to the next chief, who does the same. The glass or cup thus passes through the circle, without the liquor being tasted by any one, and is upon the point of being returned to the red clothed Mannitto, when one of the Indians, a brave man and a great warrior, suddenly jumps up and harangues the assembly on the impropriety of returning the cup with its contents.

It was handed to them, says he, by the Mannitto, that they should drink out of it, as he himself had done. To follow his example would be pleasing to him; but to return what he had given them might provoke his wrath, and bring destruction on them. And since the orator believed it for the good of the nation that the contents offered them should be drunk, and as no one else would do it, he would drink it himself, let the consequence be what it might; it was better for one man to die, than that a whole nation should be destroyed. He then took the glass, and bidding the assembly a solemn farewell, at once drank up its whole contents. Every eye was fixed on the resolute chief, to see what effect the unknown liquor would produce. He soon began to stagger, and at last fell prostrate on the ground. His companions now bemoan his fate, he falls into a sound sleep, and they think he has expired. He wakes again, jumps up and declares, that he has enjoyed the most delicious sensations, and that he never before felt himself so happy as after he had drunk the cup. He asks for more, his wish is granted; the whole assembly then imitate him, and all become intoxicated.

After this general intoxication had ceased, for they say that while it lasted the whites had confined themselves to their vessel, the man with the red clothes returned again, and distributed presents among them, consisting of beads, axes, hoes, and stockings such as the white people wear. They soon became familiar with each other, and began to converse by signs.

The Dutch made them understand that they would not stay here, that they would return home again, but would pay them another visit the next year, when they would bring them more presents, and stay with them awhile; but as they could not live without eating, they should want a little land of them to sow seeds, in order to raise herbs and vegetables to put into their broth. They went away as they had said, and returned in the following season, when both parties were much rejoiced to see each other; but the whites laughed at the Indians, seeing that they knew not the use of the axes and hoes they had given them the year before; for they had these hanging to their breasts as ornaments, and the stockings were made use of as tobacco pouches.

The whites now put handles to the former for them, and cut trees down before their eyes, hoed up the ground, and put the stockings on their legs. Here, they say, a general laughter ensued among the Indians, that they had remained ignorant of the use of such valuable implements, and had borne the weight of such heavy metal hanging to their necks, for such a length of time. They took every white man they saw for an inferior Mannitto attendant upon the supreme Deity who shone superior in the red and laced clothes. As the whites became daily more familiar with the Indians, they at last proposed to stay with them, and asked only for so much ground for a garden spot as, they said, the hide of a bullock would cover or encompass, which hide was spread before them. The Indians readily granted this apparently reasonable request; but the whites then took a knife, and beginning at one end of the hide, cut it up to a long rope, not thicker than a child's finger, so that by the time the whole was cut up, it made a great heap; they then took the rope at one end, and drew it gently along, carefully avoiding its breaking. It was drawn out into a circular form, and being closed at its ends, encompassed a large piece of ground.

The Indians were surprised at the superior wit of the whites,[59] but did not wish to contend with them about a little land, as they had still enough themselves. The white and red men lived contentedly together for a long time, though the former from time to time asked for more land, which was readily obtained, and thus they gradually proceeded higher up the Mahicannittuck, until the Indians began to believe that they would soon want all their country, which in the end proved true."

CHAPTER 3 ~
Indian relations of the conduct of the Europeans towards them

Long and dismal are the complaints which the Indians make of European ingratitude and injustice. They love to repeat them, and always do it with the eloquence of nature, aided by an energetic and comprehensive language, which our polished idioms cannot imitate. Often I have listened to these descriptions of their hard sufferings, until I felt ashamed of being a *white man*.

They are, in general, very minute in these recitals, and proceed with a great degree of order and regularity. They begin with the Virginians, whom they call the *long knives*, and who were the first European settlers in this part of the American continent. "It was we," say the Lenape, Mohicans, and their kindred tribes, "who so kindly received them on their first arrival into our country. We took them by the hand, and bid them welcome to sit down by our side, and live with us as brothers; but how did they requite our kindness? They at first asked only for a little land on which to raise bread for themselves and their families, and pasture for their cattle, which we freely gave them. They soon wanted more, which we also gave them. They saw the game in the woods, which the Great Spirit had given us for our subsistence, and they wanted that too. They penetrated into the woods in quest of game; they discovered spots of land which pleased them; that land they also wanted, and because we were loth to part with it, as we saw they had already more than they had need of, they took it from us by force, and drove us to a great distance from our ancient homes."

"By and by the *Dutchemaan*[60] arrived at *Manahachtánienk*,"[61] (here they relate with all its details what has been said in the preceding chapter.) "The great man wanted only a little, little land, on which to raise greens for his soup, just as much as a bullock's hide would cover. Here we first might have observed their deceitful spirit. The bullock's hide was cut up into little strips, and did not cover, indeed, but encircled a very large piece of land, which we foolishly granted to them. They were to raise *greens* on it, instead of which they planted *great guns*; afterwards they built strong houses, made themselves masters of the Island, then went up the river to our enemies, the Mengwe, made a league with them, persuaded us by their wicked arts to lay down our arms, and at last drove us entirely out of the country." Here, of course, is related at full length, the story which we have told in the first chapter. Then the Delawares[62] proceed.

"When the *Yengeese*[63] arrived at *Machtitschwanne*,[64] they looked about everywhere for good spots of land, and when they found one, they immediately and without ceremony possessed themselves of it; we were astonished, but still we let them go on, not thinking it worth while to contend for a little land. But when at last they came to our favourite spots, those which lay most convenient to our fisheries, then bloody wars ensued: we would have been contented that the white people and we should have lived quietly beside each other; but these white men encroached so fast upon us, that we saw at once we should lose all, if we did not resist them. The wars that we carried on against each other were long and cruel. We were enraged when we saw the white people put our friends and relatives, whom they had taken prisoners, on board of their ships, and carry them off to sea, whether to drown or sell them as slaves, in the country from which they came, we knew not, but certain it is that none of them have ever returned or even been heard of. At last they got possession of the whole of the country which the Great Spirit had given us. One of our tribes was forced to wander far beyond Quebec; others dispersed in small bodies, and sought places of refuge where they could; some came to Pennsylvania; others went far to the westward and mingled with other tribes.

"To many of those, Pennsylvania was a last, delightful asylum. But here, again, the Europeans disturbed them, and forced them to emigrate, although they had been most kindly and hospitably received. On which ever side of the *Lenapewihittuck*[65] the white people landed, they were welcomed as brothers by our ancestors,

27

who gave them lands to live on, and even hunted for them, and furnished them with meat out of the woods. Such was our conduct to the white men[66] who inhabited this country, until our elder brother, the great and good MIQUON,[67] came and brought us words of peace and good will. We believed his words, and his memory is still held in veneration among us.

But it was not long before our joy was turned into sorrow: our brother Miquon died, and those of his good counsellors who were of his mind, and knew what had passed between him and our ancestors, were no longer listened to; the strangers[68] who had taken their places, no longer spoke to us of sitting down by the side of each other as brothers of one family; they forgot that friendship which their great man had established with us, and was to last to the end of time; they now only strove to get all our land from us by fraud or by force, and when we attempted to remind them of what our good brother had said, they became angry, and sent word to our enemies, the Mengwe, to meet them at a great council which they were to hold with us at *Lœhauwake*,[69] where they should take us by the hair of our heads and shake us well. The Mengwe came; the council was held, and in the presence of the white men, who did not contradict them, they told us that we were women, and that they had made us such; that we had no right to any land, because it was all theirs; that we must be gone; and that as a great favour they permitted us to go and settle further into the country, at the place which they themselves pointed out at Wyoming."[70]

Thus these good Indians, with a kind of melancholy pleasure, recite the long history of their sufferings. After having gone through these painful details, they seldom fail to indulge in bitter, but too just reflections, upon the men of Europe. "We and our kindred tribes," say they, "lived in peace and harmony with each other before the white people came into this country; our council house[71] extended far to the north and far to the south. In the middle of it we would meet from all parts to smoke the pipe of peace together. When the white men arrived in the south, we received them as friends; we did the same when they arrived in the east. It was we, it was our forefathers, who made them welcome, and let them sit down by our side. The land they settled on was ours. We knew not but the Great Spirit had sent them to us for some good purpose, and therefore we thought they must be a good people.

We were mistaken; for no sooner had they obtained a footing on our lands, than they began to pull our council house down,[72] first at one end and then at the other, and at last meeting each other at the centre, where the council fire was yet burning bright, they put it out,[73] and extinguished it with our own blood![74] with the blood of those[75] who with us had received them! who had welcomed them in our land! Their blood ran in streams into our fire, and extinguished it so entirely, that not one spark was left us whereby to kindle a new fire;[76] we were compelled to withdraw ourselves beyond the great swamp,[77] and to fly to our good uncle, the *Delamattenos*,[78] who kindly gave us a tract of land to live on. How long we shall be permitted to remain in this asylum, the Great Spirit only knows. The whites will not rest contented until they shall have destroyed the last of us, and made us disappear entirely from the face of the earth."

I have given here only a brief specimen of the charges which they exhibit against the white people. There are men among them, who have by heart the whole history of what took place between the whites and the Indians, since the former first came into their country; and relate the whole with ease and with an eloquence not to be imitated. On the tablets of their memories they preserve this record for posterity.

I, at one time, in April, 1787,[79] was astonished when I heard one of their orators, a great chief of the Delaware nation,[80] go over this ground, recapitulating the most extraordinary events which had before happened, and concluding in these words: "I admit that there are good white men, but they bear no proportion to the bad; the bad must be the strongest, for they rule. They do what they please. They enslave those who are not of their colour, although created by the same Great Spirit who created us.[81] They would make slaves of us if they could, but as they cannot do it, they kill us! There is no faith to be placed in their words. They are not like the Indians, who are only enemies, while at war, and are friends in peace. They will say to an Indian, 'my friend! my brother!' They will take him by the hand, and at the same moment destroy him. And so you (addressing himself to the Christian Indians) will also be treated by them before long. Remember! that this day I have warned you to beware of such friends as these. I know the *long knives*; they are not to be trusted."

Eleven months after this speech was delivered by this prophetic chief, ninety-six of the same Christian Indians, about sixty of them women and children, were murdered at the place where these very words had been spoken, by the same men he had alluded to, and in the same manner that he had described. See Loskiel's History, part III., ch. 10.[82]

CHAPTER 4 ~
Subsequent fate of the Lenape and their kindred tribes

After the murder of the Conestogo Indians, the Lenni Lenape thought proper, for their safety, to withdraw altogether from the interior of the white settlements, into the wilds of the Susquehannah country; and Government, conscious that they could no longer protect any Indians, or body of Indians, whether Christians or not, in the settled parts of the province, advised the Christian Indians, whom, during the last troubles, they had with difficulty prevented from sharing the fate of the Conestogos, to retire into the back country. They did so, and settled at Wyalusing,[83] which then became the nearest settlement of Indians to the white inhabitants, being upwards of 150 miles north of Philadelphia, and about 100 miles from the frontier settlers beyond the blue mountains; all the other Indians of that nation, together with the Nanticokes, lived then higher up the Susquehannah.

For about five years, the Indians on this river enjoyed peace, and the Christian Indians lived quietly here and at another settlement they had made thirty miles higher, built good houses for themselves, together with a spacious church, planted fruit trees, and put large bodies of land under cultivation. But, while they were flattering themselves with the most favourable prospect, they were informed that the Six Nations had sold the whole country, including the land they lived on, to the English. They soon saw the object of this clandestine proceeding, of which they had not received the least notice, and foreseeing what kind of neighbours they should have, if they should stay where they were, they determined to move off in a body to the Ohio, where they had received an invitation to settle from the grand council of their nation.

Accordingly, two hundred and forty-one souls set off directly for the Muskingum river, where a large tract of land was given

31

them, out of that which the Wyandots had formerly granted and confirmed to their people; the other Indians of the same nation residing on the Susquehannah soon followed, some settling at one place, some at another; the Mouseys,[84] however, joined their own tribe, who long since had emigrated and were settled on the head waters of the Allegheny river; and so the whole country east of the Allegheny mountains was cleared of its original inhabitants.

The Delawares thus became at once released from their troublesome neighbours the Iroquois, who had calculated on their settling near them, at a place they had already fixed upon; but they were mistaken, for with all their fair speeches they could not persuade the Lenape, who gave them plainly to understand that they were no longer inclined to listen to a people who had so long and so often deceived them.

This happened in the year 1768,[85] about six years before the beginning of the revolutionary war. During which short period of tranquillity, the numbers of the Christian Indians on the Ohio rapidly increased, and never was there such a fair prospect of their being fixed in a state of prosperous civilisation. But the revolution put an end to these hopes, and this opportunity was lost, perhaps, never to return again.

It was not the fault of the American government, who were truly desirous of seeing the Indians adopt a neutral line of conduct, and repeatedly advised them not to interfere in the quarrel between the colonies and the mother country; happy would it have been if the British government had acted in the same manner; but they pursued a different plan. These poor deluded people were dragged into a war in which they had no concern, by which not only their population was gradually reduced, but they lost the desire of becoming a civilised people; for the Americans, at last, become exasperated against them, and considering all Indians as their enemies, they sent parties out from time to time to destroy them. The murder of the Christian Indians on the Muskingum in 1782, completed their alienation. Those who yet remained were driven to despair, and finally dispersed.

It is not in my power to ascertain the whole number of the Lenni Lenape, or Delaware Indians, still existing at the present time. As far as I am informed, they are very much scattered, a number of them, chiefly of the Monsey tribe, living in Upper Canada, others are in the state of Ohio, and some on the waters of the Wabash in the Indiana territory. A considerable number of them has crossed the Mississippi. Their first emigrations to that country had already begun between the years 1780 and 1790. What the numbers of this nation were when the Europeans first came into this country is difficult to tell; all I can say is, that so early as 1760, their oldest men would say that they were not then as many hundreds as they had been thousands. They have considerably decreased since that period. I saw them myself between the years 1754 and 1760, by hundreds at a time, and Loskiel in his history gives an account of upwards of 800 having been fed at Bethlehem in one year. In the year 1762, while I lived at Tuscorawas on the Muskingum, they were settled on that river and its branches, and also on the Cayahoga river, which empties into Lake Erie, in the neighbourhood of which they had since a small Christian settlement called *Pilgerruh* (Pilgrim's rest.)[86,87]

THE SHAWANOS OR SAWANOS.[88]

The history of these people is here given, principally from the relations of old Indians of the Mohican[90] tribe, who say that they formerly inhabited the Southern country, Savannah in Georgia, and the Floridas. They were a restless people, delighting in wars, in which they were constantly engaged with some of the neighbouring nations. At last their neighbours, tired of being continually harassed by them, formed a league for their destruction. The Shawanos finding themselves thus dangerously situated, asked to be permitted to leave the country, which was granted to them, and they fled immediately to the Ohio. Here their main body settled, and sent messengers to their elder brother[91] the Mohicans, requesting them to intercede for them with their grandfather the Lenni Lenape, that he might take them under his protection. This the Mohicans willingly did, and even sent a body of their own people to conduct their *younger brother* into the country of the Delawares.

The Shawanos finding themselves safe under the protection of their grandfather, did not all choose to proceed farther to the eastward, but many of them remained on the Ohio, some of whom settled even as high up that river as the long island, above which the French afterwards built Fort Duquesne, now Pittsburg. Those who proceeded farther, were accompanied by their chief, named Gachgawatschiqua, and settled principally at and about the forks of Delaware, some few between that and the confluence of Delaware and Schuylkill, and some even on the spot where Philadelphia now stands; others were conducted by the Mohicans into their own country, where they intermarried with them and became one people. When those settled near the Delaware had multiplied, they returned to Wyoming on the Susquehannah, where they resided for a great number of years.

In the mean while, those who had remained on the Ohio increased in numbers, and in process of time began again to be troublesome to their neighbours. At last, they crossed the Allegheny mountains, and falling upon the camps of the Lenape on Juniata river, they committed several murders and went off with their plunder. It was soon discovered who were the aggressors; but the Lenape had now assumed the station of "the woman," and could not engage in wars. They could only apply for protection to the Five Nations, which they did, expecting that they would immediately pursue the offenders and inflict an exemplary punishment upon them, but the Five Nations found means to evade their demand for the present. They told the Delawares that the season was too far advanced to commence a war; that it was better to put off their intended expedition until the ensuing spring; that in the mean time, both nations should put themselves in readiness, and keep their preparations secret, and that as soon as the season should open, they would march off separately and meet together at an appointed time and place on the Allegheny, then push on together for the Shawano towns below the confluence of that river and the Monongahela, where they could fall together unawares on the aggressors and punish them. The Iroquois promised, as usual, that they would place

34

themselves in the front of the battle, so that the Delawares would have nothing to do but to look on and see how bravely their protectors would fight for them, and if they were not satisfied with that, they might take their revenge themselves.

Agreeably to this plan, the Lenape remained quiet till the spring, when, with a body of their most valiant men, they marched to the appointed spot; but how great was their surprise when their pretended champions did not make their appearance? They suspected treachery, and were not mistaken; for having immediately marched forward to the Shawano towns, bent on taking an exemplary revenge, they had the disappointment to see on their arrival their enemies pushing off as fast as they could down the Ohio river in their canoes. Some of them were flying by land, as probably they had not a sufficient number of canoes to convey their whole number; these they pursued and attacked, beat them severely, and took several prisoners.

Here they had a striking instance of the treachery of the Mengwe, who had warned the Shawanos of their approach. Some time after this, the Shawanos who resided on the north branch of the Susquehannah, began to draw off by degrees, first to the west branch of that river and the Juniata, and then to the Ohio; so that at the commencement of the French war in 1755, they had all, except a few families, with whom was their chief Paxnos, retired to the Ohio, where they joined their countrymen in a war against the English.[92]

Peace was made in 1763 between Great Britain and France; but the restless spirit of the Shawanos did not permit them to remain quiet; they commenced war[93] against their southern neighbours, the Cherokees, who, while in pursuit of the aggressors, would sometimes through mistake fall upon the Lenape, who resided in the same country with the Shawanos, through whom they also became involved in a war with that nation, which lasted some time. The Mengwe being then also at war with the Cherokees, and frequently returning with their prisoners and scalps through their country, the warlike spirit was kept alive among all, until at length, in 1768, the Cherokees sought a renewal of the friendship formerly existing between them and their grandfather, the Lenape, which being effected, they, by their mediation, also brought about a peace between them and the Five Nations.

The Shawanos not being disposed to continue the war with the Cherokees by themselves, and having been reprimanded by their grandfather for being the instigators of all those troubles, willingly submitted to the dictates of the Lenape, and from that time remained at peace with all the nations until the year 1774, when they were involved in a war with the people of Virginia, occasioned by some murders which were committed on Logan's family connexions and others by white people. In this instance it cannot, I think, be said that they were the aggressors, yet their thirst for revenge was so great, and the injured Mengwe at their side called out so loudly for revenge, that they with great spirit engaged into a war with the Virginians, which, however, was of but short duration, as they were opposed with an equal degree of courage, and after a severe battle between the two rivals, at or near the mouth of the Great Kanhawa, and the destruction of many of their towns by the Virginians, the Shawanos were brought to make peace once more;[94] which did not last long, as they joined the British against the American people, some time after the commencement of the Revolution, and remained our enemies after that time, never establishing a firm peace with us, until the memorable treaty which took place in 1795, after the decisive defeat of the nations by the late General Wayne.

The Shawanos lost many of their men during these contests; but they were in a manner replaced by individuals of other nations joining them. Thus, during the Revolutionary war, about one hundred turbulent Cherokees, who could not be brought by their own nation to be at peace with the American people, and were on that account driven out of their country, came over to the Shawanos, while others from the Five Nations joined them or became their neighbours.

The Shawanos are considered to be good warriors and hunters. They are courageous, high spirited and manly, and more careful in providing a supply of ammunition to keep in reserve for an emergency, than any other nation that I have heard of. Their language is more easily learned than that of the Lenape, and has a great affinity to the Mohican, Chippeway and other kindred languages. They generally place the accent on the last syllable.

THE NANTICOKES.

The Delawares say that this nation has sprung from the same stock with them, and the fact was acknowledged by White,[95] one of their chiefs, whom I have personally known. They call the Delawares their grandfathers. I shall relate the history of the Shawanos,[96] as I had it from the mouth of White himself.

Every Indian being at liberty to pursue what occupation he pleases, White's ancestors, after the Lenape came into their country, preferred seeking a livelihood by fishing and trapping along the rivers and bays, to pursuing wild game in the forest; they therefore detached themselves, and sought the most convenient places for their purpose. In process of time, they became very numerous, partly by natural increase, and partly in consequence of being joined by a number of the Lenape, and spread themselves over a large tract of country. Thus they became divided into separate bodies, distinguished by different names; the Canai, they say, sprung from them, and settled at a distance on the shores of the Potomack and Susquehannah, where they lived when the white people first arrived in Virginia; but they removed farther on their account, and settled higher up the Susquehannah, not far from where John Harris afterwards established a ferry.[97]

The main branch, or the Nanticokes proper, were then living in what is now called the Eastern shore of Maryland. At length, the white people crowded so much upon them, that they were also obliged to seek another abode, and as their grandfather was himself retreating back in consequence of the great influx of the whites, they took the advice of the Mengwe, and bent their course at once to the large flats at Wyoming, where they settled by themselves, in sight of the Shawanos town, while others settled higher up the river, even as high as Chemenk[98] (Shenango) and Shummunk, to which places they all emigrated at the beginning of the French war. White's tribe resided there until the Revolutionary war, when they went off to a place nearer to the British, whose part they had taken, and whose standard they joined. White himself had joined the Christian Indians at Schschequon,[99] several years previous to the war, and remained with them.

Nothing, said White, had equalled the decline of his tribe since the white people had come into the country. They were destroyed in part by disorders which they brought with them, by the small pox, the venereal disease, and by the free use of spirituous liquors, to which great numbers fell victims.

The emigration of the Nanticokes from Maryland was well known to the Society of the United Brethren. At the time when these people were beginning their settlement in the forks of Delaware, the Rev. Christian[100] Pyrlæus noted down in his memorandum book, "that on the 21st day of May, 1748, a number of the Nanticokes from Maryland, passed by Shamokin in ten canoes, on their way to Wyoming." Others, travelling by land, would frequently pass through Bethlehem, and from thence through the Water Gap to Nescopeck or Susquehannah, and while they resided at Wyoming, they, together with the Shawanese, became the emissaries of the Five Nations, and in conjunction with them afterwards, endeavoured to remove the Christian Indians from Gnadenhütten, in Northampton county, to Wyoming; their private object being to have a full opportunity to murder the white inhabitants, in the war which they already knew would soon break out between the French and English.

These Nanticokes had the singular custom of removing the bones of their deceased friends from the burial place to a place of deposit in the country they dwell in. In earlier times, they were known to go from Wyoming and Chemenk, to fetch the bones of their dead from the Eastern shore of Maryland, even when the bodies were in a putrid state, so that they had to take off the flesh and scrape the bones clean, before they could carry them along. I well remember having seen them between the years 1750 and

1760, loaded with such bones, which, being fresh, caused a disagreeable stench, as they passed through the town of Bethlehem.

They are also said to have been the inventors of a poisonous substance, by which they could destroy a whole settlement of people, and they are accused of being skilled in the arts of witchcraft; it is certain that they are very much dreaded on this account. I have known Indians who firmly believed that they had people among them who could, if they pleased, destroy a whole army, by merely blowing their breath towards them. Those of the Lenape[101] and other tribes, who pretend to witchcraft, say that they learned the science from the Nanticokes; they are not unwilling to be taxed with being wizards, as it makes them feared by their neighbours.

Their national name, according to the report of their chief, White, is *Nentégo*. The Delawares call them *Unéchtgo*, and the Iroquois *Sganiateratieh-rohne*. These three names have the same meaning, and signify *tide water people*, or the *sea shore settlers*. They have besides other names, by-names, as it were, given them with reference to their occupation. The Mohicans, for instance, call them *Otayáchgo*, and the Delawares *Tawachguáno*,[102] both which words in their respective languages, signify a "bridge," a "dry passage over a stream;" which alludes to their being noted for felling great numbers of trees across streams, to set their traps on. They are also often called the *Trappers*.

In the year 1785, this tribe had so dwindled away, that their whole body, who came together to see their old chief, White, then residing with the Christian Indians on the Huron river,[103] north of Detroit, did not amount to 50 men. They were then going through Canada, to the Miami country, to settle beside the Shawanos, in consequence of an invitation they had received from them.

This once great and renowned nation has also almost entirely disappeared, as well as the numerous tribes who had descended from them; they have been destroyed by wars, and carried off by the small pox and other disorders, and great numbers have died in consequence of the introduction of spirituous liquors among them. The remainder have fled and removed in separate bodies to different parts, where they now are dispersed or mingled with other nations.

So early as the year 1762, a number of them had emigrated to the Ohio, where I became acquainted with their chief who was called by the whites "Mohican John." Others have fled to the shores of the St. Lawrence, where numbers of them incorporated themselves with the Iroquois, and where their descendants live at the present time, a mixed race, known by the name of the *Cochnewago* Indians.

Upwards of one hundred of them, who lived in the colonies of Connecticut and New York, having through the labours of the United Brethren embraced Christianity, emigrated to Pennsylvania, some time between 1742 and 1760, where they afterwards became incorporated with the Delawares.[104] A considerable number migrated from Hudson's river about the year 1734, and settled at Stockbridge, in Massachusetts; between the year 1785 and 1787, they removed to Oneida, in the country of the Six Nations, and gave to their settlement the name of New Stockbridge. Before their removal their numbers had gradually diminished. In 1791, they were reduced to 191 persons.[105] They were once very numerous in Connecticut, and in the year 1799, there still were 84 individuals of them, in the county of New London,[106] the remains of a once large and flourishing settlement. It is probable that by this time they are nearly if not entirely extinct.

It is believed that the Mahicanni are the same nation who are so celebrated in the History of New England, under the name of *Pequods* or *Pequots*.[107] The Rev. Jonathan Edwards, late

President of Union College at Schenectady, in the State of New York, published in the year 1788 in a pamphlet form, some observations on their language, which were republished at New York in 1801. This small tract, as well as the translation of the Bible into the Natick, by the venerable Eliot, and his grammar of that language, put it beyond a doubt that the idiom of the Mohicans and those of the other New England Indians proceeded from the same source with that of the Lenni Lenape.

CHAPTER 5 ~
The Iroquois

The most intelligent and credible Indians of the Lenape stock, including the Mohicans, have ever asserted, that in the whole country bounded on the north by the river St. Lawrence and the Great Lakes (including what is now Nova Scotia and New Brunswick), on the west by the Mississippi, on the east by the Great Salt-water Lake,[108] and on the south by the country of the Creeks, Cherokees, and other Florida Indians, there were but two nations, the Mengwe, and themselves. Theirs was by far the most numerous and the most extensively settled, for their tribes extended even beyond the Mississippi. On the other side of the St. Lawrence, the Algonquins, the Killistenos or Knisteneaux, and others, speaking dialects of their language, prove their origin from the same stock.

The Mengwe, on the contrary, were comparatively few, and occupied a much less portion of territory, being almost confined to the vicinity of the great lakes. But few tribes are known to be connected with them by descent and language; the principal ones are the Wyandots, otherwise called Hurons, and the Naudowessies. Almost every other nation within the boundaries described, is of the Lenape family.

Each of these two great nations, say the Delawares, had an ancient national name, and a tradition of their respective origin, handed down to them by their ancestors, and diffused among all the kindred tribes. By whatsoever names those tribes might be called, and whatever their numbers were, still they considered themselves, and were considered by others, as the offspring of the same original stock. All the tribes who had sprung from the Lenape called the mother nation *grandfather*, and received, in return, the appellation of *grandchildren*. They were all united by the strongest ties of friendship and alliance; in their own expressive language, they made but *one house, one fire, and one canoe*, that is to say, that they constituted together, one people, one family. The same thing took place between the Mengwe and the tribes descended from them. They and the Lenape had no relationship with each other, though they came over the Mississippi together at the same time. They considered each other as nations entirely distinct.

The Mengwe or Iroquois were always considered by the Lenape as only one nation, consisting of several confederated tribes. The name of Five and afterwards Six Nations, was given to them by the English, whose allies they were, probably to raise their consequence, and magnify the idea of their strength; but the Indian nations never did flatter them with that high sounding appellation, and considered them merely as confederated *tribes*.

The late Rev. Mr. Pyrlæus, in a large volume of MS. notes which he wrote between the years 1740 and 1760 (upwards of 70 years ago), has taken down on this subject the account given by the Iroquois themselves, as he had it from the mouth of an intelligent Mohawk chief,[109] whose veracity might be depended upon. After giving some details respecting the origin of their confederation, the time about which it took place, the names of the delegates from each of the confederated tribes, &c., he proceeds thus:

> "They then gave themselves the name *Aquanoshioni*, which means *one house, one family*, and consisted of the Mohawks, Oneidas, Onondagoes, Cayugas, and Senecas. This alliance having been first proposed by a Mohawk chief, the Mohawks rank in the *family* as the *eldest brother*, the Oneidas, as the *eldest son*; the Senecas, who were the last who at that time had consented to the alliance, were called the *youngest son*; but the Tuscaroras, who joined the confederacy probably one hundred years afterwards, assumed that name, and the Senecas ranked in precedence before them, as being the *next youngest son*, or as we would say, the youngest son but one."

The Rev. David Zeisberger also says:

"That the Iroquois call themselves *Aquanoschioni*, which means *united people*, having united for the purpose of always reminding each other that their safety and power consist in a mutual and strict adherence to their alliance."[110] He adds that Onondago is the chief town of the Iroquois.

Thus, in the different translations of the name which these people gave themselves, we find nothing that conveys the ideas of *nations*, it implies no more than a *family*, a *united people*, a *family compact*. The different sections take ranks in this family, of which the *Onondagoes* are the head, while the others are brothers and sons; all which tends clearly to prove, that they were originally but tribes, detached bodies of the same people, who, when brought together in close union, formed a complete family and became entitled to the name of a NATION.

We also see that self-preservation was the cause of their uniting, and that they were compelled by necessity to this measure, on which their existence depended. And though we have a right to suppose that that tribe which always takes the lead in the government of an Indian nation (the *Turtle* tribe), existed among them, yet it is evident that its authority at that time was either wholly disregarded, or at least, was too weak to give complete efficacy to its measures.

If, then, we believe the information given us by both Pyrlæus and Zeisberger to be correct, we must be fully convinced that the Iroquois confederacy did not consist of Five or Six Nations, but of as many tribes or sections of the same people, forming together one nation. These two Missionaries are known to have been men of the strictest veracity; they were both, I may say, critically acquainted[111] with the Mengwe idiom, and they had their information from the most respectable and intelligent men among that nation, the former from the Mohawk, the latter from the Onondaga tribe. There is no reason, therefore, why the truth of their statements should be doubted.

The Lenape and their kindred tribes never have called the Iroquois "the Five or Six Nations." In conversation, they call them the Mengwe, and never make use of any other but this generic name when speaking of them. In their councils, however, they occasionally distinguished them by the name *Palenach endchiesktajeet*.[113] These two words, literally translated mean "the five divisions, sections or parts together," and does not in any manner imply the idea of *nations*. Had they meant to say "the Five Nations," they would have expressed it by the words *Palenach ekhokewit*; those which they used, on the contrary, expressly imply *sectional divisions*, and leave no doubt about their meaning.

The Iroquois themselves, as we have already seen, had adopted a name, *Aquanoschioni*, merely indicative of their close union. After, however, they came to be informed of the meaning of the name which the English had given them, they were willing to let it pass as correct. The Indians are very fond of high sounding names; I have known myself chiefs who delighted to be called *Kings*, after they had learned from us that the rulers of the English and French nations were distinguished by that title.

Thus the proper name of those six united tribes is in their own language *Aquanoschioni*. By other nations they are called *Mengwe*, *Maquas*, *Mingoes*, and *Iroquois*. The Lenape call them by the first, the Mohicans and Dutch by the second, the English and Americans by the third, and the French by the fourth. I employ these different names indiscriminately in the course of this work.

As detached bodies or tribes, their names with the Lenape are the following:

1. *Sankhícani*, the Mohawks, from *Sankhican*, a gunlock, this people being the first who were furnished with muskets by the Europeans, the locks of which, with their effect in striking fire, was a subject of great astonishment to them; and thus they were named, as it were, *the fire-striking people*.
2. *W'Tássone*, the Oneidas. This name means the *stone-pipe makers*, and was given to them on account of their ingenuity in making tobacco pipes of stone.

3. *Onondágoes*, the Onondagoes. This name signifies in their own language *on the top of the hill*, their town being so situated.
4. *Queúgue*, Cayugas, thus called after a lake of the same name.
5. *Mæchachtínni*, the Senecas. This name means *Mountaineers*, and was given them because they inhabited the hilly parts of the country.
6. The *Tuscaroras*, the sixth and last tribe in the league, they call by the same name, yet I have never heard the Lenape speak of the *six divisions or tribes*; when they describe them in that manner, it is always by the number *Five*.

CHAPTER 6 ~
General character of the Indians

The Indian considers himself as a being created by an all-powerful, wise, and benevolent Mannitto;[114] all that he possesses, all that he enjoys, he looks upon as given to him or allotted for his use by the Great Spirit who gave him life: he therefore believes it to be his duty to adore and worship his Creator and benefactor; to acknowledge with gratitude his past favours, thank him for present blessings, and solicit the continuation of his good will.[115]

As beings who have control over all beasts and living creatures, they feel their importance; before they saw white people or men of a different colour from their own, they considered themselves as God's favourites, and believed that if the Great Mannitto could reside on earth he would associate with them and be their great chief.

The Indian also believes, that he is highly favoured by his Maker, not only in having been created different in shape and in mental and bodily powers from other animals, but in being enabled to controul and master them all, even those of an enormous size and of the most ferocious kinds; and therefore, when he worships his Creator in his way, he does not omit in his supplications to pray that he may be endowed with courage to fight and conquer his enemies, among whom he includes all savage beasts; and when he has performed some heroic act, he will not forget to acknowledge it as a mark of divine favour, by making a sacrifice to the great and good Mannitto, or by publicly announcing that his success was entirely owing to the courage given him by the all-powerful Spirit. Thus, habitual devotion to the great First Cause, and a strong feeling of gratitude for the benefits which he confers, is one of the prominent traits which characterise the mind of the untutored Indian.

Not satisfied with paying this first of duties to the Lord of all, in the best manner they are able, the Indians also endeavour to fulfil the views which they suppose he had in creating the world. They think that he made the earth and all that it contains for the common good of mankind; when he stocked the country that he gave them with plenty of game, it was not for the benefit of a few, but of all. Every thing was given in common to the sons of men. Whatever liveth on the land, whatsoever groweth out of the earth, and all that is in the rivers and waters flowing through the same, was given jointly to all, and every one is entitled to his share.

From this principle, hospitality flows as from its source. With them it is not a virtue but a strict duty. Hence they are never in search of excuses to avoid giving, but freely supply their neighbour's wants from the stock prepared for their own use. They give and are hospitable to all, without exception, and will always share with each other and often with the stranger, even to their last morsel. They rather would lie down themselves on an empty stomach, than have it laid to their charge that they had neglected their duty, by not satisfying the wants of the stranger, the sick or the needy. The stranger has a claim to their hospitality, partly on account of his being at a distance from his family and friends, and partly because he has honoured them by his visit, and ought to leave them with a good impression upon his mind; the sick and the poor because they have a right to be helped out of the common stock: for if the meat they have been served with, was taken from the woods, it was common to all before the hunter took it; if corn or vegetables, it had grown out of the common ground, yet not by the power of man, but by that of the Great Spirit. Besides, on the principle, that all are descended from one parent, they look upon themselves as but one great family, who therefore ought at all times and on all occasions, to be serviceable and kind to each other, and by that means make themselves acceptable to the head of the universal family, the great and good Mannitto. Let me be permitted to illustrate this by an example.

Some travelling Indians having in the year 1777, put their horses over night to pasture in my little meadow, at Gnadenhütten on the Muskingum, I called on them in the morning to learn why they had done so. I endeavoured to make them sensible of the injury they had done me, especially as I intended to mow the meadow in a day or two. Having finished my complaint, one of them replied: "My friend, it seems you lay claim to the grass my horses have eaten, because you had enclosed it with a fence: now tell me, who caused the grass to grow? Can *you* make the grass grow? I think not, and no body can except the great Mannitto. He it is who causes it to grow both for my horses and for yours! See, friend! the grass which grows out of the earth is common to all; the game in the woods is common to all. Say, did you never eat venison and bear's meat?—'Yes, very often.'—Well, and did you ever hear me or any other Indian complain about that? No; then be not disturbed at my horses having eaten only once, of what you call *your* grass, though the grass my horses did eat, in like manner as the meat you did eat, was given to the Indians by the Great Spirit. Besides, if you will but consider, you will find that my horses did not eat *all* your grass. For friendship's sake, however, I shall never put my horses in your meadow again."

The Indians are not only just, they are also in many respects a generous people, and cannot see the sick and the aged suffer for want of clothing. To such they will give a blanket, a shirt, a pair of leggings, mocksens, &c. Otherwise, when they make presents, it is done with a view to receive an equivalent in return, and the receiver is given to understand what that ought to be. In making presents to strangers, they are content with some trifle in token of remembrance; but when they give any thing to a trader, they at least expect double the value in return, saying that he can afford to do it, since he had cheated them so often.

They treat each other with civility, and shew much affection on meeting after an absence. When they meet in the forenoon, they will compliment one another with saying, "a good morning to you!" and in the afternoon, "a good evening." In the act of shaking hands with each other, they strictly attend to the distinguishing names of relations, which they utter at the time; as for instance, "a good morning, father, grandfather, uncle, aunt, cousin," and so down to a small grandchild. They are also in the habit of saluting old people no ways related to them, by the names of grandfather and grandmother, not in a tone of condescending superiority or disguised contempt, but as a genuine mark of the respect which they feel for age. The common way of saluting where no relationship exists, is that of "friend;" when, however, the young people meet, they make use of words suitable to their years or stage in life; they will say "a good morning, comrade, favourite, beloved, &c." Even the children salute each other affectionately.

"I am glad to see you," is the common way in which the Indians express themselves to one another after a short absence; but on meeting after a long absence, on the return of a messenger or a warrior from a critical or dangerous expedition, they have more to say; the former is saluted in the most cordial manner with some such expression: "I thank the Great Spirit, that he has preserved our lives to this time of our happily meeting again. I am, indeed, very glad to see you." To which the other will reply: "you speak the truth; it is through the favour of the great and good Spirit that we are permitted to meet. I am equally glad to see you." To the latter will be said: "I am glad that the Great Spirit has preserved your life and granted you a safe return to your family."

They are not quarrelsome, and are always on their guard, so as not to offend each other. When one supposes himself hurt or aggrieved by a word which has inadvertently fallen from the mouth of another, he will say to him: "Friend, you have caused me to become jealous of you," (meaning that he begins to doubt the sincerity of his friendship,) when the other explaining and saying that he had no bad intention, all is done away again.

They do not fight with each other; they say that fighting is only for dogs and beasts. They are, however, fond of play, and passing a joke, yet very careful that they do not offend.

They are ingenious in making satirical observations, which though they create laughter, do not, or but seldom give offence. For instance, seeing a bad hunter going out into the woods with his gun, they will ask him if he is going out for meat? or say to one another: "now we shall have meat, for such a one is gone a hunting," (not believing any such thing.) If they see a coward joining a war party, they will ask him ironically at what time he intends to come back again? (knowing that he will return before he has met the enemy,) or they will say to one another: "will he return this way with his scalps?"

Genuine wit, which one would hardly expect to find in a savage people, is not unfrequent among them. I have heard them, for instance, compare the English and American nations to a pair of scissors, an instrument composed of two sharp edged knives exactly alike, working against each other for the same purpose, that of *cutting*. By the construction of this instrument, they said, it would appear as if in shutting, these two sharp knives would strike together and destroy each other's edges; but no such thing: they only cut *what comes between them*. And thus the English and Americans do when they go to war against one another. It is not each other that they want to destroy, but us, poor Indians, that are between them. By this means they get our land, and, when that is obtained, the scissors are closed again, and laid by for further use.

They are remarkable for the particular respect which they pay to old age. In all their meetings, whether public or private, they pay the greatest attention to the observations and advice of the aged; no one will attempt to contradict them, nor to interfere in any manner or even to speak, unless he is specially called upon. "The aged," they say, "have lived through the whole period of our lives, and long before we were born; they have not only all the knowledge we possess, but a great deal more. We, therefore, must submit our limited views to their experience."

In travelling, one of the oldest will always take the lead, unless another is specially appointed for that purpose. If such a one stops to hunt, or in order to stay and encamp at the place for some time, all halt together, all are pleased with the spot and declare it to be judiciously chosen.

I shall expatiate further on this interesting part of the Indian character, in the sequel of this work.

They have a strong innate sense of justice, which will lead them sometimes to acts which some men will call heroic, others romantic, and not a few, perhaps, will designate by the epithet *barbarous*; a vague indefinite word, which if it means anything, might, perhaps, be best explained by *something not like ourselves*. However that may be, this feeling certainly exists among the Indians, and as I cannot describe it better than by its effects, I shall content myself with relating on this subject a characteristic anecdote which happened in the year 1793, at an Indian village called *La Chine*, situated nine miles above Montreal, and was told me in the same year by Mr. La Ramée, a French Canadian inhabitant of that place, whom I believe to be a person of strict veracity. I was then on my return from Detroit, in company with General Lincoln and several other gentlemen, who were present at the relation, and gave it their full belief. I thought it then so interesting, that I inserted it in my journal, from which I now extract it:

There were in the said village of La Chine two remarkable Indians, the one for his stature, being six feet four inches in height, and the other for his strength and activity. These two meeting together one day in the street, (a third being present,) the former in a high tone made use of some insulting language to the other, which he could not well put up with: he called him a coward, said he was his inferior in every respect, and so provoked his anger, that unable any longer to contain himself, the latter instantly replied: "You have grossly insulted me; but I will prevent you from doing the like again!" and at the same moment stabbed him through the body with his knife, so that he dropped down dead by his side.

The alarm being immediately spread through the village, a crowd of Indians assembled, and the murderer having seated himself on the ground by the side of the dead body, coolly awaited his fate, which he could not expect to be any other than immediate death, particularly as the cry of the people was, "Kill him! Kill him!" But although he placed his body and head in a proper posture to receive the stroke of the tomahawk, no one attempted to lay hands on him; but after removing the dead body from where it lay, they left him alone.

Not meeting here with his expected fate, he rose from this place for a more public part of the village, and there lay down on the ground in the hope of being the sooner despatched; but the spectators, after viewing him, all retired again. Sensible that his life was justly forfeited, and anxious to be relieved from a state of suspense, he took the resolution to go to the mother of the deceased, an aged widow, whom he addressed in these words: "Woman, I have killed thy son; he had insulted me, it is true; but still he was thine, and his life was valuable to thee. I, therefore, now surrender myself up to thy will. Direct as thou wilt have it, and relieve me speedily from misery." To which the woman answered: "Thou hast, indeed, killed my son, who was dear to me, and the only supporter I had in my old age. One life is already lost, and to take thine on that account, cannot be of any service to me, nor better my situation. Thou hast, however, a son, whom, if thou wilt give me in the place of my son, whom thou hast slain, all shall be wiped away."

The murderer then replied: "Mother, my son is yet but a child, ten years old, and can be of no service to thee, but rather a trouble and charge; but here am I, truly capable of supporting and maintaining thee: if thou wilt receive me as thy son, nothing shall be wanting on my part to make thee comfortable while thou livest." The woman approving of the proposal, forthwith adopted him as her son, and took the whole family to her house.

But we must now look to the other side of the picture. It cannot but be acknowledged that the Indians are in general revengeful and cruel to their enemies. That even after the battle is over, they wreak their deliberate revenge on their defenceless prisoners; that in their wars they are indifferent about the means which they pursue for the annoyance and destruction of their adversaries, and that surprise and stratagem are as often employed by them as open force. This is all true. Deprived of the light of the only true Christian Religion, unchecked by the precepts and unswayed by the example of the God of peace, they indulge too much, sometimes, the violence of their passions, and commit actions which force the tear from the eye of humanity. But, upon the whole, are we better than they are? I reserve this question for a separate chapter.

CHAPTER 7 ~
Government

Although the Indians have no code of laws for their government, their chiefs find little or no difficulty in governing them. They are supported by able experienced counsellors; men who study the welfare of the nation, and are equally interested with themselves in its prosperity. On them the people rely entirely, believing that what they do, or determine upon, must be right and for the public good.

Proud of seeing such able men conduct the affairs of their nation, the Indians are little troubled about what they are doing, knowing that the result of their deliberations will be made public in due time, and sure that it will receive their approbation. This result is made known to them by the chief through the orator, for which purpose they are called together and assemble at the council-house; and if it be found necessary to require a contribution of *wampum*, for carrying the decision of the chiefs into effect, it is cheerfully complied with by the whole assembly.

The chiefs are very careful in preserving for their own information, and that of future generations, all important deliberations and treaties made at any time between them and other nations. Thus, between the years 1770 and 1780, they could relate very minutely what had passed between William Penn and their forefathers, at their first meeting and afterwards, and also the transactions which took place with the governors who succeeded him. For the purpose of refreshing their own memories, and of instructing one or more of their most capable and promising young men in these matters, they assemble once or twice a year.

On these occasions they always meet at a chosen spot in the woods, at a small distance from the town, where a fire is kindled, and at the proper time provisions are brought out to them; there,

55

on a large piece of bark or on a blanket, all the documents are laid out in such order, that they can at once distinguish each particular speech, the same as we know the principal contents of an instrument of writing by the endorsement on it. If any paper or parchment writings are connected with the belts, or strings of wampum, they apply to some trusty white man (if such can be had,) to read the contents to them.

Their speaker then, who is always chosen from among those who are endowed with superior talents, and has already been trained up to the business, rises, and in an audible voice delivers, with the gravity that the subject requires, the contents, sentence after sentence, until he has finished the whole on one subject. On the manner in which the belts or strings of wampum are handled by the speaker, much depends; the *turning*[116] of the belt which takes place when he has finished one half of his speech, is a material point, though this is not common in *all* speeches with belts; but when it is the case, and is done properly, it may be as well known by it how far the speaker has advanced in his speech, as with us on taking a glance at the pages of a book or pamphlet while reading; and a good speaker will be able to point out the exact place on a belt which is to answer to each particular sentence, the same as we can point out a passage in a book. Belts and strings, when done with by the speaker, are again handed to the chief, who puts them up carefully in the speech-bag or pouch.

A message of importance is generally sent on to the place of its destination, by an inferior chief, by a counsellor, or by the speaker, especially when an immediate answer is expected. In other cases, where for instance only an answer to a speech is to be sent, two capable young men are selected for the purpose, the one to deliver the message or answer, and the other to pay attention while his companion is delivering it, that no part be forgotten or omitted. If the message be of a private nature, they are charged to draw or take it *under ground*, that is, not to make it known to any person whatsoever, except to him to whom it is directed. If they are told to enter *into the earth* with the message or speech, and rise again at the place where they are to deliver it, it is to desire them to be careful not to be seen by the way by any person, and for that purpose to avoid all paths, and travel through the woods.

No chief pays any attention to *reports*, though they may carry with them the marks of truth. Until he is *officially* and in due form apprised of the matter, he will, if questioned on the subject, reply that he had *not heard it*. It will, until then, be considered by him as the *song of a bird which had flown by*; but as soon as he is officially informed, through a string of wampum from some distant chief or leading man of the nation, whose situation entitles him to receive credit, he then will say: "I *have* heard it;" and acts accordingly.

The Indians generally, but their chiefs more particularly, have many figurative expressions in use, to understand which requires instruction. When a nation, by message or otherwise, speaks to another nation in this way, it is well understood; but when they speak to white people after this manner, who have not been accustomed to such language, explanations are necessary.

Their belts of wampum are of different dimensions, both as to the length and breadth. White and black wampum are the kinds they use; the former denoting that which is *good*, as peace, friendship, good will, &c., the latter the reverse; yet occasionally the black also is made use of on peace errands, when the white cannot be procured; but previous to its being produced for such purpose, it must be daubed all over with chalk, white clay, or any thing which changes the colour from black to white. The pipe of peace, being either made of a black or red stone, must also be whitened before it is produced and smoked out of on such occasions.

Roads from one friendly nation to another, are generally marked on the belt, by one or two rows of white wampum interwoven in the black, and running through the middle, and from end to end. It means that they are on good terms, and keep up a friendly intercourse with each other.

A black belt with the mark of a hatchet made on it with red paint, is a war belt, which, when sent to a nation together with a twist or roll of tobacco, is an invitation to join in a war. If the nation so invited smoke of this tobacco, and say it smokes well, they have given their consent, and are from that moment allies. If however they decline smoking, all further persuasion would be of no effect; yet it once[117] happened, that war messengers endeavoured to persuade and compel a nation to accept the belt, by laying it on the shoulders or thigh of the chief, who, however, after shaking it off without touching it with his hands, afterwards, with a stick, threw it after them, as if he threw a snake or toad out of his way.

Although at their councils they do not seat themselves after the manner of the white people, yet the attitude they place themselves in is not chargeable to them as a want of respect. Faithful to the trust committed to them, they are careless of ceremonies, from which the nation cannot derive any benefit. They seat themselves promiscuously around a council fire, some leaning one way, some another, so that a stranger on viewing them, might be led to conclude they were inattentive to what was said, or had become tired of attending. Not so! even sitting in this posture gives them the opportunity of being intent on what is said, and attentive to the subject under their consideration. They have no object to look at, which might draw off their attention. They are all ears, though they do not stare at the speaker! The fact is, that nothing can draw their attention from the subject they are deliberating on, unless the house they are sitting in should take fire or be attacked by an enemy.

To prove the correctness of the above assertion, I shall relate the following fact, which happened at Detroit in the winter of 1785 and 1786:

> When two most audacious murderers of the Chippeway nation, who, for many months, had put the town and whole country in fear, by the threats and the daring murders they had committed in the settlement, were taken, and brought before the commandant (their chiefs having been previously sent for, and being now assembled in the council house), heard him pronounce the words: "that according to the laws of their Father (the English)

they should[118] be punished with death," the younger of the two, who was the son of the other, sprang from his seat, and having forced his way to[119] the door, endeavoured with a knife or dagger he had hidden under his blanket, to work his way through the strong guard placed outside of the door and[120] in the street to prevent their escape; in this attempt, however, he was stabbed and fell; all which occasioned much noise and commotion without, and not a little fear and uneasiness within, among the spectators and officers of government; yet, not one of the chiefs, who were many in number, either moved from his seat, nor looked around, or even at one another; but they all remained sitting in the same posture as before, smoking their pipes as if nothing had happened.

Though there are sometimes individuals in a nation, who disregard the counsel and good advice given by the chiefs, yet they do not meet with support so as to be able to oppose the measures of government. They are generally looked upon as depraved beings, who not daring to associate with the others, lurk about by themselves, generally bent on mischief of a minor kind, such as pilfering small articles of goods and provisions. As soon, however, as they go a step further, and become known thieves and murderers, they are considered a disgrace to the nation, and being in a manner disowned by it, they are no longer entitled to their protection.

In the year 1785, an Indian of this description, murdered a Mr. Evans at Pittsburg; when, after a confinement of several months, his trial was to be brought on, the chiefs of his (the Delaware nation,) were invited to come to be present at the proceedings and see how the trial would be conducted, and, also, if they chose, to speak in behalf of the accused. These chiefs, however, instead of coming, as wished for, sent to the civil officers of that place the following laconic answer: "Brethren! You inform us that N. N. who murdered one of your men at Pittsburg, is shortly to be tried by the laws of your country, at which trial you request that some of us may be present! Brethren! knowing N. N. to have been always a very bad man, we do not wish to see him! We, therefore, advise you to try him by your laws, and to hang him, so that he may never return to us again."

I shall conclude this subject with another anecdote. When in the winter of 1788 and 1789, the Indian nations were assembling at Fort Harmer, at the mouth of the Muskingum, where a treaty was to be held, an Indian of the Seneca nation was one morning found dead on the bank of the river. The Cornplanter, chief of this nation, observing some uneasiness among the officers and people of the place, and fearing the murder at this time and place, might perhaps create much disturbance, waited in the morning on the Governor, whom he desired "not to be uneasy about what had happened the preceding night, for the man who had been killed was of no consequence." This meant in other words, that he was disowned for his bad conduct by his countrymen, and that his death would not be a loss to his nation.

CHAPTER 8 ~
Education

It may justly be a subject of wonder, how a nation without a
written code of laws or system of jurisprudence, without any form
or constitution of government, and without even a single elective
or hereditary magistrate, can subsist together in peace and
harmony, and in the exercise of the moral virtues; how a people
can be well and effectually governed without any external
authority; by the mere force of the ascendancy which men of
superior minds have over those of a more ordinary stamp; by a
tacit, yet universal submission to the aristocracy of experience,
talents and virtue! Such, nevertheless, is the spectacle which an
Indian nation exhibits to the eye of a stranger. I have been a
witness to it for a long series of years, and after much observation
and reflection to discover the cause of this phenomenon, I think I
have reason to be satisfied that it is in a great degree to be
ascribed to the pains which the Indians take to instill at an early
age honest and virtuous principles upon the minds of their
children, and to the method which they pursue in educating them.
This method I will not call a system; for systems are unknown to
these sons of nature, who, by following alone her simple dictates,
have at once discovered and follow without effort that plain
obvious path which the philosophers of Europe have been so long
in search of.

The first step that parents take towards the education of their
children, is to prepare them for future happiness, by impressing
upon their tender minds, that they are indebted for their
existence to a great, good and benevolent Spirit, who not only has
given them life, but has ordained them for certain great purposes.
That he has given them a fertile extensive country well stocked
with game of every kind for their subsistence, and that by one of
his inferior spirits he has also sent down to them from above corn,
pumpkins, squashes, beans and other vegetables for their
nourishment; all which blessings their ancestors have enjoyed for

a great number of ages. That this great Spirit looks down upon the Indians, to see whether they are grateful to him and make him a due return for the many benefits he has bestowed, and therefore that it is their duty to show their thankfulness by worshipping him, and doing that which is pleasing in his sight.

This is in substance the first lesson taught, and from time to time repeated to the Indian children, which naturally leads them to reflect and gradually to understand that a being which hath done such great things for them, and all to make them happy, must be good indeed, and that it is surely their duty to do something that will please him. They are then told that their ancestors, who received all this from the hands of the great Spirit, and lived in the enjoyment of it, must have been informed of what would be most pleasing to this good being, and of the manner in which his favour could be most surely obtained, and they are directed to look up for instruction to those who know all this, to learn from them, and revere them for their wisdom and the knowledge which they possess; this creates in the children a strong sentiment of respect for their elders, and a desire to follow their advice and example. Their young ambition is then excited by telling them that they were made the superiors of all other creatures, and are to have power over them; great pains are taken to make this feeling take an early root, and it becomes in fact their ruling passion through life; for no pains are spared to instill into them that by following the advice of the most admired and extolled hunter, trapper or warrior, they will at a future day acquire a degree of fame and reputation, equal to that which he possesses; that by submitting to the counsels of the aged, the chiefs, the men superior in wisdom, they may also rise to glory, and be called *Wisemen*, an honourable title, to which no Indian is indifferent. They are finally told that if they respect the aged and infirm, and are kind and obliging to them, they will be treated in the same manner when their turn comes to feel the infirmities of old age.

When this first and most important lesson is thought to be sufficiently impressed upon children's minds, the parents next proceed to make them sensible of the distinction between good and evil; they tell them that there are good actions and bad actions, both equally open to them to do or commit; that good acts are pleasing to the good Spirit which gave them their existence, and that on the contrary, all that is bad proceeds from the bad spirit who has given them nothing, and who cannot give them any thing that is good, because he has it not, and therefore he envies them that which they have received from the good Spirit, who is far superior to the bad one.

This introductory lesson, if it may be so called, naturally makes them wish to know what is good and what is bad. This the parent teaches him in his own way, that is to say, in the way in which he was himself taught by his own parents. It is not the lesson of an hour nor of a day, it is rather a long course more of practical than of theoretical instruction, a lesson, which is not repeated at stated seasons or times, but which is shewn, pointed out, and demonstrated to the child, not only by those under whose immediate guardianship he is, but by the whole community, who consider themselves alike interested in the direction to be given to the rising generation.

When this instruction is given in the form of precepts, it must not be supposed that it is done in an authoritative or forbidding tone, but, on the contrary, in the gentlest and most persuasive manner: nor is the parent's authority ever supported by harsh or compulsive means; no whips, no punishments, no threats are even used to enforce commands or compel obedience. The child's *pride* is the feeling to which an appeal is made, which proves successful in almost every instance. A father needs only to say in the presence of his children: "I want such a thing done; I want one of my children to go upon such an errand; let me see who is the *good* child that will do it!" This word *good* operates, as it were, by magic, and the children immediately vie with each other to comply with the wishes of their parent. If a father sees an old decrepid man or woman pass by, led along by a child, he will draw the attention of his own children to the object by saying: "What a *good* child that must be, which pays such attention to the aged! That child, indeed, looks forward to the time when it will likewise be old!" or he will say, "May the great Spirit, who looks upon him, grant this *good* child a long life!"

In this manner of bringing up children, the parents, as I have already said, are seconded by the whole community. If a child is sent from his father's dwelling to carry a dish of victuals to an aged person, all in the house will join in calling him a *good* child. They will ask whose child he is, and on being told, will exclaim: what! has the *Tortoise*, or the *little Bear* (as the father's name may be) got such a *good* child? If a child is seen passing through the streets leading an old decrepid person, the villagers will in his hearing, and to encourage all the other children who may be present to take example from him, call on one another to look on and see what a *good* child that must be. And so, in most instances, this method is resorted to, for the purpose of instructing children in things that are good, proper, or honourable in themselves; while, on the other hand, when a child has committed a *bad* act, the parent will say to him: "O! how grieved I am that my child has done this *bad* act! I hope he will never do so again." This is generally effectual, particularly if said in the presence of others. The whole of the Indian plan of education tends to elevate rather than to depress the mind, and by that means to make determined hunters and fearless warriors.

Thus, when a lad has killed his first game, such as a deer or a bear, parents who have boys growing up will not fail to say to some person in the presence of their own children: "That boy must have listened attentively to the aged hunters, for, though young, he has already given a proof that he will become a good hunter himself." If, on the other hand, a young man should fail of giving such a proof, it will be said of him "that he did not pay attention to the discourses of the aged."

In this indirect manner is instruction on all subjects given to the young people. They are to learn the arts of hunting, trapping, and making war, by listening to the aged when conversing together on those subjects, each, in his turn, relating how he acted, and opportunities are afforded to them for that purpose. By this mode of instructing youth, their respect for the aged is kept alive, and it is increased by the reflection that the same respect will be paid to them at a future day, when young persons will be attentive to what they shall relate.

This method of conveying instruction is, I believe, common to most Indian nations; it is so, at least, amongst all those that I have become acquainted with, and lays the foundation for that voluntary submission to their chiefs, for which they are so remarkable. Thus has been maintained for ages, without convulsions and without civil discords, this traditional government, of which the world, perhaps, does not offer another example; a government in which there are no positive laws, but only long established habits and customs, no code of jurisprudence, but the experience of former times, no magistrates, but advisers, to whom the people, nevertheless, pay a willing and implicit obedience, in which age confers rank, wisdom gives power, and moral goodness secures a title to universal respect. All this seems to be effected by the simple means of an excellent mode of education, by which a strong attachment to ancient customs, respect for age, and the love of virtue are indelibly impressed upon the minds of youth, so that these impressions acquire strength as time pursues its course, and as they pass through successive generations.

CHAPTER 9 ~
Languages

In all the North American territories bounded to the north and east by the Atlantic ocean, and to the south and west by the river Mississippi, and the possessions of the English Hudson's Bay company, there appears to be but four principal languages, branching out, it is true, into various dialects, but all derived from one or the other of the four mother tongues, some of which extend even beyond the Mississippi, and perhaps, as far as the Rocky Mountains. These four languages are:

I. THE KARALIT.

This language is spoken by the inhabitants of Greenland and on the Continent by the Eskimaux Indians of the coast of Labrador. Its forms and principles are sufficiently known by means of the Grammar and Dictionary of the venerable Egede,[121] and the works of Bartholinus, Wœldike, Thornhallesen,[122] Cranz[123] and others. It is much cultivated by the Missionaries of the Society of the United Brethren, by whom we may expect to see its principles still further elucidated. It is in Greenland that begin those comprehensive grammatical forms which are said to characterise the languages of the vast American continent, as far as they are known, and are the more remarkable when contrasted with the simplicity of construction of the idioms spoken on the opposite European shores, in Iceland, Denmark, Sweden and other countries. It appears evident from this single circumstance, that America did not receive its original population from Europe.

II. THE IROQUOIS.

This language in various dialects is spoken by the Mengwe or Six Nations, the Wyandots or Hurons, the Naudowessies, the Assinipoetuk, called by the French Assiniboils, Assinipoils, or Sioux, and by other tribes, particularly beyond the St. Lawrence. Father La Hontan distinguishes this class of languages by the name of the *Huron*, probably because that nation was better known to the French, whose allies they were, than the Iroquois, who were in alliance with the English.[124] All these languages, however they may be called in a general sense, are dialects of the same mother tongue, and have considerable affinity with each other. Mr. Carver is mistaken when he describes the *Naudowessie* as belonging to a class different from the Iroquois.[125] It is sufficient to compare the vocabularies that we have of these two idioms, to see the great similitude that subsists between them. We do not, unfortunately, possess a single grammar of any of these dialects; we have nothing, in fact, besides the fragment of Zeisberger's Dictionary, which I have already mentioned, but a large vocabulary of the Huron,[126] composed by Father Sagard, a good and pious French Missionary, but of very limited abilities, and who also resided too short a time among that nation to be able to give a correct account of their language. He represents it in his preface, as poor, imperfect, anomalous, and inadequate to the clear expression of ideas, in which he is contradicted by others whom we have reason to believe better informed. Zeisberger considered the Iroquois (of which the Huron is a dialect,) as a rich and comprehensive idiom. It is to be regretted that a grammar which he had composed of it, and the best part of his Dictionary, are irretrievably lost. Sir William Johnson speaks highly of the powers of this language;[127] Colden,[128] though he did not know it himself, speaks in the same manner from the information of others. Indeed, Father Sagard's Dictionary itself, when attentively read by a person acquainted with the forms of Indian languages, affords sufficient intrinsic evidence of the mistakes of the good father who composed it.

III. THE LENAPE.

This is the most widely extended language of any of those that are spoken on this side of the Mississippi. It prevails in the extensive regions of Canada, from the coast of Labrador to the mouth of Albany river which falls into the southernmost part of Hudson's bay, and from thence to the Lake of the Woods, which forms the north-western boundary of the United States. It appears to be the language of all the Indians of that extensive country, except those of the Iroquois stock, which are by far the least numerous. Farther to the north-west, in the territories of the Hudson's Bay Company, other Indian nations have been discovered, such as the Blackfoot Indians, Sussee Indians, Snake Indians, and others, whose languages are said to be different from the Iroquois and the Lenape, but we are not able to form a very correct judgment respecting those idioms from the scanty vocabularies which have been given us by Mackenzie, Umfreville and other travellers. We must wait for further light before we decide.

Out of the limits of Canada few Iroquois are found, except the remnants of those who were once settled in the vicinity of the great Lakes, in the northern parts of the now State of New York. There are yet some Wyandots in the vicinity of Detroit. All the rest of the Indians who now inhabit this country to the Mississippi, are of the Lenape stock, and speak dialects of that language. It is certain that at the time of the arrival of the Europeans, they were in possession of all the coast from the northernmost point of Nova Scotia to the Roanoke. Hence they were called *Wapanachki*, or *Abenakis*, men of the East. La Hontan gives us a list of the Indian nations of ancient Acadia, all speaking dialects of the Abenaki, or as he calls it, of the Algonquin. They were the Abenakis, Micmacs, Canibas, Mahingans (Mohicans), Openangos, Soccokis, and Etchemins, from whom all Nova Scotia, (excepting the peninsula,) and a part of the now district of Maine, were once called by the French the *country of the Etchemins*. He does not speak of the Souriquois, who are also known to have inhabited Acadia, and likewise spoke a dialect of the Lenape.

In the interior of the country we find every where the Lenape and their kindred tribes. The Miamis, or Twightwees, the Potowatomies, the Messissaugees, the Kickapoos, all those Indian nations who once inhabited, and parts of whom still inhabit the interior of our country on this side of the Mississippi and the great Lakes, are unquestionably, from their dialects, of Lenape origin. The Shawanos, it is said, formerly dwelt upon the river Savannah, in Georgia, and a part of them remaining in that country, associated with the Creeks, still retain their language.[129] As far as we are able to judge from the little knowledge that has been transmitted to us of the language of the Indians who once inhabited Maryland, Virginia, and North Carolina, they all appear to have belonged to the same stock, the Nanticokes have been shewn to have been intimately connected with the Lenape, and among those who called them *grandfather*. Two pretty copious vocabularies of their language, in the possession of the Historical Committee of the American Philosophical Society, one of them communicated by Mr. Jefferson and the other by myself, prove it beyond a doubt to have been a dialect of the Lenape.[130] The Canai or Kanhawas, who have given their name to a river in Virginia which empties itself into the Ohio, are known to have been of the same stock. The Indian names of rivers, mountains, and towns, through that vast extent of country, appear generally derived from the Lenape language.

The Baron de La Hontan, is one of the first writers, I believe, who have spoken of the universality of this idiom; but it is extraordinary that he has not said a word of the Lenni Lenape, that great and powerful nation. He calls this language the *Algonquin* tongue, although he describes that people as "an erratic sort of savages, who, like the Arabs, had no settled abode,"[131] and admits, that at the time when he wrote, their number did not exceed 200. What he says on this subject, however, is so much to my purpose, that I hope I shall be permitted to make a small extract from it.

"There are," says the Baron, "but two mother tongues in the whole extent of Canada, which I confine within the limits of the Mississippi; they are the *Huron* and the *Algonquin*. The first is understood by the Iroquois, for the difference between these two

69

is no greater than that between the Norman and the French. The second, namely the *Algonquin*, is as much esteemed among the savages as the Greek and Latin are in Europe; though it would seem that the aborigines, to whom it owes its original, disgrace it by the thinness of their nation, *for their whole number does not amount to two hundred.*"[133]

What the Baron says here of this language is very correct; but why does he call it the Algonquin, and ascribe its origin to that miserable wandering tribe? He had the Abenakis at hand, whom in another place he puts at the head of the tribes inhabiting Nova Scotia, and who still preserved the generic name of the whole nation, *Wapanachki*, which the French have softened to suit the analogy of their own tongue, by which name the different nations and tribes of the Lenape stock still recognise each other to this day. It is probable that he did not sufficiently understand their language,[134] to have much conversation with them, otherwise they would have informed him that they derived their origin from a great and powerful nation residing in the interior of the country, whom they revered as their *grandfather*, at whose door the great national council fire was kept constantly burning, whose badge was the *Turtle*, and whose supremacy was acknowledged by all the kindred tribes.

Father Charlevoix, who also speaks of the universality of this language, commits the same error in ascribing its origin to the Algonquins. "In the southern part of Hudson's Bay," says he, "the trade is carried on with the Matassins, the Monsonies, the Christinaux (Knisteneaux), and the Assinipoils, the three first of which speak the *Algonquin* language."[135] In a later publication, (I think by a Mr. Winterbotham,) of which, during my travels, some years ago, I had merely a glance, I found by some words he had put down in the language of those people, that they were *Minsi* or *Monseys*, a branch of the wolf tribe of the Lenape. So indeed, one of their names, *Monsonies*, seems of itself to indicate. The name of the Matassins, means in their language a tobacco pipe, and so it does in the Monsey to this day. And they all speak the Algonquin, a language, say both Charlevoix and La Hontan, universally known for a thousand leagues round. The last mentioned author subjoins a vocabulary of what he calls the

Algonquin tongue, which bears a greater affinity to the language of the Unamis or Turtle[136] tribe of the Lenape than that does to the idiom of the Monsey or Wolf tribe of the same nation. I find many words in the Algonquin (as given by La Hontan), which are exactly the same as in the Unami, while others bear more resemblance to the Chippeway, also a dialect of the Lenape, spoken by a tribe in connexion with the Delawares, and who call them *grandfather*.

There can be no doubt, therefore, that this universal language, so much admired and so generally spoken by the Indian nations, is that of the Lenni Lenape, and is improperly named the Chippeway by Carver, and the Algonquin by La Hontan. The celebrated Professor Vater, in his excellent continuation of Adelung's Mithridates, calls the class of languages derived from this source, "the Chippewayo-Delawarian, or Algonkino-Mohican stock."[137] It is, perhaps, indifferent for philological purposes, whether a language be called the Delaware or the Chippeway, the Algonquin or the Mohican; but every body must be sensible of the inconvenience of those long compound names, which leave no fixed or determinate idea upon the mind. For the purpose of general description it seems better to designate the languages of those connected tribes by the name of their common grandfather, the Lenni Lenape, or by the generic denomination universally adopted among them, Wapanachki, or Abenaki. I have preferred the former as a mark of respect to an ancient and once powerful nation, and in the hope that her name may be preserved, at least, in the records of philological science.

This beautiful language, and those which are derived from it, though more has been written upon them than on any of the other languages of these parts of the North American continent, are as yet but little known. The grammar of the Natick dialect published by Eliot, at Cambridge in Massachusetts, in the year 1666, has long been out of print, and is to be found only in very few libraries in the United States; Dr. Edwards's little tract on the Mohican language, although printed twice, does not appear to have had much circulation, and is not alone sufficient to give an idea of the forms and construction of these Indian dialects. Zeisberger's Delaware spelling book is but a collection of words, and does not contain any grammatical explanations. The learned Vater has taken immense pains, from the scanty helps within his reach, to discover the grounds and principles of these idioms, and what he has written on the subject is a proof of what talents and industry can effect with little means. But still the matter is not sufficiently understood. There is in the library of the society of the United Brethren in this town, an excellent MS. grammar of the Lenni Lenape, written in German by Zeisberger. I understand that the Historical Committee of the American Philosophical Society are going to publish an English translation of this valuable work. I rejoice in the prospect of this publication, which will give a clear and satisfactory view of the true genius and character of the languages of the Indian nations. At the request of the same Committee, I have endeavoured to give some further development of the principles which that grammar contains, in a series of letters to their Secretary, which, I am informed, are also to be printed. This supersedes the necessity of my entering here into more details on this interesting subject. I hope the result of these publications will be to satisfy the world that the languages of the Indians are not so poor, so devoid of variety of expression, so inadequate to the communication even of abstract ideas, or in a word so *barbarous*, as has been generally imagined.

IV. THE FLORIDIAN.

I call by this generic name, the languages spoken by those Indian nations who inhabit the southern frontier of the United States and the Spanish Province of Florida. They are the Creeks or Muskohgees, Chickesaws, Choctaws, Pascagoulas, Cherokees or Cheerakees, and several others. It is said that there once existed among them a powerful nation called the Natchez, whose language was the mother tongue of all those southern dialects. We are told also of an Apalachian nation, who it is said lived in the western parts of Louisiana, and were a part of the great nation of the Apalachians, who resided in the mountains which bear their name, and whose branches were settled under different denominations, in the vast extent of country situated between Louisiana, Canada and New England.[138] In this great *Apalachian* nation we cannot help recognising our friends the Lenape, or *Wapanachki*, whose name the French in the south have as easily corrupted into *Apalaches*, as those in the north into *Abenakis*. It was they who gave their name to the Apalachian mountains, once so called, but which of late have resumed their former appellation of Alligewi, or Allegheny. Mr. Vater thinks that the remains of those Apalachians are still to be found in the Catawbas,[139] who are sometimes named Chaktawas[140] and probably are the same who by contraction are now called Choktaws.

Other writers speak to us of the Mobilians,[141] as the nation from which the neighbouring tribes derived their origin, and whose language was their mother tongue. The fact is, that we know very little about these southern Indians, and on the subject of their languages we have nothing to guide our enquiries, but a few words given us by Adair, and some that have been collected from various sources by the late Dr. Barton. We are not, however, without the means of obtaining full and accurate information on this interesting subject, and I hope the historical committee will be successful in the measures which they are about to take to procure it. Mr. Meigs, the United States agent with the Cherokees, Mr. Mitchell, agent to the Creeks, and the Rev. John Gambold, who has long lived as a Missionary of the Society of the United Brethren with the former of these nations, are well able to satisfy their enquiries, and I have no doubt will be happy to give their aid to the advancement of the literature of their country.

It is a fact worthy of remark, and much to be regretted, that the French and English, who have been so long in possession of the immense country extending from Labrador to the Mississippi, have written so little respecting the Indian languages of this part of the American continent. Among the English, Eliot alone, and among the French, Father Sagard, can be said to have published anything on this subject that is worth notice. Zeisberger was a German, and Mr. Edwards an American. On the contrary, the Spaniards[142] have published a great number of grammars and dictionaries of the Indian languages spoken within the limits of their American possessions, and deserve much credit for these exertions. It is not yet too late for the independent Americans to retrieve the neglect of their forefathers; but no time should be lost, as the Indian nations are fast disappearing from the face of our country, and our posterity may have to regret hereafter that greater pains were not taken to preserve the memory of their traditions, customs, manners, and LANGUAGES.

CHAPTER 10 ~
Signs and Hieroglyphics

It has been asserted by many persons that the languages of the Indians are deficient in words, and that, in order to make themselves understood, they are obliged to resort to motions and signs with their hands. This is entirely a mistake. I do not know a nation of whom foreigners do not say the same thing. The fact is, that in every country, signs and motions with the hands more or less accompany discourse, particularly when delivered with a certain degree of earnestness and warmth. Foreigners, who are not very conversant with a language, pay in general as much and sometimes more attention to these motions than to the words of the speaker, in order the better to be able to understand what falls from him. Hence, almost every nation charges the others with too much gesticulation in speaking. For a similar reason, a foreign language is generally thought to be spoken quicker than our own, while the truth is, that it is our ear which is slow in distinguishing the words, not the voice which speaks that is too quick in uttering them.

The Indians do not gesticulate more when they speak than other nations do. In their public speeches they will, like our preachers and lawyers, enforce what they say by gestures and motions of the body and hands, in order to give greater weight to their observations, or to represent the subject they speak of in a more lively manner than can be done by words alone; but in common conversation they make few of those motions, and not more, I believe, than we do ourselves; even the women, who every where speak more than the men, never want words to express themselves, but rather seem to have too many, and they do not oftener employ gestures in aid of their conversation than the vivacity of their sex induces them to do every where else.

It is true that the Indians have a language of signs, by which they communicate with each other on occasions when speaking is not prudent or proper, as, for instance, when they are about to meet an enemy, and by speaking they would run the risk of being discovered. By this means they also make themselves understood to those nations of Indians whose languages they are not acquainted with, for all the Indian nations understand each other in this way. It is also, in many cases, a saving of words, which the Indians are much intent on, believing that too much talking disgraces a man. When, therefore, they will relate something extraordinary in a few words, they make use of corresponding signs, which is very entertaining to those who listen and attend to them, and who are acquainted both with the language and the signs, being very much as if somebody were to explain a picture set before them. But they never make use of signs to supply any deficiency of language, as they have words and phrases sufficient to express every thing.

I have frequently questioned Indians who had been educated at our schools, and could understand, read, write, and speak both English and German, whether they could express their ideas better in either of those languages than in their own, and they have always and uniformly answered that they could express themselves with far the greatest ease in their own Indian, and that they never were at a loss for words or phrases in which to clothe every idea that occurred to them, without being in any case obliged to gesticulate or make motions with their hands or otherwise. From the knowledge which I have acquired of their language, I have reason to be satisfied that it is so. Indeed, how can it be doubted, when we have the whole of the Bible and New Testament translated into one of their dialects, and when we see our ministers, when once familiar with the language of the nation with which they reside, preach to them without the least difficulty on the most abstruse subjects of the Christian faith? It is true, that ideas are not always expressed in those languages in the same words, or under the same grammatical forms as in our own; where we would use one part of speech, we are obliged to employ another, and one single word with them will not seldom serve a purpose for which we would have to employ several; but still, the ideas are communicated, and pass with clearness and precision from mind to mind. Thus the end of oral language is completely obtained, and more, I think, cannot be required.

The Indians do not possess our art of writing, they have no alphabets, or[143] any mode of representing to the eye the sounds of words spoken, yet they have certain hieroglyphics, by which they describe facts in so plain a manner, that those who are conversant with those marks can understand them with the greatest ease, as easily, indeed, as we can understand a piece of writing. For instance, on a piece of bark, or on a large tree with the bark taken off for the purpose, by the side of a path, they can and do give every necessary information to those who come by the same way; they will in that manner let them know, that they were a war party of so many men, from such a place, of such a nation and such a tribe; how many of each tribe were in the party; to which tribe the chief or captain belonged; in what direction they proceeded to meet the enemy; how many days they were out and how many returning; what number of the enemy they had killed, how many prisoners they had brought; how many scalps they had taken; whether they had lost any of their party, and how many; what enemies they had met with, and how many they consisted of; of what nation or tribe their captain was, &c.; all which, at a single glance, is perfectly well understood by them. In the same manner they describe a chase: all Indian nations can do this, although they have not all the same marks; yet I have seen the Delawares read with ease the drawings of the Chippeways, Mingoes, Shawanos, and Wyandots, on similar subjects.

While Indians are travelling to the place of their destination, whether it be on a journey to their distant hunting grounds or on a war excursion, some of the young men are sent out to hunt by the way, who, when they have killed a deer, bear, or other animal, bring it to the path, ready to be taken away by those who are coming along, (often with horses) to the place of encampment, when they all meet at night. Having hung up the meat by the side of the path, these young men make a kind of sun-dial, in order to inform those who are coming of the time of day it was at the time of their arrival and departure. A clear place in the path is sought for, and if not readily found, one is made by the side of it, and a circle or ring being drawn on the sand or earth, a stick of about two or three feet in length is fixed in the centre, with its upper end bent towards that spot in the horizon where the sun stood at the time of their arrival or departure. If

77

both are to be noted down, two separate sticks are set; but generally one is sufficient, namely, for the time of departure.

Hunters have particular marks, which they make on the trees, where they strike off from the path to their hunting grounds or place of encampment, which is often at the distance of many miles; yet the women, who come from their towns to fetch meat from these camps, will as readily find them as if they were conducted to the spot.

I shall conclude this chapter with an anecdote, which will at once shew how expressive and energetic is this hieroglyphic writing of the Indians. A white man in the Indian country, met[144] a Shawanos riding a horse which he recognised for his own, and claimed it from him as his property. The Indian calmly answered; "Friend! after a little while, I will call on you at your house, when we shall talk of this matter." A few days[145] afterwards, the Indian came to the white man's house, who insisting on having his horse restored, the other then told him: "Friend! the horse which you claim belonged to my uncle who lately died; according to the Indian custom, I have become heir to all his property." The white man not being satisfied, and renewing his demand, the Indian immediately took a coal from the fire-place, and made two striking figures on the door of the house, the one representing the white man taking the horse, and the other, himself, in the act of scalping him; then he coolly asked the trembling claimant "whether he could read this Indian writing?" The matter thus was settled at once, and the Indian rode off.

CHAPTER 11 ~
Oratory

The eloquence of the Indians is natural and simple; they speak what their feelings dictate without art and without rule; their speeches are forcible and impressive, their arguments few and pointed, and when they mean to persuade as well as convince, they take the shortest way to reach the heart. I know that their oratorical powers have been strongly controverted, and this is not astonishing, when we consider the prejudice that exists against their languages, which are in general believed to be poor, and inadequate to the expression of any but the most common ideas. Hence all the specimens that have been given to the world of their oratory have been viewed with a suspicious eye; the celebrated speech of Logan, authenticated as it is by the respectable authority of Col. John Gibson, has been denied to be genuine even in this country. For my part, I am convinced that it was delivered precisely as it is related to us, with this only difference, that it possessed a force and expression in the Indian language which it is impossible to transmit into our own.

I hope the exertions and researches of the Historical Committee will make the character and genius of the Indian languages better known than they have hitherto been. The world will then be better able to judge of their extent and powers, and to decide whether or not they are adequate to the purposes of oratory. In the meantime, I shall content myself with presenting another specimen of Indian eloquence; one which I did not receive at second hand, but at the delivery of which I was present in person. The translation which I offer will give but a faint idea of the strength and spirit of the original; I vouch, however, for its being as correct as it has been in my power to make it.

This speech was spoken at Detroit,[146] on the frontier of Canada, on the 9th of December,[147] 1801, by Captain Pipe,[148] a chief of the Delaware nation, and was addressed to the commanding officer of that post, then in possession of the British. The Delawares, it will be recollected, had been the steadfast friends of the French, in the war of 1756. The peace which was concluded in 1763, between the two great nations who then contended for the supremacy of this continent, was not for several years regarded by the Indians, and they continued their hostilities against the subjects and government of Great Britain. They were obliged, however, to submit to superior force; not without hopes that their father, the king of France, would soon send over a powerful army to retake Canada. They were in this situation when the war of the revolution broke out. It is well known that it was a part of the system of the British administration to employ the savages to subdue those whom they called their revolted subjects. The Delawares, in general, as I have before related, having in vain endeavoured to remain neutral, took part with the Americans.

Captain Pipe, however, with a party of the Wolf tribe, joined the English in the beginning of the war, and soon after repented it. But it was too late. He was now reluctantly compelled to go out against the Americans with the men under his command. On his return from one of those expeditions, he went to make his report to the British commandant at Detroit,[149] by whom he was received in state at the council house, in the presence of a great number of Indians, British officers and others. There were several Missionaries present, among which I was. The chief was seated in front of his Indians, facing the commandant. He held in his left hand a human scalp tied to a short stick. After a pause of some minutes he rose, and addressing the governor, delivered the following speech:

> "FATHER!" (Here the orator stopped, and turning round to the audience, with a face full of meaning, and a sarcastic look, which I should in vain attempt to describe, he went on in a lower tone of voice, as addressing himself to them;)— "I have said *father*, although, indeed, I do not know why I am to call *him* so, having never known any other father than the French, and considering the English only as *brothers*. But as this name is also *imposed* upon us,

I shall make use of it and say: (Here he fixed his eyes on the commandant.)

"FATHER! Some time ago you put a war hatchet into my hands, saying: Take this weapon and try it on the heads of my enemies the *long knives*, and let me afterwards know if it was sharp and good.

"FATHER! At the time when you gave me this weapon, I had neither cause nor inclination to go to war against a people who had done me no injury; yet in obedience to you, who say you are my father and call me your child, I received the hatchet; well knowing that if I did not obey, you would withhold from me[150] the necessaries of life, without which I could not subsist, and which are not elsewhere to be procured but at the house of my father.

"FATHER! You may, perhaps, think me a fool, for risking my life at your bidding, in a cause, too, by which I have no prospect of gaining anything; for it is *your* cause and not mine. It is *your* concern to fight the *long knives*; *you* have raised a quarrel amongst yourselves, and *you* ought yourselves to fight it out. You should not compel your children, the Indians, to expose themselves to danger for *your sakes*.

"FATHER! Many lives have already been lost on *your* account! —Nations have suffered and been weakened!—Children have lost parents, brothers and relatives!—Wives have lost husbands!—It is not known how many more may perish before YOUR war will be at an end!

"FATHER! I have said that you may, perhaps, think me a fool, for thus thoughtlessly rushing on *your* enemy! —Do not believe this, Father! Think not that I want sense to convince me, that although you *now* pretend to keep up a perpetual enmity to the long knives, you may, before long, conclude a peace with them.

81

"FATHER! You say you love your children, the Indians. — This you have often told them; and indeed it is your interest to say so to them, that you may have them at your service.

"But, FATHER! who of us can believe that you can love a people of a different colour from your own, better than those who have a *white* skin, like yourselves?

"FATHER! Pay attention to what I am going to say. While you, Father, are setting me[151] on your enemy, much in the same manner as a hunter sets his dog on the game; while I am in the act of rushing on that enemy of yours, with the bloody destructive weapon you gave me, I may, perchance, happen to look back to the place from whence you started me, and what shall I see? Perhaps, I may see my father shaking hands with the *long knives*; yes, with those very people he now calls his enemies. I may, then, see him laugh at my folly for having obeyed his orders; and yet I am now risking my life at his command! Father! keep what I have said in remembrance.

"Now, FATHER! here is what has been done with the hatchet you gave me." (Handing the stick with the scalp on it.) "I have done with the hatchet what you ordered me to do, and found it sharp. Nevertheless, I did not do *all* that I *might* have done. No, I did not. My heart failed within me. I felt compassion for *your* enemy. *Innocence*[152] had no part in your quarrels; therefore I distinguished—I spared. I took some *live flesh*,[153] which, while I was bringing to you, I spied one of your large canoes, on which I put it for you. In a few days you will receive this *flesh*, and *find that the skin is of the same colour with your own.*

"FATHER! I hope you will not destroy *what*[154] I have saved. You, Father! have the means of preserving that which with me would perish for want. The warrior is poor and his cabin is always empty; but your house, father! is always full."

82

Here we see boldness, frankness, dignity, and humanity happily blended together and most eloquently displayed. I am much mistaken if the component parts of this discourse are not put together much according to the rules of oratory which are taught in the schools, and which were certainly unknown to this savage. The peroration at the end is short, but truly pathetic, and I would even say, sublime; and then the admirable way in which it is prepared! I wish I could convey to the reader's mind only a small part of the impression which this speech made on me and on all present when it was delivered.

It is but justice here to say, that Capt. Pipe was well acquainted with the noble and generous character of the British officer to whom this speech was addressed. He is still living in his own country, an honour to the British name. He obeyed the orders of his superiors in employing the Indians to fight against us, but he did it with reluctance and softened as much as was in his power the horrors of that abominable warfare. He esteemed Captain Pipe, and I have no doubt, was well pleased with the humane conduct of this Indian chief, whose sagacity in this instance is no less deserving of praise than his eloquence. It is thus that great minds understand each other, and even in the most difficult and trying situations, find the means of making the cause of humanity triumph.

CHAPTER 12 ~
Metaphorical expressions

The Indians are fond of metaphors. They are to their discourse what feathers and beads are to their persons, a gaudy but tasteless ornament. Yet we must not judge them too severely on that account. There are other nations besides the American Indians who admire this mode of expression. Even in enlightened Europe, many centuries have not elapsed since the best and most celebrated writers employed this figure in a profuse manner, and thought it a great embellishment to their poetical and prose compositions; the immortal Shakespeare, himself, did not disdain it.

The following examples will be sufficient to give an idea of the metaphorical language of the Indians.

1. *"The sky is overcast with dark blustering clouds."*—We shall have troublesome times; we shall have war.

2. *"A black cloud has arisen yonder."*—War is threatened from that quarter, or from that nation.

3. *"Two black clouds are drawing towards each other."*—Two powerful enemies are in march against each other!

4. *"The path is already shut up!"*—Hostilities have commenced. The war is begun.

5. *"The rivers run with blood!"*—War rages in the country.

6. *"To bury the hatchet."*—To make, or conclude a peace.

7. *"To lay down the hatchet, or to slip the hatchet under the bedstead."*—To cease fighting for a while, during a truce; or, to

place the hatchet at hand, so that it may be taken up again at a moment's warning.

8. *"The hatchet you gave me to strike your enemies, proved to be very dull, or not to be sharp; my arm was wearied to little purpose!"*—You supplied me so scantily with the articles I stood in need of, that I wanted strength to execute your orders. The presents you gave me were not sufficient for the task you imposed upon me, therefore I did little!

9. *"The hatchet you gave me was very sharp!"*—As you have satisfied me, I have done the same for you; I have killed many of your enemies.

10. *"You did not make me strong!"*—You gave me nothing, or but little.

11. *"Make me very strong!"*—Give me much, pay me well!

12. *"The stronger you make me, the more you will see!"*—The more you give me, the more I will do for you!

13. *"I did as you bid me, but* SEE *nothing!"*—I have performed my part, but you have not rewarded me; or, I did my part for you, but you have not kept your word!

14. *"You have spoken with your lips only, not from the heart!"*—You endeavour to deceive me; you do not intend to do as you say!

15. *"You now speak from the heart!"*—Now you mean what you say!

16. *"You keep me in the dark!"*—You wish to deceive me; you conceal your intentions from me; you keep me in ignorance!

17. *"You stopped my ears!"*—You kept the thing a secret from me; you did not wish me to know it!

18. *"Now I believe you!"*—Done! agreed! It shall be so!

19. *"Your words have penetrated into my heart!"*—I consent! am pleased with what you say!

20. *"You have spoken good words!"*—I am pleased, delighted with what you have said!

21. *"You have spoken the truth!"*—I am satisfied with what you have said!

22. *"Singing birds!"*—Tale bearers—story tellers—liars.

23. *"Don't listen to the singing of the birds which fly by!"*—Don't believe what stragglers tell you!

24. *"What bird was it that sung that song?"*—Who was it that told that story, that lie?

25. (To a chief,) *"Have you heard the news?"*—Have you been *officially* informed?

26. *"I have not heard anything!"*—I have no *official* information.

27. *"To kindle a council fire at such a place."*—To appoint a place where the national business is to be transacted; to establish the seat of government there.

28. *"To remove the council fire to another place."*—To establish another place for the seat of government.

29. *"The council fire has been extinguished."*—Blood has been shed by an enemy at the seat of government, which has put the fire out; the place has been *polluted*.

30. *"Don't look the other way!"*—Don't lean to *that* side; don't join with those!

31. *"Look this way!"*—Join us, join our party.

32. "*I have not room to spread my blanket!*"—I am too much crowded on.

33. "*Not to have room enough for an encampment.*"—To be too much confined to a small district; not to have sufficient range for the cattle to feed on, or sufficient hunting ground.

34. "*I will place you under my wings!*"— (meaning under my arm pits) I will protect you at all hazards! You shall be perfectly safe, nobody shall molest you!

35. "*Suffer no grass to grow on the war path!*"—Carry on the war with vigor!

36. "*Never suffer grass to grow on this war path!*"—Be at perpetual war with the nation this path leads to; never conclude a peace with them.

37. "*To open a path from one nation to another, by removing the logs, brush and briars out of the way.*"—To invite the nation to which the path leads, to a friendly intercourse; to prepare the way to live on friendly terms with them.

38. "*The path to that nation is again open!*"—We are again on friendly terms; the path may again be travelled with safety.

39. "*I hear sighing and sobbing in yonder direction!*"—I think that a chief of a neighbouring nation has died.

40. "*I draw the thorns out of your feet and legs, grease your stiffened joints with oil, and wipe the sweat off your body!*"— I make you feel comfortable after your fatiguing journey, that you may enjoy yourself while with us.

41. "*I wipe the tears from your eyes, cleanse your ears, and place your aching heart, which bears you down to one side, in its proper position!*"—I condole with you; dispel all sorrow! prepare yourself for business! (N. B. This is said when condoling with a nation on the death of a chief.)

42. *"I have discovered the cause of your grief!"*—I have seen the grave (where the chief was buried.)

43. *"I have covered yon spot with*[155] *fresh earth; I have raked leaves, and planted trees thereon!"*—means literally, I have hidden the grave from your eyes; and figuratively, "you must now be cheerful again!"

44. *"I lift you up from this place, and set you down again at my dwelling place!"*—I invite you to arise from hence, and come and live where I live.

45. *"I am much too heavy to rise at this present time!"*—I have too much property! (corn, vegetables, &c.)

46. *"I will pass one night yet at this place."*—I will stay one year yet at this place.

47. *"We have concluded a peace, which is to last as long as the sun shall shine, and the rivers flow with water!"*—The peace we have made is to continue as long as the world stands, or to the end of time.

48. *"To bury the hatchet beneath the root of a tree!"*—To put it quite out of sight.

49. *"To bury deep in the earth,"* (an injury done)—To consign it to oblivion.

CHAPTER 13 ~
Indian names

The proper names of Indians are in general given to them after animals of various kinds, and even fishes and reptiles. Thus they are called the *Beaver, Otter, Sun-fish, Black-fish, Rattle-snake, Black-snake*, &c. They have also other descriptive names, from their personal qualities or appearances, and sometimes from fancy or caprice; but many of those are given them by the whites, such as *Pipe, White-eyes, Kill-buck*, &c., which are not real Indian names. They do not always preserve the names first given to them, but often assume a new one after they have come to man's estate.

Indians, who have particularly distinguished themselves by their conduct, or by some meritorious act, or who have been the subjects of some remarkable occurrence, have names given to them in allusion to those circumstances. Thus, I have known a man whose name would signify in our language *the beloved lover*, and one who was named *Met by love*. Another, a great warrior, who had been impatiently waiting for day-light to engage the enemy, was afterwards called *Cause day-light*, or *Make day-light appear*. So, one who had come in with a heavy load of turkies on his back, was called *The Carrier of Turkies*, and another whose shoes were generally torn or patched, was called *Bad Shoes*. All those names are generally expressed in one single word, in compounding which the Indians are very ingenious. Thus, the name they had for the place where Philadelphia now stands, and which they have preserved notwithstanding the great change which has taken place, is *Kúequenáku*,[156] which means, *The grove of the long pine trees*.

They have proper names, not only for all towns, villages, mountains, valleys, rivers, and streams, but for all remarkable spots, as for instance, those which are particularly infested with gnats or musquitoes, where snakes have their dens, &c. Those

89

names always contain an allusion to such particular circumstance, so that foreigners, even though acquainted with their language, will often be at a loss to understand their discourse.

To strangers, white men for instance, they will give names derived from some remarkable quality which they have observed in them, or from some circumstance which remarkably strikes them. When they were told the meaning of the name of William Penn, they translated it into their own language by *Miquon*, which means a feather or quill. The Iroquois call him *Onas*, which in their idiom means the same thing.

The first name given by the Indians to the Europeans who landed in Virginia was *Wapsid Lenape* (white people;) when, however, afterwards they began to commit murders on the red men, whom they pierced with swords, they gave to the Virginians the name *Mechanschican*, (long knives,) to distinguish them from others of the same colour.

In New England, they at first endeavoured to imitate the sound of the national name of the *English*, which they pronounced *Yengees*. They also called them *Chauquaquock*, (men of knives) for having imported those instruments into the country, which they gave in presents to the natives.[157] They thought them better men than the Virginians; but when they were afterwards cruelly treated by them, and their men shipped off to sea, the Mohicans of that country called them *Tschachgoos*; and when next the people of the middle colonies began to murder them, and called on the Iroquois to insult them and assist in depriving them of their lands, they then dropped that name, and called the whites by way of derision, *Schwannack*, which signifies *salt beings*, or *bitter beings*; for in their language the word *Schwan*, is in general applied to things that have a salt, sharp, bitter, or sour taste. The object of this name, as well as of that which the Mohicans gave to the eastern people, was to express contempt as well as hatred or dislike, and to hold out the white inhabitants of the country as hateful and despicable beings. I have, however, in many instances observed that the Indians are careful not to apply this opprobrious name to any white person whom they know to be amicably disposed towards them, and whom they are sure to be a good, honest, well-meaning man. I have heard them charge their children not to call a particular white man *Schwannack*, but *Friend*. This name was first introduced about the year 1730. They never apply it to the *Quakers*, whom they greatly love and respect since the first arrival of William Penn into the country. They call them *Quœkels*, not having in their language the sound expressed by our letter R. They say they have always found them good, honest, affable and peaceable men, and never have had reason to complain of them.

These were the names which the Indians gave to the whites, until the middle of the Revolutionary war, when they were reduced to the following three:

1. *Mechanschican* or *Chanschican* (long knives). This they no longer applied to the Virginians exclusively, but also to those of the people of the middle states, whom they considered as hostilely inclined towards them, particularly those who wore swords, dirks, or knives at their sides.

2. *Yengees.* This name they now exclusively applied to the people of New England, who, indeed, appeared to have adopted it, and were, as they still are, generally through the country called *Yankees*, which is evidently the same name with a trifling alteration. They say they know the *Yengees*, and can distinguish them by their dress and personal appearance, and that they were considered as less cruel than the Virginians or *long knives*. The proper English they[158] call *Saggenash*.

3. *Quœkels.* They do not now apply this name exclusively to the members of the Society of Friends, but to all the white people whom they love or respect, and whom they believe to have good intentions towards them.

Not only the Delawares, but all the nations round them, make use of these names, and with the same relative application. I have myself, in 1782, while at Detroit, witnessed the Chippeways, who on meeting an American prisoner, who was walking about, called out *Messamochkemaan* (long knife), though he had no knife, sword, or dirk at his side. I was one day about the same time hailed in that manner as I was walking up the river, and apprehending that I might be seized as a runaway prisoner, I immediately answered: *Kau! Saggenash*; No! an Englishman; and they passed on. I might with great propriety make this answer, as I was born in England.

In the year 1808, while I was riding with a number of gentlemen through Greentown[159] (an Indian town in the State of Ohio), I heard an Indian in his house, who through a crevice saw us passing, say in his language to his family: "See! what a number of people are coming along! —What! and among all these not one *long knife*! *All Yengees!*" Then, probably observing me, he said correcting himself, "No! one *Quœkel*."

Such are the observations which the Indians make on the white people, and the names which they give to them. They may sometimes be in the wrong; but, as they make it their particular study to become acquainted with the actions, motions, deportment, and dress of the different nations, they seldom commit mistakes, and in general, they apply their different names precisely to those whom they are meant to designate or describe.

CHAPTER 14 ~
Intercourse with each other

It is a striking fact that the Indians, in their uncivilised state, should so behave towards each other as though they were a civilised people! I have in numerous instances witnessed their meeting together, their doing business and conversing with each other for hours, their labouring together, and their hunting and fishing in bodies or parties; I have seen them divide their game, venison, bear's meat, fish, &c., among themselves, when they sometimes had many shares to make, and cannot recollect a single instance of their falling into a dispute or finding fault with the distribution, as being unequal, or otherwise objectionable. On the contrary, on such occasions they even receive what is allotted to them with thanks; they say "*anischi*" I am thankful! as if it was a present given to them.

They certainly (I am here speaking of the men) show a reverence for each other, which is visible on all occasions; they often meet for the purpose of conversation, and their sociability appears to be a recreation to them, a renewal of good fellowship. Their general principle, that good and bad cannot mingle or dwell together in one heart, and therefore must not come into contact, seems to be their guide on all occasions. So, likewise, when travelling, whether they are few, or many, they are cheerful, and resigned to the accidents which may befall them; never impatient, quarrelsome, or charging any one, or one another, with being in fault, or the occasion of what had happened; even though one should lose his all by the neglect or carelessness of the other, yet they will not fly into a passion, but patiently bear with the loss, thinking within themselves that such a one feels sorry enough already, and therefore it would be unreasonable to add to his pain. They judge with calmness on all occasions, and decide with precision, or endeavour so to do, between an accident and a wilfull act; —the *first* (they say) they are all liable to commit, and therefore it ought not to be noticed, or punished;—

the *second* being a wilful or premeditated act, committed with a bad design, ought on the contrary to receive due punishment.

To illustrate this subject, I shall relate a few of the cases of this description which have come within my knowledge. One morning early, an Indian came into the house of another who was yet abed, asking for the loan of his gun for a morning hunt, his own being out of repair; the owner readily consented, and said: "As my gun is not loaded, you will have to take a few balls out of your[160] pouch!" In taking the gun down, it, however, by some accident went off, and lodged the contents in the owner's head, who was still lying on the bed, and now expired. The gun, it appeared, was loaded, though unknown to him, and the lock left in such a condition that by a touch it went off. A cry was heard from all sides in the house: O! the *accident*! for such it was always considered to have been, and was treated as such.

A hunter went out to kill a bear, some of those animals having been seen in the neighbourhood. In an obscure part of a wood, he saw at a distance something black moving, which he took for a bear, the whole of the animal not being visible to him; he fired, and found he had shot a black horse. Having discovered the mistake, he informed the owner of what had happened, expressing at the same time his regret that he was not possessed of a single horse, with which he could replace the one he had shot. What! replied the Indian whose horse had been killed, do you think I would accept a horse from you, though you had one to give, after you have satisfied me that you killed mine *by accident*? No, indeed! for the same misfortune might also happen to me.

An aged Indian who had gone out to shoot a turkey, mistook a black hog in the bushes for one of those birds, and shot him; finding out by enquiry to whom the hog belonged, he informed the owner of the mistake he had made, offering to pay for the hog; which the other, however, not only would not accept of, but having brought the meat in, gave him a leg of the animal, because he thought that the unfortunate man, as well on account of his disappointment, in not feasting on turkey as he expected soon to do when he shot the hog, as for his honesty in informing of what he had done, was *entitled* to a share of what he had killed.

Two Indians with a large canoe, going down the Muskingum river to a certain distance, were accosted by others going by land to the same place, who requested them to take their heavy articles, as kettles, axes, hoes, &c. into their canoe, which they freely did, but unfortunately were shipwrecked at the rocks of White Eyes's falls (as the place is called,) where the whole cargo was lost, and the men saved themselves by swimming to the shore. The question being put and fully discussed, whether those men with the canoe, who had taken charge of the property of the others, and by this neglect lost the whole, were not liable to pay for the loss? it was decided in the negative, on the following grounds:

1. That the canoe men had taken the articles on board, with the pleasing hope that they thereby would oblige their fellow men, and did not expect any recompense for that service.
2. That although they might have avoided the danger and the loss, by unloading the canoe at the head of the fall, and carrying the cargo by land below it, (which was but a short distance,) as was customary, when the river was not in a proper state to run through, yet that, had those who travelled by land been in the place of those in the canoe, they might, like them, have attempted to have run through, as is sometimes done with success, and been equally unfortunate.
3. That the canoe men having had all their own property on board, which was all lost at the same time, and was equally valuable to them, it was clear that they had expected to run safely through, and could not have intentionally or designedly brought on themselves and others the misfortune which had happened, and therefore the circumstance must be ascribed entirely to *accident*.

Such is the disposition of the Indians with regard to those who inadvertently meet with a disaster, whereby others are injured. They are ready to overlook a fault, and more disposed in such cases to commiserate, than to punish; but with those who wilfully and intentionally commit aggressions and injure others, they think and act quite differently; a malicious person is generally despised, and if he intrudes himself into good company, they will, without saying a word, steal off one by one, and leave him alone to suffer the mortification which it is intended he should feel. For murderers and thieves they have no compassion, and punish them according to the nature of their crimes, if not publicly, still privately, for they are considered as a nuisance, and a disgrace to the nation, and so much so were persons of this description considered and despised in former times among the Delawares, before the white people came, that it was a rare thing to hear of any such being among them. This I have repeatedly been told, between the years 1770 and 1780, by Indians of that nation; one of whom, when a boy, resided on the spot where Philadelphia now stands, when the first house was building there, and assisted in furnishing the workmen with fish, and caught rabbits for them; the other, who was still older, lived with his parents on the spot where afterwards was built Perth Amboy in New Jersey: both were respectable men, highly esteemed by all who knew them.

I do not believe that there exists a people more attentive to paying common civilities to each other than the Indians are; but this, from a want of understanding their language, as well as their customs and manners, generally escapes the notice of travellers, although some of them, better observers than the rest, have touched upon this subject. In more than one hundred instances, I have with astonishment and delight witnessed the attention paid to a person entering the house of another, where, in the first instance, he is desired to seat himself, with the words, "sit down, my friend!" if he is a stranger, or no relation; but if a relation, the proper title is added. A person is never left standing, there are seats for all; and if a dozen should follow each other in succession, all are provided with seats, and the stranger, if a white person, with the best. The tobacco pouch next is handed round; it is the first treat, as with us a glass of wine or brandy. Without a single word passing between the man and his wife, she will go about preparing some victuals for the company, and having served the visiters, will retire to a neighbour's house, to inform the family of the visit with which her husband is honoured, never grumbling on account of their eating up the provisions, even if it were what she had cooked for her own family, considering the friendly visit well worth this small trouble and expense.

It is true, that among themselves, they expect the same attention and hospitality paid to them in return; yet that is not their main object, for I have seen a number of instances in which a return was out of the question, where poverty would not admit of it, or distance of abode put it out of the power of the visitor to return the same civilities to his host: when white people are treated in this way, with the best entertainment the house affords, they may be sure it is nothing else than a mark of respect paid to them, and that the attentions they receive do not proceed from any interested view.

CHAPTER 15 ~
Political maneuvers

In the management of their national affairs, the Indians display as much skill and dexterity, perhaps, as any people upon earth. When a political message is sent to them from a neighbouring nation,[161] they generally contrive to send an answer so ambiguously worded, that it is difficult to come at their real meaning; they conceive this to be the best way of getting rid of a proposal which they do not like, because those who sent them the message are for some time, at least, at a loss to comprehend the meaning, and not knowing whether the answer is favourable or unfavourable, their proceedings are necessarily suspended until they can discover its true sense; in this manner have operations been sometimes entirely prevented, and matters have remained in the same situation that they were in before.

It may be supposed, perhaps, that such an artful manner of treating each other might be thought provoking, and cause jealousies and disputes among the different parties; such is not, however, the case, as nothing insulting is ever contained in those messages; and as offence is not meant, it is not taken. The Indians consider it on all sides as a kind of diplomatic proceeding, an exercise which tends to invigorate the mind, of which they are very fond. It gives them opportunities to reflect and think deeply on matters of importance, and of displaying their genius, when they have found or discovered the secret of an answer sent to them, or hit upon the true meaning of an ambiguous message.

At the time of the Revolutionary war I witnessed a curious scene of diplomatic maneuvers between two great men of the Delaware nation, both of whom had in their time signalised themselves as brave and courageous men, and had acquired the character of two great war chiefs. The war that I speak of, which had but lately begun, had made it necessary for the Indians to consult their present and future safety. Captain White Eyes, of the Turtle tribe, who was placed at the head of his nation, had its welfare much at heart. He was in favour of their following the advice given them by the American Congress, which was to remain neutral, and not to meddle in the quarrel between the Americans and the parent country. He advised his people, therefore, to remain in friendship with both sides, and not to take up arms against either, as it might bring them into trouble, and perhaps, in the end, effect their ruin.

On the other hand, Captain Pipe, of the Wolf tribe, who resided at the distance of fifteen miles, where he had his council fire, was of a different opinion, and leaned on the side of the British. He was an artful, ambitious man, yet not deficient in greatness of mind, as I have shewn in a preceding chapter. But his head at that time was full of the wrongs which the Indians had suffered from the Americans, from their first coming into the country; his soul panted for revenge, and he was glad to seize the opportunity that now offered. He professed his readiness to join in proper measures to save the nation, but not such measures as his antagonist proposed; what his real object was he did not openly declare, but privately endeavoured to counteract all that was done and proposed by the other. White Eyes, however, was a sensible upright man, and never was deficient in means to support his own measures, and extricate himself from the snares with which he was on all sides surrounded by Captain Pipe. Thus they went on for upwards of two years, Pipe working clandestinely, and keeping his spies continually on the watch upon the other, while White Eyes acted openly and publicly, as though he knew nothing of what was machinating against him.

At last, a circumstance took place which apparently justified Captain Pipe in the measures he wished to pursue. In March 1778, a number of white people, of those whom we called *Tories*, among whom were M'Kee, Eliott, Girty,[162] and several others, having escaped from Pittsburg, told the Indians wherever they came, "that they must arm and be off immediately, and kill all the Americans wherever they found them, for they had determined to destroy all the Indians, and possess themselves of their country." White Eyes, not believing what these men said, advised his people to remain quiet, for this report could not be true. Pipe, on the contrary, called his men together, and in a speech which he addressed to them, pronounced every man an enemy to his country who endeavoured to dissuade them from going out against the Americans, and said that all such ought to be put to death.

Captain White Eyes was not disconcerted; he immediately assembled his warriors, and told them "that if they meant in earnest to go out, as he observed some of them were preparing to do, they should not go without him. He had taken peace measures in order to save the nation from utter destruction. But if they believed that he was in the wrong, and gave more credit to vagabond fugitives, whom he knew to be such, than to himself, who was best acquainted with the real state of things; if they had determined to follow their advice, and go out against the Americans, he would go out with them; he would lead them on, place himself in the front, and be the first who should fall. They only had to determine on what they meant to do; for his own mind was fully made up not to survive his nation, and he would not spend the remainder of a miserable life in bewailing the total destruction of a brave people, who deserved a better fate."

This spirited, and at the same time pathetic, speech of Captain White Eyes, made such an impression on the minds of the audience, that they unanimously declared that they would obey his orders, and listen to no person but himself, either white or of their own colour. Indeed, there was too much force, too much majesty in this address to be resisted; when this was reported to Pipe by his emissaries, he was absolutely confounded, and knew not what to do. A few days afterwards, the council of the Delaware nation received the most friendly and flattering messages from the commandant and Indian agent at Pittsburg, cautioning them, "not to listen to those worthless men who had ran off from them in the night, and to be assured of the steady friendship of the Government of the United States." Pipe was so put to the blush, and took this matter so much to heart, that he soon after threw off the mask, permitted his men to go out and murder the Americans, and afterwards went off with them to Sandusky, under the protection of the British Government. We have seen in a former chapter that he afterwards saw how impolitic his conduct had been, and probably wished to retrace his steps, but it was too late. He had suffered himself to be misled by his passions, excited by the remembrance of former wrongs, and thus was betrayed into his injudicious conduct. Perhaps also his jealousy of Captain White Eyes, whose superiority his proud mind could not bear, did not in a small degree contribute to it. Pipe was certainly a great man, but White Eyes was, in my opinion, the greatest of the two. I was present when he made the speech which I have related, and never shall forget the impression it made upon me.

Thus Indian politicians work and manage matters against each other without newspaper wrangles, abuse of character, personal quarrels, or open insults. Their ingenuity, when joined to a good cause, generally makes them come off victorious. In a bad cause, on the contrary, they sure[163] to meet with detection and defeat, as Captain Pipe, for his misfortune, sadly experienced.

CHAPTER 16 ~
Marriage and treatment of their wives

There are many persons who believe, from the labour that they see the Indian women perform, that they are in a manner treated as slaves. These labours, indeed, are hard, compared with the tasks that are imposed upon females in civilised society; but they are no more than their fair share, under every consideration and due allowance, of the hardships attendant on savage life. Therefore they are not only voluntarily, but cheerfully submitted to; and as women are not obliged to live with their husbands any longer than suits their pleasure or convenience, it cannot be supposed that they would submit to be loaded with unjust or unequal burdens.

Marriages among the Indians are not, as with us, contracted for life; it is understood on both sides that the parties are not to live together any longer than they shall be pleased with each other. The husband may put away his wife whenever he pleases, and the woman may in like manner abandon her husband. Therefore the connexion is not attended with any vows, promises, or ceremonies of any kind. An Indian takes a wife as it were on trial, determined, however, in his own mind not to forsake her if she behaves well, and particularly if he has children by her. The woman, sensible of this, does on her part every thing in her power to please her husband, particularly if he is a good hunter or trapper, capable of maintaining her by his skill and industry, and protecting her by his strength and courage.

When a marriage takes place, the duties and labours incumbent on each party are well known to both. It is understood that the husband is to build a house for them to dwell in, to find the necessary implements of husbandry, as axes, hoes, &c., to provide a canoe, and also dishes, bowls, and other necessary vessels for house-keeping. The woman generally has a kettle or two, and some other articles of kitchen furniture, which she brings with her. The husband, as master of the family, considers himself bound to support it by his bodily exertions, as hunting, trapping, &c.; the woman, as his *help-mate*, takes upon herself the labours of the field, and is far from considering them as more important than those to which her husband is subjected, being well satisfied that with his gun and traps he can maintain a family in any place where game is to be found; nor do they think it any hardship imposed upon them; for they themselves say, that while their field labour employs them at most six weeks in the year, that of the men continues the whole year round.

When a couple is newly married, the husband (without saying a single word upon the subject) takes considerable pains to please his wife, and by repeated proofs of his skill and abilities in the art of hunting, to make her sensible that she can be happy with him, and that she will never want while they live together. At break of day he will be off with his gun, and often by breakfast time return home with a deer, turkey, or some other game. He endeavours to make it appear that it is in his power to bring provisions home whenever he pleases, and his wife, proud of having such a good hunter for her husband, does her utmost to serve and make herself agreeable to him.

The work of the women is not hard or difficult. They are both able and willing to do it, and always perform it with cheerfulness. Mothers teach their daughters those duties which common sense would otherwise point out to them when grown up. Within doors, their labour is very trifling; there is seldom more than one pot or kettle to attend to. There is no scrubbing of the house, and but little to wash, and that not often. Their principal occupations are to cut and fetch in the fire wood, till the ground, sow and reap the grain, and pound the corn in mortars for their pottage, and to make bread which they bake in the ashes. When going on a journey, or to hunting camps with their husbands, if they have no horses, they carry a pack on their backs which often appears heavier than it really is; it generally consists of a blanket, a dressed deer skin for moccasins, a few articles of kitchen furniture, as a kettle, bowl, or dish, with spoons, and some bread, corn, salt, &c., for their nourishment. I have never known an Indian woman complain of the hardship of carrying this burden, which serves for their own comfort and support as well as of their husbands.

The tilling of the ground at home, getting of the fire wood, and pounding of corn in mortars, is frequently done by female parties, much in the manner of those husking, quilting, and other *frolics* (as they are called), which are so common in some parts of the United States, particularly to the eastward. The labour is thus quickly and easily performed; when it is over, and sometimes in intervals, they sit down to enjoy themselves by feasting on some good victuals, prepared for them by the person or family for whom they work, and which the man has taken care to provide before hand from the woods; for this is considered a principal part of the business, as there are generally more or less of the females assembled who have not, perhaps for a long time, tasted a morsel of meat, being either widows, or orphans, or otherwise in straitened circumstances. Even the chat which passes during their joint labours is highly diverting to them, and so they seek to be employed in this way as long as they can, by going round to all those in the village who have ground to till.

When the harvest is in, which generally happens by the end of September, the women have little else to do than to prepare the daily victuals, and get fire wood, until the latter end of February or beginning of March, as the season is more or less backward, when they go to their sugar camps, where they extract sugar from the maple tree. The men having built or repaired their temporary cabin, and made all the troughs of various sizes, the women commence making sugar, while the men are looking out for meat, at this time generally fat bears, which are still in their winter quarters. When at home, they will occasionally assist their wives in gathering the sap, and watch the kettles in their absence, that the syrup may not boil over.

A man who wishes his wife to be with him while he is out hunting in the woods, needs only tell her, that on such a day they will go to such a place, where he will hunt for a length of time, and she will be sure to have provisions and every thing else that is necessary in complete readiness, and well packed up to carry to the spot; for the man, as soon as he enters the woods, has to be looking out and about for game, and therefore cannot be encumbered with any burden; after wounding a deer, he may have to pursue it for several miles, often running it fairly down. The woman, therefore, takes charge of the baggage, brings it to the place of encampment, and there, immediately enters on the duties of housekeeping, as if they were at home; she moreover takes pains to dry as much meat as she can, that none may be lost; she carefully puts the tallow up, assists in drying the skins, gathers as much wild hemp as possible for the purpose of making strings, carrying-bands, bags and other necessary articles, collects roots for dyeing; in short, does every thing in her power to leave no care to her husband but the important one of providing meat for the family.

After all, the fatigue of the women is by no means to be compared to that of the men. Their hard and difficult employments are periodical and of short duration, while their husband's labours are constant and severe in the extreme. Were a man to take upon himself a part of his wife's duty, in addition to his own, he must necessarily sink under the load, and of course his family must suffer with him. On his exertions as a hunter, their existence depends; in order to be able to follow that rough employment with success, he must keep his limbs as supple as he can, he must avoid hard labour as much as possible, that his joints may not become stiffened, and that he may preserve the necessary strength and agility of body to enable him to pursue the chase, and bear the unavoidable hardships attendant on it; for the fatigues of hunting wear out the body and constitution far more than manual labour. Neither creeks nor rivers, whether shallow or deep, frozen or free from ice, must be an obstacle to the hunter, when in pursuit of a wounded deer, bear, or other animal, as is often the case. Nor has he then leisure to think on the state of his body, and to consider whether his blood is not too much heated to plunge without danger into the cold stream, since the game he is in pursuit of is running off from him with full speed. Many dangerous accidents often befall him, both as a hunter and a warrior (for he is both), and are seldom unattended with painful consequences, such as rheumatism, or consumption of the lungs, for which the sweat-house, on which they so much depend, and to which they often resort for relief, especially after a fatiguing hunt or warlike excursion, is not always a sure preservative or an effectual remedy.

The husband generally leaves the skins and peltry which he has procured by hunting to the care of his wife, who sells or barters them away to the best advantage for such necessaries as are wanted in the family; not forgetting to supply her husband with what he stands in need of, who, when he receives it from her hands never fails to return her thanks in the kindest manner. If debts had been previously contracted, either by the woman, or by her and her husband jointly, or if a horse should be wanted, as much is laid aside as will be sufficient to pay the debts or purchase the horse.

When a woman has got in her harvest of corn, it is considered as belonging to her husband, who, if he has suffering friends, may give them as much of it as he pleases, without consulting his wife, or being afraid of her being displeased; for she is in the firm belief that he is able to procure that article whenever it is wanted. The sugar which she makes out of the maple tree is also considered as belonging to her husband.

There is nothing in an Indian's house or family without its particular owner. Every individual knows what belongs to him, from the horse or cow down to the dog, cat, kitten and little chicken. Parents make presents to their children, and they in return to their parents. A father will sometimes ask his wife or one of his children for the loan of his horse to go out a hunting. For a litter of kittens or brood of chickens, there are often as many different owners as there are individual animals. In purchasing a hen with her brood, one frequently has to deal for it with several children. Thus, while the principle of community of goods prevails in the state, the rights of property are acknowledged among the members of a family. This is attended with a very good effect; for by this means every living creature is properly taken care of. It also promotes liberality among the children, which becomes a habit with them by the time they are grown up.

An Indian loves to see his wife well clothed, which is a proof that he is fond of her; at least, it is so considered. While his wife is bartering the skins and peltry he has taken in his hunt, he will seat himself at some distance, to observe her choice, and how she and the traders agree together. When she finds an article which she thinks will suit or please her husband, she never fails to purchase it for him; she tells him that it is *her* choice, and he is never dissatisfied.

The more a man does for his wife the more he is esteemed, particularly by the women, who will say: "This man surely loves his wife." Some men at their leisure hours make bowls and ladles, which, when finished, are at their wives' disposal.

If a sick or pregnant woman longs for any article of food, be it what it may, and however difficult to be procured, the husband immediately sets out to endeavour to get it. I have known a man to go forty or fifty miles for a mess of cranberries to satisfy his wife's longing. In the year 1762 I was witness to a remarkable instance of the disposition of Indians to indulge their wives. There was a famine in the land, and a sick Indian woman expressed a great desire for a mess of Indian corn. Her husband having heard that a trader at Lower Sandusky had a little, set off on horseback for that place, one hundred miles distant, and returned with as much corn as filled the crown of his hat, for which he gave his horse in exchange, and came home on foot, bringing his saddle back with him. Squirrels, ducks, and other like delicacies, when most difficult to be obtained, are what women in the first stage of their pregnancy generally long for. The husband in every such case will go out and spare no pains nor trouble until he has procured what is wanted.

In other cases, the men and their wives do not in general trouble themselves with each other's business; but the wife, knowing that the father is very fond of his children, is always prepared to tell him some diverting anecdote of one or the other of them, especially if he has been absent for some time.

It very seldom happens that a man condescends to quarrel with his wife, or abuse her, though she has given him just cause.

In such a case the man, without replying, or saying a single word, will take his gun and go into the woods, and remain there a week or perhaps a fortnight, living on the meat he has killed, before he returns home again; well knowing that he cannot inflict a greater punishment on his wife for her conduct to him than by absenting himself for a while; for she is not only kept in suspense, uncertain whether he will return again, but is soon reported as a bad and quarrelsome woman; for, as on those occasions, the man does not tell his wife on what day or at what time he will be back again, which he otherwise, when they are on good terms, never neglects to do, she is at once put to shame by her neighbours, who soon suspecting something, do not fail to put such questions to her, as she either cannot, or is ashamed to answer. When he at length does return, she endeavours to let him see by her attentions, that she has repented, though neither speak to each other a single word on the subject of what has passed. And as his children, if he has any, will on his return hang about him and soothe him with their caresses, he is, on their account, ready to forgive, or at least to say nothing unpleasant to their mother. She has, however, received by this a solemn warning, and must take care how she behaves in future, lest the next time her husband should stay away altogether and take another wife. It is very probable, that if at this time they had had no children, he would have left her, but then he would have taken his property with him at the same time.

On the return of an Indian from a journey, or long absence, he will, on entering the house, say, "I am returned!" to which his wife will reply,[164] "I rejoice!" and having cast his eyes around, he will enquire, whether all the children are well, when being answered in the affirmative, he replies, "I am glad!" which for the present is all the conversation that passes between them; nor does he relate anything at this present time that occurred on his journey, but holds himself in readiness to partake of the nourishment which his wife is preparing for him. After a while, when the men of the village have assembled at his house, his wife, with the rest, hears his story at full length.

Marriages are proposed and concluded in different ways. The parents on both sides, having observed an attachment between

108

two young persons, negotiate for them. This generally commences from the house where the bridegroom lives, whose mother is the negotiatrix for him, and begins her duties by taking a good leg of venison, or bear's meat, or something else of the same kind, to the house where the bride dwells, not forgetting to mention, that her son has killed it: in return for this the mother of the bride, if she otherwise approves of the match, which she well understands by the presents to be intended, will prepare a good dish of victuals, the produce of the labour of *woman*, such as beans, Indian corn, or the like, and then taking it to the house where the bridegroom lives, will say, "This is the produce of my daughter's field; and she also prepared it." If afterwards the mothers of the parties are enabled to tell the good news to each other, that the young people have pronounced that which was sent them *very good*, the bargain is struck. It is as much as if the young man had said to the girl, "I am able to provide you at all times with meat to eat!" and she had replied, "and such good victuals from the field, you shall have from me!" From this time not only presents of this kind are continued on both sides, but articles of clothing are presented to the parents by each party, by way of return for what they have received, of which the young people always have a share. The friendship between the two families daily increasing, they do their domestic and field work jointly, and when the young people have agreed to live together, the parents supply them with necessaries, such as a kettle, dishes or bowls, and also what is required for the kitchen, and with axes, hoes, &c. to work in the field.

The men who have no parents to negotiate for them, or otherwise choose to manage the matter for themselves, have two simple ways of attaining their object. The first is: by stepping up to the woman whom they wish to marry, saying: "If you are willing I will take you as wife!" when if she answer in the affirmative, she either goes with him immediately, or meets him at an appointed time and place.

The other mode of celebrating marriage will appear from the following anecdote:

An aged Indian, who for many years had spent much of his time among the white people, both in Pennsylvania and New Jersey, one day about the year 1770 observed, that the Indians had not only a much easier way of getting a wife than the whites, but were also more certain of getting a *good* one; "For," (said he in his broken English,) "White man court,—court,—may be one whole year!—may be two year before he marry!—well!—may be then got *very good* wife—but may be *not!*—may be *very* cross!—Well now, suppose cross! scold so soon as get awake in the morning! scold all day! scold until sleep!—all one; he must keep *him!*[165]

White people have law forbidding throwing away wife, be *he* ever so cross! must keep *him* always! Well! how does Indian do? —Indian when he see industrious Squaw, which he like, he go to *him*, place his two forefingers close aside each other, make two look like one—look Squaw in the face—see *him* smile—which is all one *he* say, *Yes!* so he take *him* home—no danger *he* be cross! no! no! Squaw know too well what Indian do if *he* cross! —
throw *him* away and take another! Squaw love to eat meat! no husband! no meat! Squaw do every thing to please husband! he do the same to please Squaw! live happy!"

CHAPTER 17 ~
Respect for the aged

There is no nation in the world who pay greater respect to old age than the American Indians. From their infancy they are taught to be kind and attentive to aged persons, and never to let them suffer for want of necessaries or comforts. The parents spare no pains to impress upon the minds of their children the conviction that they would draw down upon themselves the anger of the Great Spirit, were they to neglect those whom, in his goodness, he had permitted to attain such an advanced age, whom he had protected with his almighty power through all the perils and dangers of life, while so many had perished by wars, accidents, and sickness in various forms, by the incantations of the wizard, or the stroke of the murderer, and not a few by the consequences of their own imprudent conduct.

It is a sacred principle among the Indians, and one of those moral and religious truths which they have always before their eyes, that the Great Spirit who created them, and provided them so abundantly with the means of subsistence, made it the duty of parents to maintain and take care of their children until they should be able to provide for themselves, and that having while weak and helpless received the benefits of maintenance, education, and protection, they are bound to repay them by a similar care of those who are labouring under the infirmities of old age, and are no longer able to supply their own wants.

Thus, a strong feeling of gratitude towards their elders, inculcated and cherished from their earliest infancy, is the solid foundation on which rests that respect for old age for which Indians are so remarkable, and it is further supported by the well-founded hope of receiving the like succours and attentions in their turn, when the heavy hand of time shall have reduced them to the same helpless situation which they now commiserate in others, and seek by every means in their power to render more

111

tolerable. Hence, they do not confine themselves to acts of absolute necessity; it is not enough for them that the old are not suffered to starve with hunger, or perish with cold, but they must be made as much as possible to share in the pleasures and comforts of life. It is, indeed, a moving spectacle to see the tender and delicate attentions which, on every occasion, they lavish upon aged and decrepid persons. When going out a hunting, they will put them on a horse or in a canoe, and take them into the woods to their hunting ground, in order to revive their spirits by making them enjoy the sight of a sport in which they can no longer participate. They place them in particular situations, where they are sure that the game they are in pursuit of will pass by, taking proper measures at the same time to prevent its escape, so that their aged parents and friends may, at least, as our sportsmen call it, *be in at the death.* Nor is this all; the hoary veterans must also enjoy the honours of the chase; when the animal, thus surrounded, is come within reach of their guns, when every possibility of escape is precluded, by the woods all around being set on fire, they all, young and old, fire together, so that it is difficult to decide[166] whose ball it was that brought the animal to the ground. But they never are at a loss to decide, and always give it in favour of the oldest man[167] in the party. So, when the young people have discovered a place where the bears have their haunts, or have resorted to for the winter, they frequently take with them to the spot, such of the old men as are yet able to walk or ride, where they not only have an opportunity of witnessing the sport, but receive their full share of the meat and oil.

At home the old are as well treated and taken care of as if they were favourite children. They are cherished and even caressed; indulged in health and nursed in sickness; and all their wishes and wants are anticipated. Their company is sought by the young, to whom their conversation is considered an honour. Their advice is asked on all occasions, their words are listened to as oracles, and their occasional garrulity, nay, even the second childhood often attendant on extreme old age, is never with Indians a subject of ridicule, or laughter. Respect, gratitude, and love are too predominant in their minds to permit any degrading idea to mix itself with these truly honourable and generous feelings.

112

On every occasion, and in every situation through life, age takes the lead among the Indians. Even little boys, when going on parties of pleasure, were it only to catch butterflies, strictly adhere to this rule, and submit to the direction of the oldest in their company, who is their chief, leader and spokesman; if they are accosted on the way by any person, and asked whither they are going, or any other question, no one will presume to answer but their *speaker*. The same rule is observed when they are grown up, and in no case whatever will one of a party, club or meeting, attempt to assume authority over the leader, or even to set him right if he should mistake the road or take a wrong course; much less will any one contradict what he says, unless his opinion should be particularly asked, in which case, and no other, he will give his advice, but with great modesty and diffidence.

And yet there have been travellers who have ventured to assert that old people among the Indians are not only neglected and suffered to perish for want, but that they are even, when no longer able to take care of themselves, *put out of the way of all trouble.* I am free to declare, that among all the Indian nations that I have become acquainted with, if any one should kill an old man or woman for no other cause than that of having become useless or burdensome to society, it would be considered as an unpardonable crime, the general indignation would be excited, and the murderer instantly put to death. I cannot conceive any act that would produce such an universal horror and detestation, such is the veneration which is everywhere felt for old age.

Indeed, I have had sufficient reason to be convinced that this principle, excellent as it is in itself, is[168] even carried too far by the Indians, and that not a little inconvenience is occasioned by it. A few instances will make this better understood than any explanations that I could give.

In the year 1765, the great body of Christian Indians, after having remained sixteen months at and near Philadelphia, were permitted to return to their own country, peace having been concluded with the Indian nations, who still continued at war, notwithstanding the pacification between the European powers. They resolved to open a path through the wilderness from the

113

frontier settlements beyond the Blue Mountains, directly to Wyoming on the Susquehannah. This path they laid off and cut as they proceeded, two, three or four miles at a time, according to the nature of the ground and the convenience of water, bringing up their baggage by making two or more trips, as they had no horses to carry it.

Having arrived at the great Pine Swamp, then supposed to be about fourteen miles wide, it was found very difficult to cut a passage on account of the thickets and of the great number of fallen trees which incumbered it; they were, besides, unacquainted with that part of the country. An old Indian,[169] however, took the lead, and undertook to be their guide. After a tedious march of near two weeks, attended with much labour, he brought them across the Swamp, to the large creek which borders upon it on the opposite side. There they found a very steep mountain, through which no passage could be found either above or below. Discouraged at the prospect before them, they now saw no alternative but to return the same way they had come, and take the route by Fort Allen[170] to Nescopeck, and so up the Susquehannah to Wyoming, a distance of nearly one hundred miles round.

In this difficulty, it fortunately struck their Missionary, Mr. Zeisberger, that a certain Indian named David, who was one of their party and had followed them all the way, was acquainted with that part of the country, and might, perhaps, be able to point out to them some better and shorter road. He soon found that he was not mistaken. David was perfectly acquainted with the country, and knew a good road, through which the party might easily pass, but not having been questioned on the subject, had hitherto kept silence, and followed with the rest, though he knew all the while they were going wrong. A dialogue then took place between him and the Missionary.

> ZEISB.—*David! You are, I believe, acquainted with this country; perhaps you know a better road[171] and a shorter one than that which we are going to take.*

DAVID.—*Yes, I do; there is such a road,*[171] *which we may easily get through, and have a much shorter distance to travel than by that which is proposed; I am sure of it.*

ZEISB.—*What; David! we were all going wrong, and yet you are with us?*

DAVID.—*Yes, 'tis so.*

ZEISB.—*And yet you said nothing, and followed with the rest as if all had been right!*

DAVID.—*Yes; the guides are somewhat older than myself; they took the lead, and never asked me whether I had any knowledge of the country. If they had enquired, I would have told them.*

ZEISB.—*Will you now tell them?*

DAVID.—*No, indeed; unless they ask me. It does not become an Indian to instruct his elders.*

The question was then asked him at the instigation of Mr. Zeisberger, when he immediately told them that they must all return to a certain spot, six miles back, and then direct their course more to the north-east, which would bring them to a gap in the mountain, where they could pass through with great ease. They did so, and he followed them, and being now desired to take the lead, he did it, and brought them to the very spot he had described, and from thence led them all the way to Wyoming. This difficult part of the road, in the swamp, has been since called *David's path*, and the state road now passes through it.[172]

This anecdote was told me by Mr. Zeisberger himself, whom I have never known to say anything that was not strictly true. I therefore give it full credit; the more so, as I have myself witnessed two similar instances, with the relation of which I shall conclude this chapter.

The first happened in the year 1791. I had parted by accident from the company I was with, and lost my way in the woods. I had with me an Indian lad about twelve or thirteen years of age, and wished him to take the lead, to which, however, he would not consent. We were at last found by our party, who had gone in search of us. I complained to them of the boy, for not doing what I had bidden him; but they answered, "that he had done right, and that it did not become a *boy* to walk before a *man* and be his leader."

The second occurrence of the like kind, took place in the year 1798. I was on a journey with two young Indians, from Upper Canada to the Muskingum, round the head of Lake Erie.[173] Neither of these Indians having ever been in the country we were going to, they received their instructions from others before their departure. The leader, however, whose name was Leonhard, having once mistaken a path, we travelled several miles in a wrong direction, until, at last, I discovered the mistake, by our having the Owl creek to our left, when we ought to have had it to our right. I observed this to Christian, the young Indian in the rear, who coinciding with me in opinion, I desired him to run forward to Leonhard, who was far ahead of us, and to bring him back; but the lad answered that he *could not do it*. I asked him the reason. "It is," said he, "because I am younger than he is." "Will you then," replied I, "take *my* message to him, and tell him that *I* desire him to return to this place, where I will wait for him?" The young man immediately consented, went forward to Leonhard, and brought him back, on which we took an eastward course through the wood to the Owl creek, and, after crossing it, fell into our right path.

CHAPTER 18 ~
Pride and greatness of mind

The Indians are proud but not vain; they consider vanity as
degrading and unworthy the character of a man. The hunter
never boasts of his skill or strength, nor the warrior of his
prowess. It is not right, they say, that one should value himself
too much for an action which another may perform as well as
himself, and when a man extols his own deeds, it seems as if he
doubted his own capability to do the like again when he pleased.
Therefore, they prefer in all cases to let their actions speak for
themselves. The skins and peltry which the hunter brings home,
the deer's horns on the roof of his cabin, the horses, furniture and
other property that he possesses, his apparel and that of his
family, the visits with which he is honored by the first and best
men among his nation; all these things show what he is and what
he has done, and with this he rests satisfied.

So with the warrior; it is enough for him that he is known to be
a man of spirit and courage by the scalps and prisoners that he
brings home; he never is seen going about boasting of his warlike
exploits, and when questioned on the subject, he makes his
answer as short as possible. Even when he is entering a town
with his prisoners and scalps, he does not stare about to see
whether the people are looking at him, but walks his usual steady
pace and marches straight forward without appearing to see any
body. When at some of their particular festivals, every warrior is
called upon to relate his feats of arms, they make it a point to be
as brief as possible, leaving it to those who have done but little, to
swell their actions into importance, and give themselves credit for
what they have done. I cannot illustrate this subject better than
by a few anecdotes.

In the year 1779, two war chiefs, the one a young man of the
Shawano tribe, and the other an old warrior of the Wyandots,
living near Detroit, much celebrated for his great actions, but who

during the whole of the Revolutionary war, could not be persuaded to take the field against the Americans, met accidentally at my house on Muskingum, where they had separately come to pay me a friendly visit. The Shawano (whose nation, by the bye, are noted for much talk,) entered upon the subject of war, and with much earnestness in words and gestures, related the actions he had been engaged in, showing at the same time on his arm the mark of a bullet wound. During all this time, the Wyandot, smoking his pipe, listened with great attention and apparent surprise; and having afterwards to answer, according to custom, by relating what he had done, he laid down his pipe, and deliberately drawing off his clothes, except the breech-cloth, rose up and said: "I have been in upwards of twenty engagements with the enemy and fought with the French against the English; I have warred against the southern nations, and my body shows that I have been struck and wounded by nine balls. These two wounds I received at the same moment, from two Cherokees, who, seeing me fall, rested their guns against a tree, and ran up with their tomahawks to dispatch me, and take off my scalp. With the aid of the Great Spirit I jumped up, just at the moment when they were about to give me the stroke. I struck them and they both fell at my feet. I took their scalps and returned home." Thus this grave and respectable veteran gave a lesson to the young Shawano, which, if he well understood, he, no doubt, ever after remembered; for in a few words, and in less than five minutes, he showed him at once the contrast between great actions briefly and modestly told, and every day occurrences related and dwelt on with pompous minuteness. This contrast, indeed, was particularly striking, the more so as the modest warrior did not seem to enjoy his triumph, nor to be even conscious of the accession to his fame which must result from the publicity of the account which he had given. As both parties spoke the Shawano language, I well understood every thing they said, and I paid the most particular attention to their discourse, which was of itself sufficiently interesting.

This passion of the Indians, which I have called *pride*, but which might, perhaps, be better denominated *high-mindedness*, is generally combined with a great sense of honour, and not seldom produces actions of the most heroic kind. I am now going to relate

118

an instance of this honourable pride, which I have also witnessed. An Indian of the Lenape nation, who was considered as a very dangerous person, and was much dreaded on that account, had publicly declared that as soon as another Indian, who was then gone to Sandusky, should return from thence, he would certainly kill him. This dangerous Indian called in one day at my house on the Muskingum to ask me for some tobacco. While this unwelcome guest was smoking his pipe by my fire, behold! the other Indian whom he had threatened to kill, and who at that moment had just arrived, also entered the house. I was much frightened, as I feared the bad Indian would take that opportunity to carry his threat into execution, and that my house would be made the scene of a horrid murder. I walked to the door, in order not to witness a crime that I could not prevent, when to my great astonishment I heard the Indian whom I thought in danger, address the other in these words: "Uncle, you have threatened to kill me—you have declared that you would do it the first time we should meet. Now I am here, and we are together. Am I to take it for granted that you are in earnest, and that you are really determined to take my life as you have declared? Am I now to consider you as my avowed enemy, and in order to secure my own life against your murderous designs, to be the first to strike you and embrue my hands in your blood?—I will not, I cannot do it. Your heart is bad, it is true, but still you appear to be a generous foe, for you gave me notice of what you intended to do; you have put me on my guard, and did not attempt to assassinate me by surprise; I, therefore, will spare you until you lift up your arm to strike, and then, uncle, it will be seen which of us shall fall!" The murderer was thunderstruck, and without replying a word, slunk off and left the house.

The anecdote with which I am going to conclude this chapter, will display an act of heroism produced by this elevation of mind which I have called *pride*, which, perhaps, may have been equalled, but, I dare say, was hardly ever surpassed. In the spring of the year 1782, the war chief of the Wyandots of Lower Sandusky sent a white prisoner (a young man whom he had taken at Fort M'Intosh) as a present to another chief, who was called the *Half-king* of Upper Sandusky,[174] for the purpose of being adopted into his family, in the place of one of his sons, who

119

had been killed the preceding year, while at war with the people on the Ohio. The prisoner arrived, and was presented to the Half-king's wife, but she refused to receive him, which, according to the Indian rule, was, in fact, a sentence of death. The young man was, therefore, taken away, for the purpose of being tortured and burnt on the pile. While the dreadful preparations were making near the village, the unhappy victim being already tied to the stake, and the Indians arriving from all quarters to join in the cruel act or to witness it, two English traders,
Messrs. *Arundel* and *Robbins* (I delight in making this honourable mention of their names), shocked at the idea of the cruelties which were about to be perpetrated, and moved by feelings of pity and humanity, resolved to unite their exertions to endeavour to save the prisoner's life by offering a ransom to the war chief, which he, however refused, because, said he, it was an established rule among them, that when a prisoner who had been given as a present, was refused adoption, he was irrevocably doomed to the stake, and it was not in the power of any one to save his life. Besides, added he, the numerous war captains who were on the spot, had it in charge to see the sentence carried into execution.

The two generous Englishmen, however, were not discouraged, and determined to try a last effort. They well knew what effects the high-minded pride of an Indian was capable of producing, and to this strong and noble passion they directed their attacks: "But," said they, in reply to the answer which the chief had made them, "among all those chiefs whom you have mentioned, there is none who equals you in greatness; you are considered not only as the greatest and bravest, but as the best man in the nation." "Do you really believe what you say?" said at once the Indian, looking them full in the face. "Indeed, we do." Then, without saying another word, he blackened himself, and taking his knife and tomahawk in his hand, made his way through the crowd to the unhappy victim, crying out with a loud voice: "What have you to do with *my* prisoner?" and at once cutting the cords with which he was tied, took him to his house which was near Mr. Arundel's, whence he was forthwith secured and carried off by safe hands to Detroit, where[175] the commandant, being informed of the transaction, sent him by water to Niagara, where he was soon

120

afterwards liberated. The Indians who witnessed this act, said that it was truly heroic; they were so confounded by the unexpected conduct of this chief, and by his manly and resolute appearance, that they had not time to reflect upon what they should do, and before their astonishment was well over, the prisoner was out of their reach.

CHAPTER 19 ~
Wars and the causes which lead to them

It is a fixed principle with the Indians, that evil cannot come out of good, that no friend will injure a friend, and, therefore, that whoever wrongs or does harm to another, is his ENEMY. As it is with individuals, so it is with nations, tribes, and other independent associations of men. If they commit murder on another people, encroach on their lands, by making it a practice to come within their bounds and take the game from them, if they rob or steal from their hunting camps, or, in short, are guilty of any act of unjust aggression, they cannot be considered otherwise than as ENEMIES; they are declared to be such, and the aggrieved nation think themselves justifiable in punishing them. If murder has been perpetrated, revenge is taken in the same way. If a lesser injury has been done, a message is sent to the chief of the nation to which the wrong-doers belong, to enquire whether the act complained of was authorised, if not to give them warning not to permit the like thing to be done again. If theft or some other like offence has been committed, restitution is at the same time demanded, or such reparation as the case admits of, and the chiefs are desired to forbid their "young people" to do so any more, or that they will have to abide by the consequence.

There are tribes among the Indians, who claim the exclusive right of hunting within certain bounds, and will not suffer others to intrude and take *their* game from them, as they call it; and there have been instances, when such intruders, being found trespassing after a fair warning, have had their ears and noses cut off, and have been sent home to tell their chiefs that the next time they came again, they should be sent home *without their scalps*. While the Christian Indians of the Lenape nation were settled for a few years on the land of the Chippeways beyond Detroit, where they had taken refuge and were permitted to remain for their safety; though the Chippeways professed reverence for them, and called them *Grandfather*, yet they were

122

continually complaining of their killing their game. They had no objection to their tilling the ground, but every deer, raccoon, or other animal which they killed or took, was a cause of displeasure to their hosts; and in consequence of that, they pressed them so often to remove from their lands, that they at last went off.

When the Indians have determined to take revenge for a murder committed by another nation, they generally endeavour to make at once a bold stroke, so as to strike their enemies with terror; for which purpose, they penetrate into the hostile country as far as they can without being discovered, and when they have made their stroke, they leave a war club near the body of the person murdered, and make off as quick as possible. This war club is purposely left that the enemy may know to what nation the act is to be ascribed, and that they may not wreak their vengeance on an innocent tribe. It is meant also to let them know that unless they take measures to discover and punish the author of the original aggression, this instrument will be the means of revenging the injury, or, in other words, war will be forthwith declared against them.

If the supposed enemy is peaceably inclined, he will in such case send a deputation to the aggrieved nation, with a suitable apology. In general the chief sends word, that the act complained of was committed without his knowledge, by some of "his foolish young men;" that it was altogether unauthorised and unwarranted; that it was highly reprobated by himself and his council, and that he would be sorry that on that account a breach should be made between the two nations, but, on the contrary, wishes for peace; that he is willing to make reparation for the offence by condoling with the relations of the person slain and otherwise satisfying them. Such an offer is generally accepted, and in this manner all differences are adjusted between the parties, and they are friends again as they were before. But should the offending nation refuse to apologise and sue for peace, war is then immediately declared and is carried on with the greatest vigour.

CHAPTER 20 ~
Manner of surprising their enemies

Courage, art, and circumspection are the essential and indispensable qualifications of an Indian warrior. When war is once begun, each one strives to excel in displaying them, by stealing upon his enemy unawares, and deceiving and surprising him in various ways. On drawing near to an enemy's country, they endeavour as much as possible to conceal their tracks; sometimes they scatter themselves, marching at proper distances from each other for a whole day and more, meeting, however, again at night, when they keep a watch; at other times they march in what is called *Indian file*, one man behind the other, treading carefully in each other's steps, so that their number may not be ascertained by the prints of their feet. The nearer they suppose themselves to be to the enemy, the more attentive they are to choosing hard, stony, and rocky ground, on which human footsteps leave no impression; soft, marshy and grassy soils are particularly avoided, as in the former the prints of the feet would be easily discovered, and in the latter the appearance of the grass having been trodden upon might lead to detection; for if the grass or weeds are only bent, and have the least mark of having been walked upon, it will be almost certainly perceived, in which the sharpness and quickness of the Indians' sight is truly astonishing.

In some instances they deceive their enemies by imitating the cries or calls of some animal, such as the fawn, or turkey. They do this so admirably well, that they even draw the dam of the one and the mate of the other to the spot to which they want to come. In this manner they often succeed in decoying the enemies to the place where they are lying in ambush, or get an opportunity of surrounding them. Such stratagems, however, cannot be resorted to in all seasons; with the turkey, it only answers in the spring, and with the fawn's dam until about midsummer. In the same manner, when scattered about in the woods, they easily find each other by imitating the song of some birds, such as the quail and the rook, and at evening and morning, and particularly in the night, the cry of the owl. By this means they all join each other, though not at the same time, as they are not, perhaps, all within hearing; but the cry of the owl is repeated from time to time until they are all assembled.

It is certain that the Indians, by the prints of the feet and by other marks and signs perceivable only to themselves, can readily discover, not only that men have passed through a particular path or line of march, but they can discriminate to what particular nation those men belong, and whether they are their friends or their enemies. They also sometimes make discoveries by examining obscure places, and by that means get informed of an enemy's design. Nay, there are those among them who pretend to be able to discriminate among various marks of human footsteps the different nations of those to whom they respectively belong. I shall not undertake to assert thus far, but I shall relate an anecdote, the truth of which I firmly believe, in proof of their extraordinary sagacity in this respect.

In the beginning of the summer of the year 1755, a most atrocious and shocking murder was unexpectedly committed by a party of Indians, on fourteen white settlers within five miles of Shamokin.[176] The surviving whites, in their rage, determined to take their revenge by murdering a Delaware Indian who happened to be in those parts and was far from thinking himself in any danger. He was a great friend to the whites, was loved and esteemed by them, and in testimony of their regard, had received from them the name of *Duke Holland*,[177] by which he was generally known. This Indian, satisfied that his nation was incapable of committing such a foul murder in a time of profound peace, told the enraged settlers, that he was sure that the Delawares were not in any manner concerned in it, and that it was the act of some wicked Mingoes or Iroquois, whose custom it was to involve other nations in wars with each other, by clandestinely committing murders, so that they might be laid to the charge of others than themselves.

But all his representations were vain; he could not convince exasperated men whose minds were fully bent upon revenge. At last, he offered that if they would give him a party to accompany him, he would go with them in quest of the murderers, and was sure he could discover them by the prints of their feet and other marks well known to him, by which he would convince them that the real perpetrators of the crime belonged to the Six Nations. His proposal was accepted, he marched at the head of a party of whites and led them into the tracks. They soon found themselves in the most rocky parts of a mountain, where not one of those who accompanied him was able to discover a single track, nor would they believe that man had ever trodden upon this ground, as they had to jump over a number of crevices between the rocks, and in some instances to crawl over them. Now they began to believe that the Indian had led them across those rugged mountains in order to give the enemy time to escape, and threatened him with instant death the moment they should be fully convinced of the fraud.

The Indian, true to his promise, would take pains to make them perceive that an enemy had passed along the places through which he was leading them; here he would shew them that the moss on the rock had been trodden down by the weight of an human foot, there that it had been torn and dragged forward from its place: further he would point out to them that pebbles or small stones on the rocks had been removed from their beds by the foot hitting against them, that dry sticks by being trodden upon were broken, and even that in a particular place, an Indian's blanket had dragged over the rocks, and removed or loosened the leaves lying there, so that they lay no more flat, as in other places; all which the Indian could perceive as he walked along, without even stopping. At last arriving at the foot of the mountain on soft ground, where the tracks were deep, he found out that the enemy were eight in number, and from the freshness of the footprints, he concluded that they must be encamped at no great distance.

This proved to be the exact truth, for, after gaining the eminence on the other side of the valley, the Indians were seen encamped, some having already laid down to sleep, while others were drawing off their *leggings*[178] for the same purpose, and the scalps they had taken were hanging up to dry. "See!" said Duke Holland to his astonished companions, "there is the enemy! not of my nation, but Mingoes, as I truly told you. They are in our power; in less than half an hour they will all be fast asleep. We need not fire a gun, but go up and tomahawk them. We are nearly two to one and need apprehend no danger. Come on, and you will now have your full revenge!" But the whites, overcome with fear, did not choose to follow the Indian's advice, and urged him to take them back by the nearest and best way, which he did, and when they arrived at home late at night, they reported the number of the Iroquois to have been so great, that they durst not venture to attack them.

This account is faithfully given as I received it from *Duke Holland* himself, and took it down in writing at the time. I had been acquainted with this Indian for upwards of twenty years, and knew him to be honest, intelligent and a lover of truth. Therefore I gave full credit to what he told me, and as yet have had no reason to disbelieve or even to doubt it. I once employed him to save the life of a respectable gentleman, now residing at Pittsburg, who was in imminent danger of being killed by a war party. Duke Holland conducted him safely through the woods, from the Muskingum to the Ohio settlement. He once found a watch of mine, which had been sent to me from Pittsburg by a man who had got drunk, and lost it in the woods about fifty miles from the place where I lived. Duke Holland went in search of it, and having discovered the tracks of the man to whom it had been entrusted, he pursued them until he found the lost article, which he delivered to me.

CHAPTER 21 ~
Peace messengers

While the American Indian remained in the free and undisturbed possession of the land which God gave to them, and even for a long time after the Europeans had settled themselves in their territory, there was no people upon earth who paid a more religious respect than they did to the sacred character of the ambassadors, or (as they call them) *Messengers of peace*. It is too well known that since about the middle of the last century a great change has taken place, the cause of which, I am sorry to say, the Indians lay entirely to our charge.

The inviolability of the person of an ambassador is one of those sacred fundamental principles of the law of nature which the Almighty Creator has imprinted upon the heart of every living man. History teaches us that the most barbarous and savage nations have at all times admitted and carried it into practice. It is a lamentable truth that all the violations of it that stand upon record, are to be ascribed to civilised man or to his contagious example.

It is certain that among our Indians the person of an ambassador was formerly held most sacred and inviolable. All the nations and tribes were agreed upon this point, that a messenger, though sent by the most hostile people, was entitled not only to respect but to protection. To have, I will not say murdered, but knowingly ill treated a person of this description, was with them an unpardonable crime. War parties were always instructed, if they should find a messenger on his way from one nation to another, not only to give him protection but hospitality, and see him safely conducted to the people to whom he was sent.

In the same manner, when a messenger was sent to them by a nation with whom they were at war or at variance, though they might be ever so much exasperated against them, and even though they had firmly determined *not to listen*, that is to say, not to consent to their propositions, whatever they might be, still they would grant their protection to the man of peace, and tell him in their expressive language "that they had taken him under their wings, or placed him under their arm pits, where he was perfectly safe." It was with them a point of religious belief, that pacific messengers were under the special protection of the Great Spirit, that it was unlawful to molest them, and that the nation which should be guilty of so enormous a crime would surely be punished by being unsuccessful in war, and perhaps, by suffering a total defeat. Therefore, frequent instances happened of such messengers being sent back with the most threatening messages, such as, that it was determined to wage a war of blood and destruction, and that no quarter would be given, yet the ambassadors themselves did not meet with the least insult or disrespect; they were protected during all the time that they remained in the hostile country, and were safely conducted to their own nation, or at least, so far on their way as to be out of danger from the enemy's warriors, leaving them a sufficient time to reach their houses, before a fresh stroke was made, to give notice that the truce was at an end or that the war was begun. I have heard of messengers being sent back with a message to this effect: "I return to your bosom, safe and unmolested, the messengers you sent me. The answer to the speech they brought me from you, you will learn from my young warriors, who are gone to *see* you." The nature of the *visit* thus announced may be easily guessed at. The message was in fact a declaration of war, with a fair notice that an invasion of the enemy's country was immediately to take place.

Such were the principles, such was the manly conduct of the Indians in former times. How different it is at present I need not say. We yet remember the unhappy fate of Messrs. *Trueman*, *Freeman*, and *Hardin*. These three respectable American gentlemen, were in the year 1792, sent to the Indians with flags of truce and peace proposals, and were all wantonly murdered.[179] To whom is this horrid state of things to be attributed? I will not pretend to judge, but let us hear what the Indians say.

The principal reasons which they assign as having brought about this great change, are comprised under the following general heads

I. That the white people have intermeddled with their national concerns, by dictating to one nation how they should treat another, and even how they should speak and what they should say to them, and by this means have entirely destroyed their national independence. That they have even encouraged and supported one Indian nation in not only affecting but actually exercising dominion and supremacy over all the others.

II. That the whites have treated the Indians as a contemptible race and paid no regard themselves to the sacred character of messengers, but murdered them as well as their chiefs in numerous instances without distinction. That they even polluted what among them is esteemed most holy and inviolable, their *council fires*, extinguishing them (as they express themselves) with streams of the best blood of their nation, in violation of their professions and most solemn promises! That their whole conduct in short has appeared as if they would say to them: "We do not care for you; we despise you—all we want is your lands, and those we will have."

Nor are they at a loss when called upon to specify the particular injuries of which they complain. Amidst a long list of similar grievances, I shall select a few of the most prominent:

1. The protection given against them to the Iroquois, encouraging that nation to insult them, to treat them as women made such by conquest, and to exercise a tyrannical superiority over them.

2. The murder of the Conestogo Indians, at the very place where a *council fire* was burning at the time; where treaties had been held with them in early times, and where even a treaty had been concluded

130

in 1762, the year preceding the murder; and that too in the country of their brother *Miquon*, in the *Quaker* country, in Pennsylvania.

3. The horrid murder committed between the years 1776 and 1779, on the great and much valued Shawano chief *Cornstalk*, at Kanhawa, where it was known that he was on a friendly and interesting errand.[180]

4. The firing upon and severely wounding a noted Shawano in the year 1774, while on his return from Pittsburgh, to which place he had, out of friendship and humanity, conducted several white traders and protected them against an enraged body of Indians, on whose relations the white people had committed most horrid murders.

5. The attacking the peaceable encampment of the Delaware chiefs on the island at Pittsburgh, where one *Messenger* and several others were murdered.

6. The murder of the Christian Indians on Muskingum, by Williamson's party, together with the chief from *Achsinning*, (the standing stone,) although the persons thus murdered were known to be friends to the whites.

The Indians relate many more outrages committed on *messengers*, *visitors*, and other *friendly* Indians, of which I shall spare the painful recital to my readers. From this series of unjust and cruel acts, the Indian nations, have at last come to the conclusion that the Americans are in their hearts inimical to them, and that when they send them messengers of peace, they only mean to lull them into a fancied security, that they may the easier fall upon and destroy them. It was in consequence of this conviction that the three respectable gentlemen whom I have already mentioned, met with their unhappy fate.

CHAPTER 22 ~
Treaties

In early times, when Indian nations, after long and bloody wars, met together, for the purpose of adjusting their differences, or concluding a peace with each other, it was their laudable custom, as a token of their sincerity, to remove out of the place where the peacemakers were sitting, all warlike weapons and instruments of destruction, of whatever form or shape. "For," said they, "when we are engaged in a good work, nothing that is bad must be visible. We are met together to forgive and forget, to *bury* the destructive weapon, and put it quite out of sight; we cast away from us the fatal instrument that has caused so much grief to our wives and children, and has been the source of so many tears. It is our earnest hope and wish that it may never be dug up again." So particular were they on this point, that if a single weapon had been in sight, while a treaty was negotiating, it would have disturbed their minds by recalling the memory of past events, and instead, (as they say) of gladdening their hearts, by the prospect of a speedy peace, would, on the contrary, have filled them with sorrow.

Nor would they even permit any warlike weapons to remain within the limits of their *council fire*, when assembled together about the ordinary business of government. It might, they said, have a bad effect, and defeat the object for which they had met. It might be a check on some of the persons assembled, and perhaps, prevent those who had a just complaint or representation to make, from speaking their minds freely. William Penn, said they, when he treated with them, adopted this ancient mode of their ancestors, and convened them under a grove of shady trees, where the little birds on their boughs were warbling their sweet notes. In commemoration of these conferences (which are always to Indians a subject of pleasing remembrance) they frequently assembled together in the woods, in some shady spot as nearly as possible similar to those where they used to meet their brother *Miquon*, and there lay all his "*words*" or speeches, with those of his descendants, on a blanket or clean piece of bark, and with great satisfaction go successively over the whole. This practice (which I have repeatedly witnessed) continued until the year 1780, when the disturbances which then took place put an end to it, probably for ever.

These pleasing remembrances, these sacred usages are no more. "When we treat with the white people," do the Indians now say, "we have not the choice of the spot where the messengers are to meet. When we are called upon to conclude a peace, (and what a peace?) the meeting no longer takes place in the shady grove, where the innocent little birds with their cheerful songs, seem as if they wished to soothe and enliven our minds, tune them to amity and concord and take a part in the good work for which we are met. Neither is it at the sacred council house, that we are invited to assemble. No!—It is at some of those horrid places, surrounded with mounds and ditches, where the most destructive of all weapons, where *great guns* are gaping at us with their wide mouths, as if ready to devour us; and thus we are prevented from speaking our minds freely as brothers ought to do!"

How then, say they, can there be any sincerity in such councils? how can a treaty of this kind be binding on men thus forced to agree to what is dictated to them in a strong prison and at the cannon's mouth; where all the stipulations are on one side, where all is concession on the one part and no friendship appears on the other? From these considerations, which they urge and constantly dwell upon, the treaties which they make with the white men have lost all their force, and they think themselves no longer bound by them than they are compelled by superior power. Are they right in this or are they wrong? The impartial reader must decide.

CHAPTER 23 ~
General observations of the Indians on the white people

The Indians believe that the Whites were made by the same Great Spirit who created them, and that he assigned to each different race of men a particular employment in this world, but not the same to all. To the whites the great Mannitto gave it in charge to till the ground and raise by cultivation the fruits of the earth; to the Indians he assigned the nobler employment of hunting, and the supreme dominion over all the rest of the animal creation.

They will not admit that the whites are superior beings. They say that the hair of their heads, their features, the various colours of their eyes, evince that they are not like themselves *Lenni Lenape*, an ORIGINAL PEOPLE, a race of men that has existed unchanged from the beginning of time; but they are a *mixed* race, and therefore a *troublesome* one; wherever they may be, the Great Spirit, knowing the wickedness of their disposition, found it necessary to give them a great Book,[181] and taught them how to read it, that they might know and observe what he wished them to do and to abstain from. But they, the Indians, have no need of any such book to let them know the will of their Maker; they find it engraved on their own hearts; they have had sufficient discernment given to them to distinguish good from evil, and by following that guide, they are sure not to err.

It is true, they confess, that when they first saw the whites, they took them for beings of a superior kind. They did not know but that they had been sent to them from the abode of the Great Spirit for some great and important purpose. They therefore, welcomed them, hoping to be made happier by their company. It was not long, however, before they discovered their mistake, having found them an ungrateful, insatiable people, who, though the Indians had given them as much land as was necessary to raise provisions for themselves and their families, and pasture for their cattle, wanted still to have more, and at last would not be contented with less than the *whole country*. "And yet," say those injured people, "these white men would always be telling us of their great Book which God had given to them, they would persuade us that every man was good who believed in what the Book said, and every man was bad who did not believe in it. They told us a great many things, which they said were written in the good Book, and wanted us to believe it all. We would probably have done so, if we had seen them practise what they pretended to believe, and act according to the *good words* which they told us. But no! while they held their big Book in one hand, in the other they had murderous weapons, guns and swords, wherewith to kill us, poor Indians! Ah! and they did so too, they killed those who believed in their Book, as well as those who did not. They made no distinction!"

They, nevertheless, are sensible that they have many friends among the white people, and only regret that from their being scattered and at a distance, they cannot be useful to them and to each other. Of those whom they know to be their friends, they always speak with warmth and affection. They also speak of the *Gentellemaan* (gentlemen) as a particular class among the whites which deserves to be distinguished; but they never apply that descriptive title to a person whom they know to be their enemy, or believe to be ill disposed towards them.

The Indians have a keen eye; by looking at a person, they think that they can judge of his friendly or unfriendly disposition to their race; and, indeed, it has been allowed by many whites who have lived among them, that they are, in general, pretty good physiognomists. They are very quick among themselves in giving a name to a stranger or person of note that comes to them, and that name is always significant or descriptive of something remarkable which they have observed about his person, which serves them to remember him as a friend or otherwise, as the case may be; when they believe a person to be their friend, they will do everything in their power to oblige him, it being their principle that "good ought always to be rewarded with good." They prefer a plain man, simple in his manners and who treats them with frankness and familiarity. Such a man, they say, loves

135

them. From a proud haughty man they do not expect friendship; whatever may be his professions, they think him incapable of loving anybody but himself, or perhaps, at most, his equal, and that, they think, an Indian can, in his opinion, never be.

They sometimes amuse themselves by passing in review those customs of the white people which appear to them most striking. They observe, amongst other things, that when the whites meet together, many of them, and sometimes all, speak at the same time, and they wonder how they can thus hear and understand each other. "Among us," they say "only one person speaks at a time, and the others listen to him until he has done, after which, and not before, another begins to speak." They say also that the whites speak too much, and that much talk disgraces a man and is fit only for women. On this subject they shrewdly observe, that it is well for the whites that they have the art of writing, and can write down their words and speeches; for had they, like themselves, to transmit them to posterity by means of strings and belts of wampum, they would want for their own use all the wampum that could be made, and none would be left for the Indians.

They wonder that the white people are striving so much to get rich, and to heap up treasures in this world which they cannot carry with them to the next. They ascribe this to pride and to the desire of being called rich and great. They say that there is enough in this world to live upon, without laying anything by, and as to the next world, it contains plenty of everything, and they will find all their wants satisfied when they arrive there. They, therefore, do not lay up any stores, but merely take with them when they die as much as is necessary for their journey to the world of spirits.

They believe, or, at least, pretend to believe, that the white people have weak eyes, or are near-sighted. "For," say they, "when we Indians come among them, they crowd quite close up to us, stare at us, and almost tread upon our heels to get nearer. We, on the contrary, though, perhaps, not less curious than they are, to see a new people or a new object, keep at a reasonable distance, and yet see what we wish to see." They also remark, that when the white people meet together, they speak very loud, although near to each other, from whence they conclude that they must be hard of hearing. "As to us," they say, "we never speak loud when we come together, and yet we understand each other distinctly; we only speak in a high tone of voice before a public audience, in council, at the head of our warriors, or when we are met together for some important purpose."

The Indians also observe, that the white people must have a great many thieves among them, since they put locks to their doors, which shews great apprehension that their property otherwise would not be safe: "As to us," say they, "we entertain no such fears; thieves are very rare among us, and we have no instance of any person breaking into a house. Our Indian lock is, when we go out, to set the corn pounder or a billet of wood against the door, so that it may be seen that no body is within, and there is no danger that any Indian would presume to enter a house thus secured." Let me be permitted to illustrate this by an anecdote.

In the year 1771, while I was residing on the Big Beaver, I passed by the door of an Indian, who was a trader, and had consequently a quantity of goods in his house. He was going with his wife to Pittsburg, and they were shutting up the house, as no person remained in it during their absence. This shutting up was nothing else than putting a large hominy pounding-block, with a few sticks of wood outside against the door, so as to keep it closed. As I was looking at this man with attention while he was so employed, he addressed me in these words: "See my friend, this is an Indian lock that I am putting to my door." I answered, "Well enough; but I see you leave much property in the house, are you not afraid that those articles will be stolen while you are gone?"—"Stolen! by whom?"—"Why, by Indians, to be sure."—"No, no," replied he, "no Indian would do such a thing, and unless a white man or white people should happen to come this way, I shall find all safe on my return."

The Indians say, that when the white people encamp in the woods they are sure to lose something; that when they are gone, something or another is always found which they have lost, such as a knife, flints, bullets, and sometimes even money. They also observe that the whites are not so attentive as they are to choosing an open dry spot for their encampment; that they will at once set themselves down in any dirty and wet place, provided they are under large trees; that they never look about to see which way the wind blows, so as to be able to lay the wood for their fires in such a position that the smoke may not blow on them; neither do they look up the trees to see whether there are not dead limbs that may fall on them while they are asleep; that any wood will do for them to lay on their fires, whether it be dry or wet, and half rotten, so that they are involved during the whole night in a cloud of smoke; or they take such wood as young green oak, walnut, cherry, chestnut, &c., which throws sparks out to a great distance, so that their blankets and clothes get holes burned in them, and sometimes their whole camp takes fire. They also remark that the whites hang their kettles and pots over a fire just kindled, and before the great body of smoke has passed away.

They, however, acknowledge that the whites are ingenious, that they make axes, guns, knives, hoes, shovels, pots and kettles, blankets, shirts, and other very convenient articles, to which they have now become accustomed, and which they can no longer do without. "Yet," say they, "our forefathers did without all these things, and we have never heard, nor has any tradition informed us that they were at a loss for the want of them; therefore we must conclude that they also were ingenious; and, indeed, we know that they were; for they made axes of stone to cut with, and bows and arrows to kill the game: they made knives and arrows' points with sharp flint stones and bones, hoes and shovels from the shoulder blade of the elk and buffaloe; they made pots of clay, garments of skins, and ornaments with the feathers of the turkey, goose and other birds. They were not in want of anything, the game was plenty and tame, the dart shot from our arrows did not frighten them as the report of the gun now does; we had therefore everything that we could reasonably require; we lived happy!"

Finally, they think, that the white people have learned much of them in the art of war; for when they first began to fight the Indians, they stood all together in a cluster, and suffered themselves to be shot down like turkies. They also make a distinction between a *warrior* and a *murderer*, which, as they

138

explain it, is not much to our advantage. "It is not," say they, "the number of scalps alone which a man brings with him that prove him to be a brave warrior. Cowards have been known to return, and bring scalps home, which they had taken where they knew there was no danger, where no attack was expected and no opposition made. Such was the case with those who killed the Conestogoes at and near Lancaster, the Christian Indians on the Muskingum, the friendly Indians near Pittsburg, and a great number of scattered, peaceable men of our nation, who were all murdered by *cowards*. It was not thus that the *Black Snake*,[182] the great General Wayne acted; he was a true warrior and a brave man; he was equal to any of the chiefs that we have, equal to any that we ever had."

Thus, the Indians, while they deeply resent the wrongs and injuries which they have suffered, yet pay due homage to worth, bravery, and military skill, even in an enemy. Strong as their feelings are, they do not extinguish their sense of justice, and they are still generously disposed to allow that there are great and good individuals among a race of men, who, they believe, have doomed them to utter destruction.

CHAPTER 24 ~
Food and cookery

The principal food of the Indians consists of the game which they take or kill in the woods, the fish out of the waters, and the maize, potatoes, beans, pumpkins, squashes, cucumbers, melons, and occasionally cabbages and turnips, which they raise in their fields; they make use also of various roots of plants, fruits, nuts, and berries out of the woods, by way of relish or as a seasoning to their victuals, sometimes also from necessity.

They commonly make two meals every day, which, they say, is enough. If any one should feel hungry between meal-times, there is generally something in the house ready for him.

The hunter prefers going out with his gun on an empty stomach; he says, that hunger stimulates him to exertion by reminding him continually of his wants, whereas a full stomach makes a hunter easy, careless, and lazy, ever thinking of his home and losing his time to no purpose. With all their industry, nevertheless, and notwithstanding this strong stimulant, many a day passes over their heads that they have not met with any kind of game, nor consequently tasted a morsel of victuals; still they go on with their chase, in hopes of being able to carry some provisions home, and do not give up the pursuit until it is so dark that they can see no longer.

The morning and evening, they say, are the precious hours for the hunter. They lose nothing by sleeping in the middle of the day, that is to say, between ten o'clock in the morning and four in the afternoon, except in dark, cloudy, and rainy weather, when the whole day is nearly equally good for hunting. Therefore the hunter, who happens to have no meat in the house, will be off and in the woods before daylight, and strive to be in again for breakfast with a deer, turkey, goose, bear, or raccoon, or some other game then in season. Meanwhile, his wife has pounded her corn, now boiling on the fire, and baked her bread, which gives them a good breakfast. If, however, the husband is not returned by ten o'clock in the forenoon, the family take their meal by themselves, and his share is put aside for him when he comes home.

The Indians have a number of manners of preparing their corn. They make an excellent pottage of it, by boiling it with fresh or dried meat (the latter pounded), dried pumpkins, dry beans, and chestnuts. They sometimes sweeten it with sugar or molasses from the sugar-maple tree. Another very good dish is prepared by boiling with their corn or maize, the washed kernels of the shell-bark or hickory nut. They pound the nuts in a block or mortar, pouring a little warm water on them, and gradually a little more as they become dry, until, at last, there is a sufficient quantity of water, so that by stirring up the pounded nuts the broken shells separate from the liquor, which from the pounded kernels assumes the appearance of milk. This being put into the kettle and mixed with the pottage gives it a rich and agreeable flavour. If the broken shells do not all freely separate by swimming on the top or sinking to the bottom, the liquor is strained through a clean cloth, before it is put into the kettle.

They also prepare a variety of dishes from the pumpkin, the squash, and the green French or kidney beans; they are very particular in their choice of pumpkins and squashes, and in their manner of cooking them. The women say that the less water is put to them, the better dish they make, and that it would be still better if they were stewed without any water, merely in the steam of the sap which they contain. They cover up the pots in which they cook them with large leaves of the pumpkin vine, cabbages, or other leaves of the larger kind. They make an excellent preserve from the cranberry and crab-apple, to which, after it has been well stewed, they add a proper quantity of sugar or molasses.

Their bread is of two kinds; one made up of green corn while in the milk, and another of the same grain when fully ripe and quite dry. This last is pounded as fine as possible, then sifted and kneaded into dough, and afterwards made up into cakes of six inches in diameter and about an inch in thickness, rounded off on the edge. In baking these cakes, they are extremely particular; the ashes must be clean and hot, and if possible come out of good dry oak barks, which they say gives a brisk and durable heat. In the dough of this kind of bread, they frequently mix boiled pumpkins, green or dried, dry beans, or well pared chestnuts, boiled in the same manner, dried venison well pounded, whortleberries, green or dry, but not boiled, sugar and other palatable ingredients. For the other kind of bread, the green corn is either pounded or mashed, is put in broad green corn blades, generally filled in with a ladle, well wrapped up, and baked in the ashes, like the other. They consider this as a very delicate morsel, but to me it is too sweet.

Their *Psindamócan* or *Tassmanánc*, as they call it, is the most nourishing and durable food made out of the Indian corn. The blue sweetish kind is the grain which they prefer for that purpose. They parch it in clean hot ashes, until it bursts, it is then sifted and cleaned, and pounded in a mortar into a kind of flour, and when they wish to make it very good, they mix some sugar with it. When wanted for use, they take about a table spoonful of this flour in their mouths, then stooping to the river or brook, drink water to it. If, however, they have a cup or other small vessel at hand, they put the flour in it and mix it with water, in the proportion of one table spoonful to a pint. At their camps they will put a small quantity in a kettle with water and let it boil down, and they will have a thick pottage. With this food, the traveller and warrior will set out on long journeys and expeditions, and as a little of it will serve them for a day, they have not a heavy load of provisions to carry. Persons who are unacquainted with this diet ought to be careful not to take too much at a time, and not to suffer themselves to be tempted too far by its flavour; more than one or two spoonfuls at most at any one time or at one meal is dangerous; for it is apt to swell in the stomach or bowels, as when heated over a fire.

Their meat they either boil, roast, or broil. Their roasting is done by running a wooden spit through the meat, sharpened at each end, which they place near the fire, and occasionally turn. They broil on clean coals, drawn off from the fire for that purpose.

They often laugh at the white hunters, for baking their bread in dirty ashes, and being alike careless of cleanliness when they broil their meat. They are fond of dried venison, pounded in a mortar and dipped in bear's oil. The Delawares, Mohicans, and Shawanos are very particular in their choice of meats, and nothing short of the most pressing hunger can induce them to eat of certain animals, such as the horse, dog, wild cat, panther, fox, muskrat, wolf, &c., all which I have several times seen the Chippeways feast upon with a seemingly good appetite. The Iroquois are said to have been formerly very dirty in their eating. They dried the entrails of animals without cleaning, or even emptying them of their contents; then cut them into pieces and put them into their pottage, by way of seasoning.[183] The late Mr. Zeisberger has often related to me how he once mistook for black pepper or some other kind of spice, a certain unpleasant ingredient which he found floating in small grains on the surface of their broth.

Far different in this respect are the Lenape and their kindred tribes, particularly the three which I have named above. They are not only cleanly in their eating, but even delicate, and they will sometimes resist the pressing calls of hunger rather than eat the flesh of those animals which they consider as not being proper food for man. Of this I shall give an instance in the following anecdote.

I was travelling in the spring of 1773, from Muskingum to the Big Beaver, with more than twenty Indians, five of whom were old men and the rest women and children, all (except our guide) strangers to the country, having come but the year before from Wyalusing on the Susquehannah. Having been at one time confined two days by the overflowing of two large creeks, between which we were, we found our provisions at an end. Every man who had a gun was called upon to turn out into the woods, and try to kill something. Their endeavours, however, were to no purpose; the day passed away, and they all, except the well-known *Popunhank*[184] who had lost himself, returned to camp at night without bringing any thing of the meat kind but a wild cat, which our guide had shot. The Indians never despair, not even in the worst of times and under the severest trials; when placed in difficult situations they never use discouraging language, but always endeavour to raise their spirits and prevent them from sinking, under the hardships or dangers to which they are exposed. True to this national character, one of our old Indians immediately pronounced this wild cat to be "good, very good eating," and it was immediately ordered to be put on the spit and roasted for our supper. While this was performing, the old Indian endeavoured to divert the company by extolling in a jocular manner the country they had now got into, and where such good things were to be had; to which some one or other of the old men would reply; "all very true." At length, about nine o'clock at night, the call was given by the old cook (for so I now call him) that the meat was done and we might come in to eat. I, who had heard so much in praise of this repast, being greatly pinched with hunger, had kept myself in readiness for this expected call; but seeing nobody rise, and observing much merriment through the camp, I began to suspect that something was the matter, and therefore kept my seat.

The night was spent without any body attempting to eat of the wild cat, and in the morning a different call was given by one of the old men, signifying that a large kettle of tea had been made by some of the good women, who invited all to come and take their share of it. Every one obeyed this call, and I went with the rest, the jovial old cook taking the roasted wild cat with him to the mess. The scene was not only very diverting, but brought on an interesting discussion between the men on the propriety or impropriety of eating the flesh of all animals without restriction, some contending that they were all by the will of the great Creator ordained for some use, and therefore put in the power of man; and how were we to know which were intended for our nourishment and which not? The old cook had himself taken that position, adding that the hog and the bear fed on dirty things, and yet we ate their meat with a good appetite. The cat, however, notwithstanding all the arguments in its favour, remained untouched, and was taken back by the old hunter and cook to its former place at his fire.

But now, Popunhank, whom we believed to be lost, and our guide, who once more had gone out, and exerted himself in vain to kill a deer, came in together. The guide had been desired as he pursued his hunt to look for our lost companion, and had the good luck to find him at the distance of five or six miles, with a fine deer that he had killed. He lost no time in bringing him back to our camp.

The sight of these two men dragging a large deer along was truly joyful to us, as well on account of the recovery of our lost friend, as of the meat that he brought. All felt the cravings of hunger, all were delighted with the certain prospect of immediate relief, yet no boisterous or extraordinary rejoicing took place, but all called out with one voice: *Anischi! Anischi!* we are thankful. The wild cat, which yet remained untouched, was thrown out of the camp, and dismissed by the old cook with these words: "Go, cat, we do not want you this time!"

The woods and waters, at certain times and seasons, furnish to the Indians an abundant supply of wholesome nourishing food, which, if carefully gathered, cured and stored up, would serve them for the whole year, so that none need perish or even suffer from hunger; but they are not accustomed to laying in stores of provisions, except some Indian corn, dry beans and a few other articles. Hence they are sometimes reduced to great straits, and not seldom in absolute want of the necessaries of life, especially in the time of war. Yet, notwithstanding the numerous famines they have been visited with, they have among their traditions but one instance on record in which an human life was taken for the support of others, although they relate many cases in which numbers of them were actually starved to death. The case I allude to was so singular a circumstance, that it seems the cruel act to which it gave rise was almost unavoidable. I shall relate it here as I have received it from the most unquestionable authority.

In the winter of 1739-40, ever since remembered as the hard winter, when the ground was covered with a very deep snow, a woman with three children, was coming from beyond the Allegheny mountains on a visit to her friends or relations residing at the great island on the west branch of the Susquehannah. After she had reached that river somewhere about *Achtschingi Clammui*, which the whites have corrupted into *Chingleclamoose*,[185] the snow fell in earlier than had been before known, to such a depth, that she could not proceed any farther. She began with putting herself and her children on short allowance, in hopes that the weather might become more moderate, or the snow so hard that they could walk over it. She strove to make her little store of provisions last as long as she could, by using the grass which grew on the river's edge, and certain barks as substitutes, which she boiled to make them digestible; but more snow falling, until at last it rose to the height of a fathom or six feet, she was deprived even of that wretched food, and the wolves hovering about day and night, often attempting to rush into her little encampment, her whole time was taken up with procuring wood and making fires to prevent herself and her children from being frozen to death, and keeping those voracious animals at a distance by throwing out fire-brands to them. Her situation, at last, became intolerable. Having no alternative but that of sacrificing one of her children, she resolved on destroying the youngest, in order to preserve the others and herself from the most dreadful death. After much hesitation, she turned away her eyes and with a trembling hand gave the fatal stroke, filling at the same time the air with her loud lamentations.—She now thought she had obtained a temporary relief, and that she might be able to support herself and her surviving children until a change in the weather should take place, so that they could be able to proceed on their journey; but the wolves getting the scent of the slaughtered child, became more furious than before, her danger every moment became more imminent. She now filled the air with her cries and supplications to the Great Spirit that he would look down with compassion on their awful condition, and save them by his almighty power.—But still the danger increased, the horrid food was almost exhausted, and no relief came. Already she contemplated sacrificing another child; she looked at each of them again and again with a mother's eye, now resolving on killing the one, then changing her mind, and endeavouring to determine on the destruction of the other; she hesitated, wept, despaired, and the children, well understanding what she meant, prayed that they might all die together. While in this situation, her hand already lifted to strike the fatal stroke, the yell of two approaching Indians strikes her ear, and the murderous weapon falls from her hand. The men

146

with rackets to their feet now appear and the dreadful scene is at once closed. They had provisions with them. They made a pair of rackets for the woman to walk on, and brought her and her children along in safety to the Big Island, where my informants resided at the time. I cannot remember whether they told me that they had gone to that spot in consequence of a dream, or of some strong presentiment that they should find human creatures in distress; certain I am, however, that it was owing to one or other of these causes.

The place where this awful event took place was since called *Enda Mohátink*, which means "where human flesh was eaten." This name has been very familiar to the Indians who resided in that part of the country.

There is a spot of land at the edge of the great Pine or Beech Swamp, precisely where it is crossed by the road leading to Wyoming, which is called *the Hermit's Field*, and of which the following account is given. A short time before the white people came into Pennsylvania, a woman from some cause or other had separated herself from society, and with her young son, had taken her abode in this swamp, where she remained undiscovered until the boy grew up to manhood, procuring a livelihood by the use of the bow and arrow, in killing deer, turkeys and other animals, planting corn and vegetables, and gathering and curing nuts and berries of various kinds. When after her long seclusion she again saw Indians, she was much astonished to find them dressed in European apparel. She had become so attached to her place of abode, that she again[186] returned thither and remained there for several years. I was shewn by the Indians in the year 1765, and often afterwards, the corn hills that she had made; the ground, being a stiff clay, was not wasted or worn down, but was covered with bushes, and the traces of the labour of the female hermit were plainly discoverable.

Thus the Indians will support themselves in the midst of the greatest difficulties, never despairing of their fate, but trusting to their exertions, and to the protection of the Almighty Being who created them.

147

CHAPTER 25 ~
Dress, and ornamenting of their persons

In ancient times, the dress of the Indians was made of the skins of animals and feathers. This clothing, they say, was not only warmer, but lasted much longer than any woollen goods they have since purchased of the white people. They can dress any skin, even that of the buffaloe, so that it becomes quite soft and supple, and a good buffaloe or bear skin blanket will serve them many years without wearing out. Beaver and raccoon skin blankets are also pliant, warm and durable; they sew together as many of those skins as is necessary, carefully setting the hair or fur all the same way, so that the blanket or covering be smooth, and the rain do not penetrate, but run off. In wearing these fur blankets they are regulated by the weather; if it is cold and dry the fur is placed next the body, but in warm and wet weather, they have it outside. Some made themselves long frocks of fine fur, and the women's petticoats in the winter season were also made of them, otherwise of dressed deer skins, the same as their shirts, leggings and shoes. They say that shoes made of dressed bear skins, with the hair on and turned inside, are very warm, and in dry weather, durable. With the large rib bones of the elk and buffaloe they shaved the hair off the skins they dressed, and even now, they say that they can clean a skin as well with a well prepared rib-bone as with a knife.

The blankets made from feathers were also warm and durable. They were the work of the women, particularly of the old, who delight in such work, and indeed, in any work which shews that they are able to do their parts and be useful to society. It requires great patience, being the most tedious kind of work I have ever seen them perform, yet they do it in a most ingenious manner. The feathers, generally those of the turkey and goose, are so curiously arranged and interwoven together with thread or twine, which they prepare from the rind or bark of the wild hemp and nettle, that ingenuity and skill cannot be denied them. They show

148

the same talent and much forethought in making their *Happis*, the bands with which they carry their bags and other burdens; they make these very strong and lasting.

The present dress of the Indians is well known to consist in blankets, plain or ruffled shirts and leggings for the men, and petticoats for the women, made of cloth, generally red, blue, or black. The wealthy adorn themselves besides with ribands or gartering of various colours, beads and silver broaches. These ornaments are arranged by the women, who, as well as the men, know how to dress themselves in style. Those of the men principally consist in the painting of themselves, their head and face principally, shaving or good clean garments, silver arm spangles and breast plates, and a belt or two of wampum hanging to their necks. The women, at the expense of their husbands or lovers, line their petticoat and blue or scarlet cloth blanket or covering with choice ribands of various colours, or with gartering, on which they fix a number of silver broaches, or small round buckles. They adorn their leggings in the same manner; their mocksens, (properly *Maxen*, or according to the English pronunciation *Moxen*), are embroidered in the neatest manner, with coloured porcupine quills, and are besides, almost entirely covered with various trinkets; they have, moreover, a number of little bells and brass thimbles fixed round their ancles, which, when they walk, make a tinkling noise, which is heard at some distance; this is intended to draw the attention of those who pass by, that they may look at and admire them.

The women make use of vermilion in painting themselves for dances, but they are very careful and circumspect in applying the paint, so that it does not offend or create suspicion in their husbands; there is a mode of painting which is left entirely to loose women and prostitutes.

As I was once resting in my travels at the house of a trader who lived at some distance from an Indian town, I went in the morning to visit an Indian acquaintance and friend of mine. I found him engaged in plucking out his beard, preparatory to painting himself for a dance which was to take place the ensuing evening. Having finished his head dress, about an hour before sunset, he came up, as he said, to see me, but I and my companions judged that he came *to be seen*. To my utter astonishment, I saw three different paintings or figures on one and the same face. He had, by his great ingenuity and judgment in laying on and shading the different colours, made his nose appear, when we stood directly in front of him, as if it were very long and narrow, with a round knob at the end, much like the upper part of a pair of tongs. On one cheek there was a red round spot, about the size of an apple, and the other was done in the same manner with black. The eye-lids, both the upper and lower ones, were reversed in the colouring. When we viewed him in profile on one side, his nose represented the beak of an eagle, with the bill rounded and brought to a point, precisely as those birds have it, though the mouth was somewhat open. The eye was astonishingly well done, and the head, upon the whole, appeared tolerably well, shewing a great deal of fierceness. When we turned round to the other side, the same nose now resembled the snout of a pike, with the mouth so open, that the teeth could be seen. He seemed much pleased with his execution, and having his looking-glass with him, he contemplated his work, seemingly with great pride and exultation. He asked me how I liked it? I answered that if he had done the work on a piece of board, bark, or anything else, I should like it very well and often look at it. But, asked he, why not so as it is? Because I cannot see the face that is hidden under these colours, so as to know who it is. Well, he replied, I must go now, and as you cannot know me to-day, I will call to-morrow morning before you leave this place. He did so, and when he came back he was washed clean again.

Thus, for a single night's *frolic*, a whole day is spent in what they call dressing, in which each strives to outdo the other.

When the men paint their thighs, legs and breast, they, generally, after laying on a thin shading coat of a darkish colour, and sometimes of a whitish clay, dip their fingers' ends in black or red paint, and drawing it on with their outspread fingers, bring the streaks to a serpentine form. The garments of some of their principal actors are singular, and decorated with such a number of gewgaws and trinkets, that it is impossible to give a precise description of them. Neither are they all alike in taste, every one dressing himself according to his fancy, or the custom of the tribe to which he belongs. While the women, as I have already said, have thimbles and little bells rattling at their ancles, the men have deers' claws fixed to their braced garters or knee bands, and also to their shoes, for the same purpose; for they consider jingling and rattling as indispensably necessary to their performances in the way of dancing.

The notion formerly entertained that the Indians are beardless by nature and have no hair on their bodies, appears now to be exploded and entirely laid aside. I cannot conceive how it is possible for any person to pass three weeks only among those people, without seeing them pluck out their beards, with tweezers made expressly for that purpose. Before the Europeans came into the country, their apparatus for performing this work, consisted of a pair of muscle shells, sharpened on a gritty stone, which answered very well, being somewhat like pincers; but since they can obtain wire, of which that of brass is preferred, they make themselves tweezers, which they always carry with them in their tobacco-pouch, wherever they go, and when at leisure, they pluck out their beards or the hair above their foreheads. This they do in a very quick manner, much like the plucking of a fowl, and the oftener they pluck out their hair, the finer it grows afterwards, so that at last there appears hardly any, the whole having been rooted out. The principal reasons which they give for thus plucking out their beards and the hair next to their foreheads, are that they may have a clean skin to lay the paint on, when they dress for their festivals or dances, and to facilitate the *tattooing* themselves, a custom formerly much in use among them, especially with those who had distinguished themselves by their valour, and acquired celebrity. They say that either painting or tattooing on a hairy face or body would have a disgusting appearance.

As late as the year 1762, when I resided at Tuscorawas on the Muskingum, tattooing was still practised by some Indians; a valiant chief of that village, named *Wawundochwalend*, desirous of having another name given him, had the figure of a water-lizard engraved or tattooed on his face, above the chin, when he received the name *Twakachshawsu*, the water-lizard. The process of tattooing, which I once saw performed, is quickly done, and does not seem to give much pain. They have poplar bark in readiness burnt and reduced to a powder, the figures that are to be tattooed are marked or designed on the skin; the operator with a small stick, rather larger than a common match, to the end of which some sharp needles are fastened, quickly pricks over the whole so that blood is drawn, then a coat of this powder is laid and left on to dry. Before the whites came into this country, they scarified themselves for this purpose with sharp flint stones, or pricked themselves with the sharp teeth of a fish.

In the year 1742, a veteran warrior of the Lenape nation and Monsey tribe, renowned among his own people for his bravery and prowess, and equally dreaded by their enemies, joined the Christian Indians who then resided at this place.[187] This man, who was then at an advanced age, had a most striking appearance, and could not be viewed without astonishment. Besides that his body was full of scars, where he had been struck and pierced by the arrows of the enemy, there was not a spot to be seen, on that part of it which was exposed to view, but what was tattooed over with some drawing relative to his achievements, so that the whole together struck the beholder with amazement and terror. On his whole face, neck, shoulders, arms, thighs and legs, as well as on his breast and back, were represented scenes of the various actions and engagements he had been in; in short, the whole of his history was there deposited, which was well known to those of his nation, and was such that all who heard it thought it could never be surpassed by man.[188] Far from, murdering those who were defenceless or unarmed, his generosity, as well as his courage and skill in the art of war, was acknowledged by all. When, after his conversion, he was questioned about his warlike feats, he frankly and modestly answered, "That being now taken captive by *Jesus Christ*, it did not become him to relate the deeds he had done while in the service of the evil spirit; but that he was willing to give an account in the manner in which he had been *conquered*." At his baptism, on the 23d of December 1742, he received the name of *Michael*, which he preserved until his death, which happened on the 23rd of July 1756. He led the life of a true Christian, and was always ready and willing to relate the history of his conversion, which I heard myself from his own mouth. His age, when he died, was supposed to be about eighty years.

The cutting of the ears, which formerly was practised among the Indians, is now no longer so common with them. Their reasons for laying this custom aside, are that the operation is painful, not only when performed, but until the ears are perfectly healed, which takes a long time, and that they often lose that part of their ears which is separated from the solid part, by its being torn off by the bushes, or falling off when frost-bitten. I once heard of a gay Indian setting off on a severe cold morning for a neighbouring village not more than three miles distant, whose ears had been touched by the frost, and dropped off before he arrived at the place to which he was going. He had not even felt that he had lost them, and when told of it, he was so chagrined that he was going to destroy himself. I have seen a great many Indians with torn ears; but now the custom of cutting them is nearly if not entirely disused.

CHAPTER 26 ~
Dances, songs, and sacrifices

The dances of the Indians vary according to the purposes for which they are intended. We have seen, in the second chapter of this work, that when the Dutch first landed on New York island, the inhabitants who believed them to be celestial beings, began a solemn dance, in order to propitiate them. It is not uncommon for men who are deprived of the light of revealed religion, to believe that the divinity will be pleased with the same things from which they themselves receive pleasure.

It is a pleasing spectacle to see the Indian dances, when intended merely for social diversion and innocent amusement. I acknowledge I would prefer being present at them for a full hour, than a few minutes only at such dances as I have witnessed in our country taverns among the white people. Their songs are by no means unharmonious. They sing in chorus; first the men and then the women. At times the women join in the general song, or repeat the strain which the men have just finished. It seems like two parties singing in questions and answers, and is upon the whole very agreeable and enlivening. After thus singing for about a quarter of an hour, they conclude each song with a loud yell, which I must confess is not in concord with the rest of the music; it is not unlike the cat-bird which closes its pretty song with mewing like a cat. I do not admire this *finale*. The singing always begins by one person only, but others soon fall in successively until the general chorus begins, the drum beating all the while to mark the time. The voices of the women are clear and full, and their intonations generally correct.

Their war dances have nothing engaging; their object, on the contrary, is to strike terror in the beholders. They are dressed and painted, or rather bedaubed with paint, in a manner suitable to the occasion. They hold the murderous weapon in their hand, and imitate in their dance all the warlike attitudes, motions and

154

actions which are usual in an engagement with the enemy, and strive to excel each other by their terrific looks and gestures. They generally perform round a painted post set up for that purpose, in a large room or place enclosed or surrounded with posts, and roofed with the bark of trees; sometimes also this dance is executed in the open air. There every man presents himself in warrior's array, contemptuously looking upon the painted post, as if it was the enemy whom he was about to engage; as he passes by it he strikes, stabs, grasps, pretends to scalp, to cut, to run through; in short, endeavours to shew what he would do to a real enemy, if he had him in his power.

It was an ancient custom among the Indians to perform this dance round a prisoner, and as they danced, to make him undergo every kind of torture, previous to putting him to death. The prisoner appeared to partake in the merriment, contemptuously scoffing at his executioner, as being unskilled in the art of inflicting torments: strange as this conduct may appear, it was not without a sufficient motive. The object of the unfortunate sufferer was to rouse his relentless tormentors to such a pitch of fury, that some of them might, at an unguarded moment, give him the finishing stroke and put him out of his pain.

Previous to going out on a warlike campaign, the war-dance is always performed round the painted post. It is the Indian mode of recruiting. Whoever joins in the dance is considered as having enlisted for the campaign, and is obliged to go out with the party.

After returning from a successful expedition, a dance of *thanksgiving* is always performed, which partakes of the character of a religious ceremony. It is accompanied with singing and choruses, in which the women join. But they take no part in the rest of the performance. At the end of every song, the *scalp-yell* is shouted as many times as there have been scalps taken from the enemy.

The Indians also meet occasionally for the purpose of recounting their warlike exploits, which is done in a kind of half-singing or *recitative*. The oldest warrior recites first, then they go on in rotation and in order of seniority, the drum beating all the time, as it were to give to the relation the greater appearance of reality. After each has made a short recital in his turn, they begin again in the same order, and so continue going the rounds, in a kind of alternate chanting, until every one has concluded. On these occasions, great care must be taken not to give offence by affecting superiority over the others, for every warrior feels his own consequence, and is ready, if insulted, to shew by his actions, what he has performed in war and is still able to do. I well remember an instance of the kind, when an insulted warrior stepped out of the circle in which he was dancing, and struck dead the impudent boaster who had offended him.

Their songs are in general of the warlike or of the tender and pathetic kind. They are sung in short sentences, not without some kind of measure, harmonious to an Indian ear. The music is well adapted to the words, and to me is not unpleasing. I would not attempt to give an idea of it by means of our musical notes, as has been done by other writers, lest I should be as unsuccessful as those who have tried in the same manner to describe the melodies of the ancient Greeks. It would be well if I could describe at one and the same time the whole combination of effects which acted upon my ear, but it is vain to endeavour to do it partially. It is, indeed, much the same with their poetry; yet I cannot resist the temptation of translating as well as I can, the words of the Lenape's song, when they go out to war. They sing it, as I give it here, in short lines or sentences, not always the whole at one time, but most generally in detached parts, as time permits and as the occasion or their feelings prompt them. Their accent is very pathetic, and the whole, in their language, produces considerable effect.

THE SONG OF THE LENAPE WARRIORS GOING AGAINST THE ENEMY.

"O poor me!
Whom am going out to fight the enemy,
And know not whether I shall return again,
To enjoy the embraces of my children

156

And my wife.
O poor creature!
Whose life is not in his own hands,
Who has no power over his own body,
But tries to do his duty
For the welfare of his nation.
O! thou Great Spirit above!
Take pity on my children
And on my wife!
Prevent their mourning on my account!
Grant that I may be successful in this attempt—
That I may slay my enemy,
And bring home the trophies of war
To my dear family and friends,
That we may rejoice together.
O! take pity on me!
Give me strength and courage to meet my enemy,
Suffer me to return again to my children,
To my wife
And to my relations!
Take pity on me and preserve my life
And I will make to thee a sacrifice."

The song of the Wyandot warriors, as translated to me by an Indian trader, would read thus: "Now I am going on an errand of pleasure—O! God, take pity on me, and throw good fortune in my way—grant that I may be successful."

Thus their Almighty Creator is always before their eyes on all important occasions. They feel and acknowledge his supreme power. They also endeavour to propitiate him by outward worship, or *sacrifices*.

These are religious solemnities, intended to make themselves acceptable to the Great Spirit, to find favor in his sight, and obtain his forgiveness for past errors or offences. It is not, as some white persons would lead us to believe, that knowing the Great Spirit to be good, they are under no apprehensions from his wrath, and that they make sacrifices to the evil spirit, believing him alone to be capable of doing them hurt. This cannot be true of a people, who, as I have already said in another part, hold it as a fixed principle "that good and evil cannot and must not be united," who declare and acknowledge the great and good Spirit to be "all powerful," and the evil one to be "weak and limited in power;" who rely alone on the goodness of the author of their existence, and who, before every thing, seek by all the means in their power to obtain his favour and protection. For, they are convinced, that the evil spirit has no power over them, as long as they are in favour with the good one, and to him alone, acknowledging his continued goodness to them and their forefathers, they look for protection against the *Devil*, and his inferior spirits.

It is a part of their religious belief, that there are inferior *Mannittos*, to whom the great and good Being has given the rule and command over the elements; that being so great, he, like their chiefs, must have his attendants to execute his supreme behests; these subordinate spirits (something in their nature between God and man) see and report to him what is doing upon earth; they look down particularly upon the Indians, to see whether they are in need of assistance, and are ready at their call to assist and protect them against danger.

Thus I have frequently witnessed Indians, on the approach of a storm or thunder-gust, address the Mannitto of the air, to avert all danger from them; I have also seen the Chippeways, on the Lakes of Canada, pray to the Mannitto of the waters, that he might prevent the swells from rising too high, while they were passing over them. In both these instances, they expressed their acknowledgment, or shewed their willingness to be grateful, by throwing tobacco in the air, or strewing it on the waters.

There are even some animals, which though they are not considered as invested with power over them, yet are believed to be placed as guardians over their lives; and of course entitled to some notice and to some tokens of gratitude. Thus, when in the night, an owl is heard sounding its note, or calling to its mate, some person in the camp will rise, and taking some *Glicanican*, or

Indian tobacco, will strew it on the fire, thinking that the ascending smoke will reach the bird, and that he will see that they are not unmindful of his services, and of his kindness to them and their ancestors. This custom originated from the following incident, which tradition has handed down to them.

It happened at one time, when they were engaged in a war with a distant and powerful nation, that a body of their warriors was in the camp, fast asleep, no kind of danger at that moment being apprehended. Suddenly, the great "Sentinel" over mankind, the *owl*, sounded the alarm; all the birds of the species were alert at their posts, all at once calling out, as if saying: "Up! up! Danger! Danger!" Obedient to their call, every man jumped up in an instant; when, to their surprise, they found that their enemy was in the very act of surrounding them, and they would all have been killed in their sleep, if the owl had not given them this timely warning.

But, amidst all these superstitious notions, the supreme Mannitto, the creator and preserver of heaven and earth, is the great object of their adoration. On him they rest their hopes, to him they address their prayers and make their solemn sacrifices. These religious ceremonies are not always performed in the same manner. I had intended to have given some details upon this subject, but I find that it has been almost exhausted by other writers,[189] although I will not pretend to say that they are correct on every point. But I do not wish to repeat things which have already been told to the world over and over. Therefore, if on some subjects, relating to the manners and customs of the Indians, I should be thought to have passed over too quickly, and not to have sufficiently entered into particulars, let it be understood that I have done so to avoid the repetition of what others have said, although I am afraid I have been inadvertently guilty of it in more than one instance. I would not presume to communicate my little stock of knowledge, if I did not think that it will add something to what is already known.

I do not recollect that it has already been mentioned, that previous to entering upon the solemnity of their sacrifices, the Indians prepare themselves by vomiting, fasting, and drinking decoctions from certain prescribed plants. This they do to expel the evil which is within them, and that they may with a pure conscience attend to the *sacred performance*, for such they consider it. Nor is the object of those sacrifices always the same; there are sacrifices of prayer and sacrifices of thanksgiving, some for all the favours received by them and their ancestors from the great Being, others for special or particular benefits. After a successful war, they never fail to offer up a sacrifice to the great Being, to return him thanks for having given them courage and strength to destroy or conquer their enemies.

CHAPTER 27 ~
Scalping, whoops or yells, and prisoners

Scalping is a practice which the Indians say has obtained with their nations for ages. I need not describe the manner in which the operation is performed, it has been sufficiently done by others.[190] Indian warriors think it necessary to bring home the scalps of those they have killed or disabled, as visible proofs of their valour; otherwise they are afraid that their relations of the combat and the account they give of their individual prowess might be doubted or disbelieved. Those scalps are dried up, painted and preserved as trophies, and a warrior is esteemed in proportion to the number of them that he can shew.

It is a well known fact that the Indians pluck out all their hair except one tuft on the crown of their heads, but the reason of this exception is not, perhaps, so well understood, which is no other than to enable themselves to take off each other's scalps in war with greater facility. "When we go to fight an enemy," say they, "we meet on equal ground; and we take off each other's scalps, if we can. The conqueror, whoever he may be, is entitled to have something to shew to prove his bravery and his triumph, and it would be *ungenerous* in a warrior to deprive an enemy of the means of acquiring that glory of which he himself is in pursuit. A warrior's conduct ought to be *manly*, else he is *no man*."

As this custom prevails among all the Indian nations, it would seem, as far as I have known, to be the result of a tacit agreement among them, to leave the usual trophies of victory accessible to the contending warriors on all sides; fearing, perhaps, that if a different custom should be adopted by one nation from motives of personal safety, or to destroy the warlike reputation of their rivals or enemies, it might be easily imitated on the other side, and there would be an end to Indian valour and heroism. Indeed, it is certain, that all the weapons which the Indians make use of in war are intended for *offence*, they have no breast-plates,

161

helmets, nor any arms or accoutrements of the defensive kind, and it is not the least remarkable trait in their warlike character, that they make it even a point of honour to offer a hold of their persons to their enemy, by which if he should be possessed of greater skill or courage than themselves, he may not only the more easily destroy them, but is enabled to carry home their bloody spoils as trophies of his victory.

I once remarked to an Indian that if such was their reason for letting a tuft of hair grow on the top of their heads, they might as well suffer the whole to remain, and I could not perceive why they were so careful in plucking it out. To this observation he answered: "My friend! a human being has but one head, and one scalp from that head is sufficient to shew that it has been in my power. Were we to preserve a whole head of hair as the white people do, *several* scalps might be made out of it, which would be *unfair*. Besides, the coward might thus without danger share in the trophies of the brave warrior, and dispute with him the honour of victory."

When the Indians relate their victories, they do not say that they have taken so many "*scalps*," but so many "*heads*," in which they include as well those whom they have scalped, but left alive (which is very often[191] the case), and their prisoners, as those whom they have killed. Nor does it follow, when they reckon or number the heads of their prisoners, that they have been or are to be put to death.

It is an awful spectacle to see the Indian warriors return home from a successful expedition with their prisoners and the scalps taken in battle. It is not unlike the return of a victorious army from the field, with the prisoners and *colours*, taken from the enemy, but the appearance is far more frightful and terrific. The scalps are carried in front, fixed on the end of a thin pole, about five or six inches[192] in length; the prisoners follow, and the warriors advance shouting the dreadful *scalp-yell*, which has been called by some the *death-halloo*, but improperly, for the reasons which I have already mentioned. For every *head* taken, dead or alive, a separate shout is given. In this yell or whoop, there is a mixture of triumph and terror; its elements, if I may so speak, seem to be *glory* and *fear*, so as to express at once the feelings of the shouting warriors, and those with which they have inspired their enemies.

Different from this yell is the *alarm-whoop*, which is never sounded but when danger is at hand. It is performed in quick succession, much as with us the repeated cry of *Fire! Fire!* when the alarm is very great and lives are known or believed to be in danger. Both this and the scalp-yell consist of the sounds *aw* and *oh*, successively uttered, the last more accented, and sounded higher than the first; but in the *scalp-yell*, this last sound is drawn out at great length, as long indeed as the breath will hold, and is raised about an octave higher than the former; while in the *alarm-whoop*, it is rapidly struck on as it were, and only a few notes above the other. These yells or whoops are dreadful indeed, and well calculated to strike with terror, those whom long habit has not accustomed to them. It is difficult to describe the impression which the *scalp-yell*, particularly, makes on a person who hears it for the first time.

I am now come to a painful part of my subject; the manner in which the Indians treat the prisoners whom they take in war. It must not be expected that I shall describe here the long protracted tortures which are inflicted on those who are doomed to the fatal pile, nor the constancy and firmness which the sufferers display, singing their death songs and scoffing all the while at their tormentors. Enough of other writers have painted these scenes, with all their disgusting horrors; nor shall I, a Christian, endeavour to excuse or palliate them. But I may be permitted to say, that those dreadful executions are by no means so frequent as is commonly imagined. The prisoners are generally adopted by the families of their conquerors in the place of lost or deceased relations or friends, where they soon become domesticated, and are so kindly treated that they never wish themselves away again. I have seen even white men, who, after such adoption, were given up by the Indians in compliance with the stipulations of treaties, take the first opportunity to escape from their own country and return with all possible speed to their Indian homes; I have seen the Indians, while about delivering

163

them up, put them at night in the stocks, to prevent their escaping and running back to them.

It is but seldom that prisoners are put to death by burning and torturing. It hardly ever takes place except when a nation has suffered great losses in war, and it is thought necessary to revenge the death of their warriors slain in battle, or when wilful and deliberate murders have been committed by an enemy of[193] their innocent women and children, in which case the first prisoners taken are almost sure of being sacrificed by way of retaliation. But when a war has been successful, or unattended with remarkable acts of treachery, or cruelty on the part of the enemy, the prisoners receive a milder treatment, and are incorporated with the nation of their conquerors.

Much has been said on the subject of the preliminary cruelties inflicted on prisoners when they enter an Indian village with the conquering warriors. It is certain that this treatment is very severe when a particular revenge is to be exercised, but otherwise, I can say with truth, that in many instances, it is rather a scene of amusement, than a punishment. Much depends on the courage and presence of mind of the prisoner. On entering the village, he is shewn a painted post at the distance of from twenty to forty yards, and told to run to it and catch hold of it as quickly as he can. On each side of him stand men, women and children, with axes, sticks, and other offensive weapons, ready to strike him as he runs, in the same manner as is done in the European armies when soldiers, as it is called, run the gauntlet. If he should be so unlucky as to fall in the way, he will probably be immediately despatched by some person, longing to avenge the death of some relation or friend slain in battle; but the moment he reaches the goal, he is safe and protected from further insult until his fate is determined.

If a prisoner in such a situation shews a determined courage, and when bid to run for the painted post, starts at once with all his might and exerts all his strength and agility until he reaches it, he will most commonly escape without much harm, and sometimes without any injury whatever, and on reaching the desired point, he will have the satisfaction to hear his courage and bravery applauded. But woe to the coward who hesitates, or shews any symptoms of fear! He is treated without much mercy, and is happy, at last, if he escapes with his life.

In the month of April 1782, when I was myself a prisoner at Lower Sandusky, waiting for an opportunity to proceed with a trader to Detroit, I witnessed a scene of this description which fully exemplified what I have above stated. Three American prisoners were one day brought in by fourteen warriors from the garrison of Fort M'Intosh. As soon as they had crossed the Sandusky river, to which the village lay adjacent, they were told by the Captain of the party to run as hard as they could to a painted post which was shewn to them. The youngest of the three, without a moment's hesitation, immediately started for it, and reached it fortunately without receiving a single blow; the second hesitated for a moment, but recollecting himself, he also ran as fast as he could and likewise reached the post unhurt; but the third, frightened at seeing so many men, women and children with weapons in their hands, ready to strike him, kept begging the Captain to spare his life, saying he was a mason, and he would build him a fine large stone house, or do any work for him that he should please. "Run for your life," cried the chief to him, "and don't talk now of building houses!" But the poor fellow still insisted, begging and praying to the Captain, who, at last finding his exhortations vain, and fearing the consequences, turned his back upon him, and would not hear him any longer. Our mason now began to run, but received many a hard blow, one of which nearly brought him to the ground, which, if he had fallen, would at once have decided his fate. He, however, reached the goal, not without being sadly bruised, and he was besides bitterly reproached and scoffed at all round as a vile coward, while the others were hailed as brave men, and received tokens of universal approbation.

CHAPTER 28 ~

Bodily constitutions and diseases

The Indians are in general a strong race of men. It is very common to see a hunter come in with a whole deer on his back, fastened with a *Happis*, a kind of band with which they carry loads; it rests against the breast, that which the women use rests against the forehead. In this manner they will carry a load which many a white man would not have strength enough to raise from the ground. An Indian, named Samuel, once took the flour which was ground out of a bushel of wheat upon his back at sun-rise within two miles from Nazareth, and arrived with it in the evening of the same day at his camp at Wyoming. When the Indians build houses, they carry large logs on their shoulders from the place where the tree is cut down to where they are building.

Nevertheless, when put to agricultural or other manual labour, the Indians do not appear so strong as the whites; at least, they cannot endure it so long. Many reasons may be given for this, besides their not being accustomed to that kind of work. It is probably in part to be ascribed to their want of substantial food, and their intemperate manner of living; eating, when they have it, to excess, and at other times being days and weeks in a state of want. Those who have been brought up to regular labour, like ourselves, become robust and strong and enjoy good health. Such was the case with the Christian Indians in the Moravian settlements.

So late as about the middle of the last century, the Indians were yet a hardy and healthy people, and many very aged men and women were seen among them, some of whom thought they had lived about one hundred years. They frequently told me and others that when they were young men, their people did not marry so early as they did since, that even at twenty they were called boys and durst not wear a breech-cloth, as the men did at that time, but had only a small bit of a skin hanging before them.

Neither, did they say, were they subject to so many disorders as in later times, and many of them calculated on dying of old age. But since that time a great change has taken place in the constitution of those Indians who live nearest to the whites. By the introduction of ardent spirits among them, they have been led into vices which have brought on disorders which they say were unknown before; their blood became corrupted by a shameful complaint, which the Europeans pretend to have received from the original inhabitants of America, while these say they had never known or heard of it until the Europeans came among them. Now the Indians are infected with it to a great degree; children frequently inherit it from their parents, and after lingering for a few years at last die victims to this poison.

Those Indians who have not adopted the vices of the white people live to a good age, from 70 to 90. Few arrive at the age of one hundred years. The women, in general, live longer than the men.

The Indians do not appear to be more or less exempt than the whites from the common infirmities of old age. I have known old men among them who had lost their memory, their sight, and their teeth. I have also seen them at eighty in their second childhood and not able to help themselves.

The Indian women are not in general so prolific as those of the white race. I imagine this defect is owing to the vicious and dissolute life they lead since the introduction of spirituous liquors. Among our Christian Indians, we have had a couple who had been converted for thirty years and had always led a regular life, and who had thirteen children. Others had from six to nine. In general, however, the Indians seldom have more than four or five children.

The Indian children, generally, continue two years at the breast, and there are instances of their sucking during four years. Mothers are very apt to indulge their last child; children in this respect enjoy the same privilege alike.

I have never heard of any nation or tribe of Indians who destroyed their children, when distorted or deformed, whether they were so born or came to be so afterwards. I have on the contrary seen very particular care taken of such children. Nor have I ever been acquainted with any Indians that made use of artificial means to compress or alter the natural shape of the heads of their children, as some travellers have, I believe, pretended.

The disorders to which the Indians are most commonly subjected are pulmonary consumptions, fluxes, fevers and severe rheumatisms, all proceeding probably from the kind of life they lead, the hardships they undergo, and the nature of the food that they take. Intermitting and bilious fevers set in among them regularly in the autumn, when their towns are situated near marshy grounds or ponds of stagnant water, and many die in consequence of them. I have observed that these fevers generally make their first appearance in the season of the wild plum, a fruit that the Indians are particularly fond of. Sometimes also after a famine or long suffering for want of food, when they generally make too free an use of green maize, squashes and other watery vegetables. They are also subject to a disease which they call the *yellow vomit*, which, at times, carries off many of them. They generally die of this disease on the second or third day after the first attack.

Their old men are very subject to rheumatisms in the back and knees; I have known them at the age of 50 or 60 to be laid up for weeks and months at a time on this account, and I have seen boys 10 and 12 years of age, who through colds or fits of sickness had become so contracted that they never afterwards recovered the use of their limbs.

Worms are a very common disorder among Indian children, and great numbers of them die from that cause. They eat a great deal of green corn when in the milk, with beans, squashes, melons, and the like; their bellies become remarkably large, and it is probably in that manner that the worms are generated. I rather think that Indian children suffer less in teething than the whites.

The gout, gravel, and scrofula or king's evil, are not known among the Indians. Nor have I ever known any one that had the disorder called the *Rickets*. Consumptions are very frequent among them since they have become fond of spirituous liquors, and their young men in great numbers fall victims to that complaint. A person who resides among them may easily observe the frightful decrease of their numbers from one period of ten years to another. Our vices have destroyed them more than our swords.

CHAPTER 29 ~
Remedies

The *Materia Medica* of the Indians consists of various roots and plants known to themselves, the properties of which they are not fond of disclosing to strangers. They make considerable use of the barks of trees, such as the white and black oak, the white walnut, of which they make pills, the cherry, dogwood, maple, birch, and several others. They prepare and compound these medicines in different ways, which they keep a profound secret. Those preparations are frequently mixed with superstitious practices, calculated to guard against the powers of witchcraft, in which, unfortunately, they have a strong fixed belief. Indeed, they are too apt to attribute the most natural deaths to the arts and incantations of sorcerers, and their medicine is, in most cases, as much directed against those as against the disease itself. There are, however, practitioners among them who are free from these prejudices, or at least do not introduce them into their practice of the medical art. Still there is a superstitious notion, in which all their physicians participate, which is, that when an emetic is to be administered, the water in which the potion is mixed must be drawn up a stream, and if for a cathartic downwards. This is, at least, innocent, and not more whimsical perhaps, nor more calculated to excite a smile, than some theories of grave and learned men in civilised countries.

In fevers the Indians usually administer emetics which are made up and compounded in various ways. I saw an emetic once given to a man who had poisoned himself with the root of the May Apple.[194] It consisted of a piece of raccoon skin burned with the hair on and finely powdered, pounded dry beans and gunpowder. These three ingredients were mixed with water and poured down the patient's throat. This brought on a severe vomiting, the poisonous root was entirely discharged and the man cured.

In other complaints, particularly in those which proceed from rheumatic affections, bleeding and sweating are always the first remedies applied. The sweat oven is the first thing that an Indian has recourse to when he feels the least indisposed; it is the place

170

to which the wearied traveller, hunter, or warrior looks for relief from the fatigues he has endured, the cold he has caught, or the restoration of his lost appetite.

This oven is made of different sizes, so as to accommodate from two to six persons at a time, or according to the number of men in the village, so that they may be all successively served. It is generally built on a bank or slope, one half of it within and the other above ground. It is well covered on the top with split plank and earth, and has a door in front, where the ground is level to go or rather to creep in. Here, on the outside, stones, generally of about the size of a large turnip, are heated by one or more men appointed each day for that purpose. While the oven is heating, decoctions from roots or plants are prepared either by the person himself who intends to sweat, or by one of the men of the village, who boils a large kettleful for the general use, so that when the public cryer going his rounds, calls out *Pimook!* "go to sweat!" every one brings his small kettle, which is filled for him with the potion, which at the same time serves him as a medicine, promotes a profuse perspiration, and quenches his thirst.

As soon as a sufficient number have come to the oven, a number of the hot stones are rolled into the middle of it, and the sweaters go in, seating themselves or rather squatting round those stones, and there they remain until the sweat ceases to flow; then they come out, throwing a blanket or two about them that they may not catch cold; in the mean while, fresh heated stones are thrown in for those who follow them. While they are in the oven, water is now and then poured on the hot stones to produce a steam, which they say, increases the heat, and gives suppleness to their limbs and joints. In rheumatic complaints, the steam is produced by a decoction of boiled roots, and the patient during the operation is well wrapped up in blankets, to keep the cold air from him, and promote perspiration at the same time.

Those sweat ovens are generally at some distance from an Indian village, where wood and water are always at hand. The best order is preserved at those places. The women have their separate oven in a different direction from that of the men, and subjected to the same rules. The men generally sweat themselves once and sometimes twice a week; the women have no fixed day for this exercise, nor do they use it as often as the men.

In the year 1784,[195] a gentleman whom I had been acquainted with at Detroit, and who had been for a long time in an infirm state of health, came from thence to the village of the Christian Indians on the Huron river, in order to have the benefit of the sweat oven. It being in the middle of winter, when there was a deep snow on the ground, and the weather was excessively cold, I advised him to postpone his sweating to a warmer season; but he persisting in his resolution, I advised him by no means to remain in the oven longer than fifteen or at most twenty minutes. But when he once was in it, feeling himself comfortable, he remained a full hour, at the end of which he fainted, and was brought by two strong Indians to my house, in very great pain and not able to walk.

He remained with me until the next day, when we took him down in his sleigh to his family at Detroit. His situation was truly deplorable; his physicians at that place gave up all hopes of his recovery, and he frequently expressed his regret that he had not followed my advice. Suddenly, however, a change took place for the better, and he not only recovered his perfect health, but became a stout corpulent man, so that he would often say, that his going into the sweat oven was the best thing he had ever done in his life for the benefit of his health. He said so to me fifteen years afterwards when I saw him in the year 1798. He had not had the least indisposition since that time. He died about the year 1814, at an advanced age.

CHAPTER 30 ~
Physicians and surgeons

By these names I mean to distinguish the good and honest practitioners who are in the habit of curing and healing diseases and wounds, by the simple application of natural remedies, without any mixture of superstition in the manner of preparing or administering them. They are very different from the doctors or jugglers, of whom I shall speak in the next chapter. In one point, only, they seem to participate in their ridiculous notions, that is, in the different manner, which I have already noticed, of drawing water up or down the current of a stream, as it is to be respectively employed as a vehicle for an emetic or a cathartic. This singular idea prevails generally among the Indians of all classes. They think that as the one remedy is to work upwards and the other downwards, care should be taken in the preparation to follow the course of nature, so that no confusion should take place in the stomach or bowels of the patient.

With this only exception the Indian physicians are perhaps more free from fanciful theories than those of any other nation upon earth. Their science is entirely founded on observation, experience and the well tried efficacy of remedies. There are physicians of both sexes, who take considerable pains to acquire a correct knowledge of the properties and medical virtues of plants, roots and barks, for the benefit of their fellow-men. They are very careful to have at all times a full assortment of their medicines on hand, which they gather and collect at the proper seasons, sometimes fetching them from the distance of several days' journey from their homes, then they cure or dry them properly, tie them up in small bundles, and preserve them for use. It were to be wished that they were better skilled in the quantity of the medicines which they administer. But they are too apt, in general, to give excessive doses, on the mistaken principle that "*much* of a *good* thing must necessarily do *much good*."

Nevertheless, I must say, that their practice in general succeeds pretty well. I have myself been benefited and cured by taking their emetics and their medicines in fevers, and by being sweated after their manner while labouring under a stubborn rheumatism. I have also known many, both whites and Indians, who have with the same success resorted to Indian physicians while labouring under diseases. The wives of Missionaries, in every instance in which they had to apply to the female physicians, for the cure of complaints peculiar to their sex, experienced good results from their abilities. They are also well skilled in curing wounds and bruises.

I once for two days and two nights, suffered the most excruciating pain from a felon or whitlow on one of my fingers, which deprived me entirely of sleep. I had recourse to an Indian woman, who in less than half an hour relieved me entirely by the simple application of a poultice made of the root of the common blue violet.

Indeed, it is in the cure of external wounds that they particularly excel. Not only their professional men and women, but every warrior is more or less acquainted with the healing properties of roots and plants, which is, in a manner, indispensable to them, as they are so often in danger of being wounded in their engagements with the enemy. Hence this branch of knowledge is carried to a great degree of perfection among them.

I firmly believe that there is no wound, unless it should be absolutely mortal, or beyond the skill of our own good practitioners, which an Indian surgeon (I mean the best of them) will not succeed in healing. I once knew a noted Shawano, who having, out of friendship, conducted several white traders in safety to Pittsburgh, while they were sought for by other Indians who wanted to revenge on them the murders committed by white men of some of their people, was on his return fired at by some white villains, who had waylaid him for that purpose, and shot in the breast. This man, when I saw him, had already travelled eighty miles, with a wound from which blood and a kind of watery froth issued every time he breathed. Yet he told me he

174

was sure of being cured, if he could only reach *Waketemeki*, a place fifty miles distant, where there were several eminent Indian surgeons. To me and others who examined the wound, it appeared incurable; nevertheless, he reached the place and was perfectly cured. I saw him at Detroit ten years afterwards; he was in sound health and grown to be a corpulent man. Nine years after this I dined with him at the same place.

CHAPTER 31 ~
Doctors or jugglers

I call these men *Doctors*, because it is the name given them by their countrymen who have borrowed it from our language,[196] and they are themselves very fond of this pompous title. They are a set of professional impostors, who, availing themselves of the superstitious prejudices of the people, acquire the name and reputation of men of superior knowledge, and possessed of supernatural powers. As the Indians in general believe in witchcraft, and ascribe, as I have already said, to the arts of sorcerers many of the disorders with which they are afflicted in the regular course of nature, this class of men has risen among them, who pretend to be skilled in a certain occult science, by means of which they are able not only to cure natural diseases, but to counteract or destroy the enchantments of wizards or witches, and expel evil spirits.

These men are physicians, like the others of whom I have spoken, and like them are acquainted with the properties and virtues of plants, barks, roots, and other remedies. They differ from them only by their pretensions to a superior knowledge, and by the impudence with which they impose upon the credulous. I am sorry that truth obliges me to confess, that in their profession they rank above the honest practitioners. They pretend that there are disorders which cannot be cured by the ordinary remedies, and to the treatment of which the talents of common physicians are inadequate. They say that when a complaint has been brought on by witchcraft, more powerful remedies must be applied, and measures must be taken to defeat the designs of the person who bewitched the unfortunate patient. This can only be done by removing or destroying the deleterious or deadening substance which has been conveyed into them, or, if it is an evil spirit, to confine or expel him, or banish him to a distant region from whence he may never return.

When the juggler has succeeded in persuading his patient that his disorder is such that no common physician has it in his power to relieve, he will next endeavour to convince him of the necessity of making him *very strong*, which means, giving him a *large fee*, which he will say, is justly due to a man who, like himself, is able to perform such difficult things. If the patient who applies, is rich, the *Doctor* will never fail, whatever the complaint may be, to ascribe it to the powers of witchcraft, and recommend himself as the only person capable of giving relief in such a hard and complicated case. The poor patient, therefore, if he will have the benefit of the great man's advice and assistance, must immediately give him his *honorarium*, which is commonly either a fine horse, or a good rifle-gun, a considerable quantity of wampum, or goods to a handsome amount.

When this fee is well secured, and not before, the Doctor prepares for the hard task that he has undertaken, with as much apparent labour as if he was about to remove a mountain. He casts his eyes all round him to attract notice, puts on grave and important looks, appears wrapt in thought and meditation and enjoys for a while the admiration of the spectators. At last he begins his operation. Attired in a frightful dress, he approaches his patient, with a variety of contortions and gestures, and performs by his side and over him all the antic tricks that his imagination can suggest. He breathes on him, blows in his mouth, and squirts some medicines which he has prepared in his face, mouth and nose; he rattles his gourd filled with dry beans or pebbles, pulls out and handles about a variety of sticks and bundles in which he appears to be seeking for the proper remedy, all which is accompanied with the most horrid gesticulations, by which he endeavours, as he says, to frighten the spirit or the disorder away, and continues in this manner until he is quite exhausted and out of breath, when he retires to wait the issue.

The visits of the juggler are, if the patient requires it, repeated from time to time; not, however, without his giving a fresh fee previous to each visit. This continues until the property of the patient is entirely exhausted, or until he resolves upon calling in another doctor, with whom feeing must begin anew in the same manner that it did with his predecessor.

When at length the art of the juggling tribe has after repeated trials proved ineffectual, the patient is declared *incurable*. The doctors will say, that he applied to them too late, that he did not exactly follow their prescriptions, or sometimes, that he was bewitched by one of the greatest masters of the science, and that unless a professor can be found possessed of superior knowledge, he is doomed to die or linger in pain beyond the power of relief.

Thus these jugglers carry on their deceit, and enrich themselves at the expense of the credulous and foolish. I have known instances in which they declared a patient perfectly cured and out of all danger, who nevertheless died of his disorder a very few days afterwards, although his doctors affirmed that the evil spirit or the effects of witchcraft were entirely removed from him; on the other hand, I have seen cases in which the patient recovered after being pronounced incurable and condemned to die. In those cases, however, he had had the good sense to apply to some of the honest physicians of one or the other sex, who had relieved him by a successful application of their medicines.

The jugglers' dress, when in the exercise of their functions, exhibits a most frightful sight. I had no idea of the importance of these men, until by accident I met with one, habited in his full costume. As I was once walking through the street of a large Indian village on the Muskingum, with the chief *Gelelemend*,[197] whom we call *Kill-buck*, one of those monsters suddenly came out of the house next to me, at whose sight I was so frightened, that I flew immediately to the other side of the chief, who observing my agitation and the quick strides I made, asked me what was the matter, and what I thought it was that I saw before me. "By its outward appearance," answered I, "I would think it a bear, or some such ferocious animal, what is *inside* I do not know, but rather judge it to be the *Evil Spirit*." My friend Kill-buck smiled, and replied, "O! no, no; don't believe that! it is a man you well know, it is our *Doctor*." "A Doctor!" said I, "what! a human being to transform himself so as to be taken for a bear walking on his hind legs, and with horns on his head? You will not, surely, deceive me; if it is not a bear, it must be some other ferocious animal that I have never seen before."

The juggler within the dress hearing what passed between us, began to act over some of his curious pranks, probably intending to divert me, as he saw I was looking at him with great amazement, not unmixed with fear; but the more he went on with his performance, the more I was at a loss to decide, whether he was a human being or a bear; for he imitated that animal in the greatest perfection, walking upright on his hind legs as I had often seen it do. At last I renewed my questions to the chief, and begged him seriously to tell me what that figure was, and he assured me that although outside it had the appearance of a bear, yet inside there was a man, and that it was our doctor going to visit one of his patients who was bewitched. A dialogue then ensued between us, which I shall relate, as well as I can recollect it, in its very words:

HECKEW. *But why does he go dressed in that manner? Won't his patient be frightened to death on seeing him enter the house?*

KILLB. *No! indeed, no; it is the disorder, the evil spirit, that will be frightened away; as to the sick man, he well knows that unless the doctor has recourse to the most powerful means, he cannot be relieved, but must fall a sacrifice to the wicked will of some evil person. And, pray, don't your doctors in obstinate and dubious cases, also recur to powerful means in order to relieve their patients?*

HECKEW. *To my knowledge, there are no cases where witchcraft is assigned as the cause of a disorder, of course our doctors have nothing to do with that; and though they may sometimes have occasion to apply powerful remedies in obstinate diseases, yet it is not done by dressing themselves like wild beasts, to frighten, as you say, the disorder away. Were our doctors to adopt this mode, they would soon be left without patients and without bread; they would starve.*

KILLB. *Our doctors are the richest people among us, they have everything they want; fine horses to ride, fine clothes to wear, plenty of strings and belts of wampum, and silver arm and breast plates in abundance.*

HECKEW. *And* our *doctors have very fine horses and carriages, fine houses, fine clothes, plenty of good provisions and wines, and plenty of money besides! They are looked upon as gentlemen, and would not suffer your doctor, dressed as he is, to come into their company.*

KILLB. *You must, my friend! consider that the cases are very different. Had the white people sorcerers among them as the Indians have, they would find it necessary to adopt our practice and apply our remedies in the same manner that our doctors do. They would find it necessary to take strong measures to counteract and destroy the dreadful effects of witchcraft.*

HECKEW. *The sorcerers that you speak of exist only in your imagination; rid yourselves of this, and you will hear no more of them.*

The dress this juggler had on, consisted of an entire garment or outside covering, made of one or more bear skins, as black as jet, so well fitted and sewed together, that the man was not in any place to be perceived. The whole head of the bear, including the mouth, nose, teeth, ears, &c., appeared the same as when the animal was living; so did the legs with long claws; to this were added a huge pair of horns on the head, and behind a large bushy tail, moving as he walked, as though it were on springs; but for these accompaniments, the man, walking on all fours, might have been taken for a bear of an extraordinary size. Underneath, where his hands were, holes had been cut, though not visible to the eye, being covered with the long hair, through which he held and managed his implements, and he saw through two holes set with glass. The whole was a great curiosity, but not to be looked at by everybody.

There are jugglers of another kind, in general old men and women, who although not classed among doctors or physicians, yet get their living by pretending to supernatural knowledge. Some pretend that they can bring down rain in dry weather when wanted, others prepare ingredients, which they sell to bad hunters, that they may have good luck, and others make philters or love potions for such married persons as either do not, or think they cannot love each other.

When one of these jugglers is applied to bring down rain in a dry season, he must in the first instance receive a fee. This fee is made up by the women, who, as cultivators of the land are supposed to be most interested, but the men will slily slip something in their hands in aid of their collection, which consists of wampum beads, tobacco, silver broaches, and a dressed deer skin to make shoes of. If the juggler does not succeed in his experiment, he never is in want of an excuse; either the winds are in opposition to one another, the dry wind or air is too powerful for the moist or south wind, or he has not been made *strong enough*, (that is sufficiently paid,) to compel the north to give way to the south from whence the rain is to come, or lastly, he wants time to invoke the great Spirit to aid him on the important occasion.

In the summer of the year 1799, a most uncommon drouth happened in the Muskingum country, so that every thing growing, even the grass and the leaves of the trees, appeared perishing; an old man named *Chenos*, who was born on the river Delaware, was applied to by the women to bring down rain, and was well feed for the purpose. Having failed in his first attempt, he was feed a second time, and it happened that one morning, when my business obliged me to pass by the place where he was at work, as I knew him very well, I asked him at once what he was doing? "I am hired," said he, "to do a very hard day's work."

Q. And, pray, what work?

A. Why, to bring down rain from the sky.

Q. Who hired you to do that?

A. The women of the village; don't you see how much rain is wanted, and that the corn and every thing else is perishing?

Q. But can you make it rain?

181

A. I can, and you shall be convinced of it this very day.

He had, by this time, encompassed a square of about five feet each way, with stakes and barks so that it might resemble a pig pen of about three feet in height, and now, with his face uplifted and turned towards the north, he muttered something, then closely shutting up with bark the opening which had been left on the north side, he turned in the same manner, still muttering some words, towards the south, as if invoking some superior being, and having cut through the bark on the southwest corner, so as to make an opening of two feet, he said: "now we shall have rain enough!" Hearing down the river the sound of setting poles striking against a canoe, he enquired of me what it was? I told him it was our Indians going up the river to make a bush net for fishing. "Send them home again!" said he, "tell them that this will not be a fit day for fishing!"

I told him to let them come on and speak to them himself, if he pleased. He did so, and as soon as they came near him, he told them that they must by no means think of fishing that day, for there should come a heavy rain which would wet them all through. "No matter, Father!" answered they in a jocular manner, "give us only rain and we will cheerfully bear the soaking." They then passed on, and I proceeded to *Goschachking*, the village to which I was going.[198] I mentioned the circumstance to the chief of the place, and told him that I thought it impossible that we should have rain while the sky was so clear as it then was and had been for near five weeks together, without its being previously announced by some signs or change in the atmosphere. But the chief answered: "*Chenos* knows very well what he is about; he can at any time predict what the weather will be; he takes his observations morning and evening from the river or something in it." On my return from this place after three o'clock in the afternoon, the sky still continued the same until about four o'clock, when all at once the horizon became overcast, and without any thunder or wind it began to rain, and continued so for several hours together, until the ground became thoroughly soaked.

I am of the opinion that this man, like others whom I have known, was a strict observer of the weather, and that his prediction that day was made in consequence of his having observed some signs in the sky or in the water, which his experience had taught him to be the forerunners of rain; yet the credulous multitude did not fail to ascribe it to his supernatural power.

The ingredients for a bad hunter, to make him have good luck, are tied up in a bit of cloth, and must be worn near his skin while he is hunting. The preparations intended to create love between man and wife, are to be slily conveyed to the frigid party by means of his victuals or drink.

CHAPTER 32 ~
Superstition

Great and powerful as the Indian conceives himself to be, firm and undaunted as he really is, braving all seasons and weathers, careless of dangers, patient of hunger, thirst and cold, and fond of displaying the native energy of his character even in the midst of tortures, at the very thought of which our own puny nature revolts and shudders; this Lord of the Creation, whose life is spent in a state of constant warfare against the wild beasts of the forest and the savages of the wilderness, who, proud of his independent existence, strikes his breast with exultation and exclaims "*I am a man!*"—the American Indian has one weak side, which sinks him down to the level of the most fearful and timid being, a childish apprehension of an occult and unknown power, which, unless he can summon sufficient fortitude to conquer it, changes at once the hero into a coward.

It is incredible to what a degree the Indians' superstitious belief in witchcraft operates upon their minds; the moment that their imagination is struck with the idea that they are bewitched, they are no longer themselves; their fancy is constantly at work in creating the most horrid and distressing images. They see themselves falling a sacrifice to the wicked arts of a vile unknown hand, of one who would not have dared to face them in fair combat; dying a miserable, ignominious death; a death, to which they would a thousand times prefer the stake with all its horrors. No tale, no tradition, no memorial of their courage or heroic fortitude will go down with it to posterity; it will be thought that they were not deserving of a better fate. And, (O! dreadful thought to an Indian mind!) that death is to remain forever unrevenged;—their friends, their relations, the men of their own tribe, will seek the murderer in vain; they will seek him while, perhaps, he is in the midst of them, unnoticed and unknown, smiling at their impotent rage, and calmly selecting some new victim to his infernal art.

184

Of this extraordinary power of their conjurers, of the causes which produce it, and the manner in which it is acquired, the Indians as may well be supposed, have not a very definite idea. All they can say is that the sorcerer makes use of a "deadening substance," which he discharges and conveys to the person that he means to "*strike*," through the air, by means of the wind or of his own breath, or throws at him in a manner which they can neither understand nor describe. The person thus "*stricken*," is immediately seized with an unaccountable terror, his spirits sink, his appetite fails, he is disturbed in his sleep, he pines and wastes away, or a fit of sickness seizes him, and he dies at last a miserable victim to the workings of his own imagination.

Such are their ideas and the melancholy effects of the dread they feel of that supernatural power which they vainly fancy to exist among them. That they can destroy one another by means of poisonous roots and plants, is certainly true, but in this there is no witchcraft. This prejudice that they labour under can be ascribed to no other cause than their excessive ignorance and credulity. I was once acquainted with a white man, a shrewd and correct observer, who had lived long among the Indians, and being himself related to an Indian family, had the best opportunities of obtaining accurate information on this subject.

He told me that he had found the means of getting into the confidence of one of their most noted sorcerers, who had frankly confessed to him, that his secret consisted in exciting fear and suspicion, and creating in the multitude a strong belief in his magical powers, "For," said he, "such is the credulity of many, that if I only pick a little wool from my blanket, and roll it between my fingers into a small round ball, not larger than a bean, I am by that alone believed to be deeply skilled in the magic art, and it is immediately supposed that I am preparing the deadly substance with which I mean to strike some person or other, although I hardly know myself at the time what my fingers are doing; and if, at that moment, I happen to cast my eyes on a particular man, or even throw a side glance at him, it is enough to make him consider himself as the intended victim; he is from that instant effectually *struck*, and if he is not possessed of great fortitude, so as to be able to repel the thought, and divert his

185

mind from it, or to persuade himself that it is nothing but the work of a disturbed imagination, he will sink under the terror thus created, and at last perish a victim, not indeed, to witchcraft, but to his own credulity and folly."

But men of such strong minds are not often to be found; so deeply rooted is the belief of the Indians in those fancied supernatural powers. It is vain to endeavour to convince them by argument that they are entirely founded in delusion and have no real existence. The attempt has been frequently made by sensible white men, but always without success. The following anecdote will shew how little hope there is of ever bringing them to a more rational way of thinking.

Sometime about the year 1776, a Quaker trader of the name of John Anderson, who among the Indians was called *the honest Quaker trader*, after vainly endeavouring to convince those people by argument that there was no such thing as witchcraft, took the bold, and I might say the rash, solution to put their sorcerers to the test, and defy the utmost exertions of their pretended supernatural powers. He desired that two of those magicians might be brought successively before him on different days, who should be at liberty to try their art on his person, and do him all the harm that they could by magical means, in the presence of the chiefs and principal men of the village. The Indians tried at first to dissuade him from so dangerous an experiment; but he persisted, and at last they acceded to his demand; a conjurer was brought to him, who professed himself fully competent to the task for which he was called, but he could not be persuaded to make the attempt.

He declared that Anderson was so good and so honest a man, so much his friend and the friend of all the Indians, that he could not think of doing him an injury. He never practised his art but on bad men and on those who had injured him; the great Mannitto forbid that he should use it for such a wicked purpose as that for which he was now called upon.

The Indians found this excuse perfectly good, and retired more convinced than ever of the abilities of their conjurer, whom they now revered for his conscientious scruples.

The one who was brought on the next day was of a different stamp. He was an arch sorcerer, whose fame was extended far and wide, and was much dreaded by the Indians, not only on account of his great powers, but of the wicked disposition of his mind. Every effort was made to dissuade Mr. Anderson from exposing himself to what was considered as certain destruction; but he stood firm to his purpose, and only stipulated that the magician should sit at the distance of about twelve feet from him; that he should not be armed with any weapon, nor carry any poison or any thing else of a known destructive nature, and that he should not even rise from his seat, nor advance towards him during the operation. All this was agreed to, the conjurer boasting that he could effect his purpose even at the distance of one hundred miles. The promised reward was brought and placed in full view, and both parties now prepared for the experiment.

The spectators being all assembled, the sorcerer took his seat, arrayed in the most frightful manner that he could devise. Anderson stood firm and composed before him at the stipulated distance. All were silent and attentive while the wizard began his terrible operation. He began with working with his fingers on his blanket, plucking now and then a little wool and breathing on it, then rolling it together in small rolls of the size of a bean, and went through all the antic tricks to which the power of bewitching is generally ascribed. But all this had no effect. Anderson remained cool and composed, now and then calling to his antagonist not to be sparing of his exertions.

The conjurer now began to make the most horrid gesticulations, and used all the means in his power to frighten the honest Quaker, who, aware of his purpose, still remained unmoved. At last, while the eyes of all the spectators were fixed on this brave man, to observe the effects of the sorcerer's craft upon him, this terrible conjurer, finding that all his efforts were in vain, found himself obliged to give up the point, and alleged for his excuse "that the Americans[199] eat too much salt provisions;

187

that salt had a repulsive effect, which made the powerful invisible substance that he employed recoil upon him; that the Indians, who eat but little salt, had often felt the effects of this substance, but that the great quantity of it which the white men used effectually protected them against it."

The imposition in this instance was perfectly clear and visible, and nothing was so easy as to see through this sorcerer's miserable pretence, and be convinced that his boasted art was entirely a deception; but it was not so with the Indians, who firmly believed that the salt which the Americans[199] used was the only cause of his failure in this instance, and that if it had not been for the salted meat which Mr. Anderson fed upon, he would have fallen a victim as well as others to the incantations of this impostor.

I have received this story from the mouth of Mr. Anderson himself, who was a most respectable gentleman, and also from several credible Indians who were present at the time. After this bold and unsuccessful experiment, it is impossible to expect that the superstitious notions of the Indians on the subject of witchcraft can ever by any means be rooted out of their minds.[200]

CHAPTER 33 ~
Initiation of boys

I do not know how to give a better name to a superstitious practice which is very common among the Indians, and, indeed, is universal among those nations that I have become acquainted with. By certain methods which I shall presently describe, they put the mind of a boy in a state of perturbation, so as to excite dreams and visions; by means of which they pretend that the boy receives instructions from certain spirits or unknown agents as to his conduct in life, that he is informed of his future destination and of the wonders he is to perform in his future career through the world.

When a boy is to be thus *initiated*, he is put under an alternate course of physic and fasting, either taking no food whatever, or swallowing the most powerful and nauseous medicines, and occasionally he is made to drink decoctions of an intoxicating nature, until his mind becomes sufficiently bewildered, so that he sees or fancies that he sees visions, and has extraordinary dreams, for which, of course, he has been prepared beforehand. He will fancy himself flying through the air, walking under ground, stepping from one ridge or hill to the other across the valley beneath, fighting and conquering giants and monsters, and defeating whole hosts by his single arm. Then he has interviews with the Mannitto or with spirits, who inform him of what he was before he was born and what he will be after his death. His fate in this life is laid entirely open before him, the spirit tells him what is to be his future employment, whether he will be a valiant warrior, a mighty hunter, a doctor, a conjurer, or a prophet. There are even those who learn or pretend to learn in this way the time and manner of their death.

When a boy has been thus initiated, a name is given to him analogous to the visions that he has seen, and to the destiny that is supposed to be prepared for him. The boy, imagining all that happened to him while under perturbation, to have been real, sets out in the world with lofty notions of himself, and animated with courage for the most desperate undertakings.

The belief in the truth of those visions is universal among the Indians. I have spoken with several of their old men, who had been highly distinguished for their valour, and asked them whether they ascribed their achievements to natural or supernatural causes, and they uniformly answered, that as they knew beforehand what they could do, they did it of course. When I carried my questions farther, and asked them how they knew what they could do? they never failed to refer to the dreams and visions which they had while under perturbation, in the manner I have above mentioned.

I always found it vain to attempt to undeceive them on this subject. They never were at a loss for examples to shew that the dreams they had had were not the work of a heated imagination, but that they came to them through the agency of a mannitto. They could always cite numerous instances of valiant men, who, in former times, in consequence of such dreams, had boldly attacked their enemy with nothing but the *Tamahican*[201] in their hand, had not looked about to survey the number of their opponents, but had gone straight forward, striking all down before them; some, they said, in the French wars, had entered houses of the English filled with people, who, before they had time to look about, were all killed and laid in a heap. Such was the strength, the power and the courage conveyed to them in their supernatural dreams, and which nothing could resist.

If they stopped here in their relations, I might, perhaps, consider this practice of putting boys under perturbation, as a kind of military school or exercise, intended to create in them a more than ordinary courage, and make them undaunted warriors. It certainly has this effect on some, who fancying themselves under the immediate protection of the celestial powers, despise all dangers, and really perform acts of astonishing bravery. But it must be observed, that all that are thus initiated are not designed for a military life, and that several learn by their dreams that they are to be physicians, sorcerers, or that their lives are to be devoted to some other civil employment. And it is astonishing what a number of superstitious notions are infused into the minds of the unsuspecting youth, by means of those dreams, which are useless, at least, for making good warriors or hunters. There are even some who by that means are taught to believe in the transmigration of souls.

I once took great pains to dissuade from these notions a very sensible Indian, much esteemed by all who knew him, even among the whites. All that I could say or urge was not able to convince him that at the time of his *initiation* (as I call it) his mind was in a state of temporary derangement. He declared that he had a clear recollection of the dreams and visions that had occurred to him at the time, and was sure that they came from the agency of celestial spirits. He asserted very strange things, of his own supernatural knowledge, which he had obtained not only at the time of his initiation, but at other times, even before he was born. He said he knew he had lived through two generations; that he had died twice and was born a third time, to live out the then present race, after which he was to die and never more to come to this country again. He well remembered what the women had predicted while he was yet in his mother's womb; some had foretold that he would be a boy, and others a girl; he had distinctly overheard their discourses, and could repeat correctly every thing that they had said. It would be too long to relate all the wild stories of the same kind which this otherwise intelligent Indian said of himself, with a tone and manner which indicated the most intimate conviction, and left no doubt in my mind that he did not mean to deceive others, but was himself deceived.

I have known several other Indians who firmly believed that they knew, by means of these visions, what was to become of them when they should die, how their souls were to retire from their bodies and take their abodes into those of infants yet unborn; in short, there is nothing so wild and so extraordinary that they will not imagine and to which, when once it has taken hold of their imagination, they will not give full credit. In this they are not a little aided by certain superstitious notions which form a part of their traditionary belief, and of which I shall take notice in the next chapter.

CHAPTER 34 ~
Indian mythology

The Indians consider the earth as their universal mother. They believe that they were created within its bosom, where for a long time they had their abode, before they came to live on its surface. They say that the great, good, and all powerful Spirit, when he created them, undoubtedly meant at a proper time to put them in the enjoyment of all the good things which he had prepared for them upon the earth, but he wisely ordained that their first stage of existence should be within it, as the infant is formed and takes its first growth in the womb of its natural mother. This fabulous account of the creation of man needs only to be ascribed to the ancient Egyptians or to the Brahmins of India, to be admired and extolled for the curious analogy which it observes between the general and individual creation; but as it comes from the American savage, I doubt whether it will even receive the humble praise of ingenuity, to which, however, it appears to me to be justly entitled.

The Indian Mythologists are not agreed as to the form under which they existed while in the bowels of the earth. Some assert that they lived there in the human shape, while others, with greater consistency contend that their existence was in the form of certain terrestrial animals, such as the ground-hog, the rabbit, and the tortoise. This was their state of preparation, until they were permitted to come out and take their station on this island[202] as the Lords of the rest of the Creation.

Among the Delawares, those of the *Minsi*, or Wolf tribe, say that in the beginning, they dwelt in the earth under a lake, and were fortunately extricated from this unpleasant abode by the discovery which one of their men made of a hole, through which he ascended to the surface; on which, as he was walking, he found a deer, which he carried back with him into his subterraneous habitation; that there the deer was killed,[203] and he and his companions found the meat so good, that they unanimously determined to leave their dark abode, and remove to a place where they could enjoy the light of heaven and have such excellent game in abundance.

The other two tribes, the *Unamis* or Tortoise, and the *Unalachtigos* or Turkey, have much similar notions, but reject the story of the lake, which seems peculiar to the Minsi tribe.

These notions must be very far extended among the Indians of North America generally, since we find that they prevail also among the Iroquois, a nation so opposed to the Delawares, as has been shewn in the former parts of this work, and whose language is so different from theirs, that not two words, perhaps, similar or even analogous of signification may be found alike in both. On this subject I beg leave to present an extract from the manuscript notes of the late Reverend Christopher Pyrlæus, whom I am always fond of quoting with respect, as he was a man of great truth, and besides well acquainted with the Six Nations and their idioms.[204] The account that he here gives of the traditions of that people concerning their original existence, was taken down by him in January 1743, from the mouth of a respectable Mohawk chief named *Sganarady*, who resided on the Mohawk river.251

THE EXTRACT.

"*Traditio.*—That they had dwelt in the earth where it was dark and where no sun did shine. That though they followed hunting, they ate mice, which they caught with their hands. That *Ganawagahha* (one of them) having accidentally found a hole to get out of the earth at, he went out, and that in walking about on the earth he found a deer, which he took back with him, and that both on account of the meat tasting so very good, and the favourable description he had given them of the country above and on the earth, their mother, concluded it best for them all to come out; that accordingly they did so, and immediately set about planting corn, &c. That, however, the *Nocharauorsul*, that is, the *ground-hog*, would not come out, but had remained in the ground as before."

So far Mr. Pyrlæus. From these traditions of the Iroquois, and those of the Delawares and Mohicans, it seems to follow that they must have considered their numbers very small, when they dwelt in the earth; perhaps, no more than one family of each tribe, and that the custom of giving to their tribes the names of particular animals, must have been very ancient. The *ground-hog*, say the Mohawks, would not come out. But who was this hog? Might it not formerly have been the name of one of their tribes, who was made the subject of this fable?

However ridiculous these stories are, the belief of the Indians in them is not to be shaken. When I was a boy between twelve and fifteen years of age, I had often heard of white people conversant with the Indians, who at that time would continually come to this place, (Bethlehem) in great numbers, even by hundreds, that the Indians did not eat rabbits, because they thought them infected with the venereal disease, and that whoever ate of their flesh, was sure to take that disorder. Being then myself fond of catching those animals in traps, I asked questions on this subject of several Mohican Indians, who spoke the German language; but though they said nothing about the disease that rabbits were said to be infected with, yet they advised me by no means to eat of their flesh. They gave me no reason whatever to induce me to abstain from this food; but afterwards, in the year 1762, when I resided at Tuscorawas on the Muskingum, I was told by some of them, that there were some animals which Indians did not eat, and among them were the *rabbit* and the *ground-hog*; for, said they, they did not know but that they might be *related* to them!

I found also that the Indians, for a similar reason, paid great respect to the rattle-snake, whom they called their *grandfather*, and would on no account destroy him. One day, as I was walking with an elderly Indian on the banks of the Muskingum, I saw a large rattle-snake lying across the path, which I was going to kill. The Indian immediately forbade my doing so; "for," said he, "the rattle-snake is grandfather to the Indians, and is placed here on purpose to guard us, and to give us notice of impending danger by his rattle, which is the same as if he were to tell us 'look about!' Now," added he, "if we were to kill one of those, the others would soon know it, and the whole race would rise upon us and bite us." I observed to him that the white people were not afraid of this; for they killed all the rattle-snakes that they met with. On this he enquired whether any white man had been bitten by these animals, and of course I answered in the affirmative. "No wonder, then!" replied he, "you have to blame yourselves for that! you did as much as declaring war against them, and you will find them in *your* country, where they will not fail to make frequent incursions. They are a very dangerous enemy; take care you do not irritate them in *our* country; they and their grandchildren are on good terms, and neither will hurt the other."

These ancient notions have, however in a great measure died away with the last generation, and the Indians at present kill their grandfather the rattle-snake without ceremony, whenever they meet with him.

That the Indians, from the earliest times, considered themselves in a manner connected with certain animals, is evident from various customs still preserved among them, and from the names of those animals which they have collectively, as well as individually, assumed. It might, indeed, be supposed that those animals' names which they have given to their several tribes were mere badges of distinction, or "coats of arms" as Pyrlæus calls them; but if we pay attention to the reasons which they give for those denominations, the idea of a supposed family connexion is easily discernible. The Tortoise, or as it is commonly called, the *Turtle* tribe, among the Lenape, claims a superiority and ascendency over the others, because their *relation*, the great Tortoise, a fabled monster, the Atlas of their mythology, bears according to their traditions this great *island* on his back, and also because he is amphibious, and can live both on land and in the water, which neither of the heads of the other tribes can do.

The merits of the *Turkey*, which gives its name to the second tribe, are that he is stationary, and always remains with or about them. As to the *Wolf*, after whom the third tribe is named, he is a rambler by nature, running from one place to another in quest of his prey; yet they consider him as their benefactor, as it was by his means that the Indians got out of the interior of the earth. It was he, they believe, who by the appointment of the Great Spirit, killed the deer whom the Monsey found who first discovered the way to the surface of the earth, and which allured them to come out of their damp and dark residence. For that reason, the wolf is to be honoured, and his name preserved for ever among them. Such are their traditions, as they were related to me by an old man of this tribe more than fifty years ago.

These animals' names, it is true, they all use as national badges, in order to distinguish their tribes from each other at home and abroad. In this point of view Mr. Pyrlæus was right in considering them as "coats of arms." The Turtle warrior draws either with a coal or paint here and there on the trees along the war path, the whole animal carrying a gun with the muzzle projecting forward, and if he leaves a mark at the place where he has made a stroke on his enemy, it will be the picture of a tortoise. Those of the Turkey tribe paint only one foot of a turkey, and the Wolf tribe, sometimes a wolf at large with one leg and foot raised up to serve as a hand, in which the animal also carries a gun with the muzzle forward. They, however, do not generally use the word "wolf," when speaking of their tribe, but call themselves *Pauk-sit*[205] which means *round-foot*, that animal having a round foot like a dog.

The Indians, in their hours of leisure, paint their different marks or badges on the doors of their respective houses, that those who pass by may know to which tribe the inhabitants belong. Those marks also serve them for signatures to treaties and other documents. They are as proud of their origin from the tortoise, the turkey, and the wolf, as the nobles of Europe are of their descent from the feudal barons of ancient times, and when children spring from intermarriages between different tribes, their genealogy is carefully preserved by tradition in the family, that they may know to which tribe they belong.

I have often reflected on the curious connexion which appears to subsist in the mind of an Indian between man and the brute creation, and found much matter in it for curious observation. Although they consider themselves superior to all other animals and are very proud of that superiority; although they believe that the beasts of the forest, the birds of the air, and the fishes of the waters, were created by the Almighty Being for the use of man; yet it seems as if they ascribe the difference between themselves and the brute kind, and the dominion which they have over them, more to their superior bodily strength and dexterity than to their immortal souls.

All beings endowed by the Creator with the power of volition and self-motion, they view in a manner as a great society of which they are the head, whom they are appointed, indeed, to govern, but between whom and themselves intimate ties of connexion and relationship may exist, or at least did exist in the beginning of time. They are, in fact, according to their opinions, only the first among equals, the legitimate hereditary sovereigns of the whole animated race, of which they are themselves a constituent part. Hence, in their languages, these inflections of their nouns which we call *genders*, are not, as with us, descriptive of the *masculine* and *feminine* species, but of the *animate* and *inanimate* kinds.

Indeed, they go so far as to include trees, and plants within the first of these descriptions. All animated nature, in whatever degree, is in their eyes a great whole, from which they have not yet ventured to separate themselves. They do not exclude other animals from their world of spirits, the place to which they expect to go after death.

I find it difficult to express myself clearly on this abstruse subject, which, perhaps, the Indians themselves do not very well understand, as they have no metaphysicians among them to analyse their vague notions, and perhaps confuse them still more. But I can illustrate what I have said by some characteristic anecdotes, with which I shall conclude this chapter.

I have already observed[206] that the Indian includes all savage beasts within the number of his *enemies*. This is by no means a metaphorical or figurative expression, but is used in a literal sense, as will appear from what I am going to relate.

A Delaware hunter once shot a huge bear and broke its backbone. The animal fell and set up a most plaintive cry, something like that of the panther when he is hungry. The hunter instead of giving him another shot, stood up close to him, and addressed him in these words: "Hark ye! bear; you are a coward, and no warrior as you pretend to be. Were you a warrior, you would shew it by your firmness and not cry and whimper like an old woman. You know, bear, that our tribes are at war with each other, and that yours was the aggressor.[207] You have found the Indians too powerful for you, and you have gone sneaking about in the woods, stealing their hogs; perhaps at this time you have hog's flesh in your belly. Had you conquered me, I would have borne it with courage and died like a brave warrior; but you, bear, sit here and cry, and disgrace your tribe by your cowardly conduct."

I was present at the delivery of this curious invective; when the hunter had despatched the bear, I asked him how he thought that poor animal could understand what he said to it? "Oh!" said he in answer, "the bear understood me very well; did you not observe how *ashamed* he looked while I was upbraiding him?"

Another time I witnessed a similar scene between the falls of the Ohio and the river Wabash. A young white man, named *William Wells*,[208] who had been when a boy taken prisoner by a tribe of the Wabash Indians, by whom he was brought up, and had imbibed all their notions, had so wounded a large bear that he could not move from the spot, and the animal cried piteously like the one I have just mentioned. The young man went up to him, and with seemingly great earnestness, addressed him in the Wabash language, now and then giving him a slight stroke on the nose with his ram-rod. I asked him, when he had done, what he had been saying to this bear? "I have," said he, "upbraided him for acting the part of a coward; I told him that he knew the fortune of war, that one or the other of us must have fallen; that it was his fate to be conquered, and he ought to die like a man, like a hero, and not like an old woman; that if the case had been reversed, and I had fallen into the power of *my enemy*, I

198

would not have disgraced my nation as he did, but would have died with firmness and courage, as becomes a true warrior."

I leave the reader to reflect upon these anecdotes, which, I think, convey more real information than any further attempts that I could make to explain the strange notions which gave them rise.

CHAPTER 35 ~
Insanity, suicide

Insanity is not common among the Indians; yet I have known several who were afflicted with mental derangement. Men in this situation are always considered as objects of pity. Every one, young and old, feels compassion for their misfortune; to laugh or scoff at them would be considered as a crime, much more so to insult or molest them. The nation or colour of the unfortunate object makes no difference; the charity of the Indians extends to all, and no discrimination is made in such a lamentable case.

About the commencement of the Indian war in 1763, a trading Jew, named Chapman, who was going up the Detroit river with a batteau-load of goods which he had brought from Albany, was taken by some Indians of the Chippeway nation, and destined to be put to death. A Frenchman, impelled by motives of friendship and humanity, found means to steal the prisoner, and kept him so concealed for some time, that although the most diligent search was made, the place of his confinement could not be discovered. At last, however, the unfortunate man was betrayed by some false friend, and again fell into the power of the Indians, who took him across the river to be burned and tortured.

Tied to the stake and the fire burning by his side, his thirst, from the great heat, became intolerable, and he begged that some drink might be given to him. It is a custom with the Indians, previous to a prisoner being put to death, to give him what they call his last meal; a bowl of pottage or broth was therefore brought to him for that purpose. Eager to quench his thirst, he put the bowl immediately to his lips, and the liquor being very hot, he was dreadfully scalded. Being a man of a very quick temper, the moment he felt his mouth burned, he threw the bowl with its contents full in the face of the man who had handed it to him. "He is mad! He is mad!" resounded from all quarters. The bystanders considered his conduct as an act of insanity, and immediately untied the cords with which he was bound, and let him go where he pleased.

This fact was well known to all the inhabitants of Detroit, from whom I first heard it, and it was afterwards confirmed to me by Mr. Chapman himself, who was established as a merchant at that place.

SUICIDE is not considered by the Indians either as an act of heroism or of cowardice, nor is it with them a subject of praise or blame. They view this desperate act as the consequence of mental derangement, and the person who destroys himself is to them an object of pity. Such cases do not frequently occur. Between the years 1771 and 1780, four Indians of my acquaintance took the root of the may-apple, which is commonly used on such occasions, in order to poison themselves, in which they all succeeded, except one. Two of them were young men, who had been disappointed in love, the girls on whom they had fixed their choice, and to whom they were engaged, having changed their minds and married other lovers. They both put an end to their existence. The two others were married men. Their stories, as pictures of Indian manners, will not, perhaps, be thought uninteresting.

One of those unfortunate men was a person of an excellent character, respected and esteemed by all who knew him. He had a wife whom he was very fond of and two children, and they lived very happily together at the distance of about half a mile from the place where I resided. He often came to visit me, and as he was of a most amiable disposition, I was pleased with his visits, and always gave him a hearty welcome. When I thought he was too long about coming, I went myself to the delightful spot which he had judiciously selected for his dwelling. Here I always found the family cheerful, sociable and happy, until some time before the fatal catastrophe happened, when I observed that my friend's countenance bore the marks of deep melancholy, of which I afterwards learned the cause.

His wife had received the visits of another man; he foresaw that he would soon be obliged to separate from her, and he shuddered when he thought that he must also part from his two

201

lovely children; for it is the custom of the Indians, that when a divorce takes place between husband and wife, the children remain with their mother, until they are of a proper age to choose for themselves. One hope, however, still remained. The sugar-making season was at hand, and they were shortly to remove to their sugar-camp, where he flattered himself his wife would not be followed by the disturber of his peace, whose residence was about ten miles from thence. But this hope was of short duration.

They had hardly been a fortnight in their new habitation, when, as he returned one day from a morning's hunt, he found the unwelcome visitor at his home, in close conversation with his faithless wife. This last stroke was more than he could bear; without saying a single word, he took off a large cake of his sugar, and with it came to my house, which was at the distance of eight miles from his temporary residence. It was on a Sunday, at about ten o'clock in the forenoon, that he entered my door, with sorrow strongly depicted on his manly countenance. As he came in he presented me with his cake of sugar, saying, "My friend! you have many a time served me with a good pipe of tobacco, and I have not yet done anything to please you. Take this as a reward for your goodness, and as an acknowledgment from me as your friend." He said no more, but giving me with both his hands a warm farewell squeeze, he departed and returned to the camp.

At about two o'clock in the afternoon, a runner from thence passing through the town to notify his death at the village two miles farther, informed us of the shocking event. He had immediately on his return, remained a short time in his house, indulging in the last caresses to his dear innocent children; then retiring to some distance, had eaten the fatal root, and before relief could be administered by some persons who had observed him staggering from the other side of the river, he was on the point of expiring, and all succours were vain.

The last whom I have to mention was also a married man, but had no children. He had lived happy with his wife, until one day that she fell into a passion and made use to him of such abusive language as he could not endure. Too highminded to quarrel with a woman, he resolved to punish her by putting an end to his existence. Fortunately he was seen in the first stage of his fits, and was brought into a house, where a strong emetic diluted in lukewarm water, the composition of which I have already described,[209] was forcibly poured down his throat. He recovered after some time, but never was again the strong healthy man he had been before; his wife however took warning from this desperate act, and behaved better ever after.

CHAPTER 36 ~
Drunkenness

In treating of this subject, I cannot resist the impression of a melancholy feeling, arising from the comparison which forces itself upon my mind of what the Indians were before the Europeans came into this country, and what they have become since, by a participation in our vices. By their intercourse with us, they have lost much of that original character by which they were once distinguished, and which it is the object of this work to delineate, and the change which has taken place is by no means for the better. I am not one of those wild enthusiasts who would endeavour to persuade mankind that savage life is preferable to a state of civilisation; but I leave it to every impartial person to decide, whether the condition of the healthy sober Indian, pursuing his game through forests and plains, is not far superior to that of the gangrened drunken white man, rioting in debauchery and vice?

I have already before taken notice[210] of the assertion which our aborigines do not hesitate to make, that before the Europeans landed in those parts of the American continent, they were unacquainted with that shameful disorder which attacks generation in its sources. I am well aware that this complaint is generally believed to have been communicated by the new world to the old. I do not know upon what proofs this opinion rests, but I am disposed to give credit to the uniform assertion of our northern Indians, that this contagion was first introduced among them by emigrants from Europe. However it may be, it is a lamentable fact that they are now very generally infected with it, and that their population cannot long resist its destructive operation upon their once strong and healthy constitutions, particularly as it is associated with the abuse of strong liquors, now so prevalent among them.

Of the manner in which they have acquired this latter vice, I presume there can be no doubt. They charge us in the most positive manner with being the first who made them acquainted with ardent spirits, and what is worse, with having exerted all the means in our power to induce them to drink to excess. It is very certain that the processes of distillation and fermentation are entirely unknown to the Indians, and that they have among them no intoxicating liquors but such as they receive from us. The Mexicans have their *Pulque*, and other indigenous beverages of an inebriating nature, but the North American Indians, before their intercourse with us commenced, had absolutely nothing of the kind. The smoke of the American weed, tobacco, was the only means that they at that time had in use to produce a temporary exhilaration of their spirits.

I have related in a former chapter,[211] the curious account given by the Delawares and Mohicans of the scene which took place when they were first made to taste spirituous liquors by the Dutch who landed on New York Island. I have no doubt that this tradition is substantially founded on fact. Indeed, it is strongly corroborated by the name which, in consequence of this adventure, those people gave at the time to that island, and which it has retained to this day. They called it *Manahachtanienk*, which in the Delaware language, means *"the island where we all became intoxicated."* We have corrupted this name into *Manhattan*, but not so as to destroy its meaning, or conceal its origin. The last syllable which we have left out is only a termination, implying locality, and in this word signifies as much as *where we*. There are few Indian traditions so well supported as this.

How far from that time the dreadful vice of intoxication has increased among those poor Indians, is well known to many Christian people among us. We may safely calculate on thousands who have perished by the baneful effect of spirituous liquors. The dreadful war which took place in 1774 between the Shawanese, some of the Mingoes, and the people of Virginia, in which so many lives were lost, was brought on by the consequences of drunkenness. It produced murders, which were followed by private revenge, and ended in a most cruel and destructive war.

The general prevalence of this vice among the Indians is in a great degree owing to unprincipled white traders, who persuade them to become intoxicated that they may cheat them the more easily, and obtain their lands or[212] peltries for a mere trifle. Within the last fifty years, some instances have even come to my knowledge of white men having enticed Indians to drink, and when drunk, murdered them. The effects which intoxication produces upon the Indians are dreadful. It has been the cause of an infinite number of murders among them, besides biting off noses and otherwise disfiguring each other, which are the least consequences of the quarrels which inebriation produces between them. I cannot say how many have died of colds and other disorders, which they have caught by lying upon the cold ground, and remaining exposed to the elements when drunk; others have lingered out their lives, in excruciating rheumatic pains and in wasting consumptions, until death came to relieve them from their sufferings.

Reflecting Indians have keenly remarked, "that it was strange that a people who professed themselves believers in a religion revealed to them by the great Spirit himself; who say that they have in their houses the WORD of God, and his laws and commandments textually written, could think of making a *beson*,[213] calculated to bewitch people and make them destroy one another." I once asked an Indian at Pittsburgh, whom I had not before seen, who he was? He answered in broken English: "My name is *Black-fish*; when at home with my nation, I am a clever fellow, and when here, a *hog*." He meant that by means of the liquor which the white people gave him, he was sunk down to the level of that beast.

An Indian who had been born and brought up at Minisink, near the Delaware Water Gap, and to whom the German inhabitants of that neighbourhood had given the name of *Cornelius Rosenbaum*, told me near fifty years ago, that he had once, when under the influence of strong liquor, killed the best Indian friend he had, fancying him to be his worst avowed enemy. He said that the deception was complete, and that while intoxicated, the face of his friend presented to his eyes all the features of the man with whom he was in a state of hostility. It is impossible to express the horror with which he was struck when he awoke from that delusion; he was so shocked, that he from that moment resolved never more to taste of the maddening poison, of which he was convinced that the devil was the inventor; for it could only be the evil spirit who made him see his enemy when his friend was before him, and produced so strong a delusion on his bewildered senses, that he actually killed him. From that time until his death, which happened thirty years afterwards, he never drank a drop of ardent spirits, which he always called "the Devil's blood," and was firmly persuaded that the Devil, or some of his inferior spirits had a hand in preparing it.

Once in my travels, I fell in with an Indian and his son; the former, though not addicted to drinking, had this time drank some liquor with one of his acquaintances, of which he now felt the effects. As he was walking before me, along the path, he at once flew back and aside, calling out, "O! what a monstrous snake!" On my asking him where the snake lay, he pointed to something and said, "Why, there, across the path!" "A snake!" said I, "it is nothing but a black-burnt sapling, which has fallen on the ground." He however would not be persuaded; he insisted that it was a snake, and could be nothing else; therefore, to avoid it, he went round the path, and entered it again at some distance further. After we had travelled together for about two hours, during which time he spoke but little, we encamped for the night. Awaking about midnight, I saw him sitting up smoking his pipe, and appearing to be in deep thought. I asked him why he did not lay down and sleep? To which he replied, "O! my friend! many things have crowded on my mind; I am quite lost in thought!"

HECKEW. *"And what are you thinking about?"*

INDIAN. *"Did you say it was not a snake of which I was afraid, and which lay across the path?"*

HECKEW. *"I did say so; and, indeed, it was nothing else but a sapling burnt black by the firing of the woods."*

INDIAN. *"Are you sure it was that?"*

207

HECKEW. *"Yes; and I called to you at the time to look, how I was standing on it; and if you have yet a doubt, ask your son, and the two Indians with me, and they will tell you the same."*

INDIAN. *"O strange! and I took it for an uncommonly large snake, moving as if it intended to bite me!—I cannot get over my surprise, that the liquor I drank, and, indeed, that was not much, should have so deceived me! but I think I have now discovered how it happens that Indians so often kill one another when drunk, almost without knowing what they are doing; and when afterwards they are told of what they have done, they ascribe it to the liquor which was in them at the time, and say the liquor did it. I thought that as I saw this time a living snake in a dead piece of wood, so I might, at another time, take a human being, perhaps one of my own family, for a bear or some other ferocious beast and kill him. Can you, my friend, tell me what is in the beson that confuses one so, and transforms things in that manner? Is it an invisible spirit? It must be something alive; or have the white people sorcerers among them, who put something in the liquor to deceive those who drink it? Do the white people drink of the same liquor that they give to the Indians? Do they also, when drunk, kill people, and bite noses off, as the Indians do? Who taught the white people to make so pernicious a beson?"*

I answered all these questions, and several others that he put to me, in the best manner that I could, to which he replied, and our conversation continued as follows:

INDIAN. *"Well, if, as you say, the bad spirit cannot be the inventor of this liquor; if, in some cases it is moderately used among you as a medicine, and if your doctors can prepare from it, or with the help of a little of it, some salutary besons, still, I must believe that when it operates as you have seen, the bad spirit must have some hand in it, either by putting some bad thing into it, unknown to those who prepare it, or you have conjurers who understand how to bewitch it.—Perhaps they only do so to that which is for the Indians; for the devil is not the Indians' friend, because they will not worship him, as they do the good spirit, and therefore I believe he puts something into the beson, for the purpose of destroying them."*

208

HECKEW. *"What the devil may do with the liquor, I cannot tell; but I believe that he has a hand in everything that is bad. When the Indians kill one another, bite off each other's noses, or commit such wicked acts, he is undoubtedly well satisfied; for, as God himself has said, he is a destroyer and a murderer."*

INDIAN. *"Well, now, we think alike, and henceforth he shall never again deceive me, or entice me to drink his beson!"*

It is a common saying with those white traders who find it their interest to make the Indians drunk, in order to obtain their peltry at a cheaper rate, that they *will* have strong liquors, and will not enter upon a bargain unless they are sure of getting it. I acknowledge that I have seen some such cases; but I could also state many from my own knowledge, where the Indians not only refused liquor, but resisted during several days all the attempts that were made to induce them even to taste it, being well aware, as well as those who offered it to them, that if they once should put it to their lips, such was their weakness on that score, that intoxication would inevitably follow.

I can, perhaps, offer a plausible reason why the Indians are so fond of spirituous drinks. The cause is, I believe, to be found in their living almost entirely upon fresh meats and green vegetables, such as corn, pumpkins, squashes, potatoes, cucumbers, melons, beans, &c., which causes a longing in their stomachs for some seasoning, particularly (as is often the case) when they have been a long time without salt. They are, on those occasions, equally eager for any acid substances; vinegar, if they can get it, they will drink in considerable quantities, and think nothing of going thirty or forty miles in search of cranberries whether in season or not. They also gather crab-apples, wild-grapes, and other acid, and even bitter-tasted fruits, as substitutes for salt, and in the spring they will peel such trees as have a sourish sap, which they lick with great avidity. When for a long time they have been without salt, and are fortunate enough to get some, they will swallow at a time a table-spoonful of that mineral substance, for which they say that they and their horses are equally hungry.

The Indians are very sensible of the state of degradation to which they have been brought by the abuse of strong liquors, and whenever they speak of it, never fail to reproach the whites, for having enticed them into that vicious habit. I could easily prove how guilty the whites are in this respect, if I were to relate a number of anecdotes, which I rather wish to consign to oblivion. The following will be sufficient to confute those disingenuous traders, who would endeavour to shift the blame from themselves, in order to fix it upon the poor deluded Indians.

In the year 1769, an Indian from Susquehannah having come to Bethlehem with his sons to dispose of his peltry, was accosted by a trader from a neighbouring town, who addressed him thus: "Well! Thomas, I really believe you have turned Moravian." "Moravian!" answered the Indian, "what makes you think so?" "Because," replied the other, "you used to come to us to sell your skins and peltry, and now you trade them away to the Moravians." "So!" rejoined the Indian, "now I understand you well, and I know what you mean to say. Now hear me. See! my friend! when I come to this place with my skins and peltry to trade, the people are kind, they give me plenty of good victuals to eat, and pay me in money or whatever I want, and no one says a word to me about drinking rum—neither do I ask for it! When I come to your place with my peltry, all call to me: 'Come, Thomas! here's rum, drink heartily, drink! it will not hurt you.' All this is done for the purpose of cheating me. When you have obtained from me all you want, you call me a drunken dog, and kick me out of the room. See! this is the manner in which you cheat the Indians when they come to trade with you. So now you know when you see me coming to your town again, you may say to one another: 'Ah! there is Thomas coming again! he is no longer a Moravian, for he is coming to us to be made drunk—to be cheated—to be kicked out of the house, and be called a *drunken dog*!'"

CHAPTER 37 ~
Funerals

I believe that no sufficiently detailed account has yet been given of the manner in which the North American Indians conduct the funerals of their dead. Captain Carver tells us that the Naudowessies, among whom he was, kept those ceremonies a secret, and would not give him an opportunity of witnessing them. Loskiel, although he drew his information from the journals of our Missionaries, has treated this subject rather superficially. I therefore run little risk of repetition in describing what I have myself seen, and I hope that the particulars which I am going to relate will not be thought uninteresting.

It is well known that the Indians pay great respect to the memory of the dead, and commit their remains to the ground with becoming ceremonies. Those ceremonies, however, are not the same in all cases, but vary according to circumstances, and the condition of the deceased; for rank and wealth receive distinctions even after death, as well among savages as among civilised nations. This, perhaps, may be easily accounted for. When a great chief dies, his death is considered as a national loss; of course all must join in a public demonstration of their sorrow. The rich man, on the other hand, had many friends during his life, who cannot decently abandon him the moment the breath is out of his body; besides, his fortune supplies the means of a rich entertainment at the funeral, of which many, as may well be supposed, are anxious to partake. Thus social distinctions are found even in the state of nature, where perfect equality, if it exists any where, might with the greatest probability be supposed to be found.

Though the earth and its fruits are common to all the Indians, yet every man is permitted to enjoy the earnings of his industry, and that produces riches; and though there is no hereditary or even elective rank in their social organization, yet as power follows courage and talents, those who are generally

211

acknowledged to be possessed of those qualities, assume their station above the rest, and the distinction of rank is thus established. Politicians and philosophers may reason on these facts as they please; the descriptions that I give are from nature, and I leave it to abler men than myself to draw the proper inferences from them.

On the death of a principal chief, the village resounds from one end to the other with the loud lamentations of the women, among whom those who sit by the corpse distinguish themselves by the shrillness of their cries and the frantic expression of their sorrow. This scene of mourning over the dead body continues by day and by night until it is interred, the mourners being relieved from time to time by other women.

These honours of "mourning over the corpse" are paid to all; the poor and humble, as well as the rich, great, and powerful; the difference consists only in the number of mourners, the undistinguished Indian having few besides his immediate relations and friends, and sometimes only those. Women (notwithstanding all that has been said of their supposed inferior station and of their being reduced to the rank of slaves) are not treated after their death with less respect than the men, and the greatest honours are paid to the remains of the wives of renowned warriors or veteran chiefs, particularly if they were descended themselves of a high family, which, however strange it may appear, is not an indifferent thing among the Indians, who love to honour the merit of their great men in their relatives.

I was present in the year 1762, at the funeral of a woman of the highest rank and respectability, the wife of the valiant Delaware chief *Shingask*;[214] as all the honours were paid to her at her interment that are usual on such occasions, I trust a particular description of the ceremony will not be unacceptable. At the moment that she died, her death was announced through the village by women specially appointed for that purpose, who went through the streets crying, "*She is no more! she is no more!*" The place on a sudden exhibited a scene of universal mourning; cries and lamentations were heard from all quarters; it was truly the expression of the general feeling for a general loss.

212

The day passed in this manner amidst sorrow and desolation. The next morning, between nine and ten o'clock, two counsellors came to announce to Mr. Thomas Calhoon, the Indian trader, and myself, that we were desired to attend and assist at the funeral which was soon to take place. We, in consequence, proceeded to the house of the deceased, where we found her corpse lying in a coffin, (which had been made by Mr. Calhoon's carpenter) dressed and painted in the most superb Indian style. Her garments, all new, were set off with rows of silver broaches,[215] one row joining the other. Over the sleeves of her new ruffled shirt were broad silver arm-spangles from her shoulder down to her wrist, on which were bands, forming a kind of mittens, worked together of wampum, in the same manner as the belts which they use when they deliver speeches. Her long plaited hair was confined by broad bands of silver, one band joining the other, yet not of the same size, but tapering from the head downwards and running at the lower end to a point. On the neck were hanging five broad belts of wampum tied together at the ends, each of a size smaller than the other, the largest of which reached below her breast, the next largest reaching to a few inches of it, and so on, the uppermost one being the smallest. Her scarlet leggings were decorated with different coloured ribands sewed on, the outer edges being finished off with small beads also of various colours. Her mocksens were ornamented with the most striking figures, wrought on the leather with coloured porcupine quills, on the borders of which, round the ankles, were fastened a number of small round silver bells, of about the size of a musket ball. All these things, together with the vermilion paint, judiciously laid on, so as to set her off in the highest style, decorated her person in such a manner, that perhaps nothing of the kind could exceed it.

The spectators having retired, a number of articles were brought out of the house and placed in the coffin, wherever there was room to put them in, among which were a new shirt, a dressed deer skin for shoes, a pair of scissors, needles, thread, a knife, pewter basin and spoon, pint-cup, and other similar things, with a number of trinkets and other small articles which she was fond of while living. The lid was then fastened on the coffin with three straps, and three handsome round poles, five or six feet long, were laid across it, near each other, and one in the middle, which were also fastened with straps cut up from a tanned elk hide; and a small bag of vermilion paint, with some flannel to lay it on, was then thrust into the coffin through the hole cut out at the head of it. This hole, the Indians say, is for the spirit of the deceased to go in and out at pleasure, until it has found the place of its future residence.

Everything being in order, the bearers of the corpse were desired to take their places. Mr. Calhoon and myself were placed at the foremost pole, two women at the middle, and two men at the pole in the rear. Several women from a house about thirty yards off, now started off, carrying large kettles, dishes, spoons, and dried elk meat in baskets, for the burial place, and the signal being given for us to move with the body, the women who acted as chief mourners made the air resound with their shrill cries.

The order of the procession was as follows; first a leader or guide, from the spot where we were to the place of interment. Next followed the corpse, and close to it *Shingask*, the husband of the deceased. He was followed by the principal war-chiefs and counsellors of the nation, after whom came men of all ranks and descriptions. Then followed the women and children, and lastly two stout men carrying loads of European manufactured goods upon their backs. The chief mourners on the women's side, not having joined the ranks, took their own course to the right, at the distance of about fifteen or twenty yards from us, but always opposite to the corpse. As the corpse had to be carried by the strength of our arms to the distance of about two hundred yards, and hung low between the bearers, we had to rest several times by the way, and whenever we stopped, everybody halted until we moved on again.

Being arrived at the grave, we were told to halt, then the lid of the coffin was again taken off, and the body exposed to view. Now the whole train formed themselves into a kind of semi-lunar circle on the south side of the grave, and seated themselves on the ground. Within this circle, at the distance of about fifteen yards from the grave, a common seat was made for Mr. Calhoon and myself to sit on, while the disconsolate *Shingask* retired by himself to a spot at some distance, where he was seen weeping, with his head bowed to the ground. The female mourners seated themselves promiscuously near to each other, among some low bushes that were at the distance of from twelve to fifteen yards east of the grave.

In this situation we remained for the space of more than two hours; not a sound was heard from any quarter, though the numbers that attended were very great; nor did any person move from his seat to view the body, which had been lightly covered over with a clean white sheet. All appeared to be in profound reflection and solemn mourning. Sighs and sobs were now and then heard from the female mourners, so uttered as not to disturb the assembly; it seemed rather as if intended to keep the feeling of sorrow alive in a manner becoming the occasion. Such was the impression made on us by this long silence.

At length, at about one o'clock in the afternoon, six men stepped forward to put the lid upon the coffin, and let down the body into the grave, when suddenly three of the women mourners rushed from their seats, and forcing themselves between these men and the corpse, loudly called out to the deceased to "arise and go with them and not to forsake them." They even took hold of her arms and legs; at first it seemed as if they were caressing her, afterwards they appeared to pull with more violence, as if they intended to run away with the body, crying out all the while, "Arise, arise! Come with us! Don't leave us! Don't abandon us!" At last they retired, plucking at their garments, pulling their hair, and uttering loud cries and lamentations, with all the appearance of frantic despair. After they were seated on the ground, they continued in the same manner crying and sobbing and pulling at the grass and shrubs, as if their minds were totally bewildered and they did not know what they were doing.

As soon as these women had gone through their part of the ceremony, which took up about fifteen minutes, the six men whom they had interrupted and who had remained at the distance of about five feet from the corpse, again stepped forward and did their duty. They let down the coffin into the earth, and laid two thin poles of about four inches diameter, from which the bark had been taken off, lengthways and close together over the grave, after which they retired. Then the husband of the deceased advanced with a very slow pace, and when he came to the grave, walked over it on these poles, and proceeded forward in the same manner into an extensive adjoining prairie, which commenced at this spot.

When the widowed chief had advanced so far that he could not hear what was doing at the grave, a painted post, on which were drawn various figures, emblematic of the deceased's situation in life and of her having been the wife of a valiant warrior, was brought by two men and delivered to a third, a man of note, who placed it in such a manner that it rested on the coffin at the head of the grave, and took great care that a certain part of the drawings should be exposed to the East, or rising of the sun; then, while he held the post erect and properly situated, some women filled up the grave with hoes, and having placed dry leaves and pieces of bark over it, so that none of the fresh ground was visible, they retired, and some men, with timbers fitted beforehand for the purpose, enclosed the grave about breast-high, so as to secure it from the approach of wild beasts.

The whole work being finished, which took up about an hour's time, Mr. Calhoon and myself expected that we might be permitted to go home, as we wished to do, particularly as we saw a thundergust from the west fast approaching; but the Indians, suspecting our design, soon came forward with poles and blankets, and in a few minutes erected a shelter for us.

The storm, though of short duration, was tremendous; the water produced by the rain, flowing in streams; yet all had found means to secure themselves during its continuance, and being on prairie ground, we were out of all danger of trees being torn up or blown down upon us. Our encampment now appeared like a village, or rather like a military camp, such was the number of places of shelter that had been erected.

Fortunately, the husband of the deceased had reached the camp in good time, and now the gust being over, every one was served with victuals that had been cooked at some distance from the spot. After the repast was over, the articles of merchandise which had been brought by the two men in the rear, having been made up in parcels, were distributed among all present. No one, from the oldest to the youngest, was excepted, and every one partook of the liberal donation. This difference only was made, that those who had rendered the greatest services received the most valuable presents, and we were much pleased to see the female mourners well rewarded, as they had, indeed, a very hard task to perform. Articles of little value, such as gartering, tape, needles, beads, and the like, were given to the smaller girls; the older ones received a pair of scissors, needles and thread, and a yard or two of riband. The boys had a knife, jews-harp, awl-blades, or something of similar value. Some of the grown persons received a new suit of clothes, consisting of a blanket, shirt, breech-cloth and leggings, of the value in the whole of about eight dollars; and the women, (I mean those who had rendered essential services) a blanket, ruffled shirts, stroud and leggings, the whole worth from ten to twelve dollars. Mr. Calhoon and myself were each presented with a silk cravat and a pair of leggings. The goods distributed on this occasion, were estimated by Mr. Calhoon at two hundred dollars; the greatest part of them had, the same morning, been taken out of his store.

After we had thus remained, in a manner, under confinement, for more than six hours, the procession ended, and Mr. Calhoon and myself retired with the rest to our homes. At dusk a kettle of victuals was carried to the grave and placed upon it, and the same was done every evening for the space of three weeks, at the end of which it was supposed that the traveller had found her place of residence. During that time the lamentations of the women mourners were heard on the evenings of each day, though not so loud nor so violent as before.

I have thus described, from minutes which I took at the time, the ceremonies which take place among the Delaware Indians on the death of a person of high rank and consideration among them. The funerals of persons of an inferior station are conducted with less pomp and with less expense. When the heirs of the deceased cannot afford to hire female mourners, the duty is performed by their own immediate relations and friends. But "mourning over the corpse" is a ceremony that cannot be dispensed with.

It is always customary, when an Indian dies, of whatever rank or condition he may be, to put a number of the articles which belonged to the deceased in the coffin or grave, that he may have them when wanted. I have seen a bottle of rum or whiskey placed at the coffin head, and the reason given for it was, that the deceased was fond of liquor while living, and he would be glad of a dram when he should feel fatigued on his journey to the world of spirits.

When an Indian dies at a distance from his home, great care is taken that the grave be well fortified with posts and logs laid upon it, that the wolves may be prevented from getting at the corpse; when time and circumstances do not permit this, as, for instance, when the Indians are travelling, the body is enclosed in the bark of trees and thus laid in the grave. When a death takes place at their hunting camps, they make a kind of coffin as well as they can, or put a cover over the body, so that the earth may not sink on it, and then enclose the grave with a fence of poles.

Warriors that are slain in battle, are, if possible, drawn aside and buried, so that the enemy may not get their scalps, and also that he may not know the number of the slain. In such cases they will turn an old log out of its bed, and dig a grave so deep, that the log, when replaced, may not press too hard upon the body. If any of the fresh earth be seen, they cover it with rotten wood, brush or leaves, that its place may not be found. If they have not sufficient time for this, or the number of their dead is too great, they throw the bodies on the top of each other between large logs, and place any kind of rotten wood or other rubbish upon them. They never, when they can help it, leave their dead to be devoured by wild beasts.

When the Indians have to speak of a deceased person, they never mention him or her by name, lest they should renew the grief of the family or friends. They say, "He who was our counsellor or chief," "She who was the wife of our friend;" or they will allude to some particular circumstance, as that of the

218

deceased having been with them at a particular time or place, or having done some particular act or spoken particular words which they all remember, so that every body knows who is meant. I have often observed with emotion this remarkable delicacy, which certainly does honour to their hearts, and shews that they are naturally accessible to the tenderest feelings of humanity.

CHAPTER 38 ~
Friendship

Those who believe that no faith is to be placed in the friendship of an Indian are egregiously mistaken, and know very little of the true character of those men of nature. They are, it is true, revengeful to their enemies, to those who wilfully do them an injury, who insult, abuse, or treat them with contempt. It may be said, indeed, that the passion of revenge is so strong in them that it knows no bounds. This does not, however, proceed from a bad or malicious disposition, but from the violence of natural feelings unchecked by social institutions, and unsubdued by the force of revealed religion. The tender and generous passions operate no less powerfully on them than those of an opposite character, and they are as warm and sincere in their friendship, as vindictive in their enmities. Nay, I will venture to assert that there are those among them who on an emergency would lay down their lives for a friend: I could fill many pages with examples of Indian friendship and fidelity, not only to each other, but to men of other nations and of a different colour than themselves.

How often, when wars were impending between them and the whites, have they not forewarned those among our frontier settlers whom they thought well disposed towards them, that dangerous times were at hand, and advised them to provide for their own safety, regardless of the jealousy which such conduct might excite among their own people? How often did they not even guard and escort them through the most dangerous places until they had reached a secure spot? How often did they not find means to keep an enemy from striking a stroke, as they call it, that is to say from proceeding to the sudden indiscriminate murder of the frontier whites, until their friends or those whom they considered as such were out of all danger?

220

These facts are all familiar to every one who has lived among Indians or in their neighbourhood, and I believe it will be difficult to find a single case in which they betrayed a real friend or abandoned him in the hour of danger, when it was in their power to extricate or relieve him. The word "Friend" to the ear of an Indian does not convey the same vague and almost indefinite meaning that it does with us; it is not a mere complimentary or social expression, but implies a resolute determination to stand by the person so distinguished on all occasions, and a threat to those who might attempt to molest him; the mere looking at two persons who are known or declared friends, is sufficient to deter any one from offering insult to either.

When an Indian believes that he has reason to suspect a man of evil designs against his friend, he has only to say emphatically: "This is *my friend*, and if any one tries to hurt him, I will do to him *what is in my mind*." It is as much as to say that he will stand in his defence at the hazard of his own life. This language is well understood by the Indians, who know that they would have to combat with a spirited warrior, were they to attempt any thing against his friend. By this means much bloodshed is prevented; for it is sufficiently known that an Indian never proffers his friendship in vain. Many white men, and myself among others, have experienced the benefit of their powerful as well as generous protection.

When in the spring of the year 1774, a war broke out between the Virginians and the Shawanese and Mingoes, on account of murders committed by the former on the latter people, and the exasperated friends of those who had suffered had determined to kill every white man in their country, the Shawano chief *Silverheels*,[216] taking another Indian with him, undertook out of friendship to escort several white traders from thence to Albany,[217] a distance of near two hundred miles; well knowing at the time that he was running the risk of his own life, from exasperated Indians and vagabond whites, if he should meet with such on the road, as he did in fact on his return. I have already said how he was rewarded for this noble act of friendship and self-devotion.

In the year 1779, the noted Girty with his murdering party of Mingoes, nine in number, fell in with the Missionary Zeisberger, on the path leading from Goschacking to Gnadenhütten; their design was to take that worthy man prisoner; and if they could not seize him alive, to murder him and take his scalp to Detroit. They were on the point of laying hold of him, when two young spirited Delawares providentially entered the path at that critical moment and in an instant presented themselves to defend the good Missionary at the risk of their lives. Their determined conduct had the desired success, and his life was saved. His deliverers afterwards declared that they had no other motive for thus exposing themselves for his sake than that he was a friend to their nation, and was considered by them as a good man.

But why should I speak of others when I have myself so often experienced the benefits of Indian protection and friendship. Let me be permitted to corroborate my assertions on this subject by my own personal testimony.

In the year 1777, while the Revolutionary war was raging, and several Indian tribes had enlisted on the British side, and were spreading murder and devastation along our unprotected frontier, I rather rashly determined to take a journey into the country on a visit to my friends. Captain White Eyes, the Indian hero, whose character I have already described,[218] resided at that time at the distance of seventeen miles from the place where I lived. Hearing of my determination, he immediately hurried up to me, with his friend Captain Wingenund (whom I shall presently have occasion further to mention), and some of his young men, for the purpose of escorting me to Pittsburg, saying, "that he would not suffer me to go, while the Sandusky warriors were out on war excursions, without a proper escort and *himself* at my side." He insisted on accompanying me and we set out together.

One day, as we were proceeding along, our spies discovered a suspicious track. White Eyes, who was riding before me, enquired whether I felt afraid? I answered that while he was with me, I entertained no fear. On this he immediately replied, "You are right; for until I am laid prostrate at your feet, no one shall hurt you." "And even not then," added Wingenund, who was riding behind me; "before this happens, I must be also overcome, and lay by the side of our friend *Koguethagechton*."[219] I believed them, and I believe at this day that these great men were sincere, and that if they had been put to the test, they would have shewn it, as did another Indian friend by whom my life was saved in the spring of the year 1781.

From behind a log in the bushes where he was concealed, he espied a hostile Indian at the very moment he was levelling his piece at me. Quick as lightning he jumped between us, and exposed his person to the musket shot just about to be fired, when fortunately the aggressor desisted, from fear of hitting the Indian whose body thus effectually protected me, at the imminent risk of his own life. Captain White Eyes, in the year 1774, saved in the same manner the life of David Duncan, the peace-messenger, whom he was escorting. He rushed, regardless of his own life, up to an inimical Shawanese, who was aiming at our ambassador from behind a bush, and forced him to desist.

I could enumerate many other similar acts, but I think I have shewn enough for my purpose. Mr. Zeisberger fully agreed with me in the opinion, that it is impossible to deny to the Indians the praise of firm attachment and sincere friendship. It is not meant to say, that all will carry that feeling to the same pitch of heroism; but it is certain that there are many among them, whose strong attachments and a manly pride will induce to risk their lives in the defence of their friends. And, indeed, there is no Indian, who would not blush at being reproached that after boasting that a particular person was his friend, he had acted the coward when his friendship was put to the test, and had shrunk from venturing his own life, when there was even a chance of saving that of the man whom he professed to love.

It is not true, as some have supposed, that an Indian's friendship must be purchased by presents, and that it lasts only so long as gifts continue to be lavished upon them. Their attachments, on the contrary, are perfectly disinterested. I admit that they receive with pleasure a present from a friend's hand. They consider presents as marks of the giver's good disposition towards them. They cannot, in their opinion, proceed from an enemy, and he who befriends them, they think must love them. Obligations to them are not burdensome, they love to acknowledge them, and whatever may be their faults, ingratitude is not among the number.

Indeed, the friendship of an Indian is easily acquired, provided it is sought in good faith. But whoever chooses to obtain it must be sure to treat them on a footing of perfect equality. They are very jealous of the whites, who they think affect to consider themselves as beings of a superior nature and too often treat them with rude undeserved contempt. This they seldom forgive, while on the other hand, they feel flattered when a white man does not disdain to treat them as children of the same Creator. Both reason and humanity concur in teaching us this conduct, but I am sorry to say that reason and humanity are in such cases too little attended to. I hope I may be permitted to expatiate a little on this subject; perhaps it may be beneficial to some white persons hereafter.

The Indians are, as I have already observed before,[220] excellent physiognomists. If they are accosted by or engaged in business with a number of whites, though they may not understand the language that is spoken, they will pretty accurately distinguish by the countenance, those who despise their colour from those who are under the influence of a more generous feeling, and in this they are seldom mistaken. They fix their eyes on the whole party round, and read as it were in the souls of the individuals who compose it. They mark those whom they consider as their friends, and those whom they think to be their enemies, and are sure to remember them ever after. But what must those expect, if a war or some other circumstance should put them into the power of the Indians, who, relying on their supposed ignorance of our idiom, do not scruple even in their presence to apply to them the epithets of *dogs*, *black d—ls*, and the like? Will not these poor people be in some degree justifiable in considering those persons as decidedly hostile to their race?

Such cases have unfortunately too frequently happened, and the savages have been blamed for treating as enemies those who had so cruelly wounded their most delicate feelings! Many white men have been thus put to death, who had brought their fate on themselves by their own imprudence. On the other hand, the Indians have not failed to mark those who at the time reprobated such indecent behaviour and reproached their companions for using such improper language. In the midst of war these benevolent Christians have been treated as friends, when, perhaps, they had forgotten the humane conduct to which they were indebted for this kind usage.

Their reasoning in such cases is simple, but to them always conclusive. They merely apply their constant maxim, which I believe I have already noticed, that "good can never proceed from evil or evil from good, and that good and evil, like heterogeneous substances, can never combine or coalesce together." How far this maxim is founded in a profound knowledge of human nature, it is not my business to determine; what is certain is that they adhere to it in almost every occasion. If a person treats them ill, they ascribe it invariably to his bad heart; it is the bad spirit within him that operates; he is, therefore, a bad man. If on the contrary one shews them kindness, they say he is prompted so to act by "the good spirit within him," and that he has a *good heart*; for if he had not, he would not do good. It is impossible to draw them out of this circle of reasoning, and to persuade them that the friendship shewn to them may be dissembled and proceed from motives of interest; so convinced are they of the truth of their general principle, "that good cannot proceed from an evil source."

The conduct of the Europeans towards them, particularly within the last fifty or sixty years, has, however, sufficiently convinced them that men may dissemble, and that kind speeches and even acts of apparent friendship do not always proceed from friendly motives, but that the bad spirit will sometimes lurk under the appearance of the good. Hence, when they speak of the whites in general, they do not scruple to designate them as a false, deceitful race; but it is nevertheless true that with individuals, they frequently forget this general impression, and revert to their own honest principle; and if a white man only behaves to them with common humanity, it is still easy to get access to their simple hearts. Such are those brutes, those savages, from whom, according to some men, no faith is to be expected, and with whom no faith is to be kept; such are those *barbarous* nations, as they are called, whom God, nevertheless, made the lawful owners and masters of this beautiful country; but who, at no very remote time, will probably live, partially live, only in its history.

My object in this chapter is to prove that those men are susceptible of the noblest and finest feelings of genuine friendship. It is not enough that by a long residence among them, I have acquired the most complete conviction of this truth; facts and not opinions, I know, are expected from me. Perhaps I might rest satisfied with the proofs that I have already given, but I have only shewn the strength and have yet to display the *constancy* of their attachments; and although in the story which I am going to relate, a friend was forced to see his friend perish miserably without having it in his power to save him from the most terrible death that vengeance and cruelty could inflict, we shall not be the less astonished to see him persevere in his friendly sentiments, under circumstances of all others the most calculated, (particularly to an Indian) not only to have entirely extinguished, but converted those sentiments into feelings of hatred and revenge.

I am sorry to be so often obliged to revert to the circumstance of the cruel murder of the Christian Indians on the Sandusky[221] river[222] in the year 1782, by a gang of banditti, under the command of one Williamson. Not satisfied with this horrid outrage, the same band not long afterwards marched to Sandusky,[223] where it seems they had been informed that the remainder of that unfortunate congregation had fled, in order to perpetrate upon them the same indiscriminate murder. But Providence had so ordered it that they had before left that place, where they had found that they could not remain in safety, their ministers having been taken from them and carried to Detroit by order of the British government, so that they had been left entirely unprotected.

The murderers, on their arrival, were much disappointed in finding nothing but empty huts. They then shaped their course towards the hostile Indian villages, where being, contrary to their expectations, furiously attacked, Williamson and his band took the advantage of a dark night and ran off, and the whole party escaped, except one Colonel Crawford and another, who being taken by the Indians were carried in triumph to their village, where the former was condemned to death by torture, and the punishment was inflicted with all the cruelty that rage could invent. The latter was demanded by the Shawanese and sent to them for punishment.

While preparations were making for the execution of this dreadful sentence, the unfortunate Crawford recollected that the Delaware chief Wingenund,[224] of whom I have spoken in the beginning of this chapter, had been his friend in happier times; he had several times entertained him at his house, and shewed him those marks of attention which are so grateful to the poor despised Indians. A ray of hope darted through his soul, and he requested that Wingenund, who lived at some distance from the village, might be sent for. His request was granted, and a messenger was despatched for the chief, who, reluctantly, indeed, but without hesitation, obeyed the summons, and immediately came to the fatal spot.

This great and good man was not only one of the bravest and most celebrated warriors, but one of the most amiable men of the Delaware nation. To a firm undaunted mind, he joined humanity, kindness and universal benevolence; the excellent qualities of his heart had obtained for him the name of *Wingenund*, which in the Lenape language signifies *the well beloved*. He had kept away from the tragical scene about to be acted, to mourn in silence and solitude over the fate of his guilty friend, which he well knew it was not in his power to prevent. He was now called upon to act a painful as well as difficult part; the eyes of his enraged countrymen were fixed upon him; he was an Indian and a Delaware; he was a leader of that nation, whose defenceless members had been so cruelly murdered without distinction of age or sex, and whose innocent blood called aloud for the most signal revenge.

Could he take the part of a chief of the base murderers? Could he forget altogether the feelings of ancient fellowship and give way exclusively to those of the Indian and the patriot? Fully sensible that in the situation in which he was placed the latter must, in appearance, at least, predominate, he summoned to his aid the firmness and dignity of an Indian warrior, approached Colonel Crawford and waited in silence for the communications he had to make. The following dialogue now took place between them.

CRAWF. *Do you recollect me, Wingenund?*

WINGEN. *I believe I do; are you not Colonel Crawford?*

CRAWF. *I am. How do you do? I am glad to see you, Captain.*

WINGEN. (embarrassed) *So! yes, indeed.*

CRAWF. *Do you recollect the friendship that always existed between us, and that we were always glad to see each other?*

WINGEN. *I recollect all this. I remember that we have drunk many a bowl of punch together. I remember also other acts of kindness that you have done me.*

CRAWF. *Then I hope the same friendship still subsists between us.*

WINGEN. *It would, of course, be the same, were you in your proper place and not here.*

CRAWF. *And why not here, Captain? I hope you would not desert a friend in time of need. Now is the time for you to exert yourself in my behalf, as I should do for you, were you in my place.*

WINGEN. *Colonel Crawford! you have placed yourself in a situation which puts it out of my power and that of others of your friends to do anything for you.*

CRAWF. *How so, Captain Wingenund?*

WINGEN. *By joining yourself to that execrable man, Williamson and his party; the man who, but the other day, murdered such a number of the Moravian Indians, knowing them to be friends; knowing that he ran no risk in murdering a people who would not fight, and whose only business was praying.*

CRAWF. *Wingenund, I assure you, that had I been with him at the time, this would not have happened; not I alone but all your friends and all good men, wherever they are, reprobate acts of this kind.*

WINGEN. *That may be; yet these friends, these good men did not prevent him from going out again, to kill the remainder of those inoffensive, yet foolish Moravian Indians! I say foolish, because they believed the whites in preference to us. We had often told them that they would be one day so treated by those people who called themselves their friends! We told them that there was no faith to be placed in what the white men said; that their fair promises were only intended to allure us, that they might the more easily kill us, as they have done many Indians before they killed these Moravians.*

CRAWF. *I am sorry to hear you speak thus; as to Williamson's going out again, when it was known that he was determined on it, I went out with him to prevent him from committing fresh murders.*

WINGEN. *This, Colonel, the Indians would not believe, were even I to tell them so.*

CRAWF. *And why would they not believe it?*

WINGEN. *Because it would have been out of your power to prevent his doing what he pleased.*

CRAWF. *Out of my power! Have any Moravian Indians been killed or hurt since we came out?*

WINGEN. *None; but you went first to their town, and finding it empty and deserted you turned on the path towards us? If you had been in search of warriors only, you would not have gone thither. Our spies watched you closely. They saw you while you were embodying yourselves on the other side of the Ohio; they saw you cross that river; they saw where you encamped at night; they saw you turn off from the path to the deserted Moravian town; they knew you were going out of your way; your steps were constantly watched, and you were suffered quietly to proceed until you reached the spot where you were attacked.*

CRAWF. *What do they intend to do with me? Can you tell me?*

WINGEN. *I tell you with grief, Colonel. As Williamson and his whole cowardly host, ran off in the night at the whistling of our warrior's balls, being satisfied that now he had no Moravians to deal with, but men who could fight, and with such he did not wish to have anything to do; I say, as he escaped, and they have taken you, they will take revenge on you in his stead.*

CRAWF. *And is there no possibility of preventing this? Can you devise no way to get me off? You shall, my friend, be well rewarded if you are instrumental in saving my life.*

WINGEN. *Had Williamson been taken with you, I and some friends, by making use of what you have told me, might perhaps, have succeeded to save you, but as the matter now stands, no man would dare to interfere in your behalf. The king of England himself, were he to come to this spot, with all his wealth and treasures could not effect this purpose. The blood of the innocent Moravians, more than half of them women and children, cruelly and wantonly murdered calls aloud for revenge. The relatives of the slain, who are among us, cry out and stand ready for revenge. The nation to which they belonged will have revenge. The Shawanese, our grandchildren, have asked for your fellow-prisoner; on him they will take revenge. All the nations connected with us cry out Revenge! revenge! The Moravians whom you went to destroy having fled, instead of avenging their brethren, the offence is become national, and the nation itself is bound to take REVENGE!*

CRAWF. *Then it seems my fate is decided, and I must prepare to meet death in its worst form?*

WINGEN. *Yes, Colonel!—I am sorry for it; but cannot do anything for you. Had you attended to the Indian principle, that as good and evil cannot dwell together in the same heart, so a good man ought not to go into evil company; you would not be in this lamentable situation. You see now, when it is too late, after Williamson has deserted you, what a bad man he must be! Nothing now remains for you but to meet your fate like a brave man. Farewell, Colonel Crawford! they are coming;[225] I will retire to a solitary spot.*

I have been assured by respectable Indians that at the close of this conversation, which was related to me by Wingenund himself as well as by others, both he and Crawford burst into a flood of tears; they then took an affectionate leave of each other, and the chief immediately *hid himself in the bushes*, as the Indians express it, or in his own language, retired to a solitary spot. He never, afterwards, spoke of the fate of his unfortunate friend without strong emotions of grief, which I have several times witnessed.

Once, it was the first time that he came into Detroit after Crawford's sufferings, I heard him censured in his own presence by some gentlemen who were standing together for not having saved the life of so valuable a man, who was also his particular friend, as he had often told them. He listened calmly to their censure, and first turning to me, said in his own language: "These men talk like fools," then turning to them, he replied in English: "If king George himself, if your king had been on the spot with all his ships laden with goods and treasures, he could not have ransomed my friend, nor saved his life from the rage of a *justly* exasperated multitude." He made no further allusion to the act that had been the cause of Crawford's death, and it was easy to perceive that on this melancholy subject, grief was the feeling that predominated in his mind. He felt much hurt, however, at this unjust accusation, from men who, perhaps, he might think, would have acted very differently in his place. For,

231

let us consider in what a situation he found himself, at that trying and critical moment.

He was a Delaware Indian, and a highly distinguished character among his nation. The offence was national, and of the most atrocious kind, as it was wanton and altogether unprovoked. He might have been expected to partake with all the rest of his countrymen in the strong desire which they felt for *revenge*. He had been Crawford's friend, it is true, and various acts of sociability and friendship had been interchanged between them. But, no doubt, at that time, he believed him, at least, not to be an enemy to his nation and colour, and if he was an enemy, he might have expected him to be, like himself, a fair, open, generous foe.

But when he finds him enlisted with those who are waging a war of extermination against the Indian race, murdering in cold blood, and without distinction of age or sex, even those who had united their fate to that of the whites, and had said to the Christians: "Your people shall be *our* people, and your God *our* God,"[226] was there not enough here to make him disbelieve all the former professions of such a man, and to turn his abused friendship into the most violent enmity and the bitterest rage? Instead of this we see him persevering to the last in his attachment to a person who, to say the least, had ceased to be deserving of it; we see him in the face of his enraged countrymen avow that friendship, careless of the jealousy that he might excite; we see him not only abstain from participating in the national revenge, but deserting his post, as it were, seek a solitary spot to bewail the death of him, whom, in spite of all, he still loved, and felt not ashamed to call his *friend*.

It is impossible for friendship to be put to a severer test, and the example of Wingenund proves how deep a root this sentiment can take in the mind of an Indian, when even such circumstances as those under which the chief found himself, fail to extinguish it.

CHAPTER 39 ~
Preachers and prophets

There was a time when the preachers and prophets of the Indians, by properly exerting the unbounded influence which the popular superstitions gave them, might have excited among those nations such a spirit of general resistance against the encroachments of the Europeans, as would have enabled them, at least, to make a noble stand against their invaders, and perhaps to recover the undisturbed possession of their country. Instead of following the obvious course which reason and nature pointed out; instead of uniting as one nation in defense of their natural rights, they gave ear to the artful insinuations of their enemies, who too well understood the art of sowing unnatural divisions among them. It was not until Canada, after repeated struggles, was finally conquered from the French by the united arms of Great Britain and her colonies, that they began to be sensible of their desperate situation—this whole northern continent being now in the possession of one great and powerful nation, against whom it was vain to attempt resistance.

Yet it was at this moment that their prophets, impelled by ambitious motives, began to endeavour by their eloquence to bring them back to independent feelings, and create among them a genuine national spirit; but it was too late. The only rational resource that remained for them to prevent their total annihilation was to adopt the religion and manners of their conquerors, and abandon savage life for the comforts of civilised society; but of this but a few of them were sensible; in vain Missionaries were sent among them, who, through the greatest hardships and dangers exerted themselves to soften their misfortunes by the consolations of the Christian faith, and to point out to them the way of salvation in this world and the next; the banner of Christ was comparatively followed but by small numbers, and these were persecuted by their friends, or, at least, those who ought to have been such, as well as by their

233

enemies. Among the obstacles which the Missionaries encountered, the strong opposition which was made to them by the prophets of the Indian nations was by no means the least.

I have known several of these preachers and prophets during my residence in the Indian country, and have had sufficient opportunities to observe the means which they took to operate on the minds of their hearers. I shall content myself with taking notice here of a few of the most remarkable among them.

In the year 1762, there was a famous preacher of the Delaware nation, who resided at *Cayahaga*, near Lake Erie, and travelled about the country, among the Indians, endeavouring to persuade them that he had been appointed by the great Spirit to instruct them in those things that were agreeable to him and to point out to them the offences by which they had drawn his displeasure on themselves, and the means by which they might recover his favour for the future. He had drawn, as he pretended, by the direction of the great Spirit, a kind of map on a piece of deer skin, somewhat dressed like parchment, which he called "the great Book or Writing." This, he said, he had been ordered to shew to the Indians, that they might see the situation in which the Mannitto had originally placed them, the misery which they had brought upon themselves by neglecting their duty, and the only way that was now left them to regain what they had lost. This map he held before him while preaching, frequently pointing to particular marks and spots upon it, and giving explanations as he went along.

The size of this map was about fifteen inches square, or, perhaps, something more. An inside square was formed by lines drawn within it, of about eight inches each way, two of those lines, however, were not closed by about half an inch at the corners. Across these inside lines, others of about an inch in length were drawn with sundry other lines and marks, all which was intended to represent a strong inaccessible barrier, to prevent those without from entering the space within, otherwise than at the place appointed for that purpose. When the map was held as he directed, the corners which were not closed lay at the left hand side, directly opposite to each other, the one being at the south-east by south, and the nearest at the north-east by north.

In explaining or describing the particular points on this map, with his fingers always pointing to the place he was describing, he called the space within the inside lines "the heavenly regions," or the place destined by the great Spirit for the habitation of the Indians in future life; the space left open at the south-east corner, he called the "avenue," which had been intended for the Indians to enter into this heaven, but which was now in the possession of the white people, wherefore the great Spirit had since caused another "avenue" to be made on the opposite side, at which, however, it was both difficult and dangerous for them to enter, there being many impediments in their way, besides a large ditch leading to a gulf below, over which they had to leap; but the evil spirit kept at this very spot a continual watch for Indians, and whoever he laid hold of, never could get away from him again, but was carried to his regions, where there was nothing but extreme poverty; where the ground was parched up by the heat for want of rain, no fruit came to perfection, the game was almost starved for want of pasture, and where the evil spirit, at his pleasure, transformed men into horses and dogs, to be ridden by him and follow him in his hunts and wherever he went.

The space on the outside of this interior square, was intended to represent the country given to the Indians to hunt, fish, and dwell in while in this world; the east side of it was called the ocean or "great salt water Lake." Then the preacher drawing the attention of his hearers particularly to the south-east avenue, would say to them: "Look here! See what we have lost by neglect and disobedience; by being remiss in the expression of our gratitude to the great Spirit, for what he has bestowed upon us; by neglecting to make to him sufficient sacrifices; by looking upon a people of a different colour from our own, who had come across a great lake, as if they were a part of ourselves; by suffering them to sit down by our side, and looking at them with indifference, while they were not only taking our country from us, but this (pointing to the spot), this, our own avenue, leading into those beautiful regions which were destined for us. Such is the sad condition to which we are reduced. What is now to be done, and

235

what remedy is to be applied? I will tell you, my friends. Hear what the great Spirit has ordered me to tell you! You are to make sacrifices, in the manner that I shall direct; to put off entirely from yourselves the customs which you have adopted since the white people came among us; you are to return to that former happy state, in which we lived in peace and plenty, before these strangers came to disturb us, and above all, you must abstain from drinking their deadly *beson*, which they have forced upon us, for the sake of increasing their gains and diminishing our numbers. Then will the great Spirit give success to our arms; then he will give us strength to conquer our enemies, to drive them from hence, and recover the passage to the heavenly regions which they have taken from us."

Such was in general the substance of his discourses. After having dilated more or less on the various topics which I have mentioned, he commonly concluded in this manner: "And now, my friends, in order that what I have told you may remain firmly impressed on your minds, and to refresh your memories from time to time, I advise you to preserve, in every family, at least, such a book or writing as this, which I will finish off for you, provided you bring me the price, which is only one buckskin or two doe-skins a piece."[227] The price was of course bought,[228] and the book purchased. In some of those maps, the figure of a deer or turkey, or both, was placed in the heavenly regions, and also in the dreary region of the evil spirit; the former, however, appeared fat and plump, while the latter seemed to have nothing but skin and bones.

I was also well acquainted with another noted preacher, named *Wangomend*, who was of the Monsey tribe. He began to preach in the year 1766, much in the same manner as the one I have just mentioned. When Mr. Zeisberger first came to *Goschgoschink* town[229] on the Allegheny river, this Indian prophet became one of his hearers, but finding that the Missionary's doctrine did not agree with his own, he became his enemy. This man also pretended that his call as a preacher was not of his own choice, but that he had been moved to it by the great and good Spirit, in order to teach his countrymen, who were on the way to perdition, how they could become reconciled to their

236

God. He would make his followers believe that he had once been taken so near to heaven, that he could distinctly hear the crowing of the cocks, and that at another time he had been borne by unseen hands to where he had been permitted to take a peep into the heavens, of which there were three, one for the Indians, one for the negroes, and another for the white people. That of the Indians he observed to be the happiest of the three, and that of the whites the unhappiest; for they were under chastisement for their ill treatment of the Indians, and for possessing themselves of the land which God had given to them. They were also punished for making beasts of the negroes, by selling them as the Indians do their horses and dogs, and beating them unmercifully, although God had created them as well as the rest of mankind.

The novelty of these visions procured him hearers for a time; he found, however, at last, that the Indians became indifferent to his doctrines, particularly as he frequently warned them not to drink the *poison* brought to them by the white people, of which his congregation were very fond. Then he bethought himself of a more popular and interesting subject, and began to preach against witchcraft and those who dealt in the black art. Here he had all the passions and prejudices of the poor Indians on his side, and he did not fail to meet with the general approbation, when he declared to them that wizards were getting the upper hand, and would destroy the nation, if they were not checked in their career. He travelled in 1775, to *Goschachking*, at the forks of the Muskingum, to lay this business before the great council of the Delawares, and take their opinion upon it.

The first report which the Missionaries on the Muskingum heard on this subject, was that the chiefs had at first united in having every conjurer and witch in the nation brought to an account and punished with death, that, however, on a more mature consideration, they had thought proper in the first place to ascertain the number and names not only of those who were known, but even of those who were suspected of dealing in sorcery, and Wangomend was appointed to cause the enumeration to be made.

He accordingly hastily set off for his home; and on his arrival immediately entered on the duties of his mission; when behold! it was discovered that the number of offenders was much greater than had been at first imagined, and he found himself in danger of having his own name inserted in the black list. His zeal, in consequence, became considerably cooled, and by the time when he returned the chiefs were no longer disposed to meddle with this dangerous subject, justly fearing that it could not but terminate in the ruin of their nation. Wangomend, therefore, returned to his former mode of preaching, recommending to his hearers to purge themselves from sin by taking certain prescribed medicines, and making frequent sacrifices to the great Spirit.

The last whom I shall take notice of is the Prophet-warrior *Tecumseh*, lately so celebrated among us, and who lost his life in the last war at the battle of the Thames, on the 30th of September, 1813, at the age, it is said, of 43 years. The details of his military life have been made sufficiently known through the medium of journals and newspapers, and his famous speech to the British general Proctor delivered at Amhertsburg, a short time before the battle which decided his fate, is in every body's hands.[230] But his character as a prophet and the means that he took to raise himself to power and fame are not so well nor so particularly understood, although it is, in general, admitted that he was admirably skilled in the art of governing Indians through the medium of their passions. The sketch which I am going to draw will sufficiently prove how well this opinion is founded.

From the best information that I was able to obtain of this man, he was by nation a Shawanese, and began his career as a preacher much in the manner that others had done before him. He endeavoured to impress upon the minds of his Indian hearers, that they were a distinct people from the whites, that they had been created and placed on this soil for peculiar purposes, and that it had been ordered by the supreme being that they should live unconnected with people of a different colour from their own. He painted in vivid colours, the misery that they had brought upon themselves by permitting the whites to reside among them, and urged them to unite and expel those lawless intruders from their country.

But he soon discovered that these once popular topics no longer produced any effect on the minds of the dispirited Indians, and that it was impossible to persuade them to resort to strong measures, to oppose the progress of the whites, much less to endeavour to drive them beyond the great lake. He had long observed that whenever he touched on the subject of witchcraft, his discourses were always acceptable to his hearers, whose belief in those supernatural powers, instead of diminishing, seemed constantly to gain ground. He knew that his predecessor, Wangomend, had failed in his endeavour to gain influence and power by availing himself of these popular opinions. But his ill success did not deter him from making the same attempts. He did not, however, like him, seek the assistance of the national councils, but boldly determined to try what his talents and courage could do without any other aid.

There is a saying among the Indians, "That God ordained man to live until all his teeth are worn out, his eyesight dim and his hair grey." Of this he artfully availed himself to persuade those ignorant people, that the early deaths which constantly took place could not be attributed to any natural cause, since it was the will of God that every man should live to an advanced old age. When he found that he had thus obtained a fast hold on the minds of his hearers, by raising their fears of the powers of witchcraft to the highest pitch, he thought it was time to work on their hopes, and after gradually feeling the pulses of those he had to deal with, after successively throwing out a great number of hints and insinuations, the effects of which he had carefully observed, he at last did what no preacher before him had ventured to do, by declaring that the great Mannitto had endowed him with supernatural powers, to foretel future events, and to discover present secrets, and that he could point out with certainty, not only those, whether men or women, who were in the full possession of the art of witchcraft, but those who had even a tincture of it, however small.

His bold assertions met with implicit belief, and he obtained by that means such an unlimited command over a credulous multitude, that at last, he had only to speak the word, or even to nod, and the pile was quickly prepared by willing executioners to put to death whomsoever he thought proper to devote. Here was a wide field opened for the gratification of the worst passions. Whoever thought himself injured, denounced his enemy as a wizard; the least real or pretended cause of resentment, nay, even a paltry bribe, would bring the most innocent man to the pile or tomahawk, and no one availed himself more of this frantic delusion of the populace, than the great prophet himself. Having his spies out in every direction, he well knew who were his friends and who his enemies, and we to all who were reported to him or even suspected by him to be of the latter class! The tyrant had only to will their deaths, and his commands no one durst contradict, but all were ready to execute.

Among the number of his victims was the venerable Wyandot Chief Sha-te-ya-ron-yah, called by the whites *Leather-lips*. He was one of those who in August, 1795, signed the treaty of Greenville on behalf of the Huron tribe. His only crime was honesty, and the honourable character which he had acquired. In a fit of jealousy Tecumseh ordered him to be put to death, and his commands were but too readily obeyed. I cannot conclude this chapter better than by an account of his death, which was transmitted to me at the time (in August, 1810) by a respectable and philanthropic gentleman in the state of Ohio.

The relation which I here transcribe was accompanied with the following letter:

"DEAR SIR—

I here enclose an imperfect sketch of the execution of an unfortunate Indian. From your benevolent exertions, for many years, to ameliorate their condition, and the confidence reposed in you by them, I trust you may have it in your power successfully to oppose the wasteful influence of this prophet over these too credulous people. It is the office of humanity and worthy of the attention of the

Society of the United Brethren. I may be incorrect in the recital of some of the circumstances; it was given to me from respectable sources; sources, in my opinion, entitled to credit.

"I am, &c."

ACCOUNT OF THE DEATH OF LEATHER-LIPS.

"This unfortunate Chief of the Seneca[231] tribe, who had attained the sixty-third year of his age, had pitched his camp a few miles west of the town of Worthington in the county of Franklinton. From his constant attachment to the principles of honesty and integrity, he had obtained a certificate from an officer of the government as a testimonial of the propriety of his deportment. This aged Chief was suspected by the *Prophet*, a man of a restless, turbulent spirit, who by his exceeding address, has obtained an unbounded influence over many of the northern and western tribes of Indians, by impressing upon their minds a belief that he is endowed with supernatural knowledge, and can foretell events yet to come. This is the same prophet who gathered the Indians at Greenville a few years ago, from which meeting so much was apprehended. In order that he should no longer have anything to apprehend from him (this Indian) he issued orders for his immediate death.

These orders were given to *Crane*,[232] a chief of the Sandusky tribes, who immediately sat out with four other Indians, in quest of the old chief. About three weeks ago they found out his camp, and immediately sent his brother to him (who was one of their party) with a piece of bark, on which they had painted a tomahawk, as a token of his death! On the same day, Crane and his party spoke publicly in the settlements of the whites of their intention to kill him. When they sat out for his camp they were accompanied by five white men, amongst whom was a *justice of the peace*, no doubt to gratify their curiosity.

Upon their arrival at the camp, they informed him of the object of their mission, and that he must prepare to meet his fate! In vain did he remonstrate against the cruelty of the sentence; he told them that he was an old man, and must soon die; that if they would spare him they might have his camp, and that he would go far beyond the Mississippi, where he would never again be heard of. He also alleged that he was a man of honesty, and had done nothing to incur so hard a fate! One of the white men also made an offer of his horse, to save the old man from the impending storm. Those offers all proved ineffectual.

All hopes of a reconciliation now gone, he prepared to meet his fate with becoming dignity. While the Indians were digging his grave, he dressed himself with his best clothes in the war style, and then got his venison and refreshed himself. As soon as the grave was finished, he went to it and knelt down and prayed most fervently! He then took an affectionate leave of the Indians, and of the white men present, and when he came to the one who had offered his horse to redeem him, penetrated with gratitude, he burst into a flood of tears, and told him that *his God would reward him*. This was the only instance in which the least change could be perceived in his countenance. He was then attended to the grave by Crane—they knelt down, while Crane offered up to the great Spirit his prayers in his behalf.

The fatal period had now arrived; they arose from their knees, and proceeded a few paces, and seated themselves on the ground. The old chief inclined forward, resting his face upon his hand, his hand upon his knees; while thus seated, one of the young Indians came up and struck him twice with the tomahawk. For some time he lay senseless on the ground. The only evidence of life that yet remained, was a faint respiration. The Indians all stood around in solemn silence; finding him to respire longer than they expected, they called upon the whites to take notice how hard he died, and pronounced him a witch—no good—they struck him again and terminated his existence. He was then borne to the grave, where the last sad office was soon performed."

CHAPTER 40 ~
Short notice of the Indian Cheifs, Tamanend and Tadeuskund

The name of TAMANEND is held in the highest veneration among the Indians. Of all the chiefs and great men which the Lenape nation ever had, he stands foremost on the list. But although many fabulous stories are circulated about him among the whites, but little of his real history is known. The misfortunes which have befallen some of the most beloved and esteemed personages among the Indians since the Europeans came among them, prevent the survivors from indulging in the pleasure of recalling to mind the memory of their virtues. No white man who regards their feelings, will introduce such subjects in conversation with them.

All we know, therefore, of Tamanend is, that he was an ancient Delaware chief, who never had his equal.[233] He was in the highest degree endowed with wisdom, virtue, prudence, charity, affability, meekness, hospitality, in short with every good and noble qualification that a human being may possess. He was supposed to have had an intercourse with the great and good Spirit; for he was a stranger to everything that is bad.

When Colonel George Morgan, of Princeton in New Jersey, was, about the year 1776, sent by Congress as an agent to the western Indians, the Delawares conferred on him the name of Tamanend in honour and remembrance of their ancient chief, and as the greatest mark of respect which they could shew to that gentleman, who, they said, had the same address, affability and meekness as their honoured chief, and therefore, ought to be named after him.

The fame of this great man extended even among the whites, who fabricated numerous legends respecting him, which I never heard, however, from the mouth of an Indian, and therefore believe to be fabulous. In the Revolutionary war, his enthusiastic admirers dubbed him a saint, and he was established under the name of *St. Tammany*, the Patron Saint of America. His name was inserted in some calendars, and his festival celebrated on the first day of May in every year. On that day a numerous society of his votaries walked together in procession through the streets of Philadelphia, their hats decorated with bucks' tails, and proceeded to a handsome rural place out of town which they called the *Wigwam*, where, after a *long talk* or Indian speech had been delivered, and the *Calumet* of peace and friendship had been duly smoked, they spent the day in festivity and mirth. After dinner, Indian dances were performed on the green in front of the wigwam, the calumet was again smoked, and the company separated.

This association lasted until some years after the peace, when the public spirited owner of the wigwam, who generously had lent it every year for the honour of his favourite saint, having fallen under misfortune, his property was sold to satisfy his creditors, and this truly American festival ceased to be observed. Since that time, other societies have been formed in Philadelphia, New York, and I believe in other towns in the Union, under the name of Tammany; but the principal object of these associations being party-politics, they have lost much of the charm which was attached to the original society of St. Tammany, which appeared to be established only for pleasure and innocent diversion.

These political societies, however, affect to preserve Indian forms in their organisation and meetings. They are presided over by a Grand Sachem, and their other officers are designated by Indian titles. They meet at their "wigwam," at the "going down of the sun," in the months of snows, plants, flowers, &c. Their distinguishing appellation is always "The *Tammany* Society."

TADEUSKUND, or *Tedeuskung*, was the last Delaware chief in these parts east of the Allegheny mountains. His name makes a conspicuous figure in the history of Pennsylvania previous to the revolution, and particularly towards the commencement of the war of 1756. Before he was raised to the station of a chief, he had signalised himself as an able counsellor in his nation. In the year 1749, he joined the Christian Indian congregation, and the following year, at his earnest desire, was christened by the name of *Gideon*.[234]

He had been known before under that of *Honest John*. It was not until the year 1754, that his nation called upon him to assume a military command. The French were then stirring up the Indians, particularly the Delawares, to aid them in fighting the English, telling them that if they suffered them to go on as they before had done, they would very soon not have a foot of land to live on. The Susquehannah and Fork Indians (Delawares) were then in want of a leading character to advise and govern them, their great, good, beloved and peaceable chief *Tademe*, (commonly called *Tattemi*) having some time before been murdered in the Forks settlement by a foolish young white man.[235] They, therefore, called upon Tadeuskund to take upon himself the station of a chief, which, having accepted, he repaired to Wyoming, whither many of the Fork Indians followed him.

Whatever might have been Tadeuskund's disposition towards the English at that time, it is certain that it was a difficult task for him, and would have been such for any other chief, to govern an exasperated people, entirely devoted to the opposite interest. This may account for his not having always succeeded in gratifying our government to the extent of its wishes. Yet he did much towards lessening the cruelties of the enemy, by keeping up an intercourse with the governor of Pennsylvania, and occasionally drawing many from the theatre of war and murder, to meet the colonial authorities at Easton or Philadelphia for the negotiation of treaties, by which means fewer cruelties were committed than would otherwise have been.

His frequent visits to the governor and to the people called Quakers (to whom he was much attached, because they were known to be friendly to the Indians) excited much jealousy among some of his nation, especially the Monseys, who believed that he was carrying on some underhand work at Philadelphia detrimental to the nation at large; on which account, and as they wished the continuation of the war, they became his enemies.

From the precarious situation Tadeuskund was placed in, it was easy to foresee that he would come to an untimely end.

Perhaps no Indian chief before him ever found himself so delicately situated; mistrusted and blamed by our government and the English people generally, because he did not use his whole endeavours to keep his nation at peace, or compel them to lay down the hatchet; and accused by his own people of having taken a bribe from the English, or entered into some secret agreement with them that would be of benefit to himself alone, as he would not suffer them to inflict just punishment on that nation for the wrongs they had done them, but was constantly calling upon them to make peace. The Five Nations, on the other hand, (the enemies of the Delawares and in alliance with England,) blamed him for doing too much for the cause which they themselves supported, for making himself too busy, and assuming an authority, which did not belong to him the leader of a band of *women*, but to them, the Five Nations alone.

To do justice to this injured chief, the true secret of his apparently contradictory conduct must be here disclosed. It is said by those Indians who knew him best, and who at that time had the welfare of their own nation much at heart, that his great and sole object was to recover for the *Lenni Lenape* that dignity which the Iroquois had treacherously wrested from them; thence flowed the bitterness of the latter against him, though he seemed to be promoting the same interest which they themselves supported. He had long hoped that by shewing friendship and attachment to the English, he would be able to convince them of the justice of his nation's cause, who were yet powerful enough to make their alliance an object to the British government; but here he was greatly mistaken.

No one would examine into the grounds of the controversy between the Delawares and the Five Nations; the latter, on the contrary, were supported in their unjust pretensions as theretofore, and even called upon to aid in compelling the Lenape to make peace. This unjust and at the same time impolitic conduct, of which I have before taken sufficient notice,[236] irritated to the utmost the spirited nation of the Delawares, they felt

246

themselves insulted and degraded, and were less disposed than ever from complying with the wishes of a government which sported in this manner with their national feelings, and called in question even their right to exist as an independent people.

Surrounded as he was with enemies, Tadeuskund could not escape the fate that had long been intended for him. In the spring of 1763, when the European nations had made peace, but the Indians were still at war, he was burnt up, together with his house, as he was lying in his bed asleep. It was supposed and believed by many who were present, that this dreadful event was not accidental, but had been maturely resolved on by his enemies, whoever they were, and that the liquor which was brought to Wyoming at the time, was intended by them for the purpose of enticing him to drink, that they might the more easily effect their purpose. A number of Indians were witnesses to the fact that the house was set on fire from the outside. Suspicion fell principally upon the Mingoes, who were known to be jealous of him, and fearful of his resentment, if he should succeed in insinuating himself into the favour of the English and making good terms with them for his nation. It is said that those Indians were concerned in bringing the fatal liquor which is believed to have been instrumental to the execution of the design.

While Tadeuskund was at the head of his nation, he was frequently distinguished by the title of "King of the Delawares." While passing and repassing to and from the enemy with messages, many people called him the "War Trumpet." In his person he was a portly well-looking man, endowed with good natural sense, quick of comprehension, and very ready in answering the questions put to him. He was rather ambitious, thought much of his rank and abilities, liked to be considered as the king of his country, and was fond of having a retinue with him when he went to Philadelphia on business with the government. His greatest weakness was a fondness for strong drinks, the temptation of which he could not easily resist, and would sometimes drink to excess. This unfortunate propensity is supposed to have been the cause of his cruel and untimely death.

CHAPTER 41 ~
Computation of time; astronomical and geographical knowledge

The Indians do not reckon as we do, by days, but by nights. They say: "It is so many nights' travelling to such a place;" "I shall return home in so many nights," &c. Sometimes pointing to the heavens they say: "You will see me again when the sun stands there."

Their year is, like ours, divided into four parts: spring, summer, autumn, and winter. It begins with the spring, which, they say, is the youth of the year, the time when the spirits of man begin to revive, and the plants and flowers again put forth. These seasons are again subdivided into months or moons, each of which has a particular name, yet not the same among all the Indian tribes or nations; these denominations being generally suited to the climate under which they respectively live, and the advantages or benefits which they enjoy at the time.

Thus the Lenape, while they inhabited the country bordering on the Atlantic, called the month which we call March, "the *shad* moon," because this fish at that time begins to pass from the sea into the fresh water rivers, where they lay their spawn; but as there is no such fish in the country into which they afterwards removed, they changed the name of that month, and called it "the running of the *sap*" or "the *sugar*-making month," because it is at that time that the sap of the maple tree, from which sugar is made, begins to run; April, they call "the *spring* month," May, the *planting* month, June, the *fawn* month, or the month in which the deer bring forth their young, or, again, the month in which the hair of the deer changes to a reddish colour. They call July the *summer* month; August, the month of *roasting ears*, that is to say, in which the ears of corn are fit to be roasted and eaten. September, they call

248

the *autumnal* month, October, the gathering or *harvest* month; December, the *hunting* month, it being the time when the stags have all dropped their antlers or horns. January is called the *mouse* or *squirrel* month, for now those animals come out of their holes, and lastly, they call February the *frog* month, because on a warm day the frogs then begin to croak.

Some nations call the month of January by a name which denotes "the sun's return to them," probably because in that month the days begin to lengthen again. As I have said before, they do not call all the months by the same name; even the Monseys, a tribe of the Delawares, differ among themselves in the denominations which they give to them.

The Indians say that when the leaf of the white oak, which puts forth in the spring, is of the size of the ear of a mouse, it is time to plant corn; they observe that now the whippoorwill has arrived, and is continually hovering over them, calling out his Indian name "*Wekolis*" in order to remind them of the planting time, as if he said to them "*Hackiheck!* go to planting corn!"

They calculate their ages by some remarkable event which has taken place within their remembrance, as, for instance, an uncommonly severe winter, a very deep snow, an extraordinary freshet, a general war, the building of a new town or city by the white people, &c. Thus I have heard old Indians say more than fifty years ago, that when their brother Miquon spoke to their forefathers, they were of such an age or size, they could catch butterflies, or hit a bird with the bow and arrow. I have heard others say (alluding to the hard winter of 1739-40) that they were born at that time, or that they were then so tall, could do certain particular things, or had already some gray hair on their heads. When they could not refer precisely to some of those remarkable epochs, they would say "so many winters after."

The geographical knowledge of the Indians is really astonishing. I do not mean the knowledge of maps, for they have nothing of the kind to aid them; but their practical acquaintance with the country that they inhabit. They can steer directly through the woods in cloudy weather as well as in sunshine to the place they wish to go to, at the distance of two hundred miles and more. When the white people express their astonishment, or enquire how they can hit a distant point with so much ease and exactness, they smile and answer: "How can we go wrong when we know where we are to go to?"

There are many who conjecture that they regulate their course by certain signs or marks on the trees, as for instance, that those that have the thickest bark are exposed to the north, and other similar observations, but those who think so are mistaken. The fact is, that the Indians have an accurate knowledge of all the streams of consequence and the courses which they run; they can tell directly while travelling along a stream, whether large or small, into what larger stream it empties itself. They know how to take the advantage of dividing ridges, where the smaller streams have their heads, or from whence they take their source, and in travelling on the mountains, they have a full view of the country round, and can perceive the point to which their march is directed.

Their knowledge of astronomy is very limited. They have names for a few of the stars and take notice of their movements. The polar star points out to them by night the course which they are to take in the morning. They distinguish the phases of the moon by particular names; they say the "new moon," the "round moon" (when it is full), and when in its decline, they say it is "half round."

They ascribe earthquakes to the moving of the great tortoise, which bears the *Island* (Continent) on its back. They say he shakes himself or changes his position. They are at a loss how to account for a solar or lunar eclipse; some say the sun or moon is in a swoon, others that it is involved in a very thick cloud.

A constant application of the mind to observing the scenes and accidents which occur in the woods, together with an ardent desire to acquire an intimate knowledge of the various objects which surround them, gives them, in many respects, an advantage over the white people, which will appear from the following anecdote.

A white man had, at his camp in a dark night, shot an Indian dog, mistaking it for a wolf which had the night before entered the encampment and eaten up all the meat. The dog mortally wounded, having returned to the Indian camp at the distance of a mile, caused much grief and uneasiness to the owner, the more so as he suspected the act had been committed from malice towards the Indians. He was ordered to enquire into the matter, and the white man being brought before him, candidly confessed that he had killed the dog, believing it to be a wolf. The Indian asked him whether he could not discern the difference between the "steps" or trampling of a wolf and that of a dog, let the night be ever so dark? The white man answered in the negative, and said he believed no man alive could do that; on which the whole company burst out into laughter at the ignorance of the whites and their want of skill in so plain and common a matter, and the delinquent was freely forgiven.

CHAPTER 42 ~
General observations and anecdotes

I hope I shall be excused for bringing here together into one view a few observations and anecdotes which either could not well find their places under any of the preceding divisions of my subject, or escaped my recollection at the proper time. These additional traits will contribute something to forming a correct idea of the Indian character and manners.

I have observed a great similarity in the customs, usages, and opinions of the different nations that I have seen, however distant from each other, and even though their languages differ so much that no traces of a common origin can be found in their etymology. The uniformity which exists in the manners of the Christian nations of Europe is attributed to their common religion, and to their having once been connected together as parts of the Roman Empire. But no such bond of union appears to have subsisted between the Iroquois, for instance, and the Delawares, and yet, the language excepted, they resemble each other considerably more than the inhabitants of some European countries. I shall not endeavour to account for this remarkable fact, but I think it my duty to state it.

I have shown in a former chapter[237] that the mythological notions of the Delaware Indians prevailed in the same manner among the Wabash; it is not in that alone that those nations resemble each other, though living at a great distance. It is the custom among the Delawares that if a hunter shoots down a deer when another person is present, or even accidentally comes by before the skin is taken off, he presents it to him, saying, "Friend, skin your deer," and immediately walks off. William Wells, whom I have before spoken of, once paid me this compliment, and when I asked him the reason, he answered that it was the custom among the Indians on the Wabash.

In the year 1792, I travelled with a number of Indian chiefs of various tribes from Post Vincennes to Marietta, and I found in most instances that their usages and customs were the same that I had observed among the Delawares.[238]

The Indians in general, although they understand and speak our language, yet prefer speaking to a white man through an interpreter. For this they give various reasons. With some it is a matter of pride; as their chiefs deliver their public speeches through interpreters, they think that they appear with more dignity when they do the same. Others imagine that their words will have greater weight and effect when expressed in proper grammatical language, while some are afraid of committing mistakes when speaking in an idiom not their own. Particularly when they have a joke to pass, a hint to give, or a shrewd remark to make, they wish it to have all the advantages of a good translation, and that their wit may not be spoiled by a foreign accent, improper expression, or awkward delivery.

Though the Indian is naturally serious, he does not dislike a jest on proper occasions, and will, sometimes, even descend to a pun. Once at a dinner given at Marietta by the late Colonel Sproat,[239] to a number of gentlemen and Indian chiefs of various tribes, a Delaware chief, named George Washington, asked me what the name of our good friend, the Colonel, meant in the Lenape language? It should be observed that Colonel Sproat was remarkably tall. I told him that *Sprout* (for so the name is pronounced) meant in English a shoot, or twig of a tree. "No, no," replied the Indian, "no shoot or twig, but the *tree* itself."

I have spoken before[240] of the wit of the Indians, and the shrewd and pointed remarks which they occasionally make, but passed rather lightly on the subject. A few characteristic anecdotes will best supply this deficiency.

An Indian who spoke good English, came one day to a house where I was on business, and desired me to ask a man who was there and who owed him some money, to give an order in writing for him to get a little salt at the store, which he would take in part payment of his debt. The man, after reproving the Indian for speaking through an interpreter when he could speak such good English, told him that he must call again in an hour's time, for he was then too much engaged. The Indian went out and returned at the appointed time, when he was put off again for another hour, and when he came the third time, the other told him he was still engaged, and he must come again in half an hour.

My Indian friend's patience was now exhausted, he turned to me and addressed me thus in his own language: "Tell this man," said he, "that while I have been waiting for his convenience to give me an order for a little salt, I have had time to think a great deal. I *thought* that when we Indians want any thing of one another, we serve each other on the spot, or if we cannot, we say so at once, but we never say to any one 'call again! call again! call again! three times call again!' Therefore when this man put me off in this manner, I *thought* that, to be sure, the white people were very ingenious, and probably he was able to do what no body else could. I *thought* that as it was afternoon when I first came, and he knew I had seven miles to walk to reach my camp, he had it in his power to stop the sun in its course, until it suited him to give me the order that I wanted for a little salt. So *thought* I, I shall still have day light enough, I shall reach my camp before night, and shall not be obliged to walk in the dark, at the risk of falling and hurting myself by the way. But when I saw that the sun did not wait for him, and I had at least to walk seven miles in an obscure night, I *thought* then, that it would be better if the white people were to learn something of the Indians."

I once asked an old Indian acquaintance of mine, who had come with his wife to pay me a visit, where he had been, that I had not seen him for a great while? "Don't you know," he answered, "that the white people some time ago summoned us to a treaty, to buy land of them?"[241]—"That is true," replied I, "I had indeed forgotten it; I thought you was just returned from your fall hunt."—"No, no," replied the Indian, "my fall hunt has been lost to me this season; I had to go and get my share of the purchase money for the land we sold."—"Well then," said I, "I suppose you got enough to satisfy you?"

INDIAN. *"I can shew you all that I got. I have received such and such articles, (naming them and the quantity of each), do you think that is enough?"*

HECKEW. *"That I cannot know, unless you tell me how much of the land which was sold came to your share."*

INDIAN. (after considering a little), *"Well, you, my friend! know who I am, you know I am a kind of chief. I am, indeed, one, though none of the greatest. Neither am I one of the lowest grade, but I stand about in the middle rank. Now, as such, I think I was entitled to as much land in the tract we sold as would lie within a day's walk from this spot to a point due north, then a day's walk from that point to another due west, from thence another day's walk due south, then a day's walk to where we now are. Now you can tell me if what I have shewn you is enough for all the land lying between these four marks?"*

HECKEW. *"If you have made your bargain so with the white people, it is all right, and you probably have received your share."*

INDIAN. *"Ah! but the white people made the bargain by themselves, without consulting us. They told us that they would give us so much, and no more."*

HECKEW. *"Well, and you consented thereto?"*

INDIAN. *"What could we do, when they told us that they must have the land, and for such a price? Was it not better to take something than nothing? for they would have the land, and so we took what they gave us."*

HECKEW. *"Perhaps the goods they gave you came high in price. The goods which come over the great salt water lake sometimes vary in their prices."*

INDIAN. *"The traders sell their goods for just the same prices that they did before, so that I rather think it is the land that has fallen in value. We, Indians, do not understand selling lands* to the white people; for when we sell, the price of land is always low; land is then cheap, but when the white people sell it out among themselves, it is always dear, and they are sure to get a high price for it. I had done much better if I had stayed at home and minded my fall hunt. You know I am a pretty good hunter and might have killed a great many deer, sixty, eighty, perhaps a hundred, and besides caught many raccoons, beavers, otters, wild cats, and other animals, while I was at this treaty. I have often killed five, six, and seven deer in one day. Now I have lost nine of the best hunting weeks in the season by going to get what you see! We were told the precise time when we must meet. We came at the very day, but the great white men did not do so, and without them nothing could be done. When after some weeks they at last came, we traded, we sold our lands and received goods in payment, and when that was over, I went to my hunting grounds, but the best time, the rutting time, being over, I killed but a few. Now, help me to count up what I have lost by going to the treaty. Put down eighty deer; say twenty of them were bucks, each buckskin one dollar; then sixty does and young bucks at two skins for a dollar; thirty dollars, and twenty for the old bucks, make fifty dollars lost to me in deer skins. Add, then, twenty dollars more to this for raccoon, beaver, wild cat, black fox, and otter skins, and what does the whole amount to?"

HECKEW. "Seventy dollars."

INDIAN. "Well, let it be only seventy dollars, but how much might I have bought of the traders for this money! How well we might have lived, I and my family in the woods during that time! How much meat would my wife have dried! how much tallow saved and sold or exchanged for salt, flour, tea and chocolate! All this is now lost to us; and had I not such a good wife (stroking her under the chin) who planted so much corn, and so many beans, pumpkins, squashes, and potatoes last summer, my family would now live most wretchedly. I have learned to be wise by going to treaties, I shall never go there again to sell my land and lose my time."

I shall conclude this desultory chapter with another anecdote which is strongly characteristic of the good sense of the Indians and shews how much their minds are capable of thought and reflection.

Seating myself once upon a log, by the side of an Indian, who was resting himself there, being at that time actively employed in fencing in his corn-field, I observed to him that he must be very fond of working, as I never saw him idling away his time, as is so common with the Indians. The answer which he returned made considerable impression on my mind; I have remembered it ever since, and I shall try to relate it as nearly in his own words as possible.

"My friend!" said he, "the fishes in the water and the birds in the air and on the earth have taught me to work; by their examples I have been convinced of the necessity of labour and industry. When I was a young man I loitered a great deal about, doing nothing, just like the other Indians, who say that working is only for the whites and the negroes, and that the Indians have been ordained for other purposes, to hunt the deer, and catch the beaver, otter, raccoon and such other animals. But it one day so happened, that while a hunting, I came to the bank of the Susquehannah, where I sat down near the water's edge to rest a little, and casting my eye on the water, I was forcibly struck when I observed with what industry the *Meechgalingus*[242] heaped small stones together, to make secure places for their spawn, and all this labour they did with their mouths and bodies without hands!

Astonished as well as diverted, I lighted my pipe, sat a while smoking and looking on, when presently a little bird not far from me raised a song which enticed me to look that way; while I was trying to distinguish who the songster was, and catch it with my eyes, its mate, with as much grass as with its bill it could hold, passed close by me and flew into a bush, where I perceived them together busy building their nest and singing as they went along. I entirely forgot that I was a hunting, in order to contemplate the objects I had before me. I saw the birds of the air and the fishes in the water working diligently and cheerfully, and all this without hands! I thought it was strange, and became lost in contemplation!

I looked at myself, I saw two long arms, provided with hands and fingers besides, with joints that might be opened and shut at pleasure. I could, when I pleased, take up anything with these hands, hold it fast or let it loose, and carry it along with me as I walked. I observed moreover that I had a strong body capable of bearing fatigue, and supported by two stout legs, with which I could climb to the top of the highest mountains and descend at pleasure into the valleys. And is it possible, said I, that a being so formed as I am, was created to live in idleness, while the birds who have no hands, and nothing but their little bills to help them, work with cheerfulness and without being told to do so? Has then the great Creator of man and of all living creatures given me all these limbs for no purpose? It cannot be; I will try to go to work. I did so, and went away from the village to a spot of good land, built a cabin, enclosed ground, planted corn, and raised cattle. Ever since that time I have enjoyed a good appetite and sound sleep; while the others spend their nights in dancing and are suffering with hunger, I live in plenty; I keep horses, cows, hogs and fowls; I am happy. See! my friend; the birds and fishes have brought me to reflection and taught me to work!"

CHAPTER 43 ~
Advice to travellers

Nothing is so common as the indiscriminate charge laid upon traveller of relating strange and wonderful things for the mere purpose of exciting admiration and raising themselves into consequence. I believe for my part that this accusation is in general unjust as well as unfair, and that travellers seldom impose upon others except when they have been imposed upon themselves. The discredit which they have fallen into is more owing to their errors and mistakes than to wilful imposition and falsehood. It is therefore rendering them and the world an essential service to point out the means of avoiding those deceptions, which if not sufficiently guarded against, will at last destroy all belief in the accounts given by travellers of distant nations and of manners and customs different from our own.

The first and most important thing for a traveller is a competent knowledge of the language of the people among whom he is. Without this knowledge it is impossible that he can acquire a correct notion of their manners and customs and of the opinions which prevail among them. There is little faith to be placed in those numerous vocabularies of the languages of distant nations which are to be found in almost every book of voyages or travels; they are generally full of the most ridiculous mistakes; at least (for I must speak only of what I know) those which relate to the Indian languages of North America. I was some years ago shewn a vocabulary[243] of the idiom of the Indians who inhabited the banks of the Delaware, while Pennsylvania was under the dominion of the Swedes, which idiom was no other than the pure Unami dialect of the Lenape, and I could hardly refrain from laughing at the numerous errors that I observed in it; for instance, the Indian word given for *hand* in fact means *finger*. This is enough to shew how carelessly those vocabularies are made, and how little their authors are acquainted with the languages that they pretend to teach.

The cause of these mistakes may be easily accounted for. When pointing to a particular object you ask an Indian how it is called, he never will give you the name of the *genus*, but always that of the *species*. Thus, if you point to a tree, and ask for its name, the answer will be oak, beech, chestnut, maple, &c., as the case may be. Thus the Swedish author of the vocabulary that I have mentioned, probably happened to point to a *finger*, when he asked what was the Indian word for *hand*, and on receiving the answer, without further enquiry enriched his work with this notable specimen of Indian learning.

When I first went to reside among the Indians, I took great care to learn by heart the words *Kœcu k'delloundamen yun?* which means *What do you call this?* Whenever I found the Indians disposed to attend to my enquiries, I would point to particular objects and repeat my formulary, and the answers that they gave I immediately wrote down in a book which I kept for the purpose; at last, when I had written about half a dozen sheets, I found that I had more than a dozen names for "*tree*" as many for "*fish*," and so on with other things, and yet I had not a single generic name. What was still worse, when I pointed to something, repeating the name or one of the names by which I had been taught to call it, I was sure to excite a laugh; and when, in order to be set right, I put the question *Kœcu*, &c., I would receive for answer a new word or name which I had never heard before. This began to make me believe that everything was not as it should be, and that I was not in the right way to learn the Indian language.

It was not only in substantives or the proper names of things that I found myself almost always mistaken. Those who are not acquainted with the copiousness of the Indian languages, can hardly form an idea of the various shades and combinations of ideas that they can express. For instance, the infinitive *Mitzin* signifies *to eat*, and so does *Mohoan*. Now although the first of these words is sufficiently expressive of the act of eating something, be it what it may, yet the Indians are very attentive to expressing in one word what and how they have eaten, that is to say whether they have been eating something which needed no chewing, as pottage, mush or the like, or something that required the use of the teeth. In the latter case the proper word is *mohoan*, and in the former *guntammen*. If an Indian is asked *k'dapi mitzi?* have you eaten? he will answer *n'dapi guntammen*, or *n'dapi mohoa*, according as what he has eaten did or did not require the aid of chewing. If he has eaten of both kinds of provisions at his meal, he will then use the generic word, and say, *n'dapi mitzi*, which means generally, *I have eaten.*

These niceties of course escaped me, and what was worse, few of the words I had taken down were correctly written. Essential letters or syllables, which in the rapidity of pronunciation had escaped my ear, were almost everywhere omitted. When I tried to make use of the words which I had so carefully collected, I found I was not understood, and I was at a loss to discover the cause to which I might attribute my want of success in the earnest endeavours that I was making to acquire the Indian tongue.

At last there came an Indian, who was conversant with the English and German, and was much my friend. I hastened to lay before him my learned collection of Indian words, and was very much astonished when he advised me immediately to burn the whole, and write no more. "The first thing," said he, "that you are to do to learn our language is to get an Indian *ear*; when that is obtained, no sound, no syllable will ever escape your hearing it, and you will at the same time learn the true pronunciation and how to accent your words properly; the rest will come of itself." I found he was right. By listening to the natives, and repeating the words to myself as they spoke them, it was not many months before I ventured to converse with them, and finally understood every word they said. The Indians are very proud of a white man's endeavouring to learn their language; they help him in everything that they can, and it is not their fault if he does not succeed.

The language, then, is the first thing that a traveller ought to endeavour to acquire, at least, so as to be able to make himself understood and to understand others. Without this indispensable requisite he may write about the soil, earth and stones, describe trees and plants that grow on the surface of the land, the birds

261

that fly in the air and the fishes that swim in the waters, but he should by no means attempt to speak of the disposition and characters of the human beings who inhabit the country, and even of their customs and manners, which it is impossible for him to be sufficiently acquainted with. And indeed, even with the advantage of the language, this knowledge is not to be acquired in a short time, so different is the impression which new objects make upon us at first sight, and that which they produce on a nearer view. I could speak the Delaware language very fluently, but I was yet far from being well acquainted with the character and manners of the Lenape.

The Indians are very ready to answer the enquiries that are made respecting the usages of their country. But they are very much disgusted with the manner which they say some white people have of asking them questions on questions, without allowing them time to give a proper answer to any one of them. They, on the contrary, never ask a second question until they have received a full answer to the first. They say of those who do otherwise, that they seem as if they wished to know a thing, yet cared not whether they knew it correctly or properly. There are some men who before the Indians have well understood the question put to them, begin to write down their answers; of these they have no good opinion, thinking that they are writing something unfavourable of them.

There are men who will relate incredible stories of the Indians, and think themselves sufficiently warranted because they have Indian authority for it. But these men ought to know that all an Indian says is not to be relied upon as truth. I do not mean to say that they are addicted to telling falsehoods, for nothing is farther from their character; but they are fond of the marvellous, and when they find a white man inclined to listen to their 322 tales of wonder, or credulous enough to believe their superstitious notions, there are always some among them ready to entertain him with tales of that description, as it gives them an opportunity of diverting themselves in their leisure hours, by relating such fabulous stories, while they laugh at the same time at their being able to deceive a people who think themselves so superior to them in wisdom and knowledge. They are fond of trying white men who

262

come among them, in order to see whether they can act upon them in this way with success.

Travellers who cannot speak their language, and are not acquainted with their character, manners and usages, should be more particularly careful not to ask them questions that touch in any manner upon their superstitious notions, or, as they are often considered even by themselves "fabulous amusements." Nor should a stranger ever display an anxiety to witness scenes of this kind, but rather appear indifferent about them. In this manner he cannot be misled by interested persons or those who have formed a malicious design to deceive him. Whenever such a disposition appears (and it is not difficult to be discovered), questions of this kind should be reserved for another time, and asked in a proper manner before other persons, or of those who would be candid and perhaps let the enquirer into the secret.

I have been led to consider Carver, who otherwise is deserving of credit for the greatest part of what he has written on the character of the Indians, to have been imposed upon in the story which he relates of having learned by means of a conjurer (the chief priest of the Killistenoes, as he calls him) who pretended to have had a conversation with the great Spirit, the precise time when a canoe should come, and certain traders who had been long expected should arrive.[244] Had Carver resided a longer time among the Indians, so as to have acquired a more intimate acquaintance with their customs,[245] he would have known that they have one in particular (which I understand is universal among all the tribes), which would have easily explained to him what he thought so mysterious. Whenever they go out on a journey, whether far or near, and even sometimes when they go out on hunting parties, they always fix a day, on which they either will return, or their friends at home shall hear from them.

They are so particular and punctual in "making their word true," as they call it, that when they find that at the rate they are travelling, they would probably be at home a day or so sooner than the time appointed, they will rather lay by for that time than that their word should not be precisely made good. I have known instances when they might have arrived in very good time the day preceding that which they had appointed, but they rather chose to encamp for the night, though but a few miles distant from their home. They urge a variety of reasons for this conduct. In the first place, they are anxious not to occasion disappointment in any case when they can avoid it. They consider punctuality as an essential virtue, because, they say, much often depends upon it, particularly when they are engaged in wars. Besides, when the day of their return is certainly known, everything is prepared for their reception, and the family are ready with the best that they can provide to set before them on their arrival. If, however, unforeseen circumstances should prevent them from coming all on the same day, one, at least, or more of them, will be sure to arrive, from whom those at home will learn all that they wish to know.

On all important occasions, in which a tribe or body of Indians are concerned or interested, whether they are looking out for the return of an embassy sent to a distant nation, for messengers with an answer on some matter of consequence, for runners despatched by their spies who are watching an enemy's motions, or for traders who at stated periods every year are sure to meet them at certain places, they always take proper and efficacious measures to prevent being surprised.

The case which appears to have excited so much astonishment in Captain Carver, I believe to have been simply this. The Indians[246] had at the season that he speaks of failed to arrive at the trading place at the time appointed. The Indians who had assembled there for the purpose of meeting them could not be ignorant of the cause of their delay, as they had, no doubt, learned it by the return of some of their runners sent out for that purpose, who, as is their custom, probably informed them that another set of runners would be in the next day with further advices. The priest must have known all this, and the precise spot where those fresh runners were to encamp the night preceding their arrival, which is always well known and understood by means of the regular chain of communication that is kept up. These runners say to each other, pointing to the heavens: "When the sun stands there, I will be here or at such a particular spot," which they clearly designate. The information thus given is sure to reach in time the chiefs of the nation.

The manner in which this priest spoke to Captain Carver of his pretended intercourse with the great Spirit, clearly shews the deception that he was practising upon him. "The great Spirit," said he, "has not indeed told me when the persons we expect will be here, but to-morrow, soon after the sun has reached his highest point in the heavens, a canoe will arrive, and the people in that will inform us when the traders will come." The question, then, which he had put to the great Spirit, "when the traders would come?" was not answered, and there was no need of asking the Mannitto when the *canoes* should come, for that must have been known already, and that the people in it would tell them where the traders were, and when they might be expected to arrive.

As in or about the year 1774, I was travelling with some Christian Indians, two Indians of the same nation, but strangers to us, fell in with us just as we were going to encamp, and joined us for the night. One of them was an aged grave-looking man, whom I was pleased to see in our company, and I flattered myself with obtaining some information from him, as, according to the Indian custom, age always takes the lead in conversation. I soon, however, perceived, to my great mortification, that he dwelt on subjects which I had neither a taste for nor an ear to hear; for his topic was the supernatural performances of Indians through the agency of an unseen Mannitto. I did not pay any attention to what he said, nor did any of our Christian Indians shew marks of admiration or astonishment at the stories he was telling, but sat in silence smoking their pipes. The speaker having, after an hour's time, finished his relations, the oldest Indian in my company addressed himself to me and said: "Now you have heard what some Indians can perform. Have you ever heard the like before, and do you believe all you have heard?" "There are," I answered, "many things that I have heard of the Indians, and which I believe to be true, and such things I like to hear; but there are also things which they relate which I do not believe, and therefore do not wish to know them. While our friend here was just now telling us stories of this kind, which I cannot believe, I

265

was wishing all the time that he might soon have finished and tell us something better."

The Indian, taking the hint in good part, asked me then what things I should like to hear? On which I made this reply: "As you are a man already in years, and much older than myself, you must have seen many things that I have not seen, and heard much that I have not heard. Now I should like to hear the history of your life; where you was born, at what age you shot your first deer, what things you heard of your father and your grandfather relative to old times; where they supposed the Indians to have come from, and what traditions they had respecting them. I should like also to know how many children you have had; how far you have travelled in your lifetime, and what you have seen and heard in your travels. See!" added I, "these are the things that I should like to hear of the Indians; anything of the kind from you will give me pleasure." The Indian then, highly pleased with my candour, readily complied, and having related everything remarkable that had come within his observation and knowledge, I thanked him, saying that I should never forget him nor what he had now related to me, but that I would try to forget what he had related in the beginning. The Indians who were with me, following the thread of the conversation, continued to entertain us with rational stories, and the evening was spent very agreeably. In the morning, when we parted, the strange Indian whom I had thus rebuked, shook me cordially by the hand, saying: "Friend! you shall never be forgotten by me. Indeed I call you my *friend*."

I would take the liberty to recommend to those who may hereafter travel among the Indians, in any part of America, to be particular in their enquiries respecting the connexion of the different nations or tribes with each other, especially when the analogy of their respective languages leads to infer such *relationship*, as the Indians call it. I beg leave to suggest a few questions, which, I think, ought always to be asked. They may lead to much useful information respecting the various migrations and the original places of residence of the Indian nations, and perhaps produce more important discoveries.

1. What is the name of your tribe? Is it its original name; if not, how was it formerly called?

2. Have you a tradition of your lineal descent as a nation or tribe?

3. To what tribes are you related by blood, and where do they reside?

4. What is your character or rank in the national family?

5. Which among the tribes connected with you is that which you call *grandfather*?

6. Where is the great council fire of all the nations or tribes connected with yours?

7. How do you address the chiefs and council of such a nation or tribe?

8. What is the badge of your tribe?

From these and other similar questions, much valuable information will probably result. The nation whom another tribe calls *grandfather*, is certainly the head of the family to which they both belong. At his door burns the "great national council fire," or, in other words, at the place where he resides with his counsellors, as the great or supreme chief of the national family, the heads of the tribes in the connexion occasionally assemble to deliberate on their common interests; any tribe may have a council fire of its own, but cannot dictate to the other tribes, nor compel any of them to take up the hatchet against an enemy; neither can they conclude a peace for the whole; this power entirely rests with the great national chief, who presides at the council fire of their *grandfather*.

Indian nations or tribes connected with each other are not always connected by blood or descended from the same original stock. Some are admitted into the connexion by adoption. Such are the Tuscaroras among the Six Nations; such the

Cherokees among the Lenni Lenape. Thus, in the year 1779, a deputation of fourteen men came from the Cherokee nation to the council fire of the Delawares, to condole with their *grandfather* on the loss of their head chief.[247]

There are tribes, on the other hand, who have wandered far from the habitations of those connected with them by blood or relationship. It is certain that they can no longer be benefited by the general council fire. They, therefore, become a people by themselves, and pass with us for a separate nation, if they only have a name; nevertheless, (if I am rightly informed) they well know to what stock or nation they originally belonged, and if questioned on that subject, will give correct answers. It is therefore very important to make these enquiries of any tribe or nation that a traveller may find himself among. The analogy of languages is the best and most unequivocal sign of connexion between Indian tribes; yet the absence of that indication should not always be relied upon.

It may not be improper also to mention in this place that the purity or correctness with which a language is spoken, will greatly help to discover who is the head of the national family. For no where is the language so much cultivated as in the vicinity of the great national council fire, where the orators have the best opportunity of displaying their talents. Thus the purest and most elegant dialect of the Lenape language, is that of the Unami or Turtle tribe.

CHAPTER 44 ~
The Indians and the whites compared

If lions had painters! This proverbial saying applies with equal force to the American Indians. They have no historians among them, no books, no newspapers, no convenient means of making their grievances known to a sympathising world. Why, then, should not a white man, a Christian, who has spent among them the greatest part of his life, and was treated by them at all times with hospitality and kindness, plead their honest cause, and defend them as they would defend themselves, if they had but the means of bringing their facts and their arguments before an impartial public?

Those who have never taken the pains to enquire into the real character and disposition of the American Indians, naturally suppose, that a people who have no code of laws for their government, but where every man is at liberty to do what he pleases, where men never forget or forgive injuries, and take revenge in their own way, often in the most cruel manner, and are never satisfied until they have been revenged, must of course be *barbarians* and *savages*; by which undefined words is understood whatever is bad, wicked, and disgraceful to human nature. Imagination is immediately at work to paint them as a species of monsters, to whom cruelty is an appetite; a sort of human-shaped tigers and panthers, strangers to the finer feelings, and who commit acts of barbarity without any excitement but that of their depraved inclination, and without even suspecting that there are such things in nature as virtue on the one hand and crime on the other.

But nothing is so false as this picture of the Indians. The worst that can be said of them is, that the passion of revenge is so strong in their minds, that it carries them beyond all bounds. But set this aside, and their character is noble and great. They have no written laws, but they have usages founded on the most strict principles of equity and justice. Murder with them is punished with death. It is true, that as was the case not many centuries ago among the most civilised nations of Europe, the death of a man may be compounded for with his surviving relations; if, however, they do not choose to accept of the terms offered, any one of them may become the executioner of the murderer.

Thieves are compelled to restore what they have stolen, or to make satisfactory amends to the injured party; in their default, their nearest relations are obliged to make up the loss. If the thief, after sufficient warning, continues his bad practices, he is disowned by his nation, and any one may put him to death the next time that he is caught in the act of stealing, or that it can be clearly proved to have been committed by him. I have given two instances of the kind in a former chapter,[248] and I recollect another which will put what I have said in the strongest light. I once knew an Indian chief, who had a son of a vicious disposition, addicted to stealing, and who would take no advice. His father, tired and unable to satisfy all the demands which were made upon him for the restitution of articles stolen by his son, at last issued his orders for shooting him the next time he should be guilty of a similar act.

As to crimes and offences of an inferior nature to murder and theft, they are left to the injured party to punish in such manner as he thinks proper. Such are personal insults and threats, which among those people are not considered as slight matters. If the will and intention of the aggressor appear to be *bad*; if the insult offered is considered as the forerunner of something worse; or, as the Indians express themselves, if the "*murdering spirit*" is "*alive*" within him who offers or threatens violence to another, they think themselves justified in preventing the act meditated against them; in such a case, they consider the killing the aggressor as an act of necessity and self defence. Yet it is very rarely, indeed, that such punishments are inflicted.[249] The Indians, in general, avoid giving offence as much as possible. They firmly believe that bad thoughts and actions proceed from the evil spirit, and carefully avoid every thing that is *bad*.

Every person who is well acquainted with the true character of the Indians will admit that they are peaceable, sociable, obliging, charitable, and hospitable among themselves, and that those virtues are, as it were, a part of their nature. In their ordinary intercourse, they are studious to oblige each other. They neither wrangle nor fight; they live, I believe, as peaceably together as any people on earth, and treat one another with the greatest respect. That they are not devoid of tender feelings has been sufficiently shewn in the course of this work. I do not mean to speak of those whose manners have been corrupted by a long intercourse with the worst class of white men; they are a degenerate race, very different from the true genuine Indians whom I have attempted to describe.

If any one should be disposed to think that I have exaggerated in the picture which I have drawn of these *original people*, as they call themselves, I appeal to the numerous impartial writers who have given the same testimony respecting them. What says Christopher Columbus himself of the American Indians in his letters to his sovereign? "There are not," says he, "a better people in the world than these; more affectionate, affable, or mild. *They love their neighbours as themselves.*"

Similar encomiums were passed on them by some of the first Englishmen who came to settle in this country. The Reverend Mr. Cushman, in a sermon preached at Plymouth in 1620, says: "The Indians are said to be the most cruel and treacherous people in all those parts, even like lions; but to us they have been like lambs, so kind, so submissive and trusty, as a man may truly say, many Christians are not so kind and sincere."

The learned Dr. Elias Boudinot, of Burlington, in New Jersey (a man well remembered as one of the most eminent leaders of the American Revolution),[250] in a work[251] which, whatever opinion may be entertained of the hypothesis that he contends for, well deserves to be read, for the spirit which it breathes and the facts that it contains, has brought together in one view, the above and many other authorities of eminent men in favour of the American Indians, and in proof that their character is such as I have described. I shall not repeat after him what Las Casas, William

Penn, Bryan Edwards, the Abbé Clavigero, Father Charlevoix and others, have said on the same subject; those numerous and weighty testimonies may be found in the work to which I have referred.[252] But I cannot refrain from transcribing the opinion of the venerable author himself, to which his high character, his learning, and independence, affix a more than common degree of authority.

"It is a matter of fact," says Dr. Boudinot, "proved by most historical accounts, that the Indians, at our first acquaintance with them, generally manifested themselves kind, hospitable and generous to the Europeans, so long as they were treated with justice and humanity. But when they were, from a thirst of gain, over-reached on many occasions, their friends and relations treacherously entrapped and carried away to be sold for slaves, themselves injuriously oppressed, deceived and driven from their lawful and native possessions; what ought to have been expected, but inveterate enmity, hereditary animosity, and a spirit of perpetual revenge? To whom should be attributed the evil passions, cruel practices and vicious habits to which they are now changed, but to those who first set them the example, laid the foundation and then furnished the continual means for propagating and supporting the evil?"[253]

Such was the original character of the Indians, stamped, as it were, upon them by nature; but fifty or sixty years back, whole communities of them bore the stamp of this character, difficult now to be found within the precincts of any part of their territory bordering on the settlements of the white people!

What! will it be asked, can this be a true picture of the character of the Indians; of those brutes, barbarians, savages, men without religion or laws, who commit indiscriminate murders, without distinction of age or sex? Have they not in numberless instances desolated our frontiers, and butchered our people? Have they not violated treaties and deceived the confidence that we placed in them? No, no; they are beasts of prey in the human form; they are men with whom no faith is to be kept, and who ought to be cut off from the face of the earth!

Stop, my friends! hard names and broad assertions are neither reasons nor positive facts. I am not prepared to enter into a discussion with you on the comparative merits or demerits of the Indians and whites; for I am unskilled in argument, and profess only to be a plain *matter of fact* man. To facts therefore I will appeal. I admit that the Indians have sometimes revenged, cruelly revenged, the accumulated wrongs which they have suffered from unprincipled white men; the love of revenge is a strong passion which their imperfect religious notions have not taught them to subdue. But how often have they been the aggressors in the unequal contests which they have had to sustain with the invaders of their country? In how many various shapes have they not been excited and their passions roused to the utmost fury by acts of cruelty and injustice on the part of the whites, who have made afterwards the country ring with their complaints against the lawless savages, who had not the means of being heard in their defence? I shall not pursue these questions any farther, but let the facts that I am going to relate speak for themselves.

In the summer of the year 1763, some friendly Indians from a distant place, came to Bethlehem to dispose of their peltry for manufactured goods and necessary implements of husbandry. Returning home well satisfied, they put up the first night at a tavern, eight miles distant from this place.[254] The landlord not being at home, his wife took the liberty of encouraging the people who frequented her house for the sake of drinking to abuse those Indians, adding, "That she would freely give a gallon of rum to any one of them that should kill one of these black d——ls." Other white people from the neighbourhood came in during the night, who also drank freely, made a great deal of noise, and increased the fears of those poor Indians, who, for the greatest part, understanding English, could not but suspect that something bad was intended against their persons.

They were not, however, otherwise disturbed: but in the morning, when, after a restless night, they were preparing to set off, they found themselves robbed of some of the most valuable articles they had purchased, and on mentioning this to a man who appeared to be the bar-keeper, they were ordered to leave the house. Not being willing to lose so much property, they retired to some distance into the woods, where, some of them remaining with what was left them, the others returned to Bethlehem and lodged their complaint with a justice of the peace. The magistrate gave them a letter to the landlord, pressing him without delay to restore to the Indians the goods that had been taken from them. But behold! when they delivered that letter to the people at the inn, they were told in answer: "that if they set any value on their lives, they must make off with themselves immediately."

They well understood that they had no other alternative, and prudently departed without having received back any of their goods.[255] Arrived at Nescopeck[256] on the Susquehannah, they fell in with some other Delawares, who had been treated much in the same manner, one of them having had his rifle stolen from him. Here the two parties agreed to take revenge in their own way, for those insults and robberies for which they could obtain no redress; and that they determined to do as soon as war should be again declared by their nation against the English.

Scarcely had these Indians retired, when in another place, about fourteen miles distant from the former, one man, two women and a child, all quiet Indians, were murdered in a most wicked and barbarous manner, by drunken militia officers and their men, for the purpose of getting their horse and the goods they had just purchased.[257] One of the women, falling on her knees, begged in vain for the life of herself and her child, while the other woman, seeing what was doing, made her escape to the barn, where she endeavoured to hide herself on the top of the grain. She however was discovered, and inhumanly thrown down on the threshing floor with such force that her brains flew out.[258]

Here, then, were insults, robberies and murders, all committed within the short space of three months, unatoned for and unrevenged. There was no prospect of obtaining redress; the survivors were therefore obliged to seek some other means to obtain revenge. They did so; the Indians, already exasperated against the English in consequence of repeated outrages, and considering the nation as responsible for the injuries which it did neither prevent nor punish, and for which it did not even offer to make any kind of reparation, at last declared war, and then the injured parties were at liberty to redress themselves for the wrongs they had suffered.

They immediately started against the objects of their hatred, and finding their way, unseen and undiscovered, to the inn which had been the scene of the first outrage, they attacked it at daybreak, fired into it on the people within, who were lying in their beds. Strange to relate! the murderers of the man, two women, and child, were among them. They were mortally wounded, and died of their wounds shortly afterwards. The Indians, after leaving this house, murdered by accident an innocent family, having mistaken the house that they meant to attack, after which they returned to their homes.[259]

Now a violent hue and cry was raised against the Indians—no language was too bad, no crimes too black to brand them with. No faith was to be placed in those savages; treaties with them were of no effect; they ought to be cut off from the face of the earth! Such was the language at that time in everybody's mouth; the newspapers were filled with accounts of the cruelties of the Indians, a variety of false reports were circulated in order to rouse the people against them, while they, the really injured party, having no printing presses among them, could not make known the story of their grievances.

"No faith can be placed in what the Indians promise at treaties; for scarcely is a treaty concluded than they are again murdering us." Such is our complaint against these unfortunate people; but they will tell you that it is the white men in whom no faith is to placed. They will tell you, that there is not a single instance in which the whites have not violated the engagements that they had made at treaties. They say that when they had ceded lands to the white people, and boundary lines had been established—"firmly established!" beyond which no whites were to settle; scarcely was the treaty signed, when white intruders again were settling and hunting on their lands! It is true that when they preferred their complaints to the government, the government gave them many fair promises, and assured them that men would be sent to remove the intruders by force from the usurped lands. The men, indeed, came, but with chain and compass in their hands, taking surveys of the tracts of good land, which the intruders, from their knowledge of the country, had pointed out to them!

What was then to be done, when those intruders would not go off from the land, but, on the contrary, increased in numbers? "Oh!" said those people, (and I have myself frequently heard this language in the Western country,) "a new treaty will soon give us all this land; nothing is now wanting but a pretence to pick a quarrel with them!" Well, but in what manner is this quarrel to be brought about? A *David Owen*, a *Walker*, and many others might, if they were alive, easily answer this question. A precedent, however, may be found, on perusing Mr. Jefferson's Appendix to his Notes on Virginia. On all occasions, when the object is to murder Indians, strong liquor is the main article required; for when you have them dead drunk, you may do to them as you please, without running the risk of losing your life. And should you find that the laws of your country may reach you where you are, you have only to escape or conceal yourself for a while, until the storm has blown over! I well recollect the time when thieves and murderers of Indians fled from impending punishment across the Susquehannah, where they considered themselves safe; on which account this river had the name given to it of "*the rogue's river*." I have heard other rivers called by similar names.

In the year 1742, the Reverend Mr. Whitefield offered the Nazareth Manor (as it was then called) for sale to the United Brethren.[260] He had already begun to build upon it a spacious stone house, intended as a school house for the education of negro children. The Indians, in the meanwhile, loudly exclaimed against the white people for settling in this part of the country, which had not yet been legally purchased of them, but, as they said, had been obtained by fraud.[261] The Brethren declined purchasing any lands on which the Indian title had not been properly extinguished, wishing to live in peace with all the Indians around them. Count Zinzendorff happened at that time to arrive in the country; he found that the agents of the proprietors would not pay to the Indians the price which they asked for that tract of land; he paid them out of his private purse the whole of the demand which they made in the height of their ill temper, and moreover gave them permission to abide on the land, at their village, (where, by the by, they had a fine large peach orchard,) as long as they should think proper.

But among those white men, who afterwards came and settled in the neighbourhood of their tract, there were some who were enemies to the Indians, and a young Irishman, without cause or provocation, murdered their good and highly respected chief *Tademi*,[262] a man of such an easy and friendly address, that he could not but be loved by all who knew him. This, together with the threats of other persons, ill disposed towards them, was the cause of their leaving their settlement on this manor, and removing to places of greater safety.

It is true, that when flagrant cases of this description occurred, the government, before the Revolution, issued proclamations offering rewards for apprehending the offenders, and in later times, since the country has become more thickly settled, those who had been guilty of such offences were brought before the tribunals to take their trials. But these formalities have proved of little avail. In the first case, the criminals were seldom, if ever, apprehended; in the second, no jury could be found to convict them; for it was no uncommon saying among many of the men of whom juries in the frontier countries were commonly composed, that no man should be put to death for killing an Indian; for it was the same thing as killing a wild beast!

But what shall I say of the conduct of the British agents, or deputy agents, or by whatsoever other name they may be called, who, at the commencement of the American Revolution, openly excited the Indians to kill and destroy all the rebels without distinction? "Kill all the rebels," they would say, "put them all to death, and spare none." A veteran chief of the Wyandot nation, who resided near Detroit, observed to one of them that surely it was meant that they should kill men only, and not women and children. "No, no," was the answer, "kill all, destroy all; *nits breed lice!*"

The brave veteran[263] was so disgusted with this reply, that he refused to go out at all; wishing however to see and converse with his old brother soldiers of the Delaware nation, with whom he had fought against the English in the French war, he took the command of a body of ninety chosen men, and being arrived at the seat of the government of the Delawares, on the Muskingum, he freely communicated to his old comrades (among whom was Glikhican, whom I shall presently have occasion further to mention) what had taken place, and what he had resolved on; saying that he never would be guilty of killing women and children; that this was the first and would be the last of his going out this war; that in ten days they should see him come back with one prisoner only, no scalp to a pole, and no life lost. He kept his word. The sixteen chiefs under him, from respect and principle, agreed to all his proposals and wishes.

How different the conduct of the Indians from that of their inhuman employers! I have already related the noble speech of Captain Pipe to the British Commandant at Detroit, and I have done justice to the character of that brave officer, who surely ought not to be confounded with those Indian agents that I have spoken of. But what said Pipe to him? "Innocence had no part in your quarrels; and therefore I distinguished—I spared. Father! I hope you will not destroy what I have saved!"[264] I have also told the conduct of the two young spirited Delawares[265] who saved the life of the venerable Missionary Zeisberger, at the risk of their own. But it is not only against their own people that Indians have afforded their protection to white men, but against the whites themselves.

In the course of the Revolutionary war, in which (as in all civil commotions) brother was seen fighting against brother, and friend against friend, a party of Indian warriors, with whom one of those white men, who, under colour of attachment to their king, indulged in every sort of crimes, was going out against the settlers on the Ohio, to kill and destroy as they had been ordered. The chief of the expedition had given strict orders not to molest any of the white men who lived with their friends the Christian Indians; yet as they passed near a settlement of these converts, the white man, unmindful of the orders he had received, attempted to shoot two of the Missionaries who were planting potatoes in their field, and though the captain warned him to desist, he still obstinately persisted in his attempt. The chief, in anger, immediately took his gun from him, and kept him under guard until they had reached a considerable distance from the place. I have received this account from the chief himself, who on his return sent word to the Missionaries that they would do well not to go far from home, as they were in too great danger from the *white people*.

Another white man of the same description, whom I well knew, related with a kind of barbarous exultation, on his return to Detroit from a war excursion with the Indians in which he had been engaged, that the party with which he was, having taken a woman prisoner who had a sucking babe at her breast, he tried to persuade the Indians to kill the child, lest its cries should discover the place where they were; the Indians were unwilling to commit the deed, on which the white man at once jumped up, tore the child from its mother's arms and taking it by the legs dashed its head against a tree, so that the brains flew out all around. The monster in relating this story said, "The little dog all the time was making *wee!*" He added, that if he were sure that his old father, who some time before had died in Old Virginia, would, if he had lived longer, have turned rebel, he would go all the way into Virginia, raise the body, and take off his scalp!

Let us now contrast with this the conduct of the Indians. Carver tells us in his travels with what moderation, humanity and delicacy they treat female prisoners, and particularly pregnant women.[266] I refer the reader to the following fact, as an instance of their conduct in such cases. If his admiration is excited by the behaviour of the Indians, I doubt not that his indignation will be raised in an equal degree by that of a white man who unfortunately acts a part in the story.

A party of Delawares, in one of their excursions during the Revolutionary war, took a white female prisoner. The Indian chief, after a march of several days, observed that she was ailing, and was soon convinced (for she was far advanced in her pregnancy) that the time of her delivery was near. He immediately made a halt on the bank of a stream, where at a proper distance from the encampment, he built for her a close hut of peeled barks, gathered dry grass and fern to make her a bed, and placed a blanket at the opening of the dwelling as a substitute for a door. He then kindled a fire, placed a pile of wood near it to feed it occasionally, and placed a kettle of water at hand where she might easily use it.

He then took her into her little infirmary, gave her Indian medicines, with directions how to use them, and told her to rest easy and she might be sure that nothing should disturb her. Having done this, he returned to his men, forbade them from making any noise, or disturbing the sick woman in any manner, and told them that he himself should guard her during the night. He did so, and the whole night kept watch before her door, walking backward and forward, to be ready at her call at any moment, in case of extreme necessity. The night passed quietly, but in the morning, as he was walking by on the bank of the stream, seeing him through the crevices, she called to him and presented her babe. The good chief, with tears in his eyes, rejoiced at her safe delivery; he told her not to be uneasy, that he should lay by for a few days and would soon bring her some nourishing food, and some medicines to take. Then going to his encampment, he ordered all his men to go out a hunting, and remained himself to guard the camp.

Now for the reverse of the picture. Among the men whom this chief had under his command, was one of those white vagabonds whom I have before described. The captain was much afraid of him, knowing him to be a bad man; and as he had expressed a great desire to go a hunting with the rest, he believed him gone, and entertained no fears for the woman's safety. But it was not long before he was undeceived. While he was gone to a small distance to dig roots for his poor patient, he heard her cries, and running with speed to her hut, he was informed by her that the white man had threatened to take her life if she did not immediately throw her child into the river.

The Captain, enraged at the cruelty of this man, and the liberty he had taken with his prisoner, hailed him as he was running off, and told him, "That the moment he should miss the child, the tomahawk should be in his head." After a few days this humane chief placed the woman carefully on a horse, and they went together to the place of their destination, the mother and child doing well. I have heard him relate this story, to which he added, that whenever he should go out on an excursion, he never would suffer a white man to be of his party.

Yet I must acknowledge that I have known an Indian chief who had been guilty of the crime of killing the child of a female prisoner. It was Glikhican,[267] of whom I have before spoken, as one of the friends of the brave Wyandot who expressed so much horror at the order given to him by the Indian agents to murder women and children.[268] In the year 1770, he joined the congregation of the Christian Indians; the details of his conversion are related at large by Loskiel in his History of the Missions.[269] Before that time he had been conspicuous as a warrior and a counsellor, and in oratory it is said he never was surpassed.

This man, having joined the French, in the year 1754, or 1755, in their war against the English, and being at that time out with a party of Frenchmen, took, among other prisoners, a young woman named *Rachel Abbott*, from the Conegocheague settlement,[270] who had at her breast a sucking babe. The incessant cries of the child, the hurry to get off, but above all, the persuasions of his *white* companions, induced him, much against his inclination, to kill the innocent creature; while the mother, in an agony of grief, and her face suffused with tears, begged that its life might be spared. The woman, however, was brought safe to the Ohio, where she was kindly treated and adopted, and some years afterwards was married to a Delaware chief of respectability, by whom she had several children, who are now living with the Christian Indians in Upper Canada.

Glikhican never forgave himself for having committed this crime, although many times, and long before his becoming a Christian, he had begged the woman's pardon with tears in his eyes, and received her free and full forgiveness. In vain she pointed out to him all the circumstances that he could have

281

alleged to excuse the deed; in vain she reminded him of his unwillingness at the time, and his having been in a manner compelled to it by his French associates; nothing that she did say could assuage his sorrow or quiet the perturbation of his mind; he called himself a wretch, a monster, a *coward* (the proud feelings of an Indian must be well understood to judge of the force of this self-accusation), and to the moment of his death the remembrance of this fatal act preyed like a canker worm upon his spirits. I ought to add, that from the time of his conversion, he lived the life of a Christian, and died as such.

The Indians are cruel to their enemies! In some cases they are, but perhaps not more so than white men have sometimes shewn themselves. There have been instances of white men flaying or taking off the skin of Indians who had fallen into their hands, then tanning those skins, or cutting them in pieces, making them up into razor-straps, and exposing those for sale, as was done at or near Pittsburg sometime during the Revolutionary war. Those things are abominations in the eyes of the Indians, who, indeed, when strongly excited, inflict torments on their prisoners and put them to death by cruel tortures, but never are guilty of acts of barbarity in cold blood. Neither do the Delawares and some other Indian nations, ever on any account disturb the ashes of the dead.

The custom of torturing prisoners is of ancient date, and was first introduced as a trial of courage. I have been told, however, that among some tribes it has never been in use; but it must be added that those tribes gave no quarter. The Delawares accuse the Iroquois of having been the inventors of this piece of cruelty, and charge them further with eating the flesh of their prisoners after the torture was over. Be this as it may, there are now but few instances of prisoners being put to death in this manner.

Rare as these barbarous executions now are, I have reason to believe that they would be still less frequent, if proper pains were taken to turn the Indians away from this heathenish custom. Instead of this, it is but too true that they have been excited to cruelty by unprincipled white men, who have joined in their war-feasts, and even added to the barbarity of the scene. Can there be a more brutal act than, after furnishing those savages, as they are called, with implements of war and destruction, to give them an ox to kill and to roast whole, to dance the war dance with them round the slaughtered animal, strike at him, stab him, telling the Indians at the same time: "Strike, stab! Thus you must do to your enemy!" Then taking a piece of the meat, and tearing it with their teeth: "So you must eat his flesh!" and sucking up the juices: "Thus you must drink his blood!" and at last devour the whole as wolves do a carcass. This is what is known to have been done by some of those Indian agents that I have mentioned.

"Is this possible?" the reader will naturally exclaim. Yes, it is possible, and every Indian warrior will tell you that it is true. It has come to me from so many credible sources, that I am forced to believe it. How can the Indians now be reproached with acts of cruelty to which they have been excited by those who pretended to be Christians and civilised men, but who were worse savages than those whom, no doubt, they were ready to brand with that name?

When hostile governments give directions to employ the Indians against their enemies, they surely do not know that such is the manner in which their orders are to be executed; but let me tell them and every government who will descend to employing these auxiliaries, that this is the only way in which their subaltern agents will and can proceed to make their aid effectual. The Indians are not fond of interfering in quarrels not their own, and will not fight with spirit for the mere sake of a livelihood which they can obtain in a more agreeable manner by hunting and their other ordinary occupations. Their passions must be excited, and that is not easily done when they themselves have not received any injury from those against whom they are desired to fight. Behold, then, the abominable course which must unavoidably be resorted to—to induce them to do what?—to lay waste the dwelling of the peaceable cultivator of the land, and to murder his innocent wife and his helpless children! I cannot pursue this subject farther, although I am far from having exhausted it. I have said enough to enable the impartial reader to decide which of the two classes of men, the Indians and the whites, are most justly entitled to the epithets of brutes, barbarians, and savages. It is not for me to anticipate his decision.

But if the Indians, after all, are really those horrid monsters which they are alleged to be, two solemn, serious questions have often occurred to my mind, to which I wish the partisans of that doctrine would give equally serious answers.

> 1. Can civilised nations, can nations which profess Christianity, be justified in employing people of that description to aid them in fighting their battles against their enemies, Christians like themselves?

> 2. When such nations offer up their prayers to the throne of the most High, supplicating the Divine Majesty to grant success to their arms, can they, ought they to expect that those prayers will be heard?

I have done. Let me only be permitted, in conclusion, to express my firm belief, the result of much attentive observation and long experience while living among the Indians, that if we would only observe towards them the first and most important precept of our holy religion, "to do to others as we would be done to;" if, instead of employing them to fight our battles, we encouraged them to remain at peace with us and with each other, they might easily be brought to a state of civilisation, and become CHRISTIANS.

I still indulge the hope that this work will be accomplished by a wise and benevolent government. Thus we shall demonstrate the falsity of the prediction of the Indian prophets, who say: "That when the whites shall have ceased killing the red men, and got all their lands from them, the great tortoise which bears this island upon his back, shall dive down into the deep and drown them all, as he once did before, a great many years ago; and that when he again rises, the Indians shall once more be put in possession of the whole country."

Conclusion

I HAVE thus finished the work which was required of me by the Historical Committee of the American Philosophical Society. On reading over the printed sheets which have been kindly sent to me from Philadelphia, as they issued from the press, I have noticed several errors, some of which may be ascribed to me, others to the transcriber of the manuscript, and very few to the printer. I regret that there are among them some mistakes in dates and names of places; they are all rectified in the errata.

I am very sensible of the many defects of this little work in point of method, arrangement, composition and style. I am not an author by profession; the greatest part of my life was spent among savage nations, and I have now reached the age of seventy-five, at which period of life little improvement can be expected. It is not, therefore, as an author that I wish to be judged, but as a sincere relator of facts that have fallen within my observation and knowledge. I declare that I have said nothing but what I certainly know or verily believe. In matters of mere opinion, I may be contradicted; but in points of fact I have been even scrupulous, and purposely omitted several anecdotes for which I could not sufficiently vouch. In my descriptions of character, I may have been an unskilful painter, and ill chosen expressions may imperfectly have sketched out the images that are imprinted on my mind; but the fault is in the writer, not in the man.

It is with pleasure that I inform the reader that the parts of Mr. Zeisberger's Iroquois Dictionary which I have mentioned above, as being irretrievably lost, have most fortunately been found since this work is in the press. The book has been neatly bound in seven quarto volumes, and will remain a monument of the richness and comprehensiveness of the languages of the Indian nations. Several valuable grammatical works on the same language, by the same author and Mr. Pyrlæus, have been recovered at the same time, by means of which, the idiom of the Six Nations may now be scientifically studied.

When I spoke of the impression made by Captain Pipe's speech "on all present," I meant only on those who understood the language; for there were many who did not, and M. Baby, the Canadian interpreter, did not explain to the bystanders the most striking passages, but went now and then to the Commandant and whispered in his ear. Captain Pipe, while he spoke, was exceedingly animated, and twice advanced so near to the Commandant, that M. Baby ordered him to fall back to his place. All who were present must have at least suspected that his speech was not one of the ordinary kind, and that everything was not as they might suppose it ought to be.

I promised in my introduction to subjoin an explanatory list of the Indian nations which I have mentioned in the course of this work, but I find that I have been so full on the subject that such a list is unnecessary.

I have classed the Florida Indians together in respect of language, on the supposition that they all speak dialects of the same mother tongue; the fact, however, may be otherwise, though it will be extraordinary that there should be several languages entirely different from each other in the narrow strip of land between the Carolinas and the Mississippi, when there are but two principal ones in the rest of the United States. It is to be expected that the researches of the Historical Committee will throw light upon this subject.

ERRATA IN PART I

(Note: these page number references are from the original printing)

PAGE 26, LINE 5— Between the words "*if*" and "*what*" insert "*we can credit.*"

30, 15— For "*declaring at the same time*" read "*and declared afterwards.*"

31, 8— For "*Mohicans*" read "*Lenape.*"

67, 14— For "*1742*" read "*and November 1756.*"

72, 12— Dele "*in which.*"

77, 11— For "*Delawares*" read "*Mohicans.*"

80, 18— For "*1787*" read "*1781.*"

81, 5— For "*us*" read "*them.*"

84, 12— For "*Mouseys*" read "*Monseys.*"

23— Beginning a paragraph, for "*1768, about six*" read "*1772, a few.*"

85, 29— Of third note, for "*Shawanachau*" read "*Shawanachan.*"

90, 13— For "*Shawanos*" read "*Nanticokes.*"

91, 13— For "*schschequon*" read "*shechschequon.*"

92, 29 and 30— For "*Tawachguáno*" read "*Tayachguáno.*"

110, 12— For "*once*" read "*sometimes.*"

111, 8— For "*should*" read "*deserved to.*"

10— For "*to*" read "*out at.*"

12— Dele "*outside of the door and.*"

118, 15— For "*Thornhallesen*" read "*Thorhallesen.*"

287

122,   10— Of the first note, for "*p. 3*" read "*p. 5.*"

130,   8— For "*or*" read "*nor.*"

131,   22— For "*met*" read "*saw.*"

        25— For "*days*" read "*hours.*"

133,   5— For "*December*" read "*November.*"

140,   10— Of No. 43, for "*with*" read "*of.*"

143,   34— For "*they*" read "*the Chippeways and some other nations.*"

146,   17— For "*your*" read "*yon.*"

150,   4— After the word "*nation*" insert "*which they do not approve of.*"

153,   31— For "*they sure*" read "*they are sure.*"

160,   32— For "*reply*" read "*answer.*"

164,   26— For "*decide*" read "*say.*"

        28— For "*man*" read "*men.

166,   2— Between "*is*" and "*even*" insert "*sometimes.*"

        22— For "*an old Indian*" read "*several old men.*"

167, 11 and 13— For "*road*" read "*course.*"

174,   18— For "*where*" read "*whence.*"

178,   33— For "*Duke Holland*" read "*Luke Holland;*" the same where the name again occurs.

201,   5— Dele "*again.*"

216,   29— For "*very often*" read "*sometimes.*"

217,   2— For "*inches*" read "*feet.*"

218,   14— For "*of*" read "*on.*"

243,   3— For "*Americans*" read "*white men.*"

250,   9— For "*killed*" read "*eaten.*"

253,   37— For "*Pauk-sit*" read "*P'duk-sit.*"

263,   14— Dele "*lands or.*"

278,   35— For "*Albany*" read "*Pittsburgh.*"

283,   31— For "*Sandusky*" read "*Muskingum.*"

293,   26— For "*bought*" read "*brought.*"

313,   23— For "*them*" read "*us.*"

PART II

A
CORRESPONDENCE
BETWEEN
THE REV. JOHN HECKEWELDER.
OF BETHLEHEM,
AND
PETER S. DUPONCEAU, ESQ.,
CORRESPONDING SECRETARY OF THE
HISTORICAL AND LITERARY COMMITTEE OF
THE AMERICAN PHILOSOPHICAL SOCIETY,
RESPECTING THE
Languages of the American Indians

The following Correspondence between Mr. Heckewelder and Peter S. Du Ponceau, Esq., Corresponding Secretary of the Historical and Literary Committee of the American Philosophical Society, and subsequently, till his death in 1844, President of that Society, is appended as a fitting sequel to the preceding Account.

Introduction

THE Historical and Literary Committee of the American Philosophical Society, desirous of taking the most effectual means to promote the objects of their institution, directed their corresponding secretary to address letters in their name to such persons in the United States as had turned their attention to similar objects, and solicit their assistance.

Among other well-informed individuals, the Reverend Mr. Heckewelder of Bethlehem was pointed out by the late Dr. Caspar Wistar, President of the Society, and one of the most active and useful members of the Committee, as a gentleman whose intimate knowledge of the American Indians, their usages, manners and languages, enabled him to afford much important aid to their labours. In consequence of this suggestion, the secretary wrote to Mr. Heckewelder the letter No. 1, and Dr. Wistar seconded his application by the letter No. 2. The languages of the Indians were not at that time particularly in the view of the Committee; the manners and customs of those nations were the principal subjects on which they wished and expected to receive information. But Mr. Heckewelder having with his letter No. 4, sent them the MS. of Mr. Zeisberger's Grammar of the Delaware Language, that communication had the effect of directing their attention to this interesting subject.

This MS. being written in German, was not intelligible to the greatest number of the members. Two of them, the Reverend Dr. Nicholas Collin, and the corresponding secretary, were particularly anxious to be honoured with the task of translating it; but the secretary having claimed this labour as part of his official duty, it was adjudged to him. While he was translating that work, he was struck with the beauty of the grammatical forms of the Lenape idiom, which led him to ask through Dr. Wistar some questions of Mr. Heckewelder,[271] which occurred to him as he was pursuing his labours, and produced the correspondence now published, which was carried on by the direction and under the sanction of the Committee.

The letters which passed at the beginning between Dr. Wistar and Mr. Zeisberger,[272] and are here published in their regular order, do not, it is true, form a necessary part of this collection; but it will be perceived, that to the two letters of Dr. Wistar, Nos. 2 and 6, we are indebted for the valuable Historical Account of the Indians, which forms the first number of this volume. It is just that he should have the credit due to his active and zealous exertions.

It was intended that Mr. Zeisberger's Grammar should have immediately followed this Correspondence, which was considered as introductory to it. But it being now evident that it would increase too much the size of the volume, its publication is for the present postponed.

Correspondence respecting the Indian languages

Letter 1: Mr. Duponceau to Mr. Heckewelder

PHILADELPHIA, 9th January, 1816.

SIR.—As corresponding secretary to the Historical Committee of the American Philosophical Society, it is my duty to solicit the aid of men of learning and information, by the help of whose knowledge light may be thrown on the yet obscure history of the early times of the colonization of this country, and particularly of this State. Our much-respected President and common friend, Dr. Wistar, has often spoken to me of the great knowledge which you possess respecting the Indians who once inhabited these parts, and of your intimate acquaintance with their languages, habits and history. He had promised me, when you was last here, to do me the favour of introducing me to you, but the bad state of his health and other circumstances prevented it, which has been and still is to me the cause of much regret. Permit me, sir, on the strength of his recommendation, and the assurance he has given me that I might rely on your zeal and patriotic feelings, to request, in the name of the Historical Committee, that you will be so good as to aid their labours by occasional communications on the various subjects that are familiar to you and which relate to the early history of this country. Accounts of the various nations of Indians which have at different times inhabited Pennsylvania, their numbers, origin, migrations, connexions with each other, the parts which they took in the English and French wars and in the Revolutionary war, their manners, customs, languages, and religion, will be very acceptable, as well as every thing which you may conceive interesting, on a subject which at no distant period will be involved in obscurity and doubt, for want of the proper information having been given in time by those cotemporaries who now possess the requisite knowledge and are still able to communicate it. I hope, sir, that you will be able to find some moments of leisure to comply, at least in part, with this request, which you may do in any form that you may think proper. If that of occasional letters to Dr. Wistar or myself should be the most agreeable or convenient to you, you may adopt it, or any other mode that you may prefer. I beg you will favour me with an answer as soon as possible, that I may be able to inform the Committee of what they may expect from you. You may be assured that all your communications will be respectfully and thankfully received.

> I am, very respectfully, Sir,
> Your most obedient humble servant,
> PETER S. DUPONCEAU,
> Corresponding Secretary.

LETTER 2
Dr. C. Wistar to Mr. Heckewelder

PHILADELPHIA, 9th January, 1816.

MY DEAR SIR.—Inclosed is a letter from the corresponding secretary of the Historical Committee of our Society, which will inform you of our wishes to preserve from oblivion, and to make public, all the interesting information we can procure respecting the history of our country and its original inhabitants. I believe there is no other person now living who knows so much respecting the Indians who inhabited this part of America, as you do, and there is no one whose relations will be received with more confidence.

I hope you will approve of this method of favouring the public with your information, and we will endeavour to give you no trouble in publishing after you have favoured us with the communications. It will be particularly agreeable to the society to receive from you an account of the Lenni Lenape, as they were at the time when the settlement of Pennsylvania commenced, and of their history and misfortunes since that time; as these subjects are so intimately connected with the history of our State. The history of the Shawanese, and of the Six Nations will be very interesting to us for the same reason. But every thing which throws light upon the nature of the Indians, their manners and customs; their opinions upon all interesting subjects, especially religion and government; their agriculture and modes of procuring subsistence; their treatment of their wives and children; their social intercourse with each other; and in short, every thing relating to them which is interesting to you, will be very instructing to the Society. A fair view of the mind and natural disposition of the savage, and its difference from that of the civilised man, would be an acceptable present to the world.

You have long been a member of the Society; may we ask of you to communicate to us what you know and think ought to be published, respecting the wild animals, or the native plants of our country. The original object of our association was to bring together gentlemen like yourself, who have a great deal of information in which the public take an interest, that they might publish it together; and while an intercourse with you will give us all great pleasure, it will perhaps be a very easy way for you to oblige the world with your knowledge, as we will take the whole care of the publication. The information respecting our country which has been obtained by the very respectable Brethren of Bethlehem, and is contained in their archives, will, I believe, be more perfectly offered to the world by you at present, than probably it ever will afterwards by others; I therefore feel very desirous that you should engage in it.

The facts which Mr. Pyrlæus recorded there, relative to the confederation of the Six Nations, are so interesting that they ought to be made public.

In a few days after my return to Philadelphia, last autumn, I presented in your name to the Society the several books with which you favoured me. They were much gratified, for they considered them as truly valuable, and the secretary was requested to acknowledge the receipt of them, and to thank you in the name of the Society. I have constantly regretted the attack of influenza which deprived me of the pleasure of seeing more of you while you were last in Philadelphia. But I hope we shall meet again before a great while, and I shall be sincerely pleased if I can execute any of your commissions here, or serve you in any way; my brother joins me in assuring you of our best wishes, and of the pleasure we derived from your society.

With these I remain, your sincere friend,

C. WISTAR.

LETTER 3
Mr. Heckewelder to Dr. Wistar

BETHLEHEM, 24th March, 1816.

MY DEAR SIR.—Last evening I was favoured with a letter from you, covering one from the corresponding secretary of the Historical Committee of the American Philosophical Society, dated 9th January, and a book, for which I return my best thanks. If an apology for not having written to you since I left Philadelphia can be admitted, it must be that of my having been engaged in all my leisure hours, in completing my narrative of the Mission, a work of which, even if it is never published, I wished for good reasons, to leave a manuscript copy. I have now got through with the principal part, but have to copy the whole text, and in part to write the notes, remarks, and anecdotes which are intended for the appendix. While writing, it has sometimes struck me, that there might probably be some interesting passages in the work, as the speeches of Indians on various occasions; their artful and cunning ways of doing at times business; I had almost said their diplomatic manœuvres as politicians; their addresses on different occasions to the Great Spirit, &c., which are here noticed in their proper places. I think much of the true character of the Indian may be met with in perusing this work, and I will endeavour to forward the narrative to you and your brother for perusal, after a little while.

Were I still in the possession of all the manuscripts which I gave to my friend the late Dr. Barton, it would be an easy matter for me to gratify you and the Philosophical Society in their wishes, but having retained scarcely any, or but very few copies of what I sent him, I am not so able to do what I otherwise would with pleasure; I shall, however, make it my study to do what I can yet, though I am aware that I shall in some points, differ from what others have said and written. I never was one of those hasty believers and writers, who take the shadow for the substance: what I wished to know, I always wished to know correctly.

I approve of the mode proposed by the secretary of the Historical Committee, to make communications in the form of letters, which is for me the easiest and quickest mode. In the same way Dr. Barton received much interesting matter from me within the last 20 or 30 years. He often told me that he would publish a book, and make proper use of my communications. Had he not told me this so repeatedly, I should long since have tried to correct many gross errors, written and published, respecting the character and customs of the Indians. The Lenni Lenape, improperly called the Delawares, I shall, according to their tradition, trace across the Mississippi into this country, set forth what people they were, what parts of the country they inhabited, and how they were brought down to such a low state: perhaps, never did man take the pains that I did for years, to learn the true causes of the decline of that great and powerful nation.

The Grammar of the language of the Lenni Lenape, written by David Zeisberger, is still in my hands. By his will it is to be deposited in the Brethren's Archives in Bethlehem, but he has not prohibited taking a copy of it. Will it be of any service to the Society that it should be sent down for a few months for perusal, or if thought necessary, to take a copy? If so, please to let me know, and I shall send it with pleasure. It is, however, German and Indian, and without a translation will be understood but by few. I may perhaps find other documents interesting to the Society, as for example, copies of letters on Indian business and treaties, of which many are in the possession of Joseph Horsfield, Esq., son of the late Timothy Horsfield, through whom they have come into his hands, and who is willing to communicate them.[273] I am, dear friend,

Yours sincerely,

J. HECKEWELDER.

P. S.—Will you be so good as with my respects to mention to the secretary that I have received his letter, and shall shortly answer it—my best wishes also to your brother Richard, whom I highly esteem.

J. H.

LETTER 4 ~
From the same to the same

BETHLEHEM, 3d April, 1816.

MY DEAR FRIEND.—With Captain Mann, of your city, I send David Zeisberger's Grammar of the Language of the Lenni Lenape, (otherwise called the Delaware Indians.) As the book is not mine, but left by will, to be placed in the Library at Bethlehem, I can do no more than send it for perusal; or, if wished for, to have a copy taken from it, which, indeed, I myself would cheerfully have done for you, were it not that I must spare my weak eyes as much as possible.

I believe I have closed my last letter to you, without answering to the question you put to me, respecting, "wild animals and the native plants of our country." On this head I do not know that I could be of any service, since the animals that were in this country on the arrival of the Europeans must be pretty generally known; and respecting the native plants, I do not consider myself qualified to give any information, as all I have attended to, has been to collect plants for botanists, leaving it to them to examine and class them. But my friend Dr. Kampman of this place, who is, I believe, one of the most attentive gentlemen to botany, has promised me for you a copy of the botanical names of those plants which he, and a few others of his friends, have collected, within a great number of years, in the Forks of Delaware, with some few from New Jersey, to the number (he thinks) of about five hundred; all of which plants are in nature carefully laid up by him. Probably in two or three weeks, I shall have the pleasure of transmitting to you this promised catalogue.

I am, &c.

LETTER 5 ~
From Mr. Duponceau to Dr. Wistar

PHILADELPHIA, 14th May, 1816.

DEAR SIR. ash; When you write to your friend Mr. Heckewelder, I beg you will request him to answer the following questions:

1. What name did the French give to the Delaware nation?

2. I find in Zeisberger's Vocabulary, page 11, that *Gischuch* means the *sun*. In the Grammar, I see that the Delawares divide their year by moons, and call them *anixi gischuch*, &c. So that *gischuch* signifies *moon* as well as *sun*, how is it?

3. I find in the Grammar that the pronoun *nekama* or *neka* means *he*, but it does not appear to have any feminine. What is the proper word for *she* in the Delaware, and how is it declined?

I am, &c

LETTER 6 ~
From Dr. Wistar to Mr. Heckewelder

PHILADELPHIA, May 21st, 1816.

MY DEAR FRIEND.—I am much obliged by your kind letters, which are very interesting, and will, I hope, obtain from[274] us some of the valuable information which has been left unpublished by our ingenious colleague the late Dr. Barton. The Grammar of your venerable friend, Zeisberger, is regarded by Mr. Duponceau as a treasure. He thinks the inflections of the Indian verbs so remarkable that they will attract the general attention of the literati. Inclosed is a letter from him, by which he expects to open a correspondence with you on the subject. I will be much obliged by your writing to him as soon as your convenience will permit.

We expect soon to have materials for publishing a volume of Historical Documents, and I have proposed that we shall prefix to those which relate to Pennsylvania, all the information we can collect respecting the Indians who were here before our ancestors. The Committee agree that this will be the proper method, and my dependence for authentic information is on you; as I have never met with any person who had any knowledge to compare with yours, respecting the poor Indians. I was delighted to find that your enquiries have been directed to the history of the Lenni Lenape before they settled in Pennsylvania. The removal of the Indian tribes from our country to another is a very interesting subject. If you can tell us where they came from and what forced them away; who were here before them, and what induced their predecessors to make war for them, we shall be much obliged to you. There is no book I shall read with more pleasure than yours.

The causes of their downfall, I believe, are well known to you, and will of course have a place. The manner in which they were treated by the Six Nations, after their conquest, will be an interesting article, as it will shew the Indian policy. An account of the political rights which were still allowed them, and, in short, of everything which is connected with their conquest, will add to the interest of the work. As occupants of Pennsylvania before the whites, ought not the Shawanese and the Six Nations also to be described?

I have been told that the Shawanese were more refined than any other Indians in this part of America, and that the place where Chilicothe now stands, was the seat of Indian civilisation.

I have the pleasure of forwarding to you an instructing work by Dr. Drake, a physician at Cincinnati, which he sends you.

He also sends a small package and a letter to Mr. Steinhauer.

I send them by a wagon which goes from Mr. Bolling's, but I am not without some expectation of paying another visit to Bethlehem very soon, where it will be a great gratification to meet with my friend.

        Affectionately yours,

        CASPAR WISTAR.

LETTER 7 ~
Mr. Heckewelder to Mr. Duponceau

BETHLEHEM, 27th May, 1816.

DEAR SIR.—I was this morning favoured with a letter from my friend Dr. Wistar, inclosing some questions which you wish me to answer. I lose no time in complying with your desire.

Your first question is, "what name the French did give to the Delaware nation?"

I believe the Baron de La Hontan meant them when he spoke of the Algonkins, whom he describes as a people whose language was understood by many nations or tribes. So is certainly that of the Delawares.

While I was residing on the Muskingum, between the years 1773 and 1781, I cannot precisely remember the year, there came a French gentleman who was travelling on some business among the different Indian tribes, and could speak more or less of several Indian languages, among which was that of the Delawares. I had much conversation with him respecting the Indians, and observed that he called the Delawares *les Lenopes*, (a word evidently derived from their real name *Lenni Lenape*.) He told me that the language of that nation had a wide range, and that by the help of it, he had travelled more than a thousand miles among different Indian nations, by all of whom he was understood. He added, that the Baron La Hontan, when speaking of the Algonkins, must either have alluded to that nation, or to some one descended from them. In other instances, in the course of the four years that I resided in Upper Canada, I generally heard the French Canadians call them Lénôpé, while the English called them Delawares. Nevertheless, I do not doubt but that they have been called by different names by the French and other travellers, and if my memory serves me, some of the French people called them *les Loups*, a name probably derived from one of their tribes called the *Wolf*, if it is not a corruption of Lenape or Lenope.

303

Your next question is, "whether the Delaware word *gischuch*, signifies the sun or moon, or both together?" The Indian name "*gischuch*," is common to "the two great luminaries which send down light from above." The moon is called "*nipawi gischuch*," as it were "the sun which gives light in the night." It is also called in one word "*nipahum*." "*Gischuch*," singly, is often used for the moon; the Indian year is divided into thirteen lunar months, and in this sense, the word "*gischuch*," is used; as for instance, "*schawanáki*[275] *gischuch*" or, in the Minsi or Monsey dialect, "*chwani*[276] *gischuch*" the *shad moon*, answering to the month which we call March, at which time the fish called "shad" passes from the sea into the fresh water rivers. The inferior "stars" have a different name; they are called in the singular *alank*; plural, *alankewak*, and by contraction, *alanquak*.

Lastly, you ask whether the Delawares have a word answering to the English personal pronoun "*she*," and what it is? I beg leave to answer you somewhat in detail.

In the Indian languages, those discriminating words or inflections which we call *genders*, are not, as with us, in general, intended to distinguish between male and female beings, but between animate and inanimate things or substances. Trees and plants (annual plants and grasses excepted) are included within the generic class of animated beings. Hence the personal pronoun has only two modes, if I can so express myself, one applicable to the animate, and the other to the inanimate gender; "*nekama*" is the personal pronominal form which answers to "he" and "she" in English. If you wish to distinguish between the sexes, you must add to it the word "man" or "woman." Thus "*nekama lenno*," means "*he*" or "*this man;*" "*nekama ochqueu*," "*she*" or "*this woman*." This may appear strange to a person exclusively accustomed to our forms of speech, but I assure you that the Indians have no difficulty in understanding each other.

Nor must you imagine that their languages are poor. See how the Delaware idiom discriminates between the different ages of man and woman!

LENNO, *a man.*Wuskilenno, *a young man.*Pilapeu, *a lad.*Pilawesis, or pilawétzitsch, *a boy.*Pilawétit, *a male infant babe.*Kigeyilenno, *an aged man.*Mihilusis, *an old man, worn out with age.*OCHQUEU, *a woman.*Wusdóchqueu, *a young woman, a virgin.*Ochquetschitsch, *a girl.*Quetit, *a female infant babe.*Gichtochqueu, *an aged woman.*Chauchschìsis, *a very old woman.*

Note "*len*" or "*lenno*" in the male, and "*que*" or "*queu*" in the female, distinguish the sexes in compound words; sometimes the *L* alone denotes the male sex, as in "pi*l*apeu," "mihi*l*usis," &c.

The males of quadrupeds are called "*lenno wéchum*," and by contraction "*lennochum*;" the females "*Ochqueu wéchum*," and by contraction "*ochquéchum*," which is the same as saying *he* or *she* beasts. With the winged tribe, their generic denomination "*wehelle*" is added to the word which expresses the sex; thus, "*lenno wehelle*" for the male, and "*ochquechelle*" (with a little contraction) for the female. There are some animals the females of which have a particular distinguishing name, as "*Nunschetto*" a *doe*, "*Nunscheach*" a *she bear*. This, however, is not common.

Thus I have endeavoured to answer your questions, and I hope, have done it to your satisfaction. I shall always be willing and ready to give you any further information that you or the Philosophical Society may require; I mean, always to the best of my knowledge and abilities.

I am, &c.

LETTER 8 ~
Mr. Duponceau to Mr. Heckewelder

PHILADELPHIA, 10th June, 1816.

DEAR SIR.—Your favour of the 27th ult. has done me the greatest pleasure. I am very thankful for the goodness you have had to answer the questions which I took the liberty of putting to you through our common friend Dr. Wistar. I shall not fail to avail myself of your kind offer to answer such further questions as I may ask, as in so doing I shall fulfil a duty which the Historical Committee of the Philosophical Society has imposed upon me, and at the same time I am satisfied that I shall derive a great deal of pleasure to myself. But I must acknowledge that I am entirely ignorant of the subject on which I have been directed to obtain information from you, so much so that I am even at a loss what questions to ask. As I have, however, undertaken the task, I must endeavour to go through it as well as I can, and rely on the instruction which I shall receive from your letters, to point out to me further enquiries. I am fortunately employed in translating the late Mr. Zeisberger's Grammar of the Lenni Lenape, which will lead me a little into the right path, and I read at the same time such books as I can find in our scanty libraries respecting the languages of the American Indians. This study pleases me much, as I think I perceive many beauties in those idioms, but the true enjoyment of those beauties is, I presume, only accessible to those to whom the languages are familiar.

From what I have above stated, you will easily perceive that my questions to you must necessarily be desultory, and without any regular order or method. But you will diffuse light through this chaos, and every thing at last will find its proper place.

I cannot express to you how delighted I am with the grammatical forms of the Indian languages, particularly of the Delaware, as explained by Mr. Zeisberger. I am inclined to believe that those forms are peculiar to this part of the world, and that they do not exist in the languages of the old hemisphere. At least, I am confident that their development will contribute much to the improvement of the science of universal grammar. About fifty years ago, two eminent French philosophers published each a short treatise on the origin of language. One of them was the celebrated mathematician Maupertuis, and the other M. Turgot, who afterwards was made a minister of state, and acquired considerable reputation by his endeavours to introduce reform into the administration of the government of his own country. M. Maupertuis, in his Essay, took great pains to shew the necessity of studying the languages even of the most distant and barbarous nations, "because," said he, "we may chance to find some that are formed on *new plans of ideas*." M. Turgot, instead of acknowledging the justness of this profound remark, affected to turn it into ridicule, and said he could not understand what was meant by "*plans of ideas*." If he had been acquainted with the Delaware language, he would have been at no loss to comprehend it.

I presume that by this expression M. Maupertuis meant the various modes in which ideas are combined and associated together in the form of words and sentences, and in this sense it is to me perfectly intelligible. The associations expressed by words must be first formed in the mind, and the words shew in what order of succession the ideas were conceived, and in what various groups they arranged themselves before utterance was given to them. The variety of those groups which exist in the different languages forms what M. Maupertuis meant by "plans of ideas," and indeed, this variety exists even in one and the same language. Thus when we say, "lover," and "he who loves," the same group of ideas is differently combined, and of course, differently expressed, and it may well be said that those ideas are arranged "on different plans."

This difference is strongly exemplified in the Delaware language; I shall only speak at present of what we call the "declension of nouns." What in our European idioms we call the "objective cases" are one or more words expressive of two prominent ideas, that of the object spoken of, and that of the manner in which it is affected by some other object or action operating upon it. This is done in two ways; by inflecting the substantive, or by affixing to it one or more of those auxiliary words which we call "prepositions." Thus when we say in English "*of Peter*" and in German "*Peters*," the same two principal ideas are expressed in the former language by two words and in the latter by one, and the termination or inflexion *s* in German conveys the same meaning as the preposition "*of*" in English. It is clear that these two ideas, before they were uttered in the form of words, were grouped in the minds both of the German and the Englishman; in the one, as it were at once, and in the other successively: for it is natural to suppose that they were conceived as they are expressed. Again, when you say in Latin *amo Petrum*, (I love Peter,) the termination *um* is expressive of the action of the verb *love*, upon the object, *Peter*. In the English and German this accessory idea is not expressed by sound, but still it exists in the mind. In every language there are more ideas, perhaps, understood, than are actually expressed. This might be easily demonstrated, if it were here the place.

Let us now consider how the same ideas are combined and expressed in the Delaware language, according to Mr. Zeisberger. When the accessory idea which we call "*case*" proceeds from the operation of a verb upon a noun or word significant of an object, that idea is not affixed as with us to the noun but to the verb, or in other words, it is not the *noun* but the *verb* that is declined by inflexions or cases. Thus when you say "*getannitowit n'quitayala*, I fear God;" the first word, *getannitowit*, which is the substantive, is expressed, as we should say, in the nominative case, while the termination of the verb *yala*, expresses its application to the object. It is precisely the same as if in Latin, instead of saying, *Petrum amo*, I love Peter, we carried the termination *um* to the verb, and said *Petrus amum*. Does not this shew that many various combinations of ideas may take place in the human mind, of which we, Europeans by birth or descent, have not yet formed a conception? Does this not bid defiance to our rules or canons of universal grammar, and may we not say with M. Maupertuis, that in extending our study of the languages of man, we shall probably find some formed upon "plans of ideas" different from our own?

But I perceive that instead of asking you questions, as it is my duty to do, I am losing myself in metaphysical disquisitions; I return, then, to my principal object. A very interesting German book has lately fallen into my hands. It is entitled "*Untersuchungen ueber Amerikas Bevælkerung ans dem alten Kontinente*,"[277] and it is written by Professor Vater, of Leipzig. The author, after justly observing that the language of the Delawares is exceedingly rich in grammatical forms, and making the same observation on that of the Naticks, from the venerable Eliot's translation of the Bible into that idiom, says that, on the contrary, that of the Chippeways is very poor in that respect. "*Die Chippewæer*," he says, "*haben fast keine formen*."[278] This appears to me very strange, because on examining the various Indian languages from Nova Scotia to Chili, I have been surprised to find that they appear all formed on the same model, and if Professor Vater is correct, the Chippeway dialect will form an exception. I beg, therefore, you will inform me whether there is such a great difference as he states between that and the Delaware. I am much inclined to think that the learned Professor is mistaken. I must take this opportunity, however, to express my astonishment at the great knowledge which the literati of

Germany appear to possess of America, and of the customs, manners and languages of its original inhabitants. Strange! that we should have to go to the German universities to become acquainted with our own country.

Another German Professor, of the name of Rudiger, has compiled an interesting work, in which he gives specimens of all the languages in the world, as far as they are known, and among them does not forget those of the Indian nations of America. He gives the numerals of the Delaware language, from a vocabulary of that idiom, printed at Stockholm, in 1696, and made while the Swedes were in possession of that part of this country which they principally inhabited. I find a considerable difference between those numerals and these given by Zeisberger. That you may see in what it consists, I insert them both.

DELAWARE NUMERALS.

According to the Swedish Vocabulary.		According to Zeisberger.	
1.	Ciutte.	1.	Ngutti.
2.	Nissa.	2.	Nischa.
3.	Naha.	3.	Nacha.
4.	Nawo.	4.	Newo.
5.	Pareenach.	5.	Palenach.
6.	Ciuttas.	6.	Guttasch.
7.	Nissas.	7.	Nischasch.
8.	Haas.	8.	Chasch.
9.	Pæschun.	9.	Peschkonk.
10.	Thæræn.	10.	Tellen.
20.	Nissinacke.	20.	Nishinachke.
100.	Ciutabpach.	100.	Nguttapachki.

Now, there can be no doubt that these two sets of numerals belong to the same language, but I am astonished at seeing the same words written so differently by a Swede and a German, when there is so little difference in the powers of the alphabetical signs of their languages. I am particularly struck with some words that are written with *R* by the Swede and with *L* by the German author. In all Zeisberger's Grammar I have not been able to find the letter *R* in one single Delaware word, neither is it to be found in any of the words of his Delaware spelling book. No doubt you can inform me of the reason of this difference.

A greater one is still to be found in the Algonkin numerals given by the Baron La Hontan, and those of the Delaware proper. I place them here again in opposition to each other.

Algonkin numerals from La Hontan.	Delaware numerals from Zeisberger.
1. Pegik.	1. Ngutti.
2. Ninch.	2. Nischa.
3. Nissoue.	3. Nacha.
4. Neou.	4. Newo.
5. Narau.	5. Palenach.
6. Ningoutouassou.	6. Guttasch.
7. Ninchouassou.	7. Nischasch.
8. Nissouassou.	8. Chasch.
9. Changassou.	9. Peschkonk.
10. Mitassou.	10. Tellen.

There is certainly a family resemblance between some of these words, while in others no kind of similarity can be traced. As you believe that the Delawares and the Algonkins are the same people, I beg you will be so good as to point out to me the cause of the difference which I have observed.

I am, &c.

310

LETTER 9 ~
From the same to the same

PHILADELPHIA, 13th June, 1816.

DEAR SIR.—I take the liberty of submitting to you a few questions, which have occurred to me in perusing Mr. Zeisberger's Grammar. I beg you will be so good as to answer them at your leisure.

I am, &c.

QUERIES.

1. In Mr. Zeisberger's Grammar, double consonants are frequently used, as in *Pommauchsin, Lenno, Lenni Lenape*.

QUÆRE: Are the two consonants fully and distinctly sounded, thus: *pom-m-auchsin—Len-n-o*, as in the Italian language, or is only one of the consonants heard, as if it were thus written: *pomauchsin, leno*. In this latter case what is the reason for using two consonants, if only one is sounded?

2. Mr. Zeisberger frequently puts a comma or apostrophe (') before or after the letter N in the present of the indicative verbs, *'npommauchsi*, and sometimes *n'pommauchsi*. Sometimes he writes the word without: *ndappiwi, ndappiwitsch*; what is the reason of this variation? Is there any necessity for the comma before or after the *N* in the first person, or after the *K* and *W*, in the second and third? Is it not best to simplify as much as possible the orthography of such a difficult language?

3. What is the difference in pronunciation between *ke* and *que*; say, *pomauchsijenke* and *pomauchsijeque*? Is the latter sounded like *cue* or *kue*, or is it sounded as *ke*?

311

4. The conjunctive mood is expressed in German by "*wenn;*" 370 does it mean in English "*if*" or "*when*"? Does "*n'pomauchsijane,*" mean "when I live" or "if I live," or both? I find it sometimes expressed "*wenn,*" oder "*da,*" oder "*als,*" which inclines me to think it signifies both "*when*" and "*if.*"

5. I find some terminations in the tenses of the verbs, sometimes written "*cup,*" sometimes "*kup,*" and sometimes "*gup;*" thus *epiacup,* "where I was," *elsijakup,* "when or if I was so situated;" and *pommauchsijengup,* "if or when we have lived." Are these different sounds, or does this difference in writing arise from the Germans being accustomed to confound the sounds of K and G hard?

6. I find some words written sometimes with one *I* and sometimes with two; thus *elsia,* and *elsija.* Are the two *i*'s separately articulated, or do they sound only as one?

7. I find the second person of the singular in verbs sometimes written with a *K*, sometimes with a *G*, thus *kneichgussi,* du wirst gesehen (thou art seen); *kdaantschi,* du wirst gehen (thou wilt go); *gemilgussi,* dir wird gegeben (it is given to thee). Why is it not written *kemilgussi*? see query 5. I find sometimes a double *aa*—Is it merely to express length of quantity, or are the two *a*'s sounded distinctly?

8. What is the difference in sound between *ch* and *hh*, do they both represent the same guttural sound like *ch* in German? If so, why express this sound in two different ways; if otherwise, what is the real difference between the two sounds?

EXAMPLES.

*Ach*pil, bleibe du (remain thou); ach*pich*tique, wenn sie nicht da sind (if they are not ere); nda*hh*enap, wir waren gegangen (we had gone); kda*hh*imo, ihr gehet (you go).

I am, &c.

LETTER 10 ~
Mr. Heckewelder to Mr. Duponceau

BETHLEHEM, 20th June, 1816.

DEAR SIR.—Your favors of the 10th and 13th inst. have been duly received. I shall now endeavour to answer the first. The second shall in a few days be attended to.

I am glad to find that you are so much pleased with the forms of our Indian languages. You will be still more so as you become more familiar with the beautiful idiom of the Lenni Lenape. It is certain that many of those forms are not to be found either in the German or English; how it is with the other languages of Europe, Asia, and Africa, I cannot say, not being acquainted with them, and never having made philology my particular study. I concur with you in the opinion that there must be in the world many different ways of connecting ideas together in the form of words, or what we call *parts of speech*, and that much philosophical information is to be obtained by the study of those varieties. What you observe with regard to the verbs being inflected in lieu of affixing a case or termination to the noun is very correct, but the ground or principle on which it is done, is not perhaps known to you. The verbs in the Indian languages are susceptible of a variety of forms, which are not to be found in any other language that I know. I do not mean to speak here of the positive, negative, causative, and a variety of other forms, but of those which Mr. Zeisberger calls *personal*, in which the two pronouns, governing and governed, are by means of affixes, suffixes, terminations, and inflections, included in the same word. Of this I shall give you an instance from the Delaware language. I take the verb *ahoalan*, to love, belonging to the fifth of the eight conjugations, into which Mr. Zeisberger has very properly divided this part of speech.

INDICATIVE, PRESENT, POSITIVE.

Singular.   **Plural.**

313

N'dahoala, *I love,* n'dahoalaneen, *we love,*
k'dahoala, *thou*— k'dahoalohhimo, *you*—
w'dahoala,}
or ahoaleu } *he*— ahoalewak, *they*—

Now for the personal forms in the same tense.

FIRST PERSONAL FORM.
I.

Singular.   *Plural.*
K'dahoatell, *I love thee,*   K'dahoalohhumo, *I love you,*
n'dahoala, *I love him or her.* n'dahoalawak,—*them.*

SECOND PERSONAL FORM.
THOU.

Singular.   *Plural.*
K'dahoali, *thou lovest me,* k'dahoalineen, *thou lovest us,*
k'dahoala,—*him or her.*   k'dahoalawak,—*them.*

THIRD PERSONAL FORM.
HE, (*or* SHE.)

Singular.   *Plural.*
N'dahoaluk, *he loves me,* w'dahoalguna, *he loves us,*
k'dahoaluk,—*thee,*   w'dahoalguwa,—*you,*
w'dahoalawall—*him.*   w'dahoalawak,—*them.*

314

FOURTH PERSONAL FORM.
WE.

Singular.   *Plural.*

K'dahoalenneen, *we love thee,* k'dahoalohummena, *we love you,*
n'dahoalawuna,—*him.*   n'dahoalowawuna,—*them.*

FIFTH PERSONAL FORM.
YOU.

Singular.   *Plural.*

K'dahoalihhimo, *you love me,* k'dahoalihhena, *you love us.*
k'dahoalanewo,—*him.*   k'dahoalawawak,—*them.*

SIXTH PERSONAL FORM.
THEY.

Singular.   *Plural.*

N'dahoalgenewo, *they love me,* n'dahoalgehhena, *they love us.*
k'dahoalgenewo,—*thee,*   k'dahoalgehhimo,—*you.*
w'dahoalanewo,—*him.*   w'dahoalawawak,—*them.*

In this manner verbs are conjugated through all their moods and tenses, and through all their negative, causative, and various other forms, with fewer irregularities than any other language that I know of.

These conjugations, no doubt, you have found, or will find in Mr. Zeisberger's grammar, but the few examples that I have above put together, are necessary to understand the explanation which I am about to give.

The words you quote are: "*getannitowit n'quitayala*," *I fear God*, or rather, according to the Indian inversion, *God I fear*. Your observation is that the inflection or case of the noun substantive *God*, is carried to the verb. This is true; but if you enquire for the reason or the manner in which it takes place, you will find that *ala* is the inflection of the second or last person of the verb, in the first personal form; thus as you have seen that *n'dahoala* means *I love him*, so *n'quitayala*, in the same form and person means *I fear him*; it is therefore the same as if you said *God I fear him*. This is not meant in the least to doubt or dispute the correctness of your position, but to shew in what manner the combination of ideas is formed that has led to this result. You have now, I believe, a wider field for your metaphysical disquisitions.

I pass on to the other parts of your letter. I believe with you that Professor Vater is mistaken in his assertion that the language of the Chippeways is deficient in grammatical forms. I am not skilled in the Chippeway idiom, but while in Upper Canada, I have often met with French Canadians and English traders who understood and spoke it very well. I endeavoured to obtain information from them respecting that language, and found that it much resembled that of the Lenape. The differences that I observed were little more than some variations in sound, as *b* for *p*, and *i* for *u*. Thus, in the Delaware, *wapachquiwan* means a *blanket*, in the Chippeway it is *wabewian*; *gischuch* is Delaware for a *star*, the Chippeways say *gischis*; *wape* in Delaware *white*; in the Chippeway, *wabe*. Both nations have the word *Mannitto* for God, or the Great Spirit, a word which is common to all the nations and tribes of the Lenape stock.

There is no doubt that the Chippeways, like the Mahicanni, Naticks, Wampanos, Nanticokes, and many other nations, are a branch of the great family of the Lenni Lenape, therefore I cannot believe that there is so great a difference in the forms of their languages from those of the mother tongue. I shall, however, write on the subject to one of our Missionaries who resides in Canada, and speaks the Chippeway idiom, and doubt not that in a short time I shall receive from him a full and satisfactory answer.

On the subject of the numerals, I have had occasion to observe that they sometimes differ very much in languages derived from the same stock. Even the Minsi, a tribe of the Lenape or Delaware nation, have not all their numerals like those of the Unami tribe, which is the principal among them. I shall give you an opportunity of comparing them.

Numerals of the Minsi.

1. Gutti.
2. Nischa.
3. Nacha.
4. Newa.
5. *Nalan,* (algonk. *narau.*)
6. Guttasch.
7. *Nischoasch,* (algonk. *nissouassou.*)
8. Chaasch.
9. *Nolewi.*
10. *Wimbat.*

Numerals of the Unami.

1. N'gutti.
2. Nischa.
3. Nacha.
4. Newo.
5. Palenach.
6. Guttasch.
7. Nischasch.
8. Chasch.
9. *Peschkonk.*
10. *Tellen.*

You will easily observe that the numbers five and ten in the Minsi dialect, resemble more the Algonkin, as given by La Hontan, than the pure Delaware. I cannot give you the reason of this difference. To this you will add the numerous errors committed by those who attempt to write down the words of the Indian languages, and who either in their own have not alphabetical signs adequate to the true expression of the sounds, or want an *Indian ear* to distinguish them. I could write a volume on the subject of their ridiculous mistakes. I am, &c.

LETTER 11 ~
From Mr. Heckewelder

BETHLEHEM, 24th June, 1816.

DEAR SIR.—I now proceed to answer the several queries contained in your letter of the 13th inst.

1. The double consonants are used in writing the words of the Delaware language, for the sole purpose of indicating that the vowel which immediately precedes them is short, as in the German words *immer*, *nimmer*, *schimmer*, and the English *fellow*, *terrible*, *ill*, *butter*, &c. The consonant is not to be articulated twice.

2. The apostrophe which sometimes follows the letters *n* and *k*, is intended to denote the contraction of a vowel, as *n'pommauchsi*, for *ni pommauchsi*, *n'dappiwi*, for *ni dappiwi*, &c. If Mr. Zeisberger has placed the apostrophe in any case before the consonant, he must have done it through mistake.

3. There is a difference in pronunciation between *ke* and *que*; the latter is pronounced like *kue* or *kwe*. In a verb, the termination *ke* indicates the first person of the plural, and *que* the second.

4. The word *wenn*, employed in the German translation of the tenses of the conjunctive mood of the Delaware verbs, means both *when*, and *if*, and is taken in either sense according to the content of the phrase in which the word is used. Examples: *Ili gachtingetsch pommauchsiane*, "IF I live until the next year"—*Payane Philadelphia*, "WHEN I come to Philadelphia."

5. Sometimes the letters *c* or *g*, are used in writing the Delaware language instead of *k*, to shew that this consonant is not pronounced too hard; but in general *c* and *g* have been used as substitutes for *k*, because our printers had not a sufficient supply of types for that character.

318

6. Where words are written with *ij*, both the letters are to be articulated; the latter like the English *y* before a vowel. For this reason in writing Delaware words I often employ the *y* instead of *j*, which Mr. Zeisberger and the German Missionaries always make use of. Thus *Elsija* is to be pronounced like *Elsiya*.

7. Answered in part above, No. 5. The double vowels are merely intended to express length of sound, as in the German.

8. *Ch*, answers to the X of the Greeks, and *ch* of the Germans. *Hh*, like all other duplicated consonants, indicates only the short sound of the preceding vowels.

      I am, &c.

LETTER 12 ~
To Mr. Heckewelder

PHILADELP , 13th July, 1816.

DEAR SIR.—I have received your kind letters of the 20th and 24th ult. It is impossible to be more clear, precise, and accurate, than you are in your answers to my various questions. The information which your letters contain is of the highest interest to me, and I doubt not will prove so to the Committee, by whose orders I have engaged in this Correspondence, on a subject entirely new to me, but with which I hope in time and with your able assistance, to become better acquainted.

M. de Volney has said somewhere in his excellent Descriptive View of the United States, that it were to be wished that five or six eminent linguists should be constantly employed at the public expense to compile Indian Grammars and Dictionaries. I cannot suppose that the Count meant literally what he said, as he must have been sensible of the difficulties attending on the execution of such a plan, but at any rate, here is a noble display of enthusiasm for our favourite science, and a sufficient encouragement for us to pursue our philological enquiries. Alas! if the beauties of the Lenni Lenape language were found in the ancient Coptic, or in some ante-diluvian Babylonish dialect, how would the learned of Europe be at work to display them in a variety of shapes and raise a thousand fanciful theories on that foundation! What superior wisdom, talents and knowledge would they not ascribe to nations whose idioms were formed with so much skill and method! But who cares for the poor American Indians? They are savages and barbarians and live in the woods; must not their languages be savage and barbarous like them?

Thus reason those pretended philosophers who court fame by writing huge volumes on the origin of human language, without knowing, perhaps, any language but their own, and the little Latin and Greek that they have been taught at College. You would think, when you read their works, that they had lived in the first ages of the creation and had been intimately acquainted with the family of our first parents. They know exactly what words were first uttered when men began to communicate their ideas to each other by means of articulated sounds; they can tell you how the various parts of speech, in perfect regular order, were successively formed, and with a little encouragement, they would, I have no doubt, compile a Grammar and Dictionary of the primitive language, as one Psalmanazar did once in England of a supposed Formosan tongue. It is a pity, indeed, that the Delawares, the Wyandots and the Potowatamies, with languages formed on a construction which had not been before thought of, come to destroy their beautiful theories. What then? are we to suppress the languages of our good Indians, or to misrepresent them, that the existing systems on Universal Grammar and the origin of language may be preserved? No, my friend, we shall on the contrary, I hope, labour with all our might to make them known, and provide, at least, additional facts for future theorists.

I have been led into this chain of ideas by reading the ponderous work of a Scotch Lord named Monboddo, who has dreamt of languages more than any other writer that I know. On the authority of a Father Sagard, (a French Missionary) he represents the language of the Hurons as the most incoherent and unsystematical heap of vocables that can possibly be conceived. Their words have no regular formation or derivation, no roots or radical syllables, there is no analogy whatever in the construction or arrangement of this language. He says, for instance, that there is a word for "two years" entirely different from those which signify one, three, four or ten years; that "*hut*," "*my hut*," and "*in my hut*," are severally expressed by words entirely different from each other. He adduces several other examples of the same kind, with which I shall not trouble you, and concludes with saying, that "the Huron language is the most imperfect of any that has been yet discovered." (Orig. of Lang., Vol. I., p. 478.)

Before we proceed further, let us suppose that a Huron or a Delaware is writing a treatise on the origin of language, and in the pride of pompous ignorance attempts to make similar observations on the English idiom. Following Lord Monboddo's course of reasoning, he will say: "The English is the most imperfect language upon earth, for its words have no kind of analogy to each other. They say, for instance, '*a house*,' and the things that belong to a house they call '*domestic*.' They say '*a year*,' and 'an *annual* payment,' for a sum of money payable every *year*. That is not all; if the payment is to be made in *two* years, it is then called *biennial*, in which you find no trace of either the word *two* or the word '*year*,' of which in a regular language it should be compounded. What belongs to a *King* is royal; to a *woman*, feminine; to *ship*, naval; to a *town*, urban; to the *country*, rural. Such another irregular, unmethodical dialect never existed, I believe, on the back of the great tortoise!!"

Such would be the language of our Huron philosopher, and he would be about as right as Lord Monboddo. I have read this work of Father Sagard, of which there is a copy in the Congress library. It appears to me that the good Father was an honest, well meaning, but most ignorant friar, of one of the mendicant orders. His residence among the Hurons was very short, not more than a twelve-month; he was, I know not for what reason, called home by his superiors, and left America with great regret. He has collected a number of words and phrases of the Huron language in the form of a vocabulary, which he improperly calls a dictionary. I have had it copied and shall shew it to you when you come to town. You will be satisfied when you see it, that the good man not only never analysed the language of the Hurons, but was incapable of doing it. He was perfectly bewildered in the variety of its forms, and drew the very common conclusion that what he could not comprehend was necessarily barbarous and irregular. From an attentive perusal of his "dictionary," I am inclined to draw the opposite conclusion from that which he has drawn. There appears to me to be in it sufficient internal evidence to shew that the Huron language is rich in grammatical forms, and that it is constructed much on the same plan with the Delaware. I shall be very glad to have your opinion on it, with such information as you are able and willing to give. I beg particularly that you will let me know whether there are roots and derivations in the Indian languages, analogous to those of our own?

I am, &c.

LETTER 13 ~
To Mr. Heckewelder

PHILADELPHIA, 18th July, 1816.

DEAR SIR.—In your letter of the 27th of May you have said that you believed the Delaware nation were those whom the Baron La Hontan meant to designate by the name of *Algonkins*. In a subsequent letter, (June 20th,) you seem to consider them as distinct nations, but nearly allied to each other; you say you are not well acquainted with their language, which is not the same with that of the Lenape, though there is a considerable affinity between them. Upon the whole I suppose that you have meant to apply the denomination Algonkins, not only to the Delawares proper, but to all the nations and tribes of the same family.

This has led me to consider who those Algonkins might be that La Hontan speaks of, and upon the best investigation that I have been able to make of the subject, I am inclined to believe that La Hontan's Algonkins are properly those whom we call *Chippeways*, a family or branch of the Delawares, but not the Delawares themselves. I first turned to Dr. Barton's "New Views of the Origin of the Nations and Tribes of America," in which I found that he considered the Delawares and Chippeways as two distinct people; but when I came to the specimens which he gives of their languages in his Vocabularies, I found no difference whatever in the idioms of the two nations. Pursuing the enquiry further, I compared the Vocabulary of the Chippeway language given by Carver in his travels, and that of the Algonkin by La Hontan, and was much astonished to find the words in each language exactly alike, without any difference but what arises from the French and English orthography. The words explained by the two authors, happen also to be precisely the same, and are arranged in the same alphabetical order. So that either Carver is a gross plagiarist, who has pretended to give a list of Chippeway words and has only copied the Algonkin words given by La Hontan, or the Chippeways and Algonkins are one and the same people. I shall be very glad to have your opinion on this subject.

323

I find in Zeisberger's Grammar something that I cannot well comprehend. It is the verb "*n'dellauchsi*" which he translates "I live, move about," or "I so live that I move about." Pray, is this the only verb in the Delaware language, which signifies "*to live*," and have the Indians no idea of "life," but when connected with "*locomotion*"?

Is the *W* in the Delaware, as your Missionaries write it, to be pronounced like the same letter in German, or like the English *W* and the French *ou*? If this letter has the German sound, then it is exactly the same as that of our *V*; in that case I am astonished that the Delawares cannot pronounce the *F*, the two sounds being so nearly alike.

I am, &c.

LETTER 14 ~
FROM MR. HECKEWELDER

BETHLEHEM, 22d July, 1816.

DEAR SIR.—I received at the same time your two letters of the 13th and 18th inst., the last by our friend Dr. Wistar. I think you are wrong to complain of the little importance attached by the learned of Europe to the study of Indian languages and of the false ideas which some of them have conceived respecting them. The truth is that sufficient pains have not been taken in this country to make them known. Our Missionaries have, indeed, compiled grammars and dictionaries of those idioms, but more with a view to practical use and to aid their fellow-labourers in the great work of the conversion of the Indians to Christianity, than in order to promote the study of the philosophy of language. They have neither sought fame nor profit, and therefore their compositions have remained unknown except in the very limited circle of our religious society. It belongs to the literary associations of America to pursue or encourage those studies in a more extended point of view, and I shall be happy to aid to the utmost of my power the learned researches of the American Philosophical Society.

Your remarks on Lord Monboddo's opinion respecting the Indian languages, and on Father Sagard's work, on which that opinion is founded, I believe to be correct. I am not acquainted with the language of the Hurons, which I have always understood to be a dialect of that of the Iroquois, or at least to be derived from the same stock, and I cannot conceive why it should be so poor and so imperfect as the good Father describes it, while its kindred idiom, the Iroquois, is directly the reverse. At least, it was so considered by Mr. Zeisberger, who was very well acquainted with it. Sir William Johnson thought the same, and I believe you will find his opinion on the subject in one of the Volumes of the Transactions of the Royal Society of London.[279] Colden, in his History of the Five Nations, says "that the verbs of that language are varied, but in a manner so different from the Greek and Latin, that his informant could not discover by what rule it was done."[280] I suspect his informant had not yet acquired a very profound knowledge of the Iroquois; but from his imperfect description of their verbs, I am very nearly convinced that they are formed on the same model with those of the Lenni Lenape, which Mr. Zeisberger has well described in his Grammar of that language. Colden praises this idiom in other respects; he says that "the Six Nations compound their words without end, whereby their language becomes sufficiently copious." This is true also of the Delawares.

The Hurons are the same people whom we call Wyandots; the Delawares call them *Delamattenos*. I am inclined to believe that the tribe whom we call *Naudowessies*, and the French *Sioux*, who are said to live to the west or north-west of Lake Superior, are a branch of the Hurons; for the rivers which we call *Huron*, (of which there are three)[281] are called by the Chippeways, *Naduwewi*, or *Naudowessie Sipi*. But of this I cannot be sure; though I would rather conclude that *Naudowessie* is the Chippeway name for all the Wyandots or Hurons. It is a fact which, I think, deserves to be ascertained. It is a very common error to make several Indian nations out of one, by means of the different names by which it is known.

I proceed to answer the questions contained in your letter of the 18th.

As it seems to me probable that the Naudowessies and Hurons, though called by different names, are the same people; so it may be the case with the Chippeways and the Algonkins, although I have no greater certainty of this hypothesis than of the former. I have no doubt, however, of their being both derived from the same stock, which is that of the Lenni Lenape: that their languages are strikingly similar is evident from the two vocabularies that you mention, and I had rather believe that they both speak the same language, than that Captain Carver was a plagiarist. The accounts which he gives of the Indians I have found in general correct; which is the more remarkable, that from his own account, it appears that he did not reside very long among them. He must have been, therefore, a very attentive and accurate observer.

It is very probable that I did not express myself with sufficient precision in the passages of my letters of the 27th of May and 20th of June to which you refer. The Lenni Lenape, or Delawares, are the head of a great family of Indian nations who are known among themselves by the generic name of *Wapanachki*, or "Men of the East." The same language is spread among them all in various dialects, of which I conceive the purest is that of the chief nation, the Lenape, at whose residence the grand national councils meet, and whom the others, by way of respect, style *grandfather*. The Algonkins are a branch of that family, but are not, in my opinion, entitled to the pre-eminence which the Baron La Hontan ascribes to them. He applied the name "Algonkin," in a more extensive sense than it deserves, and said that the Algonkin language was the finest and most universally spread of any on the continent; a praise to which I think the Lenni Lenape idiom alone is entitled. In this sense only I meant to say that the Baron included the Delawares in the general descriptive name of "Algonkins."

I have yet to answer your questions respecting the language, which I shall do in a subsequent letter.

I am, &c.

LETTER 15 ~
From the same

BETHLEHEM, 24th July, 1816.

DEAR SIR.—I have now to answer your question on the subject of the Delaware verb, *n'dellauchsi*, which Zeisberger translates by "I live, or move about," or "I so live that I move about." You ask whether this is the only verb in the language which expresses "*to live*," and whether the Indians have an idea of *life*, otherwise than as connected with *locomotion*?

Surely they have; and I do not see that the contrary follows from Mr. Zeisberger's having chosen this particular verb as an example of the first conjugation. I perceive you have not yet an adequate idea of the copiousness of the Indian languages, which possess an immense number of comprehensive words, expressive of almost every possible combination of ideas. Thus the proper word for "*to live*" is in the pure Unami dialect *lehaleheen*. An Unami meeting an aged acquaintance, whom he has not seen for a length of time, will address him thus: "*Ili k'lehelleya?*"[282] which means, "are you yet alive?" The other will answer "*Ili n'papomissi*,"[283] "I am yet able to walk about." The verb *n'dellauchsin*, which Mr. Zeisberger quotes, is more generally employed in a spiritual sense, "*n'dellauchsin Patamawos wulelendam*," "I live up, act up to the glory of God." This verb, like *pommauchsin*, implies action or motion, connected with *life*, which is still the principal idea. I do not know of any thing analogous in the English language, except, perhaps, when we say "To *walk* humbly before God;" but here the word *walk* contains properly no idea in itself but that of locomotion, and is not coupled with the idea of *life*, as in the Indian verb which I have cited. The idea intended to be conveyed arises in English entirely from the *figurative* sense of the word, in the Delaware from the *proper* sense.

I should never have done, were I to endeavour to explain to you in all their details the various modes which the Indians have of expressing ideas, shades of ideas, and combinations of ideas; for which purpose the various parts of speech are successively called to their aid. In the conjugations of the verbs, in Zeisberger's Grammar, you will find but three tenses, present, past, and future; but you will be much mistaken if you believe that there are no other modes of expressing actions and passions in the verbal form as connected with the idea of time. It would have been an endless work to have given all those explanations in an elementary grammar intended for the use of young Missionaries, who stood in need only of the principal forms, which they were to perfect afterwards by practice. Let me now try to give you a faint idea of what I mean by a few examples in the Delaware language.

N'mitzi, *I eat.*[284]N'mamitzi, *I am eating, or am in the act of eating.*N'mitzihump, *I have eaten.*Metschi n'gischi mitzi, *I am come from eating.*N'dappi mitzi, *I am returned from eating.*

The first two *n'mitzi* and *n'mamitzi*, both mean *I eat*, but the one is used in the indefinite, and the other in the definite sense, and a good speaker will never employ the one instead of the other. The three last expressions are all past tenses of the verb "I eat," and all mean, "*I have eaten*," but a person just risen from table, will not say, "*n'dappi mitzi;*" this expression can only be used after leaving the place where he has been eating, in answer to a person who asks him "where he comes from." The word "*n'dappi*" is connected with the verb *apatschin*, to return. There is another distinction, proper to be mentioned here. If the place where the person comes from is near, he says "*n'dappi,*" if distant "*n'dappa.*" Thus:

N'dappi pihm, *I am come from sweating (or from the sweat oven.)*
N'dappihackiheen, *I am come from planting.*
N'dappi wickheen, *I am come from building a house.*
N'dappimanschasqueen, *I am come from mowing grass.*
N'dappi notamæsin, *I am come from striking fish with a spear.*
N'dappallauwin, *I am come (returned) from hunting.*

N'dappachtopalin, *I am come (returned) from making war.*

In the future tense I could shew similar distinctions, but it would lead me too far.

I must now take notice of what Father Sagard says, as you have mentioned in your letter of the 13th inst., that the Indian languages have "no *roots*, and that there is no regularity in the formation of their words." It is certain that the manner in which the Indians in general form their words is different from that of the Europeans, but I can easily prove to you that they understand the manner of forming them from "*roots.*" I take, for instance, the word *wulit*, good, proper, right, from which are derived:

Wulik, *the good.* Wulaha, *better.* Wulisso, *fine, pretty.* Wulamoewagan, *truth.* Wulatenamuwi, *happy.* Wulatenamoagan, *happiness.* Wulapensowagan, *blessing.* Wulapan, *fine morning.* Wuliechen, *it is good, or well done.* Wulittol, *they are good.* Wuliken, *it grows well, thrives.* Wuliechsin, *to speak well.* Wulelendam, *to rejoice.* Wulamallsin, *to be well, happy.*

Wulandeu,}Wuligischgu,}*a fine day.*

Wulapeyu, *just, upright.* Wuliwatam, *to be of good understanding.* Wuliachpin, *to be in a good place.* Wulilissin, *to do well.* Wulilissu, *he is good.* Wulilissick, *behave ye well.* Wulinaxin, *to look well.* Wulamoeyu, *it is true.* Wulantowagan, *grace.* Wulatopnachgat,[285]*a good word.* Wulatopnamik, *good tidings.* Wulatonamin,[286]*to be happy.* Wulissowagan, *prettiness, handsome appearance.* Wulihilleu, *it is good.* Wulineichquot, *it is well to be seen.* Wulelemileu, *it is wonderful.* Wulitehasu, *well cut or hewed.* Wuliwiechinen, *to rest well.* Welsit Mannitto, *the Good Spirit.* From Machtit, *bad.* Machtitsu, *nasty.* Machtesinsu, *ugly.* Machtschi *or* Matschi Mannitto *or* Machtando, *the evil Spirit, the Devil*, &c.

330

You will naturally observe that the words derived from the root *Wulit*, imply in general the idea of what is good, handsome, proper, decent, just, well, and so pursuing the same general object to *happiness* and its derivatives; *happiness* being considered as a good and pleasant feeling, or situation of the mind, and a person who is *happy*, as being well. This does not, as you might suppose, make the language ambiguous; for the Indians speak and understand each other with great precision and clearness.

I have yet to answer your question about the *f* and *w*. There are in the Delaware language no such consonants as the German *w*, or English *v*, *f*, or *r*. Where *w* in this language is placed before a vowel, it sounds the same as in English; before a consonant, it represents a *whistled* sound of which I cannot well give you an idea on paper, but which I shall easily make you understand by uttering it before you when we meet.

I am, &c.

LETTER 16 ~
To Mr. Heckewelder

PHILADELPHIA 31st July, 1816.

DEAR SIR.—I have received with the geatest pleasure your two favours of the 24th and 26th inst.; the last, particularly, has opened to me a very wide field for reflection. I am pursuing with ardour the study of the Indian languages (I mean of their grammatical forms) in all the authors that I can find that have treated of the subject, and am astonished at the great similarity which I find between those different idioms from Greenland even to Chili. They all appear to me to be compounded on a model peculiar to themselves, and of which I had not before an idea. Those personal forms of the verbs, for instance, which you mention in your letter of the 20th of June, I find generally existing in the American languages. The Spanish-Mexican Grammarians call them *transitions*, but they are not all equally happy in their modes of explaining their nature and use. The word "*transition*," however, I think extremely well chosen, as it gives at once an idea of the passage of the verb from the pronoun that governs to that which is governed, from "I love" to "I love you." The forms of the Indian verbs are so numerous, that a proper technical term is very much wanted to distinguish this particular class, and I adopt with pleasure this appropriate Spanish name, at least, until a better one can be found.

I am sufficiently satisfied from the examples in your last letter that the Indians have in their languages "roots," or radical words from which many others are derived; indeed, I never doubted it before, and only meant to shew you by the instances of Father Sagard, and Lord Monboddo, what false ideas the Europeans have conceived on this subject. The various meanings of the word "*wulit*" and its derivatives, obtained, as you have shewn, by easy or natural transitions from one kindred idea to another, are nothing new in language. The Greek has the word "*kalos*," which in its various meanings is very analogous to "*wulit*." Instances of similar "transitions" from different European idioms might be cited without end. There is one in the French which strikes me at this moment with peculiar force. In that language, an honest man is "*just*" in his dealings and a judge in his judgments; but a pair of shoes is so likewise, when made exactly to fit

332

the foot, and by a natural transition, when the shoes are too tight, they are said to be too *just* (trop justes). A foreigner in France is reported to have said to his shoemaker, complaining of the tightness of a pair of new made shoes: "*Monsieur, ces souliers sont trop équitables.*" I remember also an English song, beginning with the words "*Just like love,*" where you see the word "*just*" is employed without at all implying the idea of *equity* or *justice*. But justice is strict, exact, correct, precise, and therefore the word *just* is employed for the purpose of expressing these and other ideas connected with that to which it was first applied.

I have made these trite observations, because I am well aware that many *a priori* reasoners would not fail to find in so many words of different meanings derived from the same root, a proof of the poverty of the Indian languages. They would say that they are poor, because they have but few radical words, a conclusion which they would infallibly make without taking the pains of ascertaining the fact. If they were told that the Greek (the copiousness of which is universally acknowledged) has itself but a comparatively small number of roots, they would not be at a loss to find some other reason in support of their pre-conceived opinion. I have read somewhere (I cannot recollect in what book), that there was not a greater proof of the barbarism of the Indian languages, than the comprehensiveness of their locutions. The author reasoned thus: Analysis, he said, is the most difficult operation of the human mind; it is the last which man learns to perform. Savage nations, therefore, express many ideas in a single word, because they have not yet acquired the necessary skill to separate them from each other by the process of analysis, and to express them simply.

If this position were true, it would follow that all the languages of savage nations have been in the origin formed on the same model with those of the American Indians, and that simple forms have been gradually introduced into them by the progress of civilisation. But if we take the trouble of enquiring into facts, they will by no means lead us to this conclusion. It is not many centuries since the Scandinavian languages of the North of Europe were spoken by barbarous and savage nations, but we do not find that in ancient times they were more comprehensive in their grammatical forms than they are at present, when certainly they are the least so, perhaps, of any of the European idioms; on the other hand, the Latin and Greek were sufficiently so by means of the various moods and tenses of their verbs, all expressed in one single word, without the use of auxiliaries; and yet these two nations had attained a very high degree, at least, of civilisation. I do not, therefore, see as yet, that there is a necessary connexion between the greater or lesser degree of civilisation of a people, and the organisation of their language. These general conclusions from insulated facts ought constantly to be guarded against; they are the most fruitful sources of error in the moral as well as in the natural sciences. Facts ought to be collected and observations multiplied long before we venture to indulge in theoretical inferences; for unobserved facts seem to lie in ambush, to start up at once in the face of finespun theories, and put philosophers in the wrong.

I wish very much that some able linguist would undertake to make a good classification of the different languages of the world (as far as they are known) in respect to their grammatical forms. It was once attempted in the French Encyclopedia, but without success, because the author had only in view the Latin and Greek, and those of the modern languages which he was acquainted with. His division, if I remember right, was formed between those idioms in which inversions are allowed, and those in which they are not. Of course, it was the Latin and Greek on the one side, and the French, Italian, &c., on the other. This meagre classification has not been generally adopted, nor does it, in my opinion, deserve to be. A greater range of observation ought to be taken.

I do not pretend to possess talents adequate to carrying into execution the plan which I here suggest; but I beg you will permit me to draw a brief sketch of what I have in view.

I observe, in the first place, in the eastern parts of Asia, a class of languages formed on the same model, of which I take that which is *spoken* in the empire of China, as it stood before its conquest by the Tartars, to be the type. In this language, there is but a very small number of words, all monosyllables. As far as I am able to judge from the excellent grammars of this idiom of which we are in possession, the words convey to the mind only the principal or leading ideas of the discourse, unconnected with many of those accessory ideas that are so necessary to give precision to language, and the hearer is left to apply and arrange the whole together as well as he can. It has but few or no grammatical forms, and is very deficient in what we call the connecting parts of speech. Hence it is said that the words spoken are not immediately understood by those to whom they are addressed, and that auxiliary modes of explanation, others than oral communication, are sometimes resorted to, when ambiguities occur. As I am no Sinologist, I will not undertake to say that the description which I have attempted to give of this language, from the mere reading of grammars and dictionaries, is very accurate, but I venture to assert that it differs so much from all others that we know, that with its kindred idioms, it deserves to form a *genus* in a general classification of the various modes of speech. From its great deficiency of grammatical forms, I would give to this genus the name *asyntactic*.

My second class of languages would consist of those which possess, indeed, grammatical forms, sufficient to express and connect together every idea to be communicated by means of speech, but in which those forms are so organized, that almost every distinct idea has a single word to convey or express it. Such are the Icelandic, Danish, Swedish, and even the German and English. Those forms of the nouns and verbs which are generally called declensions and conjugations, are in these languages the result of an analytical process of the mind, which has given to every single idea, and sometimes to a shade of an idea, a single word to express it. Thus, when we say "*of the man*," here are three ideas, which, in the Latin, are expressed by one single word "*hominis*." In the locution "*I will not*," or "*I am not willing*," and in the verbal form "*I will go*," three or four ideas are separately expressed in English, which, in Latin, are conveyed together by single words "*nolo*," "*ibo*." From this peculiar quality of sufficiently, yet separately, expressing all the necessary ideas, I would denominate this class of languages *analytical*, or *analytic*.

The third class would, of course, be that in which the principal parts of speech are formed by a synthetical operation of the mind, and in which several ideas are frequently expressed by one word. Such are what are called the Oriental languages, with the Latin, Greek, Slavonic, and others of the same description. These I would call *synthetic*.

The French, Italian, Spanish, and Portuguese, with their various dialects, in which conquest has in a great degree intermingled the modes of speech of the second and third class, would together form a fourth, which I would call "*mixed*."

In these various classes I have not found a place for the Indian languages, which richly deserve to form one by themselves. They are "*synthetic*" in their forms, but to such a degree as is not equalled by any of the idioms which I have so denominated, and which are only such in comparison with others where *analytic* forms prevail. That they deserve to make a class by themselves cannot be doubted. They are the very opposite of the Chinese, of all languages the poorest in words, as well as in grammatical forms, while these are the richest in both. In fact, a great variety of forms, necessarily implies a great multiplicity of words; I mean, complex forms, like those of the Indians; compound words in which many ideas are included together, and are made to strike the mind in various ways by the simple addition or subtraction of a letter or syllable. In the Chinese much is understood or guessed at, little is expressed; in the Indian, on the contrary, the mind is awakened to each idea meant to be conveyed, by some one or other of the component parts of the word spoken. These two languages, therefore, as far as relates to their organisation, stand in direct opposition to each other; they are the top and bottom of the idiomatic scale, and as I have given to the Chinese, and its kindred dialects, the name of *asyntactic*, the opposite name, *syntactic*, appears to me that which is best suited to the languages of the American Indians. I find that instead of asking you questions, as I ought to do, I am wandering again in the field of metaphysical disquisitions. I shall try to be more careful in my next letter.

I am, &c.

LETTER 17 ~
To the same

PHILADELPHIA, 3d August, 1816.

DEAR SIR.—I now return to my proper station of a scholar asking questions of his master. In your letter of the 24th ult., you have fully satisfied me that the Indians have a great number of words derived from "*roots*," much in the same manner as in the languages of Europe, but you have said at the same time "that the manner in which the Indians in general form their words, is different from that of the Europeans." I am very anxious to have this manner[287] explained, and I shall be very much obliged to you for all the information that you can give me on the subject.

I have told you already that I thought I had reason to believe that all the American languages were formed on the same general plan. If I am correct in my supposition, I think I have found in the language of Greenland, the identical manner of compounding words which I am now calling upon you to explain. You will tell me whether I have judged right, and you will at once destroy or confirm my favourite hypothesis. According to the venerable Egede, words are formed in the Greenland language by taking and joining together a part of each of the radical words, the ideas of which are to be combined together in one compound locution. One or more syllables of each simple word are generally chosen for that purpose and combined together, often leaving out the harsh consonants for the sake of euphony. Thus from "*agglekpok*," he writes, "*pekipok*," he mends or does better, and "*pinniarpok*," he endeavours, is formed the compound word "*agglekiniaret*," which means, "endeavour to write better." The first syllable "*agl*," is taken from "agl*ekpok*," the second "*ek*" from the same word, and also from the first syllable of "*pekipok*," leaving out the *p* to avoid harshness, and the third "*inniar*" from "Pinniar*pok*," also leaving out the initial consonant for the same reason. It seems to me that I find something like it in the Delaware language. According to Zeisberger, *wet*ooch*wink* signifies "father." Now taking the second syllable *ooch*, and placing *n* before it, you have "*nooch*," my father. To be sure, it is not the first syllable that is borrowed, as in the above example

337

from the Greenlandish, but the principle appears, nevertheless, to be the same in both languages.

On the subject of this word "*father*" I observe a strange contradiction between two eminent writers on Indian languages, evidently derived from the stock of the Lenni Lenape or Delaware. One of them, Roger Williams, in his Key to the Language of the New England Indians, says "*osh*" (meaning probably *och* or *ooch*, as the English cannot pronounce the guttural *ch*) father; "*nosh*" my father; "*kosh*" thy father, &c. On the other hand, the Rev. Jonathan Edwards, in his observations on the language of the *Muhhekanew* (Mohican) Indians, speaks as follows: "A considerable part of the appellations is never used without a pronoun affixed. The Mohegans say, my father, '*nogh*' (again *noch* or *nooch*) thy father '*kogh*,' &c., but they cannot say absolutely '*father.*' There is no such word in their language. If you were to say '*ogh*,' you would make a Mohegan both stare and smile." (page 13.)

Which of these two professors is right? It seems that either Rogers invented the word *osh* for "father," from analogy, or that Edwards is not correct when he says that *ogh* or *ooch* singly, mean nothing in the Indian language. Is he not mistaken when he says that there is no word whatever answering to "father," or "the father," in an abstract sense; and if an Indian would stare and smile when a white man says *ooch*, would he smile in the same manner if he said *wetoochwink*? Is it possible to suppose that this respectable author had only a partial knowledge of the language on which he wrote, and that he was not acquainted with the radical word from which *nooch* and *kooch* had been formed? Or is there no such radical word, and has Zeisberger himself committed a mistake?

I beg leave to submit to you also another observation that I have made. It appears from the work of the late Dr. Barton, who quotes your authority for it, that the name of the *Lenni Lenape*, means "*the original people*," and that "*Lenno*" in the Delaware language signifies "man," in the general sense, (*Mensch*.) Now, it appears that in the language of the *Micmacs* (a tribe of Nova Scotia,) they call an Indian "*Illenoh*," and in that of the Canadian mountaineers (whom some believe to be the Algonkins proper) they say "*Illenou*." (Mass. Histor. Coll. for the year 1799, pp. 18, 19.) I am apt to believe that those names are the same with "*Lenno*," and that it is from them that the French have formed the name "*Illinois*," which extends even beyond the Mississippi. In the speech of the Indian chief *Garangula*, to the Governor of Canada, related by La Hontan, the warrior says: "You must know, Onontio, that we have robbed no Frenchmen, but those who supplied the '*Illinois*,' and the '*Oumamis*,' our enemies, with powder and ball." I am inclined to believe that Garangula when he spoke of the *Illinois* meant the *Lenni Lenape*, and by the name of *Oumamis*, intended to describe their chief tribe, the *Unamis*. Of this, however, I leave you to judge. But I strongly suspect that "*Lenno*," "*Lenni*," "*Illenoh*," "*Illenou*," "*Illinois*," are the same name, and all apply to that great nation whom the Baron La Hontan takes to be the *Algonkins*, who, it would seem, are only called so by way of discrimination, but consider themselves as a branch of the great family of the "*Illenou*." If I am correct in this, how do you make out that *Lenni Lenape* means "*original people*"?

The Greenlanders, according to Egede, call themselves *Innuit*, which in their language also signifies *men*. It appears to me to be very much akin to *Illenoh*, *Illeun*. Could the Greenlanders be in any way connected with the *Lenni Lenape*?

Pray tell me from what languages are derived the words *squaw*, *sachem*, *tomahawk*, *calumet*, *wampum*, *papoose*, which are so much in use among us? Are they of the Delaware or the Iroquois stock?

   I am, &c.

LETTER 18
From Mr. Heckewelder

BETHLEHEM 12th August, 1816.

DEAR SIR.—I have duly received your two letters of the 31st of July and 3d of August last. I am much pleased with your metaphysical disquisitions, as you call them, and I beg you will indulge in them with perfect freedom, whenever you shall feel so disposed. I agree with you that a proper classification of human languages would be a very desirable object; but I fear the task is too hard ever to be accomplished with the limited knowledge of man. There are, no doubt, many varieties in language yet to be discovered.

As you wish to be acquainted with the manner in which our North American Indians compound their words, I shall endeavour to satisfy you as well as I am able. The process is much the same as that which Egede has described with respect to the Greenland language, and this strongly corroborates your opinion respecting the similarity of forms of at least of those of North America. In the Delaware and other languages that I am acquainted with, parts or parcels of different words, sometimes a single sound or letter, are compounded together, in an artificial manner, so as to avoid the meeting of harsh or disagreeable sounds, and make the whole word fall in a pleasant manner upon the ear. You will easily conceive that words may thus be compounded and multiplied without end, and hence the peculiar richness of the American languages. Of this I can give you numerous examples. In the first place, the word "*nadholincen.*" It is a simple short word, but means a great deal. The ideas that are conveyed by it are these: "Come with the canoe and take us across the river or stream." Its component parts are as follows: The first syllable "*nad*" is derived from the verb "*naten,*" to fetch; the second, "*hol,*" from "*amochol,*" a canoe or boat; "*ineen*" is the verbal termination for "*us,*" as in *milineen*, "give us;"—the simple ideas, therefore, contained in this word, are "*fetch canoe us,*" but in its usual and common acceptation it means, "come and fetch us across the river with a canoe." I need not say that this verb is conjugated through all its moods and tenses. *Nadholawall* is the form of the third person of the

340

singular of the indicative present, and means "He is fetched over the river with a canoe," or simply, "He is fetched over the river."

From *wunipach*, a leaf, *nach*, a hand, and *quim*, a nut growing on a tree (for there is a peculiar word to express nuts of this description and distinguish them from other nuts) is formed *wunachquim*, an acorn, and the ideas which by this name are intended to be conveyed are these: "The nut of the tree the leaves of which resemble a hand, or have upon them the form of a hand." If you will take the trouble to examine the leaves of an oak tree, you will find on them the form of a hand with outspread fingers. On the same principle are formed

M'sim, *hickory*
nut.Ptucquim, *walnut*.Wapim, *chestnut*.Schauwemin, *beech nut*,
and many others.

The tree which we call "*Spanish oak*," remarkable for the largeness of its leaves, they call "*Amanganaschquiminschi*," "the tree which has the largest leaves shaped like a hand." If I were to imitate the composition of this word in English and apply it to our language, I would say *Largehandleafnuttree*, and softening the sounds after the Indian manner, it would perhaps make *Larjandliffentree*, or *Larjandlennuttree*, or something like it. Of course, in framing the word, an English ear should be consulted. The last syllable of that which I have last cited, is not taken from the proper name for *tree*, which is *hittuck*; but from "*achpansi*,"[288] which means the "stock, trunk or body of a tree" (in German "*der stamm*"). The last syllable of this word, "*si*," is in its compound converted into *schi*, probably for the sake of euphony, of which an Indian ear in this case is the best judge.

Again, "*nanayunges*," in Delaware means "a horse." It is formed from *awesis*, a beast, from which the last syllable *es* is taken, and *nayundam*, to carry a burden on the back or shoulders; for when something is carried in the hands or arms, the proper verb is "*gelenummen*." The word which signifies "horse," therefore, literally means, "the beast which carries on its back," or in other words, "a beast of burden." Were asses or camels known to the Indians, distinctive appellations for them would soon and easily be formed.

Thus much for the names of *natural substances*, and words which relate to visible objects. Let us now turn to the expression of ideas which affect the moral sense.

341

You will remember that I have told you before that "*wulik*" or "*wulit*" signifies "good," and in the various derivations which flow from it means almost every thing that is good, just, proper, decent, pleasing or agreeable. When an Indian wishes to express that he is pleased with something that you have told him, he will say in his metaphorical language: "You have spoken *good* words." Now let us see how this compound idea is expressed. "*Kolamoe*" is one of the forms of the past tense of a verb which means "to speak the truth," and properly translated signifies "thou hast spoken the truth," or "thou hast spoken good words." *K*, from *ki*, expresses the second person, "*ola*" is derived from *wulit* and conveys the idea of *good*; the rest of the word implies the action of speaking.

In the third person, "*wulamoe*" means "he has spoken the truth;" from which is formed the noun substantive *wulamoewagan*, "*the* truth:" *wagan* or *woagan* (as our German Missionaries sometimes write it to express the sound of the English *w*) being a termination which answers to that of "*ness*" in English, and "*heit*" or "*keit*" in German. Pursuing further the same chain of ideas, *wulistamoewagan* or *wulamhittamoewagan*, means "faith" or "belief," the belief of what a man has seen or heard; for *glistam* is a verb which signifies "to hear, hearken, listen;" hence "*wulista*," believe it, *wulistam*, he believes; *wulisto*, believe ye, &c. The Indians say *klistawi!* hear me! *nolsittammen*, I believe it; *ammen* or *tammen* abridged from *hittammen*, where they are employed as terminations, mean "to do, perform, adopt." See what a number of ideas are connected together in single words, and with what regularity they are compounded, with proper terminations indicating the part of speech, form, mood, tense, number and person, that they respectively belong to! The various shades of thought that those different modes of speech discriminate are almost innumerable; for instance, *wulistammen* means simply to believe; *wulamsittammen* to believe with full conviction. I would never have done, if I were to point out to you all the derivatives from this source, or connected with the idea of *belief*, which word I bring forward merely by way of example, there being many others equally fruitful. There is *wulamoinaquot*, credible, worthy of belief (sometimes used as an impersonal verb, "it is credible, it deserves to be believed"); *welsittawot*, a believer; *welsittank*, a believer in the religious sense, &c.

The syllable *pal* or *pel* prefixed to some words, implies denial, and also frequently denotes wrong and is taken in a bad sense. Hence *palsittamoewagan*, unbelief; *palsittammen*, to disbelieve; *pelsittank*, an unbeliever; *pelsittangik*, unbelievers. Again, *palliwi*, otherwise; *palliton*,

342

to spoil, to do something wrong; *palhiken*, to make a bad shot, to miss the mark in shooting; *palhitechen*, to aim a stroke and miss it; *pallahammen*, to miss in shooting at *game*; *pallilissin*, to do something amiss or wrong.

M. de Volney has very justly observed on the Miami language, which is a dialect of the Lenape, that *m* at the beginning of a word implies in general something bad or ugly. It is certainly so in the Delaware, though not without exceptions, for *mannitto*, a spirit, by which name God himself, the great and good Spirit is called, begins with that ill-omened letter. Nevertheless the words "*machit*," bad, and "*medhick*," evil, have produced many derivatives, or words beginning with the syllables *med*, *mach*, *mat*, *mui*, *me*, *mas*, &c., all of which imply something bad, and are taken in a bad sense. For instance, *mekih* and *melih*, corruption; *machtando*, the devil; *machtageen*, to fight, kill; *machtapan*, a bad, unpleasant morning; *machtapeek*, bad time, time of war; *machtonquam*, to have a bad dream, &c. I mention this merely to do justice to the sagacity of M. Volney, whose few observations upon the Indians induce us to regret that he was not in a situation to make more.

I begin to feel fatigued, and therefore shall take leave of you for the present and reserve the remainder of my answer for my next letter.

I am, &c.

LETTER 19 ~
From the same

BETHLEHEM, 15th August, 1816.

DEAR SIR.—I sit down to conclude my answer to your letter of the 3d inst.

Before I begin this task, let me give you some examples that now occur to me to shew the regularity of the formation of Indian words.

1. The names of reptiles generally end in *gook* or *gookses*.

Achgook, *a snake.*Suckachgook, *a black snake* (from *suck* or *suckeu*, black.)Mamalachgook, *spotted snake.*Asgaskachgook, *green snake.*

2. The names of fishes in *meek* (*Namæs*, a fish.)

Maschilameek, *a trout* (spotted fish.)Wisameek, *cat-fish* (the fat fish.)Suckameek, *black fish.*Lennameek, *chub fish.*

3. The names of other animals, have in the same manner regular terminations, *ap*, or *ape*, for walking in an erect posture; hence *lenape*, man; *chum*, for four-legged animals, and *wehelleu*, for the winged tribes. I need not swell this letter with examples, which would add nothing to your knowledge of the principle which I have sufficiently explained.

I now proceed to answer your letter.

Notwithstanding Mr. Edwards's observation (for whom I feel the highest respect), I cannot help being of opinion, that the monosyllable *ooch*, is the proper word for *father*, abstractedly considered, and that it is as proper to say *ooch*, father, and *nooch*, my father, as *dallemons*, beast, and *n'dallemons*, my beast; or *nitschan*, child, or a child, and *n'nitschan*, my child. It is certain, however, that there are few occasions for using these words in their abstract sense, as there are so many ways of associating them

344

with other ideas. *Wetoochwink* and *wetochemuxit* both mean "the father," in a more definite sense, and *wetochemelenk* is used in the vocative sense, and means "thou our father." I once heard Captain Pipe, a celebrated Indian chief, address the British commandant at Detroit, and he said *nooch!* my father!

The shades of difference between these several expressions are so nice and delicate, that I feel great difficulty in endeavouring to explain them. *Wetochemuxit*, I conceive to be more properly applicable to the heavenly Father, than to an earthly one. It implies an idea of power and authority over his children, superior to that of mere procreation, therefore I think it fittest to be used in prayer and worship. *Wetoochwink*, on the contrary, by the syllable *we* or *wet*, prefixed to it, implies progeny and ownership over it;[289] and *wink* or *ink* conveys the idea of the actual existence of that progeny. Yet Mr. Zeisberger, who well understood the language, has used *wetoochwink* in the spiritual sense. Thus, in his Delaware Hymn Book,[290] you find, page 15, *Pennamook Wetoochwink milquenk!* which is in English "Behold what the Father has given us!" Again, in the same book, page 32, we read, "*Hallewiwi wetochemuxit;*" which means "The Father of Eternity." Upon the whole I believe that *ooch* is a proper word for "father" or "a father," but *wetoochwink* may also be used in the same sense, notwithstanding its more definite general acceptation. There is little occasion, however, to use either with this abstract indefinite meaning.

I agree with you that *lenni, lenno, illenoh, illenou, illinois,* appear to have all the same derivation, and to be connected with the idea of *man, nation,* or *people*. *Lenno*, in the Delaware language, signifies man, and so does *Lenape*, in a more extended sense. In the name of the Lenni *Lenape*, it signifies *people*; but the word *lenni*, which precedes it, has a different signification and means *original*, and sometimes *common, plain, pure, unmixed*. Under this general description the Indians comprehend all that they believe to have been first created in the origin of things. To all such things they prefix the word *lenni*; as, for instance, when they speak of *high* lands, they say *lenni hacki* (original lands), but they do not apply the same epithet to *low* lands, which being generally formed by the overflowing or washing of rivers, cannot, therefore, be called *original*. Trees which grow on high lands are also called *lenni hittuck*, original trees. In the same manner they designate Indian corn, pumpkins, squashes, beans, tobacco, &c., all which they think were given by the Great Spirit for their use, *from the beginning*. Thus, they call Indian corn[291] *lenchasqueem*, from *lenni* and *chasqueem*; beans, *lenalachksital*,

345

from *lenni* and *malachksital*; tobacco, *lenkschatey*, from *lenni* and *kschatey*; which is the same as if they said *original corn, original beans, original tobacco*. They call the linden tree *lennikby*, from *lenni* and *wikby*; the last word by itself meaning "the tree whose bark peels freely," as the bark of that tree peels off easily all the year round. This bark is made use of as a rope for tying and also for building their huts, the roof and sides of which are made of it. A house thus built is called *lennikgawon*, "original house or hut," from *lennikby*, original, or linden tree, *wikheen*, to build, and *jagawon* or *yagawon*, a house with a flat roof. It is as if they said "a house built of *original* materials."

Lennasqual, in the Minsi dialect, means a kind of grass which is supposed to have grown on the land from the beginning. English grasses, as timothy, &c., they call *schwannockasquall*, or white men's grass. The chub fish they call *lennameek*, because, say they, this fish is in all fresh water or streams, whereas other fish are confined to certain particular waters or climates.

They also say *lenni m'bi*, "pure water;" *leneyachkhican*, a fowling piece, as distinguished from a rifle, because it was the *first* fire-arm they ever saw; a rifle they call *tetupalachgat*. They say, *lenachsinnall*, "common stones," because stones are found every where, *lenachpoan*, "common bread," (*achpoan* means "bread"); *lenachgook*, a common snake, such as is seen every where (from *achgook*, a snake); *lenchum*, the original, common dog, not one of the species brought into the country by the white people. I think I have sufficiently explained the name "*Lenni Lenape*."

As I do not know the Greenland language, I cannot say how far the word "*innuit*" is connected with *lenni* or *lenno*, or any of the words or names derived from them.

The words *squaw, sachem, tomahawk*, and *wigwam*, are words of Delaware stock, somewhat corrupted by the English. *Ochqueu*, woman; *sakima*, chief; *tamahican*, hatchet;[292] *wickwam* (both syllables long, as in English *weekwawm*), a house. Hence, *nik*, my house; *kik*, thy house; *wikit*, his house; *wikichtit*, their houses; *wikia*, at my house; *wiquahemink*, in the house; again, *wickheen*, to build a house; *wikhitschik*, the builders of a house; *wikheu*, he is building a house; *wikhetamok*, let us build a house; *wikheek* (imperative), build a house; *wikhattoak*, they are building (a house or houses).

Calumet is not an Indian word; M. Volney thinks it is an English word for a tobacco pipe; it is certainly not proper English, but I have always thought that it was first used by the English or the French. The Delaware for a tobacco pipe is *Poakan* (two syllables).

Wampum is an Iroquois word, and means a marine shell.

Papoose, I do not know; it is not a word of the Delaware language, yet it is possible that it may be used by some Indian nations, from whom we may have borrowed it. I have been told that the Mahicanni of New England made use of this word for a *child*. I am, &c.

LETTER 20 ~
To Mr. Heckewelder

Philadelphia, 21st August, 1816.

Dear Sir.—I have read with the greatest pleasure your two interesting letters of the 12th and 15th. I need not tell you how pleased the Historical Committee are with your correspondence, which is laid before them from time to time. I am instructed to do all in my power to induce you to persevere in giving to your country the so much wanted information concerning the Indians and their languages. The Committee are convinced that the first duty of an American Scientific Association is to occupy themselves with the objects that relate to our own country. It is on these subjects that the world has a right to expect instruction from us.

I am busily employed in studying and translating the excellent Delaware Grammar of Mr. Zeisberger; I hope the Historical Committee will publish it in due time. The more I become acquainted with this extraordinary language, the more I am delighted with its copiousness and with the beauty of its forms. Those which the Hispano-Mexican Grammarians call *transitions* are really admirable. If this language was cultivated and polished as those of Europe have been, and if the Delawares had a Homer or Virgil among them, it is impossible to say with such an instrument how far the art could be carried. The Greek is admired for its compounds; but what are they to those of the Indians? How many ideas they can combine and express together in one single locution, and that too by a regular series of grammatical forms, by innumerably varied inflexions of the same radical word, with the help of pronominal affixes! All this, my dear sir, is combined with the most exquisite skill, in a perfectly regular order and method, and with fewer exceptions or anomalies than I have found in any other language. This is what really astonishes me, and it is with the greatest difficulty that I can guard myself against enthusiastic feelings. The verb, among the Indians, is truly the *word* by way of excellence. It combines itself with the pronoun, with the adjective, with the adverb; in short, with almost every part of speech. There are forms both positive and negative which include the two pronouns, the governing and the governed; *ktahoatell*,[293] "I love thee;" *ktahoalowi*, "I do not love thee." The

348

adverb "not," is comprised both actively and passively in the negative forms, *n'dahoalawi*, "I do not love;" *n'dahoalgussiwi*, "I am not loved;" and other adverbs are combined in a similar manner. From *schingi*, "unwillingly," is formed *schingattam*, "to be unwilling," *schingoochwen*, "to go somewhere unwillingly," *schingimikemossin*, "to work unwillingly;" from *wingi*, "willingly," we have *wingsittam*, "to hear willingly," *wingachpin*, "to be willingly somewhere," *wingilauchsin*, "to live willingly in a particular manner;" from the adverb *gunich*,[294] "long," comes *gunelendam*, "to think one takes long to do something;" *gunagen*, "to stay out long;" and so are formed all the rest of the numerous class of *adverbial verbs*. The *adjective verbs* are produced in the same way, by a combination of adjective nouns with the verbal form. Does *guneu* mean "long" in the adjective sense, you have *guneep*, it was long, *guneuchtschi*, it will be long, &c.; from *kschiechek*, "clean," is formed *kschiecheep*, "it was clean;" from *machkeu*, "red," *machkeep*, "it was red;" and so on through the whole class of words. Prepositions are combined in the same manner, but that is common also to other languages. What extent and variety displays itself in those Indian verbs, and what language, in this respect, can be compared to our savage idioms?

Nor are the participles less rich or less copious. Every verb has a long series of participles, which when necessary can be declined and used as adjectives. Let me be permitted to instance a few from the causative verb *wulamalessohen*, "to make happy." I take them from Zeisberger.

Wulamalessohaluwed, *he who makes happy.*
Wulamalessohalid, *he who makes me happy.*
Wulamalessohalquon, *he who makes thee happy,*
Wulamalessohalat, *he who makes him happy.*
Wulamalessohalquenk, *he who makes us happy.*
Wulamalessohalqueek, *he who makes you happy.*
Wulamalessohalquichtit, *he who makes them happy.*

Now comes another participial-pronominal-vocative form; which may in the same manner be conjugated through all the *objective* persons. *Wulamalessohalian!* THOU WHO MAKEST ME HAPPY!

I will not proceed further; but permit me to ask you, my dear sir, what would Tibullus or Sappho have given to have had at their command a word at once so tender and so expressive? How delighted would be Moore, the poet of the loves and graces, if his language, instead of five or six tedious words slowly following in the rear of each other, had furnished him with an expression like this, in which the lover, the object beloved, and the delicious sentiment which their mutual passion inspires, are blended, are fused together in one comprehensive appellative term? And it is in the languages of savages that these beautiful forms are found! What a subject for reflection, and how little do we know, as yet, of the astonishing things that the world contains!

In the course of my reading, I have often seen the question discussed which of the two classes of languages, the *analytical* or the *synthetical* (as I call them), is the most perfect or is preferable to the other. Formerly there seemed to be but one sentiment on the subject, for who cannot perceive the superiority of the Latin and Greek, over the modern mixed dialects which at present prevail in Europe? But we live in the age of paradoxes, and there is no opinion, however extraordinary, that does not find supporters. To me it would appear that the perfection of language consists in being able to express much in a few words; to raise at once in the mind by a few magic sounds, whole masses of thoughts which strike by a kind of instantaneous intuition. Such in its effects must be the medium by which immortal spirits communicate with each other; such, I should think, were I disposed to indulge in fanciful theories, must have been the language first taught to mankind by the great author of all perfection.

All this would probably be admitted if the Latin and Greek were only in question: for their supremacy seems to stand on an ancient legitimate title not easy to be shaken, and there is still a strong prepossession in the minds of the learned in favour of the languages in which Homer and Virgil sang. But since it has been discovered that the barbarous dialects of savage nations are formed on the same principle with the classical idioms, and that the application of this principle is even carried in them to a still greater extent, it has been found easier to ascribe the beautiful organisation of these languages to stupidity and barbarism, than to acknowledge our ignorance of the manner in which it has been produced. Philosophers have therefore set themselves to work in order to prove that those admirable combinations of ideas in the form of words, which in the ancient languages of Europe used to be considered as some of the greatest efforts of the human mind, proceed in the savage idioms from the absence or weakness of mental powers in those who originally framed them.

350

Among those philosophers the celebrated Dr. Adam Smith stands pre-eminent. In an elegant treatise on the origin and formation of language, he has endeavoured to shew that synthetical forms of speech were the first rude attempts which men made to communicate their ideas, and that they employed comprehensive and generic terms, because their minds had not yet acquired the powers of analysis and were not capable of discriminating between different objects. Hence, he says every river among primitive men was *the river*, every mountain *the mountain*, and it was very long before they learned to distinguish them by particular names. On the same principle, he continues, men said in one word *pluit* (it rains,) before they could so separate their confused ideas as to say *the rain* or *the water is falling*. Such is the sense and spirit of his positions, which I quote from memory.

This theory is certainly very ingenious; it is only unfortunate that it does not accord with facts, as far as our observations can trace them. You have shown that the comprehensive compounds of the Delaware idiom are formed out of other words expressive of single ideas; these simple words, therefore, must have been invented before they were compounded into others, and thus analysis presided over the first formation of the language. So far, at least, Dr. Smith's theory falls to the ground; nor does he appear to be better supported in his supposition of the pre-existence of generic terms. For Dr. Wistar has told me, and quotes your authority for it, that such are seldom in use among the Indians, and that when a stranger pointing to an object asks how it is called, he will not be told a *tree*, a *river*, a *mountain*, but an ash, an oak, a beech; the Delaware, the Mississippi, the Allegheny. If this fact is correctly stated, it is clear that among those original people every tree is not *the tree*, and every mountain *the mountain*, but that, on the contrary, everything is in preference distinguished by its specific name.

It is no argument, therefore, against the synthetical forms of language, that they are in use among savage nations. However barbarous may be the people by whom they are employed, I acknowledge that I can see nothing barbarous in them, but think, on the contrary, that they add much to the beauty of speech. This is neither the time nor the place to enter into an elaborate discussion of this subject, but I beg leave to be allowed to illustrate and support my opinion by a lively example taken from the Latin tongue.

Suetonius relates that the Roman Emperor Claudius (one of the most barbarous tyrants that ever existed,) once gave to his courtiers the spectacle of a naval combat on the Fucine lake, to be seriously performed by gladiators. When the poor fellows saw the Emperor approaching, they hailed him with "*Ave, Imperator,* MORITURI *te salutant!*" In English this means, "Hail, Cæsar! THOSE WHO ARE GOING TO DIE salute thee!" The tyrant was so moved, or rather struck with this unexpected address, that before he had time to reflect he returned the salutation *Avete vos!* "Fare ye well!" This gracious reply, from the mouth of an Emperor, amounted to a pardon, and the gladiators, in consequence, refused to fight. But the monster soon returned to his natural ferocity, and after hesitating for a while whether he would destroy them all by fire and sword, he rose from his seat, and ran staggering along the banks of the lake, in the most disgusting agitation, and at last, partly by exhortations and partly by threats, compelled them to fight.[295] Thus far Suetonius.

Now, my dear sir, I put the question to you; if the gladiators, instead of *morituri*, had said in English *those who are about or going to die*; would the Emperor even have hesitated for a moment, and would he not at once have ordered those men to fight on? In the word *morituri*, he was struck at the first moment with the terrible idea of death placed in full front by means of the syllable MOR; while the future termination ITURI with the accessory ideas that it involves was calculated to produce a feeling of tender compassion on his already powerfully agitated mind, and in fact did produce it, though it lasted only a short time. But if, instead of this rapid succession of strong images, he had been assailed at first with five insignificant words *Those—who—are—going—to*, foreseeing what was about to follow, he would have had time to make up his mind before the sentence had been quite pronounced, and I doubt much whether the gladiators would have been allowed time to finish it. In German, *Diejenigen welche am sterben sind,* would have produced much the same effect, from the length of the words *diejenigen* and *welche*, which have no definite meaning, and could in no manner have affected the feelings of the tyrant Claudius. *Ceux qui vont mourir,* in French, is somewhat shorter, but in none of the modern languages do I find anything that operates on my mind like the terrible and pathetic *morituri*. May we not exclaim here with the great Gœthe: *O, eine Nation ist zu beneiden, die so feine Schattirungen in einem Worte auszudruecken weiss!* "O, how a nation is to be envied, that can express such delicate shades of thought in one single word!"[296]

I hope, indeed I do not doubt, that there is a similar word in the Delaware language; if so, please to give it to me with a full explanation of its construction and meaning.

I thank you very much for the valuable information you have given on the subject of the word "*father;*" the distinction between *wetochemuxit,* and *wetoochwink,* appears to me beautiful, and Zeisberger seems to have perfectly understood it. When he makes use of the first of these words, he displays the "*Father of Eternity*" in all his glory; but when he says, "*Behold what the Father has given us!*" he employs the word *wetoochwink,* which conveys the idea of a *natural father,* the better to express the paternal tenderness of God for his children. These elegant shades of expression shew in a very forcible manner the beauty and copiousness of the Indian languages, and the extent and the force of that natural logic, of those powers of feeling and discrimination, and of that innate sense of order, regularity and method which is possessed even by savage nations, and has produced such an admirable variety of modes of conveying human thoughts by means of the different organs and senses with which the Almighty has provided us.

Will you be so good as to inform me whether the Delaware language admits of inversions similar or analogous to those of the Latin tongue; and in what order words are in general placed before or after each other? Do you say "*bread give me,*" or "*give me bread*"?

I am, &c.

LETTER 21 ~
From Mr. Heckewelder

BETHLEHEM, 26th August, 1816.

DEAR SIR.—Your letter of the 21st inst. has done me the greatest pleasure. I see that you enter the spirit of our Indian languages, and that your mind is struck with the beauty of their grammatical forms. I am not surprised to find that you admire so much *wulamalessohalian*, it is really a fine expressive word; but you must not think that it stands alone; there are many others equally beautiful and equally expressive, and which are at the same time so formed as to please the ear. Such is *eluwiwulik*, a name which the Indians apply to Almighty God, and signifies "the most blessed, the most holy, the most excellent, the most precious." It is compounded of *allowiwi*, which signifies "*more*" and *wulik*, the meaning of which has been fully explained in former letters. It is, as it were *allowiwi wulik*; the vowel *a*, in the first word being changed into *e*. By thus compounding this word *allowiwi* with others the Delawares have formed a great number of denominations, by which they address or designate the Supreme Being, such are:

Eliwulek,[297] }Allowilen,[298]}*He who is above every thing.*[299]

Eluwantowit,[300]*God above all;* ("getannitowit" means *God.*)Elewassit,[301]*the most powerful, the most majestic.*Eluwitschanessik, *the strongest of all.*Eluwikschiechsit, *the supremely good.*[302]Eluwilissit, *the one above all others in goodness.*

I have no doubt you will admire these expressions; our Missionaries found them of great use, and considered them as adding much to the solemnity of divine service, and calculated to promote and keep alive a deep sense of devotion to the Supreme Being. I entirely agree with you in your opinion of the superior beauty of compound terms; the Indians understand very well how to make use of them, and a great part of the force and energy of their speeches is derived from that source: it is very difficult, I may even say impossible, to convey either in German or English, the whole

354

impressiveness of their discourses; I have often attempted it without success.

The word "*morituri*" which you cite from the Latin, affords a very good argument in support of the position which you have taken. It is really very affecting, and I am not astonished at the effect which it produced upon the mind of the cruel emperor. We have a similar word in the Delaware language, "*Elumiangellatschik*," "those who are on the point of dying, or who are about to die." The first part of it, *elumi*, is derived from the verb *n'dallemi*, which means "I am going about" (something). *N'dallemi mikemosi*, "I am going to work," or "about to work." *N'dallemi wickheen*, "I am going to build." *N'dallemi angeln*, "I am about dying," or "going to die." The second member of the word, that is to say *angel*, comes from *angeln*, "to die;" *angloagan*, "death," *angellopannik*, "they are all dead." The remainder is a grammatical form; *atsch*, indicates the future tense; the last syllable *ik*, conveys the idea of the personal pronoun "*they*." Thus *elumiangellatschik*, like the Latin *morituri*, expresses in one word "they or those who are going or about to die," and in German "*Diejenigen welche am sterben sind*."

I am pleased to hear that you discover every day new beauties as you proceed with the study of the Indian languages, and the translation of Mr. Zeisberger's Grammar. You have, no doubt, taken notice of the reciprocal verb exemplified in the fifth conjugation, in the positive and negative forms by "*ahoaltin*," "to love each other." Permit me to point out to you the regularity of its structure, by merely conjugating one tense of it in the two forms.

INDICATIVE PRESENT.

Positive Form.	Negative Form.
N'dahoaltineen, *we love one another.*	Mat n'dahoaltiwuneen, *we do not love one another.*
K'dahoaltihhimo, *you love one another.*	Matta kdahoaltiwihhimo, *you do not love one another.*
Ahoaltowak, *they love one another.*	Matta ahoaltiwiwak, *they do not love one another.*

355

You will find the whole verb conjugated in Zeisberger, therefore I shall not exemplify further. You see there is no singular voice in this verb, nor is it susceptible of it, as it never implies the act of a single person. In the negative form, "matta" or "atta" is an adverb which signifies "no" or "not," and is always prefixed; but it is not that alone which indicates the negative sense of the verb. It is also pointed out by *wu* or *wi*, which you find interwoven throughout the whole conjugation, the vowel immediately preceding being sometimes changed for the sake of sound, as from "ahol*a*wak," "they love each other," is formed "ahoalt*i*wiwak," "they do not love each other."

I will point out further, if you have not already observed it, what I am sure you will think a grammatical curiosity; it is a concordance in tense of the adverb with the verb. Turn to the future of the same negative conjugation in Zeisberger, and you will find:

Mattatsch n'dahoaltiwuneen, *we shall or will not love each other*.Mattatsch k'dahoaltiwihhimo, *you*—Mattatsch ahoaltiwiwak, *they*—

I have said already that *atsch* or *tsch* is a termination which in the conjugation of verbs indicates the future tense. Sometimes it is attached to the verb, as in *matta ktahoaliwitsch*, "thou shalt or wilt not love me," but it may also be affixed to the adverb as you have seen above, by which means a variety is produced which adds much to the beauty and expressiveness of the language.

You have asked me whether the Delaware language has inversions corresponding with those of the Latin? To this question, not being a Latin scholar, I am not competent to give an answer; I can only say that when the Indian is well or elegantly spoken, the words are so arranged that the prominent ideas stand in front of the discourse; but in familiar conversation a different order may sometimes be adopted. We say, in Delaware, *Philadelphia epit*, "Philadelphia at," and not, as in English, "at Philadelphia." We say "bread give me," and not "give me bread," because *bread* is the principal object with which the speaker means to strike the mind of his hearer.

In the personal forms, or as you call them, *transitions* of the active verbs, the form expressive of the pronoun governed is sometimes placed in the beginning, as in *k'dahoatell*, "I love thee," which is the same as *thee I love*;

for *k* (from *ki*), is the sign of the second person; sometimes, however, the governing pronoun is placed in front, as in *n'dahoala*, "I love him," *n'* being the sign of the first person, I. In these personal forms or transitions, one of the pronouns, governing or governed, is generally expressed by its proper sign, *n'* for "I" or "me," *k'* for "thou" or "thee," and *w'* for "he or him;" the other pronoun is expressed by an inflexion, as in *k'dahoalohhumo*, I love you, *k'dahoalineen*, thou lovest us, *k'dahoalowak*, thou lovest them. You may easily perceive that the governing pronoun is not always in the same relative place with the governed.

That these and other forms of the verbs may be better understood, it will not be amiss to say something here of the personal pronouns. They are of two kinds: separable and inseparable. The separable pronouns are these:

Ni, *I.*Ki, *thou.*Neka, *or* nekama, *he or she.*Kiluna, *we.*Kiluwa, *you.*Neka mawa, *they.*

There are other personal pronouns, which I believe to be peculiar to the Indian languages; such are:

Nepe, *I also.*Kepe, *thou also.*Nepena, *or* kepena, *we also.*Kepewo, *you also.*Kepoak, *they also.*

The inseparable pronouns are *n* for the first person, *k* for the second, and *w* or *o* for the third, both in the singular and the plural. They are combined with substantives in the possessive forms, as in *nooch*, my father, *kooch*, thy father; the third person is sometimes expressed by the termination *wall*, as *ochwall*, his or her father, and at other times by *w*, as in *wtamochol*, his or her canoe. In the plural, *nochena*, our father, *kochuwa*, your father, *ochuwawall*, their father.

The verbal transitions are compounded of the verb itself, combined with the inseparable pronouns and other forms or inflexions, expressive of time, person, and number. To understand these properly requires attention and study.

These things are not new to you, but they may be of use to those members of the Committee who have not, like yourself, had the opportunity of studying a grammar of this language.

I am, &c.

LETTER 22 ~
From the same

BETHLEHEM, 27th August, 1816.

DEAR SIR.—I promised you in one of my former letters that I would write to a gentleman well acquainted with the Chippeway language, to ascertain whether it is true, as Professor Vater asserts, that it is almost without any grammatical forms. I wrote in consequence to the Rev. Mr. Dencke, a respectable Missionary of the Society of the United Brethren, who resides at Fairfield in Upper Canada, and I have the pleasure of communicating to you an extract from his answers to the different questions which my letter contained.

EXTRACT.

1. "According to my humble opinion, and limited knowledge of the Indian languages, being chiefly acquainted with the Delaware and Chippeway, of ich alone I can speak with propriety, those two idioms are of one and the same grammatical structure, and rich in forms. I am inclined to believe that Mr. Duponceau is correct in his opinion that the American languages in general resemble each other in point of grammatical construction; for I find in that of Greenland nearly the same inflections, prefixes, and suffixes, as in the Delaware and the Chippeway. The inflexions of nouns and conjugations of verbs are the same. The pronominal accusative is in the same manner incorporated with the verb, which, in this form, may be properly called *transitive*. See Crantz's History of Greenland, in German, page 283. These forms, though they are very regular, are most difficult for foreigners to acquire. I might give examples of conjugations in the various forms, but as they have not been expressly called for, I do not think necessary to do it.

"The Greenlanders, it seems, have three numbers in the conjugation of their verbs, the singular, dual, and plural; the Delawares and Chippeways have also three, the singular, the *particular*, and the plural. For instance, in the Delaware language we say in the plural, '*k'pendameneen*,' which means

359

'we *all* have heard;' and in the particular number we say, '*n'pendameneen,*' 'we, who are now specially spoken of, (for instance, this company, the white people, the Indians,) have heard.' Upon the whole, Crantz's History of Greenland has given me a great insight into the construction of the Indian languages; through his aid, I have been able to find out the so necessary *infinitive* of each particular verb. By means of the transitions, Indian verbs have nine or ten different infinitives, whence we must conclude that it is very difficult to learn the Indian languages. There is also a peculiarity in them, by means of the duplication of the first syllable, as '*gattopuin,*' 'to be hungry;' '*gagattopuin,*' to be very hungry.

2. "Carver's Vocabulary of the Chippeway, I believe is not correct, though I have it not at present before me.

3. "The numerals in the Chippeway up to ten, are as follows. I write them according to the German orthography. 1. Beschik. 2. Nisch. 3. Nisswi. 4. Newin. 5. Nanán. 6. N'guttiwaswi. 7. Nischschwaswi. 8. Schwaschwi. 9. Schenk. 20. Quetsch."

Thus far Mr. Dencke. I do not recollect whether I have already explained to you what he says about the "*particular*" number in the conjugation of the Delaware verbs. There is a distinction in the plural forms. "*K'pendameneen,* (*k'* from *kiluna,* 'we,') means generally 'we have heard,' or 'we all have heard,' not intending to allude to a particular number of persons; in '*n'pendameneen,*' the '*n*' comes from '*niluna,*' which means '*we,*' in particular, our family, nation, select body, &c. '*Niluna yu epienk,*' 'we who are here assembled,' *n'penameneen,* (for *niluna penameneen*) we see (we who are together see); *n'pendameneen,* we hear (we who are in this room hear). But when no discrimination is intended to be made, the form *kiluna,* or its abridgement *k'* is used. *Kiluna elenapewit,* 'we, the Indians' (meaning *all* the Indians); *kiluna yu enda lauchsienk,* 'we all that live upon earth;' '*k'nemeneen sokelange,*' we see it rain, (we *all* see it rain); *k'nemeneen waselehelete,* we *all* see the light, (we and all who live upon earth see the light.)"

I believe Mr. Zeisberger does not mention this distinction in his Grammar; but he could not say every thing.

I am, &c.

LETTER 23 ~
To Mr. Heckewelder

PHILADELPHIA, 30th August, 1816.

DEAR SIR.—I thank you for your two favours of the 26th and 27th inst. I am very much pleased to find from the valuable extract of Mr. Dencke's letter, which you have had the goodness to communicate, that the Chippeways have grammatical forms similar to those of the Delawares. Indeed, as far as my researches have extended, I have found those forms in all the Indian languages from Greenland to Cape Horn. The venerable Eliot's Grammar shews that they exist in the idiom of the New England Indians, as he calls it, which is believed to be that of the Natick tribe. Crantz and Egede prove in the most incontrovertible manner that the language of Greenland is formed on the same *syntactic* or *polysynthetic* model. So are the various dialects of Mexico, as far as I can judge from the Grammars of those languages that are in our Society's library. Indeed, the authors of those Grammars are the first who have noticed the personal forms of the Indian verbs, and given them the name of *transitions*. I find from Father Breton's Grammar and Dictionary of the Caribbee language, that those forms exist also in that idiom, and the Abbé Molina, in his excellent History of Chili, has shewn that the Araucanian belongs to the same class of languages. All the genuine specimens that we have seen of the grammatical forms of the Indians from north to south, on the continent, and in the islands, exhibit the same general features, and no exception whatever that I know of has yet been discovered. Father Sagard's assertions about the Huron are not founded in fact, and are even disproved by the examples which he adduces, and Mr. Dencke's testimony is sufficient to counterbalance the naked supposition of Professor Vater that the language of the Chippeways has no forms. Too much praise cannot be given to this learned author for the profound researches that he has made on the subject of American languages with a view to discover the origin of the ancient inhabitants of this continent, but not being on the spot, he had not the same means of ascertaining facts that we possess in this country. Had he lived among us, he would not so easily have been persuaded that there was such a difference between the different languages of the American Indians; that some of them were exceedingly rich in grammatical forms, and appeared to have been framed with the greatest skill, while others were so very poor in that respect that they might be compared to the idioms of the most savage nations in north-eastern Asia and Africa.[303] In Philology, as well as in every other science, authorities ought to be weighed, compared, and examined, and no assertion should be lightly believed that is not supported by evident proof faithfully drawn from the original sources.

I do not positively assert that all the languages of the American Indians are formed on the same grammatical construction, but I think I may safely advance that as far as our means of knowledge extend, they appear to be so, and that no proof has yet been adduced to the contrary. When we find so many different idioms, spoken by nations which reside at immense distances from each other, so entirely different in their etymology that there is not the least appearance of a common derivation, yet so strikingly similar in their forms, that one would imagine the same mind presided over their original formation, we may well suppose that the similarity extends through the whole of the languages of this race of men, at least until we have clear and direct proof to the contrary. It is at any rate, a fact well worthy of investigation, and this point, if it should ever be settled, may throw considerable light on the origin of the primæval inhabitants of this country.

The most generally established opinion seems to be, that the Americans are descended from the Tartars who inhabit the north-easternmost parts of Asia. Would it not be then well worth the while to ascertain this fact by enquiring into the grammatical forms and construction of the languages of those people? The great Empress Catharine employed a learned professor to compile a comparative vocabulary of those languages which are spoken within the vast extent of the Russian Empire. This was but the first step towards a knowledge of the character and affinities of those idioms. If something may be discovered by the mere similarity of words, how much farther may not we proceed by studying and comparing the "plans of men's ideas," and the variety of modes by which they have contrived to give them body and shape through articulate sounds. This I consider to be the most truly philosophical view of human language generally considered, and before we decide upon the Tartar origin of the American Indians, we ought, I think, to study the grammars of the Tartar languages, and ascertain whether their thoughts flow in the same course, and whether their languages are formed by similar associations of ideas, with those of their supposed descendants. If essential differences should be found between them in this respect, I do not see how the hypothesis of Tartar origin could afterwards be maintained.

Professor Vater is of opinion that the language of the Cantabrians, whom we call Biscayans or Basques, a people who inhabit the sea coast at the foot of the Pyrenean mountains, is formed on the same model with that of the American Indians. We have in our Society's library, a translation into that idiom of Royaumont's History of the Bible. I acknowledge, that by comparing it with the original, I have found sufficient reason to incline in favour of the Professor's assertion. This is a very curious fact, which well deserves to be inquired into. This Basque language, it is to be presumed, was once spoken in a considerable part of the ancient world, and probably branched out into various dialects. How comes it that those polysynthetic forms which distinguish it, have disappeared from all the rest of the continent of Europe, and are only preserved in a single language no longer spoken but by a handful of mountaineers? How comes it that the Celtic which appears no less ancient is so widely different in its grammatical construction? Are we to revive the story of the Atlantis, and believe that the two continents of America and Europe were once connected together? At least, we will not forget that the Biscayans were once great navigators, and that they were among the first who frequented the coasts of Newfoundland.

But let us leave these wild theories, and not lose sight of our object, which is to ascertain facts, and let others afterwards draw inferences from them at their pleasure. In Father Breton's Grammar and Dictionary of the Caribbee language, I have been struck with a fact of a very singular nature. It seems (and indeed there appears no reason to entertain the least doubt on the subject) that in that idiom the language of the men and that of the women differ in a great degree from each other. This difference does not merely consist in the inflexions or terminations of words, but the words themselves, used by the different sexes, have no kind of resemblance. Thus the men call an enemy *etoucou*, and the women *akani*; a friend in the masculine dialect is *ibaouanale*, in the female *nitignon*. I might adduce a much greater number of examples to shew the difference between these two modes of speaking. It does not, however, pervade the whole language; sometimes the termination of the words only differs, while in many cases the same words are used exactly alike by both sexes. But those which differ entirely in the two idioms are very numerous, and are in general terms of common use, such as names of parts of the body, or of relationship as father, mother, brother, sister, and many others. It is said a tradition prevails in the Caribbee islands that their nation was once conquered by another people, who put all the males to death and preserved only the females, who retained their national language, and would not adopt that of the conquerors. I am not much disposed to believe this story; the more so as I find similar instances in other idioms of different words being employed by the men and

363

women to express the same thing. Thus among the Othomis, (a Mexican tribe) the men call a brother-in-law *naco*, and the women *namo*; a sister-in-law is called by the men *nabehpo*, and by the women *namuddu*. (Molina's Grammar of the Othomi language, p. 38.) In the Mexican proper, the men add an *e* to the vocative of every proper name, and say *Pedroe* for *Pedro*; while the women leave out the *e* and distinguish the vocative only by an affected pronunciation. (Rincon's Mexican Grammar, p. 6.) It is said also that among the Javanese, there is a language for the nobles and another for the common people.[304] These are curious facts, and a discovery of their causes would lay open an interesting page of the great hidden book of the history of man.

As I have determined to abstain from every hypothesis, I shall leave it to others to discover and point out the causes of these extraordinary facts; but I shall be obliged to you for informing me whether in any of the Indian languages that you know, there is any such difference of dialect between the two sexes, and in what it particularly consists. I cannot believe this story of the conquest of the Caribbee islands and of its producing that variety of language. I find it related by one Davis, an English writer, in whom I place no reliance; for he has pretended to give a Vocabulary of the Caribbee language, which he has evidently taken from Father Breton, without even taking the trouble of substituting the English for the French orthography. Carver acted with more skill in this respect.

I thank you for the explanation which you have given of what Mr. Dencke calls the "*particular* plural," of the Chippeway and Delaware languages, of which I had no idea, as Zeisberger does not make any mention of it. It appears to me that this numerical form of language (if I can so express myself,) is founded in nature, and ought to have its place in a system of Universal Grammar. It is more natural than the Greek dual, which is too limited in its comprehension, while the particular plural expresses more, and may be limited in its application to two, when the context or the subject of the conversation requires it. I find this plural in several of the modern European languages; it is the *nosotros* of the Spanish, the *noi altri* of the Italian, and the French *nous autres*. There is nothing like it in English or German, nor even in the Latin. I am disposed to believe that this form exists also in the Greenland language, and has been improperly called *dual* by those who have written on it. The Abbé Molina speaks also of a Dual in the Araucanian idiom, which he translates by *we two*. But he may have used a term generally known, to avoid the explanations which a new one would have required. However this may be, the particular plural is well worthy of notice.

I shall be obliged to you for a translation of the Lord's prayer in the Delaware language, with proper explanations in English. I suspect that in Loskiel is not correct.

In reading some time ago one of the Gospels, (I think St. Mark's,) in one of the Iroquois dialects, said to be translated by the celebrated chief Captain Brandt, I observed that the word *town* was translated into Indian by the word *Kanada*, and it struck me that the name of the province of *Canada* might probably have been derived from it. I have not been able to procure the book since, but I have now before me a translation of the English common prayer-book into the Mohawk, ascribed to the same chief, in which I find these words: "*Ne* KANADA-*gongh konwayatsk Nazareth*," which are the translation of "in a CITY called Nazareth," (Matth. ii. 23.) The termination *gongh* in this word appears evidently to be a grammatical form or inflexion, and *Kanada* is the word which answers for "*city*." I should be glad to know your opinion of this etymology.

I find in Zeisberger's grammar, in the conjugation of one of the forms of the verb *n'peton* "I bring," *n'petagep* in one place, and in another *n'petagunewoakup*, both translated into German by "*sie haben mir gebracht*," "they have brought to me." Are these words synonyma, or is there some difference between them, and which?

      I am, &c.

LETTER 24 ~
From Mr. Heckewelder

BETHLEHEM, 5th September, 1816.

DEAR SIR.—I have received your favour of the 30th ult. I answer it first at the end, and begin with your etymology of the word *Canada*. In looking over some of Mr. Zeisberger's papers, who was well acquainted with the language of the Onondagoes, the principal dialect of the Iroquois, to which nation the Mohawks belong, I find he translates the German word *stadt* (town) into the Onondago by "*ganatage*." Now, as you well know that the Germans sometimes employ the G instead of the K, and the T instead of the D, it is very possible that the word *Kanada* may mean the same thing in some grammatical form of the Mohawk dialect. As you have seen it so employed in Captain Brandt's translation, there cannot be the least doubt about it. This being taken for granted, it is not improbable that you have hit upon the true etymology of the name *Canada*. For nothing is more certain than what Dr. Wistar once told you on my authority, that the Indians make more use of *particular* than of *generic* words. I found myself under very great embarrassment in consequence of it when I first began to learn the Delaware language. I would point to a tree and ask the Indians how they called it; they would answer an *oak*, an *ash*, a *maple*, as the case might be, so that at last I found in my vocabulary more than a dozen words for the word *tree*. It was a good while before I found out, that when you asked of an Indian the name of a thing, he would always give you the specific and never the generic denomination. So that it is highly probable that the Frenchman who first asked of the Indians in Canada the name of their country, pointing to the spot and to the objects which surrounded him, received for answer *Kanada*, (town or village), and committing the same mistake that I did, believed it to be the name of the whole region, and reported it so to his countrymen, who consequently gave to their newly acquired dominions the name of *Canada*.

I had never heard before I received your letter that there existed a country where the men and the women spoke a different language from each other. It is not the case with the Delawares or any Indian nation that I am acquainted with. The two sexes with them speak exactly the same idiom.

366

The women, indeed, have a kind of lisping or drawling accent, which comes from their being so constantly with children; but the language which they speak does not differ in the least from that which is spoken by their husbands and brothers.

The question you ask about *n'petageep* and *n'petagunewoakup*, both of which Zeisberger translates by *sie haben mir gebracht*, is easily answered. The translation is correct in both cases, according to the idiom of the German language, from which alone the ambiguity proceeds. *N'petageep* means "they have brought to me," but in a general sense, and without specifying by whom the thing has been brought. *Es ist mir gebracht worden*, or "it has been brought to me," would have explained this word better, while *n'petagunewoakup* is literally rendered by *"they,"* (alluding to particular persons,) "have brought to me," or *sie haben mir gebracht*. You have here another example of the nicely discriminating character of the Indian languages.

I believe I have never told you that the Indians distinguish the genders, animate and inanimate, even in their verbs. *Nolhatton* and *nolhalla*, both mean "*I possess*," but the former can only be used in speaking of the possession of things inanimate, and the latter of living creatures. NOLHATTON *achquiwanissall*, "I have or possess blankets;" *cheeli kœcu n'nolhattowi*, "many things I am possessed of," or "I possess many things;" *woak nechenaunges nolhallau*, "and I possess a horse," (and a horse I possess.) The *u* which you see at the end of the verb *nolhalla*, conveys the idea of the pronoun *him*, so that it is the same as if you said, "and a horse I possess *him*." It is the accusative form on which you observed in one of your former letters and is annexed to the *verb* instead of the *noun*.

In the verb "*to see*," the same distinction is made between things animate and inanimate. *Newau*, "I see," applies only to the former, and *nemen* to the latter. Thus the Delawares say: *lenno newau*, "I see a man;" *tscholens newau*, "I see a bird;" *achgook newau*, "I see a snake." On the contrary they say, *wiquam nemen*, "I see a house;" *amochol nemen*, "I see a canoe," &c.

It is the same with other verbs; even when they speak of things lying upon the ground, they distinguish between what has life and what is inanimate; thus they say, *icka* schingieschin[305] *n'dallemans* "there lies my beast," (the verb *schingieschin*[305] being only used when speaking of animate things;) otherwise they will say: *icka* schingieschen *n'tamahican*, "yonder lies my

367

ax." The *i* or the *e* in the last syllable of the verb, as here used in the third person, constitutes the difference, which indicates that the thing spoken of has or has not life.

It would be too tedious to go through these differences in the various forms which the verb can assume; what I have said will be sufficient to shew the principle and the manner in which this distinction is made.

I inclose a translation of the Lord's Prayer into Delaware, with the English interlined according to your wishes. I am, &c.

THE LORD'S PRAYER IN THE DELAWARE LANGUAGE.

Ki	*Thou*
Wetóchemelenk	*our Father*
talli	*there*
épian	*dwelling*
Awosságame,	*beyond the clouds,*
Machelendásutsch	*magnified or praised be*
Ktellewunsowágan	*thy name*
Ksakimowagan	*thy kingdom*
peyewiketsch	*come on*
Ktelitehewágan	*thy thoughts, will, intention, mind,*
léketsch	*come to pass*
yun	*here*
Achquidhackamike	*upon or all over the earth,*
elgiqui	*the same*
leek	*as it is*
talli	*there*
Awosságame	*in heaven or beyond the clouds,*
Milineen	*give to us*
eligischquik	*on or through this day*

gunagischuk	*the usual, daily*
Achpoan	*bread,*
woak	*and*
miwelendammauwineen	*forgive to us*
n'tschannauchsowagannéna	*our transgressions* (faults),
elgiqui	*the same as*
niluna	*we* (particular plural) *we who are here*
miwelendammáuwenk	*we mutually forgive them,*
nik	*who or those*
tschetschanilawequéngik	*who have transgressed or injured us* (past participle)
woak	*and*
kátschi	*let not*
n'páwuneen	*us come to that*
li	*that*
achquetschiechtowáganink	*we fall into temptation;* (ink, *into*),
shuckund	*but* (rather)
ktennineen	*keep us free*
untschi	*from*
medhicking	*all evil*
Alod	*for*
Knihillátamen	*thou claimest*
ksakimowágan[306]	*thy kingdom*
woak	*and*
ktallewussoágan	*the superior power*
woak	*and*
ktallowilissowágan	*all magnificence*
ne	*from*
wuntschi	*heretofore*
hallemiwi,	*ever* (always)

Nanne leketsch.

Amen. (so be it; so may it come to pass.)

LETTER 25 ~
To Mr. Heckewelder

PHILADELPHIA, 1st October, 1816

DEAR SIR.—Various professional avocations have prevented me from answering sooner your kind letter of the 5th ult. I thank you for the Delaware translation of the Lord's prayer; it does not differ much from that in Loskiel, but the English explanations which you have given add greatly to its value.

The information which your letter contains on the subject of the annexation to the verb of the form or inflexion indicative of the gender, is quite new to me. Though I was already acquainted with the principle on which this takes place, I was not fully aware of the extent of its application. We have already noticed and remarked upon the combination of the pronominal form with the active verb[307] in "*getannitowit n'quitayala*, I fear God;" in which the pronoun *him* is expressed by the last syllable *ala* or *yala*, so that it is the same as if you said "*God I fear him*," in Latin *Deus timeo eum*, and by contraction, *Deus timeum*. With this it is not difficult to pursue the same course or "plan of ideas," by connecting not only the subject pronoun, but its gender, animate, or inanimate, with the verbal form. The idea of the sexes, if the language admitted of it, might be expressed in the same manner. Thus also Latin words might be compounded on the Delaware plan. If I wished to express in that manner "*I see a lion*," I would say *leo video eum*, and by contraction *videum*; and if the object was of the feminine gender, I would say *videam*, for *video eam*. The difference between the Latin and the Delaware is that in the former the ideas of the pronoun and its gender are expressed by a *nominal* and in the latter by a *verbal* form. I consider *leonem video*, as a contraction of *leo eum video*; the *n* being interposed between *leo* and *eum*, and the *u* in *eum* left out for euphony's sake. In the same manner *fœminam* appears to me to be contracted from *fœmina eam*;[308] whence we may, perhaps, conclude that in the formation of different languages, the same ideas have occurred to the minds of those who framed them; but have been differently combined, and consequently differently expressed. Who would have thought that the barbarous idioms of the American savages could have thrown light on the

371

original formation of the noble and elegant language of ancient Rome? Does not this very clearly shew that nothing is indifferent in science, and above all, that we ought by no means to despise what we do not know?

I thought we had exhausted all the verbal forms of the Delaware language, when I accidentally fell upon one which Zeisberger has not mentioned in his grammar, but of which he gives an example in his vocabulary or spelling-book. It is a curious combination of the relative pronoun "*what*" or "*that which*" with an active verb, regularly conjugated through the several transitions or personal forms. The author thus conjugates the present of the indicative.

FIRST TRANSITION.

Singular.	*Plural.*
Elan, *what I tell thee,*	ellek, *what I tell you*
elak, *what I tell him.*	elachgup, *what I tell them.*

SECOND TRANSITION.

Singular.	*Plural.*
Eliyan, *what thou tellest me,*	eliyenk, *what thou tellest us,*
elan, *what thou tellest him.*	elachtup, *what thou tellest them.*

THIRD TRANSITION.

Singular.	*Plural.*
Elit, *what he tells me,*	elquenk, *what he tells us,*
elquon, *what he tells thee,*	elquek, *what he tells you,*
elat, elguk, *what he tells him.*	elatup, elatschi, *what he tells them.*

FOURTH TRANSITION.

Singular.   *Plural.*

Elenk, *what we tell you,* ellek, *what we tell you,*
elank, *what we tell him.* elanquik, *what we tell them.*

FIFTH TRANSITION.

Singular.   *Plural.*

Eliyek, *what you tell me,*   eliyenkup, *what you tell us,*
elatup, *what you tell him.* elaachtitup, *what you tell them.*

SIXTH TRANSITION.

Singular.   *Plural.*

Elink, *what they tell me,*   elgeyenk, *what they tell us,*
elquonnik, *what they tell thee,* elgeyek, *what they tell you,*
elaachtit, *what they tell him.*   elatschik, *what they tell us.*

Thus I have given myself the pleasure of transcribing this single tense of
one of the moods of this beautiful verb, which I find is used also in the
sense of "*as I tell thee*," &c., and is a striking example of the astonishing
powers of this part of speech in the Delaware language. Can you tell me
where those powers end? Is there anything which a Delaware verb will not
express in some form or other? I am no longer astonished to find that Mr.
Zeisberger has not displayed in his grammar all the richness of this idiom.
A single verb, with its various forms and transitions, would almost fill a
volume, and there are no less than eight conjugations, all of which were to
be explained and illustrated by examples!

But it is not in the verbs alone that consist the beauties of this language. The
other parts of speech also claim our attention. There I find, as well as in the
verbs, forms and combinations of which I had not before conceived an idea.
For instance, Zeisberger tells us that there are nouns substantive in the

Delaware which have a *passive mood*! Strange as this may appear to those who are unacquainted with Indian forms, it is nevertheless a fact which cannot be denied; for our author gives us several examples of this *passive noun*, all ending with the substantive termination *wagan*, which, as you have informed me, corresponds with the English *ness*, in "happiness," and the German *heit* or *keit*, in the numerous words ending with these syllables. Permit me to select some of the examples given by Zeisberger.

Machelemuxowagan, *honour, the being honoured.*
Gettemagelemuxowagan, *the receiving favour, mercy, tenderness.*
Mamschalgussiwagan,[309]*the being held in remembrance.*
Witahemgussowagan, *the being assisted or helped.*
Mamintochimgussowagan,[310]*the being esteemed.*
Wulakenimgussowagan, *the being praised.*
Machelemoachgenimgussowagan, *the receiving honour and praise.* Amangachgenimgussowagan, *the being raised or elevated by praise.* Schingalgussowagan, *the being hated.*
Mamachtschimgussowagan, *the being insulted.*

You will, I am afraid, be disposed to think that we have changed places, and that I am presuming to give you instruction in the Delaware language; but I am only repeating to you the lessons that I have learned from Zeisberger, to save you the trouble of explaining what I can obtain from another source; to be corrected, if I have committed mistakes, and to receive from you the information which my author does not give. Besides, as our correspondence is intended for the use of the Historical Committee, my occasional extracts from Zeisberger, and the observations to which they give rise, are addressed to them as well as to you, and under your correction, may contribute to give them a clearer idea of the forms of the Indian languages. Our letters thus form a kind of epistolary conference between the scholar and his master, held before a learned body, who profit even by the ignorance of the student, as it draws fuller and more luminous explanations from the teacher. Had I proceeded otherwise, your task would have been much more laborious and troublesome, and it would have been ungenerous to have exacted it from you.

In this manner I have relieved you from the trouble of explaining the *passive substantives* of Zeisberger, unless I should have mistaken his meaning, in which case, you will, of course, set me right. But this author does not tell us whether there are on the other hand *active substantives*, such

374

as "*the honouring*," "*the favouring*," "*the remembering*," "*the praising*," "*the insulting*," "*the hating*." Here I beg you will be so good as to supply his deficiency, and explain what he has left unexplained.

I find also that there are diminutive words in the Delaware, as in the Italian, such as *lennotit*, a little man, (from *lenno*); *amementit*, a little child, (from *amemens*); *wiquames*, a little house, (from *wiquam*), &c. Pray, are there also augmentatives? Is there any difference between the diminutive terminations *tit* and *es*, and what is it?

I have been told that you intend soon to visit Philadelphia; I shall rejoice to find it true, and to form a personal acquaintance with you, which, I hope, will produce a lasting friendship.

I am, &c.

LETTER 26 ~
From Mr. Heckewelder

BETHLEHEM, 10th October, 1816.

DEAR SIR.—I have hesitated whether I should answer your favour of the 1st inst., being very soon to set out for Philadelphia, where I shall be able to explain to you verbally everything that you wish to know in a much better manner than I can do in writing. As there are, however, but few questions in your letter, and those easily answered, I sit down to satisfy your enquiry, which will for the present close our correspondence. If you think proper to resume it after my return to this place, you will find me as ready as ever to continue our Indian disquisitions.

In the first place, it cannot, I think, properly be said that substantives in general in the Delaware language have a passive mood; but there are substantives which express a passive situation, like those which you have cited, after Mr. Zeisberger. I do not know of any words which express the same thing *actively*, except the infinitives of active verbs, which are in that case substantively used. Such are,

Shingalgundin, *to hate*; or *the hating*.Machelemuxundin, *to honour*; or *the honouring*.Mamachkimgundin, *to insult* (by words); or *the insulting*.

The diminutive forms in the Indian are *tit* and *es*; the former is generally applied to animate, and the latter to inanimate things. Thus we say *lennotit*, a little man; *amementit*, a little child; *wiquames*, a small house; and *amocholes*, a small canoe. This rule does not hold, however, in all cases; for the little fawn of a deer, although animate, is called *mamalis*, and a little dog among the Minsi is called *allumes*, (from *allum*, a dog.) *Chis* or *ches*, is also a diminutive termination, which is sometimes applied to beasts; *achtochis* and *achtoches*, "a small deer."

Augmentatives are compounded from the word *chingue*, which signifies large; and sometimes the two words are separately used.

376

Chingue, or m'chingue puschis, *a large cat.*Chingewileno (for *chingue lenno*), *a tall stout man.*Chingotœney (for *chingue otœney*), *a large town.*Chingi wiquam, *a large house.*Chingamochol, *a large canoe.*Chingachgook, *a large snake,* &c.

There are a few augmentatives formed in a different manner; for instance, from *pachkshican* or *kshican*, "a knife," are formed *pachkschicanes*, "a small knife," and *m'chonschicanes*,[311] "a large knife;" still it is easy to see that *m'chon*, in the latter word, is derived from *chingue*, large or great, which, with a little variation, brings it within the same rule with the others.

You have, no doubt, observed in Zeisberger the terminations *ink* and *unk*, which express the idea of locality, coupled with a substantive, as for instance:

Utenink, or otœnink, *from* otœney, *a town; in the town.*

Utenink n'da, *I am going to town, or into the town.*

Utenink noom, *I am coming from within the town.*

Sipunk, (*from* sipo) *to or into the river.*

M'bink, (*from* m'bi) *in the water.*

Hakink, (*from* hacki) *in or on the earth.*

Awossagamewunk, (*from* awossageme), *in heaven.*

Wachtschunk n'da, *I am going up the hill.*

Wachtschunk noom, *I come from the hill.*

Hitgunk, *on or to the tree.*

Ochunk, *at his father's.*

As you must have observed that many of our Indian names of places end with one or other of these terminations, such as *Minisink, Moyamensing, Passyunk,* &c., you will understand that all these names are in what we might call the *local* case, which accounts for the great number of those which end in this manner.

I beg you will not write to me any more for the present, as I do not know how soon I may have the pleasure of seeing you. I anticipate great satisfaction from your acquaintance, and hope it will be improved into a true *Indian* friendship.

I am, &c.
J. HECKEWELDER.

PART III

WORDS, PHRASES, AND SHORT DIALOGUES,

IN THE LANGUAGE OF THE

LENNI LENAPE, OR DELAWARE INDIANS.

BY THE REV. JOHN HECKEWELDER,

OF BETHLEHEM

Words, phrases, etc., of the Lenni Lenape, or Delaware Indians.

N'mítzi, *I eat.*

N'gáuwi, *I drink.*

N'wachpácheli, *I awake.*

N'ménne, *I drink.*

N'papommíssi, *I walk.*

N'gagelícksi, *I laugh.*

N'mamentschi, *I rejoice.*

N'dáschwil, *I swim.*

N'manúnxi, *I am angry.*

N'mikemósi, *I work.*

N'delláchgusi, *I climb.*

N'nanipauwi, *I stand.*

N'lemáttáchpi, *I sit.*

Nópo, nóchpo, n'hóppo, *I smoke.*

N'schiweléndam, *I am sorry.*

N'gattópui, *I am hungry.*

N'gattósomi, *I am thirsty.*

N'pálsi, *I am sick.*

Nolamálsi, *I am well.*

N'nipitíne, *I have the tooth-ache.*

N'wilíne, *I have a head-ache.*

N'wischási, *I am afraid.*

N'wiquíhhalla, *I am tired.*

N'tschittanési, *I am strong.*

N'schawússi, *I am weak, feeble.*

N'túppocu, *I am wise.*

N'nanólhand, *I am lazy.*

N'pomóchksi, *I creep.*

N'dellemúske, *I am going away.*

N'gattúngwan, *I am sleepy.*

Oténink n'da, *I am going to town.*

Gelóltowak, *they are quarrelling.*

K'dahólel, *I love you.*

Kschingálel, *I hate you.*

Ponihi, *let me alone.*

Palli áal, *go away.*

Gótschemunk, *go out of the house.*

Ickalli áal, *away with you.*

Kschaméhella, *run.*

Ne nipauwi, *stop there.*

Undach áal, *come here.*

Kpáhi, *shut the door.*

Tauwúnni, *open the door, lid*, &c.

Pisellissu, *soft.*

Pisalatúlpe, *soft-shelled tortoise.*

Kulupátschi, *otherwise, on the other hand, else, however.*

Nahalíwi, }Eiyelíwi, }*both* (of them.)

Leu, *true.*Attáne léwi, *it is not true.*

Alla gaski lewi, *it cannot be true.*

Bíschi, bíschihk, *yes, indeed,* (it is so.)

N'wingalláuwi, *I like to hunt.*

N'winggi mikemósi, *I like to work.*

N'schíngi mikemósi, *I don't like to work.*

M'wingínammen, *I like it.*

N'wingándammen, *I like the taste* (of it).

N'wíngachpihn, *I like to be here.*

N'schíngachpihn, *I dislike being here.*

N'mechquihn, *I have a cold, cough.*

Undach lénni, *reach it hither.*

Undach lénnemáuwil, *reach it to me.*

N'gattópui, *I am hungry.*

N'gattosomi, *I am thirsty.*

N'wiquíhilla, *I am tired, fatigued.*

N'tschitannéssi, *I am strong.*

N'schauwihilla, *I am weak, faint.*

N'wischási, *I am afraid.*

N'daptéssi, *I sweat.*

N'dágotschi, *I am cold, freezing.*

N'dellennówi, *I am a man.*

N'dochquéwi, *I am a woman.*

N'damándommen, *I feel.*

N'leheléche, *I live, exist, draw breath.*

Lécheen, *to exist, breathe, draw breath, be alive*.

Lechéwon, *breath*. *Note*. As we would ask a person whom we had not seen for a long time: "Are you *alive* yet?"—or, is such and such a one yet *alive*? the Indian would say: Ili klehelêche? *do you draw breath yet?*

Leheléche íli nítis, N. N.? *does my favourite friend* N. N. *yet draw breath?*

Gooch ili lehelecheu? *does your father draw breath yet?*

Gáhawees ili lehelecheu? *does your mother draw breath yet?*

N'tschu! *my friend*.N'tschútti, *dear, beloved friend*.

Nitis, *confidential friend*.

Geptschat, *a fool*.

Geptschátschik, *fools*.

Leppóat, *wise*.Leppoeu, *he is wise*.

Leppoátschik, *wise men, wise people*.

Sókelaan, *it rains*.

K'schilaan, *it rains hard*.

Pélelaan, *it begins to rain*.

Achwi sókelaan, *it rains very hard*.

Alla sókelaan, *it has left off raining*.

Peelhácquon, *it thunders*.

Sasapeléhelleu, *it lightens*.

Petaquíechen, *the streams are rising*.

M'chaquiéchen, *the streams are up, high*.

Choppécat, *the water is deep*.

Meetschi higíhelleu, *the waters are falling*.

Síchilleu meétschi, *the waters have run off*.

Tatehúppecat, *shallow water*.

Gahan, *very low water, next to being dried up*.

K'schuppéhelleu, *a strong current, riffle*.

Pulpécat, *deep dead water, as in a cove or bay*.

Clampéching, *a dead running stream, the current imperceptible*.

Kscháchan, *the wind*.

Ta úndchen? *from whence blows the wind?*

Lowannéunk úndchen, *the wind comes from the north*.

Schawannéunk úndchen, *the wind comes from the south*.

Schawanáchen, *south wind*.

Lowannáchen, *north wind*.

Wundchennéunk, *in the west*.

Gachpatteyéunk, *in the east*.

Moschháquot, *a clear sky*.

Kschiechpécat, *clear water, clear, pure water*.

Achgumhócquat, *cloudy*.

Páckenum, *dark*, (very.)

Pekenink, *in the dark*.

Pisgeu, *it is dark*.

Pisgéke, *when it becomes dark*, (is dark.)

Mah! *there, take it*!

Yuni, *this*.

Nanni, nan, *that*.

Wullíh, *yonder*.

Wáchelemi, *afar off*.

Wáchelemat? *is it afar off, a great way off?*

Péchuat, *near, nigh.*

Pechuwíwi, *near,* (not far off.)

Pechútschi, *near.*

Pechu lennitti, *directly, presently.*

Pechu, *soon, directly.*

Alíge, *if so, nevertheless.*

Alíge n'dallemúsca, *I will go for all, nevertheless I will go.*

Yu úndachqui! *this way, to this side!*

Icka úndachqui, *to yon side.*

Ickalli úndachqui! *still further on that way!*

Wullih! *yonder!*

Wullíh táh! *beyond that!*

Pennó wullíh! *look yonder!*

Nachgiéchen, *it has hit against something,* (cannot move or be driven forward,) *as a joist, a pin in a building.*

Clagáchen, *it rests on something in the water, is grounded.*

Clagáchen amóchol, *the canoe is aground, rests on something.*

Clagáchen aschwitchan, *the raft has grounded.*

Tauwihilla, *sunk, it has sunk.*

N'dámochol k'tauwíhille, *my canoe sunk.*

Gachpattol amóchol, *take the canoe out of the water.*

Gachpallátam, *let us get out and go on shore.*

Pusik! *embark!* (ye.)

Pusil! *embark!* (thou.)

Wischíksil! *be thou vigilant, quick, in earnest and exert thyself!*

Wischíksik! *be ye vigilant, in earnest, quick!* (about it.) *Note.* The word wischíksi or wischíxi is by the white people interpreted as signifying "*be strong*," which does not convey the true meaning of this word: it comprehends more; it asks for *exertions to be made, to fulfil the object.*

N'petalogálgun! *I am sent as a messenger!*

N'sagimáum petalogálgun yu pétschi, *my chief has sent me as a messenger to you.*

Matta nutschquem'páwi, *I am not come for nothing*, (meaning, being on an errand.)

Pechu k'pendammenéwo wentsche payan, *you will soon hear why I am come here.*

Tschingetsch kmátschi? *when do you return home again?*

Sédpook! *at day break!*

N'dellgun lachpi gatta páame, *I was told to hasten, and return quickly.*Lachpí, *quick*, (without delay.)

N'mauwi pihm, *I am going to take a sweat* (at the sweat house).

N'dapi pihm, *I am come from sweating* (from the sweat house).

N'dapelláuwi, *I am come from hunting.*

N'dápi notamœsi, *I come from taking fish with the spear.*

N'dapi áman, *I come from fishing with the hook and line.*

N'dapi achquáneman, *I come from bushnet fishing.*

Notameshícan, *a fishing spear, gig.*

Aman, *a fish hook.*

Achquáneman, *a bush net.*

Apatschiáne, *when I return.*

Góphammen, }K'páhammen,}*to shut up anything close, a door, &c.*

Kpáhi, *shut the door.*

Kpáskhamen, *to plug up tight.*

Tauwún, *open the door.*

Tauwúnni, *open the door for me.*

M'biák, *a whale,* (fish.)

Yuh' allauwítan! *come, let us go a hunting!*

Nclema n'metenaxíwi, *I am not yet ready.*

K'metenaxi yúcke? *are you now ready?*

Nélema ta! *not yet!*

Pechu lenítti, *by and by.*

Laháppa pehil! *wait a little for me!*

Nelema n'gischambíla níwash! *I have not yet done tying up my pack!*

Yúh' yehúcke allemuskétam! *well now let us go on!*

Schuck sokeláan gachtáuwi! *but it will rain!*

Quanna ta! *even if it does, no matter if it does!*

Alla kschilánge, *when the shower is over.*

Ta hatsch gemauwikéneen? *at what place shall we encamp?*

Wdiungoakhánnink, *at the white oak run.*

Enda gochgochgáchen, *at the crossing, fording-place.*

Enda tachtschaúnge, *at the narrows,* (where the hill comes close on the river.)

Meechek achsinik, *at the big rock.*

Gauwáhenink, *at the place of the fallen timbers.*

Sikhéunk, *at the salt spring.*

Pachséyink, *in the valley.*

Wachtschúnk, *on the hill.*

Yapéwi, *on the river bank.*

Gámink, *on the other side of the river.*

Eli shíngeek, *on the flat,* (level upland.)

Mahónink, *at the lick,* (deer lick.)

Oténink, *in the town.*

Tékenink, *in the woods.*

Hachkihácanink, *in the field.*

Pockhapóckink, *at the creek between the two hills.*

Menatheink, *on the island.*

Enda lechauhánne, *at the forks of the river.*

Enda lechauwíechen, *at the forks of the road.*

Sakunk, *at the outlet of the river,* (mouth of the river.)

T'huppecúnk, *at the cold spring.*

K'mésha? *did you kill a deer?*

Atta, n'palléha! *no, I missed him!*

Yuh' allácqui! *what a pity!*

Biesch knéwa? *then you did see one?*

Nachen n'newa achúch, *three times I saw deer.*

Quonna eet kpúngum machtit, *perhaps your powder is bad.*

Na leu, *that is true, so it turned out to be.*

Achtschíngi pockteu, *it scarcely took fire.*

Achtuchuíke wérnan? *are there plenty of deer where you was?*

Atta ta húsca, *not a great many.*

Nángutti schuck n'peenhálle, *I saw but few tracks.*

Machk kpenhálle? *did you track any bears?*

Biesch n'penhálle mauchsu, *I tracked but one.*

Schuck n'dállemons mekane, *but my dog.*

Palli uchschíha, *drove him off.*

N'gatta amochólhe, *I want to make a canoe.*

Wítschemil! *help me!*

N'pachkamen gachláuwi, *I want to get bled.*

Yuh, nanne léketsch, *well do so, let it be so.*

N'matamálsi, *I feel unwell.*

Woak n'nipitíne, *and have the tooth-ache.*

Wítschemil! *help me!*

Poníhil, *let me alone.*

Tschitgússil! *be still, hold your tongue!*

Kscháhel! *strike hard, lay on well!* (on wood, &c.)

Míleen, *to give, the giving.*

Mil, *give.*

Mili, *give me.*

Milineen, *give us.*

Miltin, *given,* (was already.)

Miltoágan, *a present.*

N'milgun, *it was given to me.*

Milo, *give him.*

Milátamo, *let us give him.*

Sehe! *hush, be quiet!*

Elke! *O dear, wonderful!*

389

Ekesa! *miserable, for shame!*

Suppínquall, *tears*.

Lepácku, *he cries*.

E gohán, *yes, indeed*.

Kéhella, *aye, yes*.

Kehellá? *so, is it possible?*

Kehella lá! *O yes, so it is!*

Yuh kehella! *well, then!*

La kella! *to be sure, 'tis so!*

Kehella kella! *yes, yes!*

E-E, *yes, (a lazy yes.)*

Mátta, *no.*Tá, *no, (a lazy no.)*

Tagú, *no, not*.

Atta ta, *no, no*.

Eekhockewítschik mamachtagéwak, *the nations are warring against each other*.

Yuh allácqui na lissichtit, *indeed it is a pity they do so*.

Napenaltowaktsché, *they will be scalping each other*.

Auween won gintsch pat? *who is that who just now came?*

Taktáani, *I don't know*.

Mauwi pennó, *go and see*.

Auween kháckev? *who are you?* (of what nation.)

Lennápe n'hackey, *I am an Indian*, (of the Lenni Lenape.)

Ta kóom? *where do you come from?*

Oténink nóom, *I come from the town*.

Auween kpetschi, witscheuchgun? *who came with you here?*

Na nípauwit, *he who stands there.*

Lennápe? *is he an Indian?* (a Lenni Lenape.)

Tah, Mengwe, *no, he is a Mingo, an Iroquois.*

Kpetschi witscheuchgun otenink untschi? *did he come with you from the town?*

Matta! n'mattelúkgun, *no! he fell in with me* (by the way).

Ta tallí? *where?*

Wulli tah achtschaúnge! *yonder at the narrows!*

Ki gieschquíke? *this day?* (to-day.)

Atta! welaquíke, *no! last evening.*

Kœcu undochwe wentschi yu páat? *what is he come here for, what is he after?*

Taktani, schuck n'tschupínawe! *I don't know, but I mistrust him!*

Tcshpináxu gáhenna, *he appears suspicious, has a suspicious appearance.*

Gichgemotket quónna, *probably he is a thief.*

Wewitschi eet, *most likely,* (he is such.)

N'gemotemúke n'dállemons nechnaúnges, *my horse has been stolen from me.*

Wichwínggi gemotgéwak Menge, *the Mingoes are very fond of stealing.*

Yuh amachgídieu, *they are vagabonds.*Gachtíngetsch, *next year.*

Lehelechejane, *If I live,* (or am alive.)

Gamhackinktsch n'da, *I will go across the sea,* (or more properly) *to the country beyond the sea.*

Clámachphil! *sit still!*

391

Schíki a na Lenno, *that is a fine, pretty man.*

Quatsch luppackhan? *why do you cry?*

N'nilchgun na nipauwit, *he that stands there struck me.*

Uchschímo meetschi, *he has already ran off, made away with himself.*

T'chúnno! *catch him!*

Gachbílau! *tie him!*

Lachénau! *let him loose!*

Weemi, *or* wemi auween lue, *everybody says.*

Wigwingi geloltóak schwánnakwak, *that the white people are fond of quarrelling.*

N'matúnguam, *I had a bad dream.*

N'mátschi, *I will go home.*

Siquonne lappitsch knewi lehellecheyan! *in the spring you will see me again if I am alive!*

Yuh, schuck mámschali! *well, but do remember me!*

Natsch leu, *it shall be so, that shall be done.*

N'nuntschímke, *I have been called.*

Auween guntschimgun? *who called you?*

N'dochquéum, *my wife.*

N'nitsch undach aal! *come hither my child!*

Lachpi! *quick!*Nayu nípauwi (or nípawi), *there stand.*

Pelláh, *indeed, surely, so so.*

Petalamo auween, *somebody sounds* (calls out) *the alarm yell,* (signifying danger at hand.)

Yuh, shimoítam! *come, let us run off!*

Nélema ta! *not yet!*

Quanna eet auween gatta napenálgun! *perhaps somebody is coming to attack and scalp us!*

Wewitschi eet, *probably, may-be.*

Pennáu! *look!*Wulli ta pépannik! *yonder they are coming!*

Auween knéwa? *who do you see?*

Machelook, *or* chelook schwánnakwak, *many white people.*

Papomiscuak? *are they on foot?*

Alénde, *some of them.*

Schuk matta weémi, *but not all of them.*

Gachtonalukguntsch matta uchschimuiénge, *we shall be attacked if we do not make off with ourselves.*

Yuh, uchschimuítam alíge, *well then, let us make off at any rate.*

Mattapewíwak nik schwannakwak, *the white people are a rascally set of beings.*

Kilunéwak wingi, *they are giving to lying.*

Kschinggálguna gehenna, *they hate us truly.*

Gemotemukguna wíngi, *they like, are disposed to rob us, are thieves upon us.*

Yuh, gachtonalátam! *well, let us fall upon them, attack them.*

Longundowináquot, *it looks likely for peace, there is a prospect of peace.*

Pennau won! *look at that one!*

Achgíeuchsu, *he is drunk.*

Achgepíngwe, *he is blind.*

Achgépcheu, *he is deaf.*

Kpítscheu, *he is foolish.*

Sópsu, *he is naked.*

Mamanúnxu, *he is angry.*

Scháaksu, *he is covetous.*

Pihmtónheu, *he has a crooked mouth.*

Ilau, *he is a great war-captain.*

Sakímau, *he is a chief.*

Kschamehellátam, *let us run together.*

Típaas, *a hen.*

Tipátit, *a chicken.*

Tschólens, *a bird.*

Tscholéntit, *a little bird.*

FOOTNOTES:

1 The annotations in brac s are by the Editor.

2 Between the words *"if"* and *"what"* insert *"we can credit."*

3 A figurative expression, denoting the territory claimed by them, and occupied at the time.

4 Alluding to the white people settling those countries.

5 [The book referred to here and elsewhere frequently in the course of his narrative by the author, was written by the Rev. George Henry Loskiel, a clergyman of the Continental Province of the Moravian Church, and was published at Barby, Saxony, in 1789. It is entitled "Geschichte der Mission der Evangelischen Brüder unter den Indianern in Nordamerika," and is a faithful record of the Christian work in which the Moravians engaged chiefly among the Lenape and Iroquois stocks of the aborigines, in the interval between 1735 and 1787. The material on which the author wrought in the preparation of his history was furnished mainly from the archives of his church at Herrnhut, to which duplicates of the missionaries' journals were statedly forwarded. In this way he was enabled to produce a narrative which is marvellously accurate, even touching minor points of topography, despite the fact that the shifting scenes of his drama were laid in another hemisphere. The preface was written at Strickenhof, in Livonia, in May of 1788. In it Mr. Loskiel acknowledges his indebtedness for valuable assistance to the venerable Bishop Augustus G. Spangenberg, who had superintended the Moravian Mission in the New World in the interval between 1744 and 1762; and to the veteran missionary David Zeisberger, at that time still in its service. It was the latter who supplied the larger portion of the material relating to the history, traditions, manners, and customs of the North American Indians, found in the ten chapters introductory to the history of the Mission. This valuable work was translated into English by the Rev. Christian Ignatius Latrobe, of London, in 1793, and published there, in 1794, by "The Brethren's Society for the Furtherance of the Gospel." It is now a rare book. Having been consecrated a Bishop for the American Province of his Church in 1802, Mr. Loskiel came to this country, settled at Bethlehem, Pa., where he died in 1814.]

6 Figurative expression. See Loskiel's History, Part I. c. 10.²]

7 For "*declaring at the same time*" read "*and declared afterwards*."

8 [John Christopher Pyrlœus was sent by the heads of the Moravian Church at Herrnhut, Saxony, to Bethlehem, Pa., in the autumn of 1741, to do service in the Indian Mission. Having assisted Count Zinzendorf, during his sojourn in the Province in 1742, in the work of the ministry among a portion of the German population of Philadelphia, we find him, in January of 1743, prosecuting the study of the Mohawk under the direction of Conrad Weiser, the provincial interpreter, at Tulpehocken, (near Womelsdorf, Berks County, Pa.) This was in view of fitting himself for the office of corresponding secretary of the Mission Board at Bethlehem, and for the duties of an evangelist among the Iroquois stock of Indians, to whom it was purposed by the Moravians to bring the Gospel. At the expiration of three months he returned to Bethlehem, and in the following June, accompanied by his wife, who was a daughter of John Stephen Benezet, a well-known merchant of Philadelphia, set out for the Mohawk country, his destination being the Mohawk castle of Canajoharie. Here he remained upwards of two months, in which interval of time he visited the remaining Mohawk castles, and by constant intercourse with the Indians strove assiduously to perfect himself in their language. Such was his progress then and subsequently, that in 1744 he felt himself competent to impart instruction in that important dialect of the Iroquois to several of his brethren at Bethlehem, who were training for missionaries. In 1748, while settled at Gnadenhütten, on the Mahoning, (Lehighton, Carbon County, Pa.,) he rendered similar service. Meanwhile he had acquired a knowledge of the Mohican, and in 1745 there appeared his first translations of German hymns into that tongue— the beginnings of a collection for use in Divine worship in the Mission churches. Eight of the eleven years of his stay in this country were mainly spent in labors of the kind just enumerated. Having been liberally educated, Mr. Pyrlœus was well qualified for the work in which he engaged. Several of his contributions to this novel department of philology, in manuscript, are deposited in the library of the American Philosophical Society in Philadelphia. Among these are essays on the grammatical structure of the Iroquois dialects, and a collection of notes on Indian traditions. The former Mr. Heckewelder names on a subsequent page, and from the latter he makes frequent extracts. In 1751 Mr. Pyrlœus sailed for England, where he was active in the ministry of his Church until his recall to Germany in 1770. He died at Herrnhut in 1785.]

9 [The passage referred to by Mr. Heckewelder is quoted in full by way of annotation on a subsequent page.]

10 [Norman's Kill, named after Albert Andriese Bratt De Norman, an early settler of Beverwyck, rises in Schenectady County, has a south-east course of about twenty-eight miles, and empties into the Hudson, two miles south of Albany, in the town of Bethlehem. In records of 1677 it is called Bethlehem's Kil. The Indian name of the stream was Tawalsantha. In the spring of 1617 the United New Netherlands Company erected a fort near the banks of Norman's Kill, and in 1621 the Dutch made a solemn alliance and treaty of peace with the Five Nations, near its mouth.—*Munsell's Collections of the History of Albany*. Albany, 1870.]

11 For "*Mohicans*" read "*Lenape*."

12 ["*The History of the Five Indian Nations depending on the Province of New York in America*, by *Cadwallader Colden*." The first edition of this rare book was dedicated by the author to his Excellency, William Burnet, Esq., and was printed and sold by William Bradford in New York, 1727. Colden emigrated from Scotland in 1708, and first settled in Pennsylvania, engaging in the practice of medicine. Removing to New York in 1718, he was some time surveyor-general, subsequently a member of the King's Council, and in 1761 commissioned Lieutenant-Governor of the Province. This commission he held at the time of his death at his seat on Long Island, in September of 1776.]

13 [The proceedings of these conferences and treaties with the Indians are spread upon the minutes of the Provincial Council of Pennsylvania, which were authorized to be printed by the Act of Legislature of April 4th, 1837, and published subsequently in seven volumes. They are known as "The Colonial Records."]

14 At a Treaty, at Easton, in July and November, 1756.

15 [Should be *Thomson*.]

16 Loskiel's History, Part I., ch. 10.

17 The Iroquois were at that time a confederacy of only Five Nations; they became Six afterwards when they were joined by the Tuscaroras.

18 Meaning, that the Five Nations would assist the white people in getting the country of their enemies, the Delawares, &c., to themselves.

19 Loskiel, Part I., ch. 10.

20 [The Indian converts attached to the Moravian Mission, whom Mr. Heckewelder invariably designates "Christian Indians" throughout his history. The Moravian Indians at this date were settled with their missionaries in three towns on the Tuscarawas branch of the Muskingum (now the Tuscarawas River), all within the limits of the present Tuscarawas County, Ohio.]

21 Loskiel, Part III., ch. 9.

22 The proper name is *Wtáwas*, the *W* is whistled.

23 [In the summer of 1794, Gen. Wayne moved an army into the Ohio country, and on the 20th of August defeated the confederated Indians near the rapids of the Maumee, or Miami of the Lake. The result of this campaign was a treaty of peace, which was ratified at Greenville, the present county seat of Darke County, Ohio, in August of 1795, between the United States Government, represented by Wayne, and the Shawanese, Delawares, Wyandots, Ottawas, Potawattomies, Miamis and smaller tribes, at which treaty about two-thirds of the present state of Ohio was ceded to the United States.]

24 [The missionary David Zeisberger, in a collection of Delaware vocables incorporated in "*An Essay of a Delaware and English Spelling Book for the use of the Schools of the Christian Indians on the Muskingum River*," printed at Philadelphia, by Henry Miller, in 1776, defines *Lennilenape*, "Indians of the same nation."]

25 Colden.

26 La Hontan.

27 The Dutch called them Mahikanders; the French Mourigans, and Mahingans; the English, Mohiccons, Mohuccans, Mohegans, Muhheekanew, Schatikooks, River Indians.

28 "Night's encampment" is a halt of one year at a place.

29 The Mississippi, or *River* of *Fish*; *Namœs*, a *Fish*; *Sipu*, a *River*.

30 The Iroquois, or Five Nations.

31 [Col. John Gibson, to whom Mr. Heckewelder frequently alludes, was born at Lancaster, Pa., in 1740. At the age of eighteen, he made his first campaign under Gen. Forbes, in the expedition which resulted in the acquisition of Fort Du Quesne from the French. At the peace of 1763 he settled at that post (Fort Pitt) as a trader. Some time after this, on the resumption of hostilities with the savages, he was captured by some Indians, among whom he lived several years, and thus became familiar with their language, manners, customs, and traditions. In the expedition against the Shawanese under Lord Dunmore, the last royal governor of Virginia, in 1774, Gibson played a conspicuous part. On the breaking out of the Revolutionary war, he was appointed to the command of one of the Continental regiments raised in Virginia, and served with the army at New York and in the retreat through New Jersey. He was next employed in the Western department, serving under Gen. McIntosh in 1778, and under Gen. Irvine in 1782. At one time he was in command at Pittsburgh. In 1800 Col. Gibson was appointed Secretary and acting Governor of the territory of Indiana, a position which he filled for a second time between 1811 and 1813. Subsequently he was Associate Judge of Allegheny County, Pa. He died near Pittsburgh in 1822. He was an uncle of the late John B. Gibson, Chief Justice of the Supreme Court of Pennsylvania between 1827 and 1851.]

32 Loskiel's History of the Mission of the United Brethren, Part I., ch. I.

33 [In 1789 Mr. Heckewelder, accompanied by Abraham Steiner, (subsequently a missionary to the Cherokees of Georgia,) visited the mission at New Salem, on the Petquotting, (now the Huron,) in Erie County, Ohio, on business relating to the survey of a tract of land on the Tuscarawas, which Congress had conveyed to the Moravians in trust for their Indians. This was to indemnify them for losses incurred at their settlements during the border-war of the Revolution.]

34 The *Glades*, that is to say that they crossed the mountains.

35 Meaning the river Susquehannah, which they call "the great Bay River," from where the west branch falls into the main stream.

36 The word "Hittuck," in the language of the Delawares, means a rapid stream; "Sipo," or "Sipu," is the proper name for a river.

37 [The Indians of this town proved troublesome neighbors to a small company of Moravians, who, in the spring of 1740, were employed by Whitefield to erect a large dwelling near its site, which he designed for a school for negroes. The town lay near the centre of a tract of 5,000 acres (now Upper Nazareth township, Northampton County, Pennsylvania), which Whitefield bought of William Allen, which he named Nazareth, and which, in 1741, he conveyed to the Moravians. Captain John and his clan of Delawares vacated their plantation in the autumn of 1742, and in the following year, the Moravians commenced their first settlement, and named it Nazareth. Whitefield's house is still standing.]

38 Loskiel, part I., ch. 10.

39 The Reverend C. Pyrlœus, a pupil of Conrad Weiser, of whom he learned the Mohawk language, and who was afterwards stationed on the Mohawk River, as a Missionary, has, in a manuscript book, written between the years 1742 and 1748, page 235, the following note which he received from a principal chief of that nation, viz.: "The Five Nations formerly did eat human flesh; they at one time ate up a whole body of the French King's soldiers; they say, *Eto niocht ochquari*; which is: Human flesh tastes like bear's meat. They also say, that the hands are not good eating, they are *yozgarat*, bitter."

Aged French Canadians have told me, many years since, while I was at Detroit, that they had frequently seen the Iroquois eat the flesh of those who had been slain in battle, and that this was the case in the war between the French and English, commonly called the war of 1756.

400

At a treaty held at the Proprietors house in Philadelphia, July 5th, 1742, with the Six Nations, none of the Senecas attended; the reason of their absence being asked, it was given for answer, "that there was a famine in their country, and that a father had been obliged to kill two of his children, to preserve the lives of the remainder of the family." See Colden's History of the Five Nations, part II., page 52. See also the minutes of that treaty, printed at Philadelphia, by B. Franklin, in 1743, p. 7, in the Collection of Indian Treaties in the library of the American Philosophical Society.

40 Loskiel, part I., ch. 1.

41 The Rev. C. Pyrlœus, in his manuscript book, page 234, says: "The alliance or confederacy of the Five Nations was established, as near as can be conjectured, one age (or the length of a man's life) before the white people (the Dutch) came into the country. *Thannawage* was the name of the aged Indian, a Mohawk, who first proposed such an alliance." He then gives the names of the chiefs of the Five Nations, which at that time met and formed the alliance, viz.: "*Toganawita*, of the Mohawks; *Otatschéchta*, of the Oneidas; *Tatotarho*, of the Onondagos; *Togaháyon*, of the Cayugas; *Ganiatariò* and *Satagarùyes*, from two towns of the Senecas, &c.," and concludes with saying: "All these names are forever to be kept in remembrance, by naming a person in each nation after them," &c., &c.

42 Loskiel, part I., ch. 10.

43 Loskiel, part I., ch. 10.

44 Ibid.

45 [The following is the passage from Loskiel, which that historian copied from David Zeisberger's "Collection of Notes on the Indians," compiled by the missionary during his residence in the valley of the Tuscarawas, about 1778. "According to the account of the Delawares, they were always too powerful for the Iroquois, so that the latter were at length convinced that if they continued the war, their total extirpation would be inevitable. They therefore sent the following message to the Delawares: 'It is not profitable that all the nations should be at war with each other, for this will at length be the ruin of the whole Indian race. We have therefore considered a remedy by which this evil may be prevented. One nation shall be the *woman*. We will place her in the midst, and the other nations who make war shall be the man, and live around the woman. No one shall touch or hurt the woman, and if any one does it, we will immediately say to him, "Why do you beat the woman?" Then all the men shall fall upon him who has beaten her. The woman shall not go to war, but endeavor to keep peace with all. Therefore, if the men that surround her beat each other, and the war be carried on with violence, the woman shall have the right of addressing them, "Ye men, what are ye about? why do you beat each other? We are almost afraid. Consider that your wives and children must perish, unless you desist. Do you mean to destroy yourselves from the face of the earth?" The men shall then hear and obey the woman.' The Delawares add, that, not immediately perceiving the intention of the Iroquois, they submitted to be the *woman*. The Iroquois then appointed a great feast, and invited the Delaware nation to it; when, in consequence of the authority given them, they made a solemn speech containing three capital points. The first was, that they declared the Delaware nation to be the *woman* in the following words: 'We dress you in a woman's long habit, reafilled ching down to your feet, and adorn you with ear-rings;' meaning that they should no more take up arms. The second point was thus expressed: 'We hang a calabash with oil and medicine upon your arm. With the oil you shall cleanse the ears of the other nations, that they may attend to good and not to bad words, and with the medicine you shall heal those who are walking in foolish ways, that they may return to their senses and incline their hearts to peace.' The third point, by which the Delawares were exhorted to make agriculture their future employ and means of subsistence, was thus worded: 'We deliver into your hands a plant of Indian corn and a hoe.' Each of these points was confirmed by delivering a belt of wampum, and these belts have been carefully laid up, and their meaning frequently repeated.

"The Iroquois, on the contrary, assert that they conquered the Delawares, and that the latter were forced to adopt the defenceless state and appellation of a *woman* to avoid total ruin.

"Whether these different accounts be true or false, certain it is that the Delaware nation has ever since been looked to for preservation of peace, and entrusted with the charge of the great belt of peace and chain of friendship, which they must take care to preserve inviolate. According to the figurative explanation of the Indians, the middle of the chain of friendship is placed upon the shoulder of the Delaware, the rest of the Indian nations holding one end and the Europeans the other."]

46 [*The Life and Times of David Zeisberger, the Western Pioneer and Apostle to the Indians, by Edmund de Schweinitz, Phila.*, 1870, reviews the Moravian mission among the North American Indians from its beginnings to recent times, besides very fully portraying the career of the veteran missionary, who spent upwards of sixty years of his life as an evangelist to the Indians, thirty-six of which were passed within the limits of the present State of Ohio. He died on the 17th of November, 1808, at Goshen, on the Tuscarawas, in the 88th year of his age. Zeisberger, in the course of his long life in the Indian country, mastered the Delaware and the Onondaga of the Iroquois, into the former of which he made translations of a number of devotional books, while he studied both critically, as his literary efforts in that direction, partly published and partly in MS., amply testify.]

47 Mr. Proud, in his History of Pennsylvania, relates that, some time after the establishment of William Penn's government, the Indians used to supply the family of one John Chapman, whose descendants still reside in Bucks County, with all kinds of provisions, and mentions an affecting instance of their kindness to that family. Abraham and John Chapman, twin children about nine or ten years old, going out one evening to seek their cattle, met an Indian in the woods, who told them to go back, else they would be lost. They took his advice and went back, but it was night before they got home, where they found the Indian, who had repaired thither out of anxiety for them. And their parents, about that time, going to the yearly meeting at Philadelphia, and leaving a young family at home, the Indians came every day to see whether anything was amiss among them. Such (says Proud) in many instances was the kind treatment of the Aborigines of this country to the English in their first and early settlement. Proud's Hist., Vol. I., pp. 223, 224.

48 [For "Easton in Pennsylvania," read *Philadelphia*. Easton, the county-seat of Northampton County, was laid out in the spring of 1752.]

49 For "1742," read "*and November, 1756.*" [The latter was held at Easton.]

50 [The so-called French and Indian war, the fourth and last of the inter-colonial wars, which originated in disputes between the French and English concerning territorial claims, and which, after a seven years' contest, resulted in establishing the supremacy of the latter over the civilized portions of North America.]

51 [The Conestogas remained on their ancestral seats, near the mouth of the Conestoga, in Manor township, Lancaster County, Penna., long after the other Indians on the Susquehanna had been crowded by the advance of civilization beyond Shamokin. Here the remnant of this tribe was fallen upon by Scotch-Irish partizans of Paxton township (now within the limits of Dauphin County) in December of 1763, all that were at the settlement killed, and their cabins burnt to the ground. Ten days later, the remainder of this inoffensive people, who had been lodged in the jail at Lancaster, were inhumanly butchered by the same band of lawless frontiersmen. In Heckewelder's "Narrative of the Mission of the United Brethren among the Delaware and Mohegan Indians," there is a statement by an eye-witness, touching the last scene in this bloody tragedy.]

52 [White Eyes, alias Koquethagachton, a celebrated captain and counsellor of the Delawares of the Ohio country, was first met by Heckewelder at his home, near the mouth of the Beaver (above Pittsburg), when the latter was on his way to the Tuscarawas, in the spring of 1762. When Zeisberger entered the valley of that river, in 1772, and built Schönbrunn, the chieftain was residing six miles below Gekelemukpechunk, the then capital of his nation, in the present Oxford township, Coshocton County. In Dunmore's war, as well as in the war of the Revolution, White Eyes strove strenuously to keep the Delawares neutral. Failing in this in the latter contest, and seeing himself necessitated to take sides, he declared for the Americans, joined Gen. McIntosh's command, but died at Fort Laurens, on the Tuscarawas, in November of 1778, before the projected expedition, which was aimed at the Sandusky towns, moved. White Eyes was a warm friend of the Moravian mission, and was deeply interested in the progress of his people in the arts of civilized life.]

53 Indian chiefs, in their public speeches, always speak on behalf of their nation in the singular number and in the first person, considering themselves, in a manner, as its representatives.

54 [In August of 1779, Col. Daniel Brodhead, then commandant of Fort Pitt, moved with some troops up the Allegheny, and in the forks of that river destroyed several settlements, inhabited by Monsey and Seneca Indians. "The Delawares," he writes in his report to the War Department, "are ready to follow me wherever I go."]

55 Loskiel, part II., ch. 8.

56 Henry Hudson, a British navigator and discoverer in the employ of the Dutch East India Company, sailed from Amsterdam in command of the Half Moon, in April of 1609, in search of a north-eastern passage. Foiled by the ice in the higher latitudes, he turned southwards, and in September anchored in New York bay.

57 Dele "*in which*."

58 Hackhack is properly a gourd; but since they have seen glass bottles and decanters, they call them by the same name.

59 These Dutchmen were probably acquainted with what is related of Queen Dido in ancient history, and thus turned their classical knowledge to a good account.

60 The Hollanders.

61 Manhattan, or New York Island.

62 For "*Delawares*" read "*Mohicans*."

63 An Indian corruption of the word *English*, whence probably the nickname *Yankees*.

64 This word means "a cluster of islands with channels every way, so that it is in no place shut up or impassable for craft." The Indians think that the white people have corrupted this word into *Massachusetts*. It deserves to be remarked as an example of the comprehensiveness of the Indian languages.

65 The Delaware river. I have said above, p. 51, that *Hittuck* means a rapid stream. I should have added that it means so only when placed at the end of another word, and used as a compound. Singly, it signifies a *tree*.

66 The Swedes and Dutch.

67 William Penn.

68 Land traders and speculators.

69 Easton, Northampton County, Pa.

70 This actually took place at a treaty held at Easton in July and November, 1756.

71 *Council house* here means "Connexion District."

72 *Pulling the council house down.* Destroying, dispersing the community, preventing their further intercourse with each other, by settling between them on their land.

73 *Putting the fire out.* Murdering them or their people, where they assemble for pacific purposes, where treaties are held, &c.

74 *Our own blood.* The blood flowing from the veins of some of our community.

75 Alluding to the murder of the Conestogo Indians, who, though of another tribe, yet had joined them in welcoming the white people to their shores.

In a narrative of this lamentable event, supposed to have been written by the late Dr. Franklin, it is said: "On the first arrival of the English in Pennsylvania, messengers from this tribe came to welcome them with presents of venison, corn, and skins, and the whole tribe entered into a treaty of friendship with the first proprietor, William Penn, which was to last as long as the sun should shine, or the waters run in the rivers."

76 *The fire was entirely extinguished by the blood of the murdered running into it; not a spark was left to kindle a new fire.* This alludes to the last fire that was kindled by the Pennsylvania government and themselves at Lancaster, where the last treaty was held with them in 1762, the year preceding this murder, which put an end to all business of the kind in the province of Pennsylvania.

77 *The great Swamp.* The Glades on the Allegheny mountains.

78 *Delamattenos.* The Hurons or Wyandots, whom they call their uncle. These, though speaking a dialect of the Iroquois language, are in connexion with the Lenape.

79 For "1787" read "1781."

80 [These were the words of a war-chief of the Delawares, Pachgantschihilas by name, in the course of an address to the Moravian Indians at Gnadenhütten, in which he sought to persuade them to remove from their exposed position on the Tuscarawas to a place of safety among the Wyandots of the Maumee.]

81 For "*us*" read "*them*."

82 [The massacre of Moravian Indians at Gnadenhütten was perpetrated on the 8th of March, 1782, by militia led by Col. David Williamson, of Washington County, Pa. The details of this atrocious affair are very minutely given by De Schweinitz in *The Life and Times of David Zeisberger*. While such of the borderers as had suffered from Indian forays sought to extenuate the deplorable transaction, it was at the same time made the subject of an investigation at the head-quarters of the department. With what result, however, is inferable from the following extract from a letter written by Gen. Irvine to His Excellency William Moore, President of the Supreme Executive Council of Pennsylvania, and dated *Fort Pitt, May 9, 1782:*—"Since my letter of the 3d inst. to your excellency, Mr. Pentecost and Mr. Cannon have been with me. They, and every intelligent person whom I have consulted with on the subject, are of opinion that it will be almost impossible ever to obtain a just account of the conduct of the militia at Muskingum. No man can give any account, except some of the party themselves; if, therefore, an inquiry should appear serious, they are

407

not obliged, nor will they give evidence. For this and other reasons, I am of opinion farther inquiry into the matter will not only be fruitless, but in the end may be attended with dangerous consequences. A volunteer expedition is talked of against Sandusky, which, if well conducted, may be of great service to this country, if they behave well on this occasion. It may also in some measure atone for the barbarity they are charged with at Muskingum. They have consulted me, and shall have every countenance in my power, if their numbers, arrangements, &c., promise a prospect of success." *MS. in the Irvine Collection.*]

[The following is a letter from Col. John Gibson, to the Right Rev. Nathaniel Seidel, senior Bishop of the Moravian Church at Bethlehem, dated *Fort Pitt, May 9, 1782.*

"Sir:—Your letter by Mr. Shebosh of the 11th ult., came safe to hand. I am happy to find that the few small services I rendered to the gentlemen of your society in this quarter, meet with the approbation of you and every other worthy character.

"Mr. Shebosh will be able to give you a particular account of the late horrid massacre perpetrated at the towns on Muskingum, by a set of men the most savage miscreants that ever degraded human nature. Had I have known of their intention before it was too late, I should have prevented it by informing the poor sufferers of it.

"I am in hopes in a few days to be able to send you a more particular account than any that has yet transpired, as I hope to obtain the deposition of a person who was an eye-witness of the whole transaction, and disapproved of it. Should any accounts come to hand from Mr. Zeisberger, or the other gentlemen of your society, you may depend on my transmitting them to you. Please present my compliments to Mr. William Henry, Jr., &c.

> "Believe me, with esteem, your most
> obedient servant,
> "Jno. Gibson,
> "Col. 7th Virginia Reg't."]

83 [For a full account of this exodus, the reader is referred to a paper entitled "Wyalusing and the Moravian Mission at Friedenshütten," by

W. C. Reichel, in Part 5 (1871) of the Transactions of the Moravian Historical Society.]

84 For "*Mouseys*" read "*Monseys.*"

85 For "1768, *about six*," read "1772, *a few.*"

86 Loskiel, part III., ch. 12.

87 [Pilgerruh on the Cuyahoga, within the limits of what is now Independence township, Cuyahoga County, Ohio, was the seat of the mission during the time of the dispersion in the interval between May of 1786, and April of 1787.]

88 General John Gibson thinks that *Sawano* is their proper name; they are so called by the other Indian nations, from their being a southern people. *Shawaneu*, in the Lenape language, means the south; *Shawanachau*,[89] the south wind, &c. We commonly call them the *Shawanese*.

89 For "*Shawanachau*" read "*Shawanachan.*"

90 The Shawanos call the Mohicans their *elder brother*.

91 Loskiel, part II., ch. 10.

92 While these people lived at Wyoming and in its vicinity, they were frequently visited by missionaries of the Society of the United Brethren, who, knowing them to be the most depraved and ferocious tribe of all the Indian nations they had heard of, sought to establish a friendship with them, so as not to be interrupted in their journies from one Indian Mission to another. Count Zinzendorf being at that time in the country, went in 1742 with some other missionaries to visit them at Wyoming, stayed with them 20 days, and endeavoured to impress the gospel truths upon their minds; but these hardened people, suspecting his views, and believing that he wanted to purchase their land, on which it was reported there were mines of silver, conspired to murder him, and would have effected their purpose, but that Conrad Weiser, the Indian interpreter, arrived fortunately in time to prevent it. (Loskiel, part II., ch. 1.) Notwithstanding this, the Brethren frequently visited them, and Shehellemus, a chief of great influence, having become their friend (Loskiel, ibid., ch. 8), they could now travel with greater safety. He died at Shamokin in 1749; the Brethren were, however, fortunate enough to obtain the friendship of Paxnos or Paxsinos, another chief of the Shawanos, who gave them full proof of it by sending his sons to escort one of them to Bethlehem from Shamokin, where he was in the most perilous situation, the war having just broke out. (Loskiel, ibid., ch. 12.)

93 Loskiel, part I., ch. 10.

94 [After the peace of 1763 there was comparative quiet on the Western frontiers, until the inauguration of the "Dunmore War," in the spring of 1774—a contest which the last royal governor of Virginia is said to have excited, in order to divert the attention of the colonists from the oppressive acts of England towards them. The initial military movement in this war was Col. Angus McDonald's expedition against the Shawanese town of Waketameki, just below the mouth of the Waketameki Creek, within the limits of the present county of Muskingum, Ohio. The battle fought on the 10th of October, 1774, at the junction of the Great Kanawha and the Ohio, between the garrison of Point Pleasant, under General Andrew Lewis, and the flower of the Shawanese, Delawares, Mingoes, and Wyandots, led by the Cornstalk, the Shawano king, in which the confederate Indians were routed, was speedily followed by a peace.]

95 See, in Loskiel's History, part II., ch. 10, his account of the visit of this chief to the Christian Indian Congregation at Bethlehem.

96 For "*Shawanos*" read "*Nanticokes.*"

97 [In 1726, John Harris, a Yorkshireman, settled at the mouth of the Paxton Creek, traded largely with the neighboring Indians, cleared a farm, and kept a ferry. John Harris, Jr., his son, born on the Paxton in the above-mentioned year, inherited from his father 700 acres of land, on a part of which Harrisburg was laid out in 1785.]

98 *Zeningi*, according to Loskiel.

99 For "*Schschequon*" read "*Shechschequon.*"

100 [For "*Christian*" read "*Christopher.*"]

410

101 Loskiel, part I., ch. 9.

102 For "*Tawachguáno*" read "*Tayachguáno.*"

103 [Now the Clinton, on whose banks New Gnadenhütten was built by David Zeisberger in the summer of 1782.]

104 [The first mission established by the Moravians among the northern tribes of Indians, was among a clan of Mohegans, in the town of Pine Plains, Dutchess County, New York, where Christian Henry Rauch, of Bethlehem, began his labors as an evangelist in July of 1740.]

105 Collections Massach. Histor. Soc., vol. I., p. 195; vol. IV., p. 67; vol. IX., p. 92.

106 Collections Massach. Histor. Soc., vol. IX., p. 76.

107 Coll. Mass. Hist. Soc., vol. IX., p. 77. Trumbull's History of Connecticut, vol. I., p. 28.

108 The Atlantic Ocean.

109 P. 235.—This MS. is in the library of the Society of the United Brethren at Bethlehem.

110 Loskiel, part II., ch. 9.

111 Mr. Zeisberger wrote a complete dictionary of the Iroquois language, in three quarto volumes, the first of which, from A to the middle of H, is unfortunately lost. The remainder, which is preserved, contains upwards of 800 pages, which shews that, at least, the Indian languages are not so *poor* as is generally imagined. It is German and Indian, beginning with the German.[112]]

112 [This work, entitled "*Deutch und Onondagaishes Wörterbuch,*" i. e., Lexicon of the German and Onondaga Languages, complete in 7 vols., MS., is deposited in the Library of the American Philosophical Society, at Philadelphia. Also a complete grammar of the Onondaga by the same author.]

113 This word should be pronounced according to the powers of the German Alphabet.

114 Being, or Spirit.

115 An old Indian told me about fifty years ago, that when he was young, he still followed the custom of his father and ancestors, in climbing upon a high mountain or pinnacle, to thank the Great Spirit for all the benefits before bestowed, and to pray for a continuance of his favour; that they were sure their prayers were heard, and acceptable to the Great Spirit, although he did not himself appear to them.

116 When, between the years 1760 and 1768, the noted war-chief Pontiac had concerted a plan of surprising and cutting off the garrison and town of Detroit, while in the act of delivering an impressive peace oration, to the then commandant Major Gladwyn, the *turning of the belt* was to have been the signal of the attack by his forces, who all had their guns, which previously had been cut off to large pistol length, hidden under their blankets. So I have been informed by some of the most respectable inhabitants of Detroit, and by the Indians themselves.

117 For "*once*" read "*sometimes.*"

118 For "*should*" read "*deserved to.*"

119 For "*to*" read "*out at.*"

120 Dele "*outside of the door and.*"

121 Grammatica Grœnlandico-Danico-Latina, edita à P. Egede, Hafniœ, 1760, 8vo.

Dictionarium Grœnlandico-Danico-Latinum, adornatum à P. Egede, Hafniœ, 1750, 8vo.

122 For "*Thornhallesen*" read "*Thorhallesen.*"

123 [The Moravians have been conducting a successful mission in Greenland since 1733. In 1761, David Crantz, one of their clergymen, sailed for that distant country to collect material for a history, touching its physical aspect and resources, the manners and customs of the native tribes. Crantz's work was published at Barby, Saxony, in 1765, under the title of "*Historie von Grönland, enthaltend die Beschreibung des Landes und der Einwohner insbeomdere, die Geschichte der dortigen Mission der evangelischen Brüder zu Neu-Herrnhut und Lichtenfels.*" An English Translation appeared in London, in 1766.]

124 The Hurons, a great while, perhaps centuries ago, became disunited from the Iroquois; many wars took place between them, and the former withdrew at last to remote places, where they settled, and were discovered by French Missionaries and traders: of this last I was repeatedly assured during my residence at Detroit, between 1781 and 1786.

125 Carver says that there are in North America, four different languages, the Iroquois to the east, the Chippeway or Algonkin to the northwest, the Naudowessie to the west, and the Cherokee, &c. to the south. Travels, ch. 17, Capt. Carver, though he appears to have been in general an accurate observer, resided too short a time among the Indians to have a correct knowledge of their languages. [Mr. Heckewelder quotes here and elsewhere from "*Three Years' Travels through the Interior Parts of North America for more than Five Thousand Miles, &c.,*" by Capt. *Jonathan Carver of the Provincial Troops in America, Phila.,* 1796. Those tribes of the Naudowessies among whom Carver resided for five months, dwelt about the River St. Pierre, 200 miles above its junction with the Mississippi. This was the extreme westerly point reached by the adventurous traveller. The entire nation of the Naudowessies, according to Carver, mustered upwards of 2000 fighting men.]

126 Le grand Voyage du pays des Hurons, par Samuel Sagard, Paris, 1632. To which is added, a Dictionary of the Huron language, with a preface.

127 Philos. Trans. Abr., vol. lxiii., p. 142.

128 Hist. of the Five Nations, p. 14.

129 Barton's New Views, Ed. 1798. Prelim. Disc., p. 32.

130 The late Dr. Barton, in the work above quoted, append., p. 3,[132] seems to doubt this fact, and relies on a series of numerals which I once communicated to him, and was found among the papers of the late Rev. Mr. Pyrlæus. But it is by no means certain that those numerals were taken from the language of the Nanticokes, and the vocabularies above mentioned leave no doubt as to the origin of that dialect.

131 Letter v.

132 For "*page* 3" read "*page* 5."

133 Letter xxv.

134 He says that it is not copious, and is only adapted to the necessities and conveniences of life. These are the ideas which strangers and philosophers, reasoning *à priori*, entertain of Indian languages; but those who are well acquainted with them think very differently. And yet the Baron says that the Algonquin is "the finest and the most universal language on the Continent."

135 Letter xi., p. 276.

136 It should be properly *Tortoise*; but this word seems in a fair way to be entirely superseded by *Turtle*, as well in England as in this country.

137 *Chippewäisch-Delawarischer, oder Algonkisch-Moheganischer, Stamm.* Mithrid., part III., vol. iii., p. 337.

138 Vater in Mithrid., part III., vol. 3, p. 283, quotes De Laet, Novus Orbis, pp. 98, 103, Du Pratz, vol. 2, pp. 208, 9, Rochefort, Histoire Natur. des Antilles, pp. 351, 394, and Hervas, *Catologo delle Lingue*, p. 90; none of which works I have it in my power to consult.

139 Mithrid., ibid.

140 Loskiel, part I., ch. 1.

141 Duvallon, Vue de la Colonie Espagnole du Mississippi, quoted by Vater, in Mithrid., ibid., p. 297.

142 The Bibliotheca Americana records 45 grammars and 25 dictionaries of the languages spoken in Mexico only, and 85 works of different authors on religious and moral subjects written or translated into some of those languages.

143 For "*or*" read "*nor.*"

144 For "*met*" read "*saw.*"

145 For "*days*" read "*hours.*"

146 Loskiel, part III., ch. 9.

147 For "*December*" read "*November.*"

148 [Pipe, a leader of the Wolf tribe of the Monseys, was residing in the Ohio country at the time of Bouquet's expedition against the Delawares and Shawanon of the Muskingum and Scioto, in 1764. When the Moravians entered the valley of the former river, he was at home on the Walhonding, about 15 miles above the present Coshocton. In the border wars of the Revolution, he at first declared against the Americans, withdrawing with the disaffected Delawares to the Tymochtee creek, a branch of the Sandusky, within the limits of the present Crawford County. While here, he was a serviceable tool in the hands of the British at Detroit. To the Moravian mission among his countrymen he was for many years unjustifiedly hostile. Eventually, however, he regarded the work apparently with favor. It was the Pipe who doomed Col. William Crawford to torture, after the failure of the latter's expedition against Sandusky in the summer of 1782. After the treaty of Fort Harmar in January of 1789, Pipe threw all his influence on the side of those of his people who now resolved at all hazards to uphold peace with the United States. He died a few days before the defeat of the confederated Indians by Wayne, near the rapids of the Maumee.]

149 See Loskiel, part III., ch. 9, p. 704, German text, and p. 165, Eng. Trans.

150 It will be understood that he speaks here throughout for himself and his nation or tribe, though always in the first person of the singular, according to the Indian mode.

151 Meaning his nation, and speaking, as usual, in the first person.

152 Meaning women and children.

153 Prisoners.

154 To make his language agree with the expression *live flesh*.

155 For "*with*" read "*of*."

156 According to the powers of the English alphabet, it should be written Koo-ek-wen-aw-koo.

157 Rogers's Key into the Language of the Indians of New England, ch. vi.

158 For "*they*" read "*the Chippeways and some other nations*."

159 [In Green township, in what is now Ashland County.]

160 For "*your*" read "*yon*."

161 After the word "*nation*" insert "*which they do not approve of*."

162 [Alexander McKee, Matthew Elliott, and Simon Girty,—the first some time a British agent among the Indians, the second with a captain's commission from the commandant at Detroit, the third as brutal, depraved, and wicked a wretch as ever lived,—deserted with a squad of soldiers from Fort Pitt, in March of 1778. This trio of renegade desperadoes, henceforth, in the capacity of emissaries of the British at Detroit (with their savage allies), wrought untold misery on the frontiers, even till the peace of 1795.]

163 For "*they sure*" read "*they are sure*."

164 For "*reply*" read "*answer*."

165 The pronouns in the Indian language have no feminine gender.

166 For "*decide*" read "*say*."

167 For "*man*" read "*men*."

168 Between "*is*" and "*even*" insert "*sometimes*."

169 For "*an old Indian*" read "*several old men*."

170 [The fort, built by Franklin in the early winter of 1756, stood on the site of Weissport, on the left bank of the Lehigh, in Carbon County, Penna. The well of the fort alone remains to mark its site.]

171 For "*road*" read "*course*."

172 [The road from Easton, via Ross Common and the Pocono, to Wilkes-Barré, formerly called the Wilkes-Barré turnpike.]

173 [Mr. Heckewelder had been despatched by the Mission Board at Bethlehem to Fairfield, on the Retrenche, (Thames,) in Upper Canada, where the Moravian Indians settled in 1792, to advise with them and their teachers, concerning a return to the valley of the Tuscarawas, in which the survey of a grant of 12,000 acres of land, made by Congress, had recently been completed. Pursuant to his instructions, he proceeded from Fairfield to the Tuscarawas, to make the necessary preparations for a colony that was to follow in the ensuing autumn, and re-founded Gnadenhütten. The village of Goshen, seven miles higher up the river, was built in October, on the arrival of David Zeisberger and the expected colony from the Retrenche.]

174 [The Wyandot village of Upper Sandusky was three miles in a south-easterly direction from the site of the present town of Upper Sandusky, the county-seat of Wyandot County, Ohio. Lower Sandusky, a trading-post and Wyandot town, was situated at the head of navigation on the Sandusky. Fremont, the county-seat of Sandusky County, marks its site. Here the Moravian missionaries and their families were most hospitably entertained by Arundel and Robbins for upwards of three weeks, while awaiting the arrival of boats from Detroit, on which they were to be taken as prisoners of war to that post. It was through British influence that the Mission on the Muskingum had been overthrown in the early autumn of 1781, and that its seat was transferred to the Sandusky. Fort McIntosh stood on the present town of Beaver, Beaver County,

Pennsylvania. It was erected in October of 1778 by General McIntosh, then in command of the Western Department.]

175 For "*where*" read "*whence.*"

176 [On the 18th October, 1755, a party of Indians fell upon the settlers on the Big Mahanoy, (now Penn's Creek, in Union County, Penna.,) killed and carried off twenty-five persons, and burned and destroyed all the buildings and improvements.—*Colonial Records, vol. 6, p. 766.*]

177 For "*Duke Holland*" read "*Luke Holland;*" the same where the name again occurs.

178 Indian stockings.

179 [The three Commissioners set out from Fort Washington (Cincinnati) for the Indian country in June of 1792, but never returned. Despite the failure of this mission, General Rufus Putnam was without delay despatched on a similar errand, and at Post Vincennes, on the Wabash, in September of the above mentioned year, concluded a treaty of peace with a number of the Western tribes. Mr. Heckewelder was associated by the War Department with Putnam in this perilous undertaking.]

180 [Cornstalk, the well-known Shawano king, while held by the Americans in the fort at Point Pleasant, at the mouth of the Kanhawa, was murdered by some soldiers of the garrison, in revenge for the loss of one of their companions, who had met his death while hunting, at the hands of a British Indian.]

181 The Bible.

182 The Indians gave this name to General Wayne, because they say that he had all the cunning of this animal, who is superior to all other snakes in the manner of procuring his food. He hides himself in the grass with his head only above it, watching all around to see where the birds are building their nests, that he may know where to find the young ones when they are hatched.

183 This is not applicable to the Iroquois of the present time.

184 [A Monsey of Wyalusing, at whose persuasion the Moravian Indians settled on that stream in 1765, who became one of their number, following them to the Big Beaver and the Tuscarawas, where he died in May of 1775. Papunhank's name occurs frequently in the annals of Provincial history between 1762 and 1765.]

185 [The Chinglacamoose, now the Moose, empties into the Susquehannah in Clearfield County, Penna.]

186 Dele *again*.

187 Bethlehem.

188 ["The serenity of Michael's countenance," writes Loskiel, "when he was laid in his coffin, contrasted strangely with the figures scarified upon his face when a warrior. These were as follows: upon the right cheek and temple, a large snake; from the under lip a pole passed over the nose, and between the eyes and the top of the forehead, ornamented at every quarter of an inch with round marks, representing scalps; upon the upper cheek, two lances crossing each other; and upon the lower jaw, the head of a wild boar."]

189 See Loskiel, part I., ch. 3.

190 See Loskiel, part I., ch. 11.

191 For "*very often*" read "*sometimes.*"

192 For "*inches*" read "*feet.*"

193 For "*of*" read "*on.*"

194 Podophyllum peltatum.

195 [Mr. Heckewelder was in this year residing at New Gnadenhütten on the Huron (now the Clinton), Michigan, where the Moravian Missionaries ministered to their converts for upwards of three years, subsequent to their compulsory evacuation of the Tuscarawas valley.]

196 They call them *Doctols*; because the Indians cannot pronounce the letter R. The Minsi or Monseys call them "Mĕdéu," which signifies "conjuror."

197 [Gelelemend, *i. e., a leader,* (whose soubriquet among the whites was Kill-buck,) a grandson of the well-known Netawatwes, was sometime chief counsellor of the Turkey tribe of the Delaware nation, and after the death of Captain White Eyes, installed temporarily as principal chief. He was a strenuous advocate of peace among his people in the times of the Revolutionary war; and being a man of influence, drew upon himself, in consequence, the implacable animosity of those of his countrymen who took up arms against the Americans. Even after the general peace concluded between the United States and the Indians of the West in 1795, his life was on several occasions imperilled by his former opponents. Gelelemend united with the Moravian Indians, at Salem, on the Petquotting in the summer of 1788, where, in baptism, he was named William Henry, after Judge William Henry, of Lancaster. He died at Goshen, in the early winter of 1811, in the eightieth year of his age. He is said to have been born in 1737, in the neighborhood of the Lehigh Water Gap, Carbon County, Pa. William Henry Gelelemend was one of the last converts of distinction attached to the Moravian Mission among the Indians.]

198 [Goschachking, sometime the capital of the Delaware nation, stood on the Muskingum, immediately below the junction of the Tuscarawas and the Walhonding. On its site stands Coshocton. The town was destroyed by Gen. Brodhead in 1781.]

199 For "*Americans*" read "*white men.*"

200 The following extract from the Detroit Gazette, shews that this superstitious belief of the Indians in the powers of witchcraft, still continues in full force, even among those who live in the vicinity of the whites, and are in the habit of constant intercourse with them.

From the Detroit Gazette of the 17th of August, 1818.

On the evening of the 22d ult. an Indian of the Wyandot tribe was murdered by some of his relatives, near the mouth of the river Huron, on lake Erie. The circumstances, in brief, are as follows:

"It appears that two Wyandots, residing at Malden, and relatives to the deceased, had been informed by Captain Johnny, an Indian living on the Huron river, and also a relative, that a Shawanee Indian had come to his death by the witchcraft of an old Indian woman and her son Mike, and that in order to avert the vengeance of the Shawanee tribe, it would be necessary to kill them—and furthermore, that the death of Walk-in-the-water, who died last June, was caused by the same old woman's witchcraft. It was determined to kill the old woman and her son—and for that purpose they crossed over on the 22d ult. and succeeded in the course of the evening in killing the latter in his cabin. The old woman was not at home. The next day, while endeavouring to persuade her to accompany them into the woods, as they said, to drink whiskey, they were discovered by Dr. William Brown and Mr. Oliver Williams, who had received that morning intimations of their intentions, and owing to the exertions of these gentlemen, the old woman's life was preserved and one of the Indians taken, who is now confined in the jail of this city—the others escaped by swiftness of foot.

"On the examination of the Indian taken, it appeared that the old woman, shortly after the death of the Shawanee, had entered his cabin, and in a voice of exultation, called upon him, saying—'Shawanee man! where are you?—You that mocked me; you thought you would live forever—you are gone and I am here—come—Why do you not come?' &c.—She is said to have made use of nearly the same words in the cabin of Walk-in-the-water, shortly after his death."

201 War-hatchet: from which we have made *tomahawk*.

202 The Indians call the American continent an island; believing it to be (as in fact, probably, it is) entirely surrounded with water.

203 For "*killed*" read "*eaten*."

204 Mr. Pyrlœus lived long among the Iroquois, and was well acquainted with their language. He was instructed in the Mohawk dialect by the celebrated interpreter Conrad Weiser. He has left behind him some manuscript grammatical works on that idiom, one of them is entitled: *Affixa nominum et verborum Linguœ Macquaicœ*, and another, *Adjectiva, nomina et pronomina*

421

Linguæ Macquaicæ. These MSS. are in the library of the Society of the United Brethren at Bethlehem.

205 For "*Pauksit*" read "*P'duk-sit*."

206 See page 101.

207 Probably alluding to a tradition which the Indians have of a very ferocious kind of bear, called the *naked bear*, which they say once existed, but was totally destroyed by their ancestors. The last was killed in the New York state, at a place they called *Hoosink*, which means the *Basin*, or more properly the *Kettle*.

208 The same whom Mr. de Volney speaks of in his excellent "View of the Soil and Climate of the United States." Supplement, No. VI., page 356, Philadelphia Edition, 1804.

209 See ch. 29, p. 225.

210 See ch. 28, p. 221.

211 See ch. 2.

212 Dele "*lands or*."

213 This word means *liquor*, and is also used in the sense of a medicinal draught, or other compound potion.

214 [Shingask, which signifies *boggy or marshy ground overgrown with grass*, a brother of Tamaqua, or King Beaver, ranked first among Indian warriors in the times of the so-called French and Indian war. The frontiers of Pennsylvania suffering severely from the forays of this Delaware and his braves, Governor Denny, in 1756, set a price of £200 upon his head or scalp. Mr. Heckewelder, in a "Collection of the Names of Chieftains and Eminent Men of the Delaware Nation" states that Shingask, although an implacable foe in battle, was never known to treat a prisoner with cruelty. "One day," he goes on to say, "in the summer of 1762, while passing with him near by where two prisoners of his—boys of about twelve years of age—were amusing themselves with his own boys, as the chief observed that my attention was arrested by them, he asked me at what I was looking. Telling him in reply that I was looking at his prisoners, he said, 'When I first took them, they were such; but now they and my children eat their food from the same bowl or dish;' which was equivalent to saying that they were in all respects on an equal footing with his own children, or alike dear to him."]

215 A kind of round buckle with a tongue, which the Indians fasten to their shirts. The traders call them *broaches*. They are placed in rows, at the distance of about the breadth of a finger one from the other.

216 The same whom I have spoken of above, page 184, No. 4.

217 For "*Albany*" read "*Pittsburg*."

218 See ch. 15, p. 151.

219 The Indian name of Capt. White Eyes.

220 Page 188.

221 For "*Sandusky*" read "*Muskingum*."

222 See above, pages 81, 184.

223 [Williamson did not lead the expedition against Sandusky, nor was it organized for the destruction of the Moravian Indians, then in the Sandusky country. It was led by Colonel William Crawford. Sanctioned by General Irvine, then in command of the Western Department, the undertaking was intended to be effectual in ending the troubles upon the western frontiers of Pennsylvania and Virginia, by punishing the Wyandots, Shawanese, Delawares, and Mingoes, whose war-parties were wont to come from their settlements in Sandusky, to kill and devastate along the borders. See Butterfield's *Crawford's Campaign against Sandusky*, for full details touching the fitting out of this expedition, its disastrous termination, and the awful death by torture of its commanding officer.

In a letter written by Washington to General Irvine, and dated *Headquarters, 6th August, 1782*, he expresses himself in the following words: "I lament the failure of the expedition, and am particularly affected with the disastrous fate of Colonel Crawford. No other than the extremest torture which could be inflicted by the savages, could, I think, have been expected by those who were unhappy enough to fall into their hands, especially under the present exasperation of their minds from the treatment given their Moravian friends. For this reason, no person should at this time suffer himself to fall alive into the hands of the Indians."—*MS. in the Irvine Collection.*]

224 This name, according to the English orthography, should be written *Winganoond* or *Wingaynoond*, the second syllable accented and long, and the last syllable short.

225 The people were at that moment advancing, with shouts and yells, to torture and put him to death.

226 Ruth, i. 16.

227 Of the value of one dollar.

228 For "*bought*" read "*brought*."

229 [A Monsey settlement near the mouth of the Tionesta, within the limits of the present Venango County. It was visited by Mr. Zeisberger for the first time in the autumn of 1767; in the following year it became the seat of a mission. In 1770, the Allegheny was exchanged by the missionary and his converts for the Beaver. Zeisberger's labors at Goschgoschink furnished the subject for Schüssele's historical painting, "The Power of the Gospel."]

230 See Nile's Weekly Register, vol. i., p. 141, vol. v., p. 174, and vol. vi., p. 111.

231 This appears to be a mistake; Leather-lips, as has been stated above, was a chief of the Wyandots or Hurons, and is so styled in the treaty of Greenville, otherwise called Wayne's Treaty, where he was one of the representatives of that nation.

232 The Indian name of this chief was Tar-he; he was also a Wyandot or Huron, and one of the signers of the Greenville treaty. How great must have been the power of Tecumseh, who trusted the execution of Leather-lips to a chief of the same nation!

233 [The earliest record of Tamanen is the affix of his mark to a deed, dated 23d day of the 4th month, 1683, by which he and Metamequan conveyed to old Proprietor Penn a tract of land, lying between the Pennypack and Neshaminy creeks, in Bucks County.— *Pennsylvania Archives*, vol. i., p. 64. Heckewelder gives the signification of the Delaware word "tamanen" as *affable*.]

234 [Tadeuskund was baptized at the Gnadenhütten Mission, (Lehighton, Carbon County, Pa.,) by the Moravian Bishop Cammerhoff, of Bethlehem, in March of 1750. For additional notices of this prominent actor in the French and Indian war, extracted from manuscripts in the Archives of the Moravian Church at Bethlehem, the reader is referred to *Memorials of the Moravian Church*, vol. i., edited by *W. C. Reichel, Philadelphia, 1870*.]

235 [Moses Tatemy was a convert of, and sometime an interpreter for, David Brainerd, during that evangelist's career among the Delawares of New Jersey and Pennsylvania, who were settled on both sides of their great river, between its forks and the Minisinks. A grant of upwards of 200 acres of land, lying on the east branch of Lehietan or Bushkill, within the limits of the present Northampton County, Pa., was confirmed to the chief about the year 1737, by the Proprietaries' agents, for valuable services rendered. On this reservation, Tatemy was residing as late as 1753, and probably later. He was there a near neighbour of the Moravians at Nazareth. In the interval between 1756 and 1760, he participated in most of the numerous treaties and conferences between the Governors of the Province and his countrymen, frequently in the capacity of an interpreter. Subsequent to the last-mentioned year, his name ceases to appear on the Minutes of the Provincial Council. He probably died in 1761. Such being the facts in the case, Mr. Heckewelder is in error when he states that Tatemy lost his life at the hands of a white man *prior to 1754*. That a *son* of the old chieftain, *Bill Tatemy* by name, was mortally wounded in July of 1757, by a young man in the Ulster-Scot settlement, (within the limits of Allen township, Northampton County,) while straying from a body of Indians, who were on their way from Fort Allen to Easton, to a treaty, is on record in the official papers of that day. This unprovoked assault upon one of their countrymen, as was to be expected, incensed the disaffected Indians to such a degree, that Governor Denny was fain to assure them, at the opening of the treaty, that the offender should be speedily brought to justice; at the same time, he condoled with the afflicted father. *Bill*

Tatemy died near Bethlehem, from the effects of the gun-shot wound, within five weeks. He had been sometime under John Brainerd's teaching, at Cranberry, N. J., and was a professing Christian.]

236 See above page 67, and see the Errata with reference to that page.

237 Ch. 34, pp. 255, 256.

238 [These chiefs were representatives of the seven nations with whom Gen. Putnam concluded a treaty in September of the above-mentioned year, and were on their way to Philadelphia.

Note.—The following is a copy of the letter written by the Secretary of War to Mr. Heckewelder, advising him of Putnam's request that he might be associated with him in his mission to the western Indians:

"War Department, *18 May, 1792.*

"Sir.—I have the honour to inform you that the United States have for some time past been making pacific overtures to the hostile Indians north-west of the Ohio. It is to be expected that these overtures will soon be brought to an issue under the direction of Brigadier-General Putnam, of Marietta, who is specially charged with this business.

"He is now in this city, and will be in readiness to set out on Monday next, and being acquainted with you, he is extremely desirous that you should accompany him in the prosecution of this good work.

"Being myself most cordially impressed with a respect for your character and love of the Indians, on the purest principles of justice and humanity, I have cheerfully acquiesced in the desire of Gen. Putnam.

"I hope sincerely it may be convenient for you to accompany or follow him soon, in order to execute a business which is not unpromising, and which, if accomplished, will redound to the credit of the individuals who perform it.

"As to pecuniary considerations, I shall arrange them satisfactorily with you.

> "With great respect, I am, sir, your most
> obedient servant,
> "H. KNOX,
> *Secretary of War.*"]

239 [Col. Ebenezer Sproat was one of the colony which, under the auspices of the recently formed Ohio Company, and led by Gen. Putnam, emigrated to the Ohio country in the spring of 1788, and founded Marietta.]

240 Ch. 6, p. 104.

241 For "*them*" read "*us.*"

242 Sun-fish.

243 Vocabularium Barbaro-Virgineorum, bound with an Indian translation from the Swedish of Luther's Catechism. Stockholm, 1696, duod.

244 Carver's Travels, Introduction, p. 72. Boston Edit., 1797.

245 Carver was only 14 months in the Indian country, during which time he says he travelled near 4000 miles and visited twelve different nations of Indians.

246 For "*Indians*" read "*traders.*"

247 [They were sent to Goschschoking (Coshocton), the then capital of the Delaware nation, to condole with that people on the death of White Eyes.]

248 Ch. 7, p. 111.

249 See above, ch. 18, p. 172.

250 Dr. Boudinot was long a member, and once President, of the Continental Congress, and his talents were very useful to the cause which he had embraced. At a very advanced age, he now enjoys literary ease in a dignified retirement.

251 A Star in the West, or a humble attempt to discover the long lost ten tribes of Israel, preparatory to their return to their beloved city, Jerusalem. Trenton (New Jersey), 1816.

252 See page 140, and following.

253 Star in the West, p. 138.

254 This relation is authentic. I have received it from the mouth of the chief of the injured party, and his statement was confirmed by communications made at the time by two respectable magistrates of the county.

255 [This outrage was committed at the public house of John Stenton, which stood on the road leading from Bethlehem to Fort Allen, a short mile north of the present Howertown, Allen township, Northampton County. Stenton belonged to the Scotch-Irish, who settled in that region as early as 1728.]

256 [Nescopeck was an Indian settlement on the highway of Indian travel between Fort Allen and the Wyoming Valley.]

257 Justice Geiger's letter to Justice Horsefield proves this fact

258 [These unprovoked barbarities were perpetrated by a squad of soldiers who, in command of Captain Jacob Wetterholt, of the Provincial service, were in quarters at the Lehigh Water Gap, Carbon County, Pa.]

259 [In this paragraph, Mr. Heckewelder briefly alludes to the *last foray* made by Indians into old Northampton County, south of the Blue Mountain. It occurred on the 8th of October, 1763. An account of the affair at Stenton's, on the morning of that day, in which Stenton was shot dead, and Captain Jacob Wetterholt and several of his men seriously or mortally wounded, was published in Franklin's *Pennsylvania Gazette*, of October 18th, 1763. Leaving Stenton's, after the loss of one of their number, the Indians crossed the Lehigh, and on their way to a store and tavern on the Copley creek, (where they also had been wronged by the whites,) they murdered several families residing within the limits of the present Whitehall township, Lehigh County. Laden with plunder, they then struck for the wilderness north of the Blue Mountain. Upwards of twenty settlers were killed or captured on that memorable day, and the buildings on several farms were laid in ashes.]

260 [The 5,000 acres at Nazareth, which Whitefield sold to the Moravians in 1741, were first held by Lœtitia Aubrey, to whom it had been granted by her father, William Penn, in 1682. The right of erecting this tract, or any portion thereof, into a manor, of holding court-baron thereon, and of holding views of frankpledge for the conservation of the peace, were special privileges accorded to the grantee by the grantor. It was one of few of the original grants similarly invested. The royalty, however, in all cases remained a dead letter.]

261 Alluding to what was at that time known by the name of the *long day's walk.*

262 See above, p. 302.

263 The same of whom I have spoken above, p. 171.

264 See above, pp. 135, 136.

265 Above, p. 279.

266 Carver's Travels, ch. 9, p. 196. Edit. above cited.

267 [Glikhican, one of the converts of distinction attached to the Moravian mission, was a man of note among his people, both in the council chamber and on the war-path. When the Moravians first met him he resided at Kaskaskunk, on the Beaver, and at Friedenstadt, on that river, he was baptized by David Zeisberger in December of 1770. Subsequently he became a "national assistant" in the work of the Gospel, lived consistently with his profession, and met his death at the hands of Williamson's men at Gnadenhütten in March of 1782.]

268 See above, p. 338.

269 Loskiel, p. 3, ch. 3.

270 [The valley of the Conecocheague, which stream drains Franklin County, Pennsylvania, was explored and settled about 1730 by Scotch-Irish pioneers, among whom were three brothers of the name of Chambers. The site of Chambersburg was built on by Joseph Chambers. The Conecocheague settlement suffered much from the Indians after Braddock's defeat in 1755.]

271 Letter V.

272 For "*Zeisberger*" read "*Heckewelder.*"

273 These papers have been communicated.

274 For "*from*" read "*for.*"

275 For "*schawanáki*" read "*schwanameki.*"

276 For "*chwani*" read "*chwami.*"

277 An Enquiry into the Question, whether America was peopled from the Old Continent?

278 The Chippeways have hardly any grammatical forms.

279 See Philos. Trans. abridged; vol. lxiii., 142.

280 Colden's Hist. of the Five Nations. Octavo ed., 1747, p. 14.

281 One of them empties itself into the north side of Lake St. Clair, another at the west end of Lake Erie, and a third on the south side of the said lake, about twenty-five miles east of Sandusky river or bay.

282 For "*K'lehelleya*" read "*K'lehellecheya.*"

283 From the verb *Pommauchsin.*

284 In the original it is *N'mizi*; the German z being pronounced like *tz*, which mode of spelling has been adopted in this publication.

285 For "*Wulatopnachgat*" read "*Wulaptonachgat.*"

286 For "*Wulatonamin*" read "*Wulatenamin*."

287 For "*manner*" read "*matter*."

288 For "*achpansi*" read "*achpanschi*."

289 *Wenitschanit*, the parent or owner of a child naturally begotten; *wetallemansit*, the owner of the beast.

290 [*A Collection of Hymns, for the use of the Christian Indians of the Missions of the United Brethren, in North America*. Philadelphia: Printed by Henry Sweitzer, at the corner of Race and Fourth Streets, 1803. A second edition of this work abridged, and edited by the Rev. Abraham Luckenbach, was published at Bethlehem in 1847.]

291 For "*Indian corn*" read "*a particular species of Indian corn*."

292 All words ending in *ican, hican, kschican*, denote a sharp instrument for cutting. *Pachkschican*, a knife; *pkuschican*, a gimlet, an instrument which cuts into holes; *tangamican*, or *tangandican*, a spear, a sharp-pointed instrument; *poyachkican*, a gun, or an instrument that cuts with force.

293 For "*Ktahoatell*" read "*Ktahoalell*."

294 For "*gunich*" read "*gunih*."

295 Quin et emissurus Fucinum lacum, naumachiam ante commisit. Sed cum proclamantibus naumachiariis "Ave, Imperator! morituri te salutant," respondisset "Avete vos!" neque post hanc vocem, quasi veniâ datâ, quisquam dimicare vellet, diù cunctatus an omnes igni ferroque absumeret, tandem è sede sua prosiluit, ac per ambitum lacûs, non sine fœdâ vacillatione discurrens, partim minando, partim adhortando, ad pugnam compulit. Sueton. in Claud. 21.

296 Gœthe, in Wilhelm Meister.

297 For "*Eliwulek*" read "*Eluwilek*."

298 For "*Allowilen*" read "*Allowilek*."

299 For the English translation of these two words substitute "*the most extraordinary, the most wonderful*."

300 For "*Eluwantowit*" read "*Eluwannitlowit*."

301 For "*Elewassit*" read "*Elewussit*."

302 For "*the supremely good*" read "*the most holy one*."

303 Bey vielen Amerikanischen Sprachen finden wir theils einen so künstlichen und zusammengesetzten bau, und einem so grossen reichthum an grammatischen formen, wie ihn selbst bey dem verbum wenige sprachen der Welt haben: theils scheinen sie so arm an aller grammatischen ausbildung, wie die sprachen der rohesten Völker in Nord-Ost-Asia und in Afrika seyn mögen. *Untersuchungen über Amerikas bevölkerung*, S. 152.

304 Among the Mbayas, a nation of Paraguay, it is said that young men and girls, before their marriage, speak a language differing in many respects from that of married men and women. Azara, c. 10.

305 For "*schingieschin*" read "*schingiechin*."

306 The *k* which is prefixed to this and the following substantives, conveys the idea of the pronoun *thy*; it is a repetition (as it were) of the beginning of the phrase "for *thine*" &c., and enforces its meaning. *Ksakimowagan*, may be thus dissected: *k*, thy, *sakima*, king or chief, *wagan*, substantive termination, added to *king*, makes *kingdom*.

307 See Letters 8 and 10.

308 M. Raynouard, in his excellent Researches on the Origin and Formation of the corrupted Roman Language, spoken before the year 1000, has sufficiently proved that the French articles *le*, the Spanish *el*, and the Italian *il*, are derived from the Latin demonstrative pronoun *ille*, which began about the sixth century to be prefixed to the substantive. Thus they said: ILLI *Saxones*, "THE SAXONS;" ILLI *negociatores de Longobardia*, "THE Lombard merchants," &c. So natural is the use of the pronominal form to give clearness and precision to language. *Recherches*, &c., p. 39.

309 For "*Mamschalgussiwagan*" read "*Mamschalgussowagan*."

310 For "*Mamintochimgussowagan*" read
"*Mamintschimgussowagan*."

311 For "*M'chonschicanes*" read "*M'chonschican*."

We hope you have enjoyed what we believe to be the best kind of history book: firsthand accounts of our ancestors. It is our hope that you will make room in your home for a library filled with the true history books of America, and Western Civilization as a whole.

Knowledge Keepers is dedicated to the preservation of print materials to be passed on to future generations. Please visit our website for more history reprints, plus book lists and blog posts about the importance of preserving our history:

Knowledgekeepersbookstore.com

Please be so kind as to leave a review wherever you purchased this book!

Originally published in 1838, it features the biographies of every man who signed the Declaration of Independence, as well as George Washington and Patrick Henry. The author, L. Carroll Judson, knew or met almost every single man in this book. It is such a treasure! Not only is each biography included, but with each one, Judson describes the traits that were so necessary to produce such men. Also included are the first draft and final draft of the Declaration of Independence, The United States Constitution (at 1838), and George Washington's Farewell Address.

This version is updated with a photo of each signer, a photo of their autographs, and some footnotes. Order your copy on Amazon.com or KnowledgeKeepersBookstore.com.

Originally published in 1872, author John S. C. Abbott weaves the story of the original Plymouth Colony in 1620. The history of this little settlement is full of adventure, sadness, and miracles, and lays the foundation for what would become the United States of America. Drawing liberally from the firsthand accounts of William Bradford, William Brewster, Edward Winslow, John Robinson, Abbott puts the details into a wonderful chronological narrative, from the persecution of the Puritans in England to the death of their beloved Captain, Miles Standish.

This is a must-read for any student of history, and anyone who wants to get the facts from those who made history. Order your copy on Amazon.com or KnowledgeKeepersBookstore.com.

MILES STANDISH
THE PURITAN CAPTAIN
BY JOHN S. C. ABBOTT

1620   *Knowledge* KEEPERS
HOME LIBRARY SERIES

Originally published in 1916, this Book of Nebraska Pioneer Reminiscences was issued by the Daughters of the American Revolution of Nebraska, and:

"dedicated to the daring, courageous, and intrepid men and women—the advance guard of our progress—who, carrying the torch of civilization, had a vision of the possibilities which now have become realities.

Order your copy on Amazon.com or KnowledgeKeepersBookstore.com.

Made in the USA
Middletown, DE
06 November 2023

42032271R00267